ARCHITECTURE IN COMMUNION

ARCHITECTURE *in* COMMUNION

Implementing the Second Vatican Council through Liturgy and Architecture

by

STEVEN J. SCHLOEDER

IGNATIUS PRESS　SAN FRANCISCO

COVER ART: *Ascending,* by Rosemarie Evans
Watercolor, 1990

Cover design by Roxanne Mei Lum

Contents

Acknowledgments

During the past nine years of researching Catholic church architecture and liturgy, I have benefited greatly from the advice, encouragement, and critique of many friends and colleagues. Without their help and support, this present work would be impoverished indeed.

From its inception, this book owes much to Cherie Peacock, without whom the ideas would never have achieved the clarity and structure they have; to Professor John Saward, who has labored over it with me for many years and who has been a constant source of encouragement and direction; to Professor Michael Brawne, who first helped me to define the problems in contemporary church architecture; to Richard and Carol Downer for their friendship and support, the use of their extensive personal library, and particularly Carol's deft handling of obscure medieval Latin translations. And I owe a special note of thanks to the Rotary International Foundation, which funded the initial research.

I am most grateful to those who are leading the way toward a true revival of authentic Catholic culture rooted in the fullness of the Second Vatican Council, who have believed in this book, and who have given me the encouragement to persevere toward its publication— among them, again Professor Saward, Mr. Stratford Caldecott, Dr. Scott Hahn, and Joseph Fessio, S.J.

I have had the humbling opportunity to learn from the sapient critiques of some of the finest theological minds our Church has formed, including Rev. Louis Bouyer, who kindly read the manuscript, and several Dominican fathers who have brought their formidable intellects to bear in sharpening this work: Michael Carey, O.P., Giles Dimock, O.P., Aidan Nichols, O.P., and Gregory Tatum, O.P.

Several scholars, liturgists, and architects have taken interest in my work and given invaluable advice and friendship, among them Rev. Roger Wojcik, Mr. Edward Cullinan, Mr. Henry Hardinge Menzies, Dr. John X. Evans, and Professors Robert Tavernor, Joseph Rykwert, Thomas Gordon Smith, and Duncan Stroik.

Finally, I am grateful to those who have lent of their resources for illustrations, particularly Msgr. Francis Mannion, for the photographs of the beautiful renovation of Cathedral of the Madeleine in Salt Lake City; Thomas Gordon Smith of the University of Notre Dame, who kindly gave me access to the School of Architecture's extensive slide library; and also to Pierbattista Pizzaballa, O.F.M., of the Studium Biblicum Franciscanum and Dr. Michael Greenhalgh of the Australian National University's ARTSERVE image library, both of whom gave me kind permission to reproduce the images from their excellent Internet sites. I am likewise indebted for the contributions of Mr. Darrin Merlino, C.M.F., Mr. William Burks, AIA, the Conrad Schmitt Studios, and Martin de Porres Walsh, O.P. I am grateful to Mrs. Rosemarie Evans, a wonderfully gifted artist, for permission to reproduce her magnificent watercolor *Ascending* on the cover.

Even with all the immense resources of which I have had the benefit, I accept all responsibility for any errors or omissions in the work. Finally, I realize that the ideas in this book, insofar as they reflect the true mind of the Church, are not mine per se, but have been given to me. The great saints, theologians, architects, builders, Council fathers, and churchmen of the past have laid out clearly the ideas of what "church" means. I am merely following in their path. They have laid a road that has become obscured by architectural and liturgical debris since the beginning of the twentieth century. Today this road is being rediscovered and cleared by such groups as Adoremus: Society for the Renewal of the Sacred Liturgy, the Society for Catholic Liturgy, the Fra Angelico Guild, the Centre for Faith and Culture, and by the many men and women dedicated to the promotion of authentically Catholic culture, liturgy, and architecture in the fullness of Vatican Council II. I hope this book likewise helps to clear that road.

I.1 Heiligsten Dreifaltigkeitkirche, Vienna,
by F. Wotruba, 1965.

I.3 Wells Cathedral, *c.* 1185–1239.

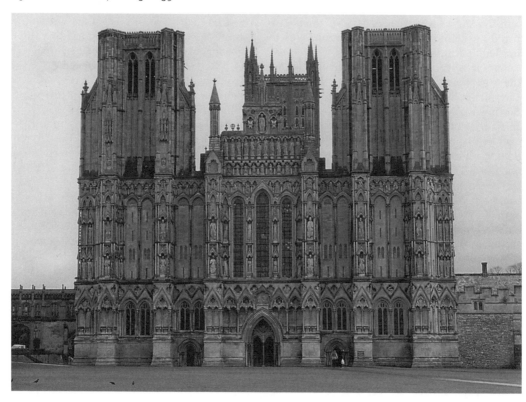

Introduction

Direct thy steps to the perpetual ruins;
the enemy has destroyed everything in the sanctuary!
Thy foes have roared in the midst of thy holy place;
they have set up their own signs to proclaim their victory.

Psalm 74:3–4

I have undertaken this work because I find many—or rather *most*—recent Catholic churches to be banal, uninspiring, and frequently even liturgically bizarre [fig. I.1]. Set against the background of a historical survey of churches —St. John Lateran [fig. I.2], San Vitale, Hagia Sophia, Wells [fig. I.3], Chartres, Orvieto [fig. I.4], Santa Maria Novella, San Carlo alle Quattro Fontane [fig. I.5], and Il Redentore , to name but a few—the twentieth century is certainly architecturally impoverished with respect to ecclesiastical buildings. The few truly outstanding and acclaimed churches of this century, such as Perret's Notre-Dame-le-Raincy, the chapels at Ronchamp, and La Tourette by Le Corbusier [fig. I.6], or Schwarz's Corpus Christi in Aachen, are all the more outstanding because they stand apart from the mundane. Yet even these buildings, while perhaps great examples of modern architecture, are not necessarily great *Catholic churches*.

Particularly since the Second Vatican Council it seems Western Catholicism has been moving even farther away from the centuries-old tradition of great ecclesiastical architecture. There are many reasons ascribed for this phenomenon: a disordered desire to "keep with the times", clericalism, the insignificance of the Church in the modern world, and the intellectual poverty of modern architecture are but a few commonplace explanations. I think,

I.2 St. John Lateran, Rome, *c.* 313–320.

however, the true problem—and therefore the solution—lies elsewhere.

There is a certain history, a tradition, involved in crafting Catholic churches. It is a process that is rooted in Catholic thought and seeks to express Catholic values. Over the centuries there has evolved a rich, complex, and subtle "language" of symbols—of building forms, of details, of shapes, of location, and of emphases—that seeks to convey theological and liturgical ideas through the artful use of materials. This "language", which predates Christianity, is a language of meal and of

9

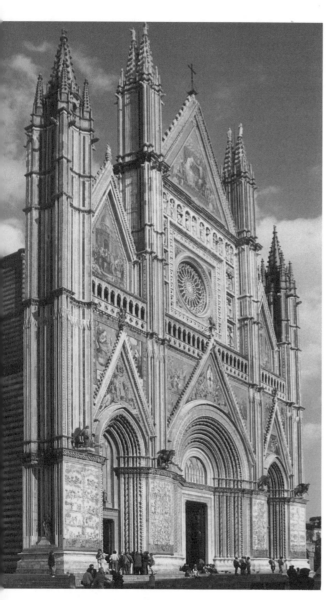

I.4 Orvieto Cathedral, 1290.

sacrifice. It was adopted by the builders of the early Church and continued to develop across the patristic, medieval, Renaissance, Baroque, and Revivalist ages. Much of this tradition has been neglected (if not discarded outright) in the wake of the Modern movement in architecture and with the liturgical experimentation of the twentieth century. The "language" still whispers to us, albeit vestigially, but is gagged by the neo-iconoclastic agenda of the Modernists.

Admittedly, Modernism, which Pius X regarded as the summation of all heresy, has had baneful effects on the Church, first in regard to philosophy, then to theology, and subsequently in regard to architecture. Many prominent Catholic thinkers have not discerningly separated the wheat from the chaff and have accepted certain secondary issues as primary ones. Parallel problems have surfaced in liturgical theology and, therefore, liturgical design. Because of these confusions, much of the tradition of Catholic church design has gone by the wayside. Nowadays there is a dubious distinction drawn between understanding the church building as "the house of God" and understanding it as "the house of God's people" (dubious because it ignores the reality of the "Body of Christ"). A similar false distinction is drawn between the Eucharist as a sacrifice (and therefore a *sacrificial meal*) and the Eucharist as a communal meal, as if the two could be opposed. No longer is the essential difference between the ministerial priesthood and the common priesthood of the faithful seen as a positive and necessary distinction. Too often that distinction has been obscured in the thinking and writing of liturgists. These misunderstandings and oversights have consequently found architectural expression—they are often attributed to the Second Vatican Council and, ironically enough, implemented "in the spirit of the Council". It is my firm conviction, however, that many of these positions are not only indemonstrable from the teachings of Vatican II but are also often antithetical to the expressed intention of the Council.

In fact, it becomes clear from an integrated reading of Vatican II that the changes in exter-

I.5 San Carlo alle Quattro Fontane, Rome, by F. Borromini, 1634–1682.

nal forms proposed by the Council were relatively few—and always in the context of an organic growth from existing forms. The nature of the Church, of the Eucharist, and the liturgy of course remains constant even if emphases change. Since the *Church* remains the same, one should question why *church buildings* have changed so radically since the Council. Vatican II did not change the substance of the faith or the liturgy but offered some fresh insights into both. Similarly, the buildings in which we worship and the expression of the liturgy itself should be open to responsible developments but should always reflect the Church's magisterial understanding of the Body of Christ in all its manifestations. My goal, therefore, is to read the documents of the Second Vatican Council with the intention of finding the "continuity in tradition" of which the documents speak and to apply the appropriate theological and liturgical principles to the design of church buildings.

Let it be made clear that I am not seeking a return to any previous *style* of building. There is no single "Catholic style of architecture".

Furthermore, there is still great advancement to be made in church design. Each age has to find a common ground to reconcile the tension between the need for preserving the Faith and the need to make it relevant to contemporary society. We have at our hands a tradition, a rich, varied, and subtle language of church architecture. We have new methods of construction, new technologies, and new ways of thinking about buildings. And the Church herself has given us new ways of understanding the organic union of clergy and laity within the one Body of Christ. These developments make for a potent dialectic, which can advance both the architectural and the liturgical dialogues. Any true progress, however, can come about only by first respecting the intentions of the Council.

This vision, then, is the heart and purpose of this book: to find appropriate arrangements and considerations for church buildings that are infused with the true spirit of the Second Vatican Council. Our goal is to enliven the parish community—which is the true Church built of living stones in Christ—with a material church building designed to serve and further the primary vocation to become a community of love, which must mean a people of sacrifice

I.6 Notre-Dame-du-Haut, Ronchamp, France, by Le Corbusier, 1955.

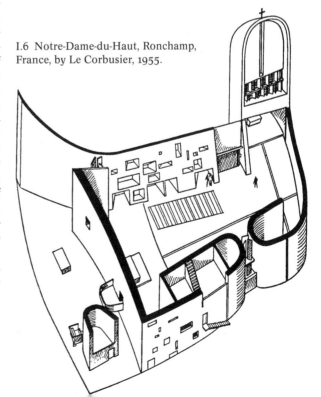

and redemption. Throughout the book the reader is asked to be mindful of this idea. More than a mere monument to God, the church building finds its true purpose as a means to the sanctification of his people. We must all learn to love him and our brothers and sisters in communities of love: this learning takes place as we are strengthened and sanctified and bound together by our sacrificial participation in the eucharistic liturgy. Thus we may become more like our Lord in our humanity, so that we may come to share in his divinity. These three goals, the sanctification of believers, the building of communities of love and service, and the true humanizing of the individual and of society, are focal points of this book because they are the vision of the Vatican Council.

The book is structured simply. The first three chapters place the modern Catholic church building in its proper theological, sociological, historical, and liturgical settings. These chapters provide a common understanding of the agenda of the Second Vatican Council, the relationship of the Church to the arts and her artists and architects, and a discussion of the nature and dynamics of the Eucharistic Sacrifice.

The next three chapters examine the specific architectural requirements of the church building. Chapter 4 examines the sanctuary furnishings in terms of their liturgical, canonical, and symbolic components. Chapter 5 looks at the architectural needs of the other sacraments and rites; and chapter 6 considers the social and communal aspects of the parish buildings.

The last three chapters are ordered to help the architect and the community regain an iconographic understanding of the church building. To help achieve this understanding, the idea of sacred images is discussed in chapter 7: the history and theology of the icon, as well as the place of the sacred image in the church today, are considered. In chapter 8, the building as a whole is considered in its symbolic aspects, from both liturgical and historical perspectives. Finally, chapter 9 examines the questions about the form of the church building. Here the relationships between architectural massing, function, location, detail, and symbol are explored, with positive suggestions for regaining an iconic– a *sacramental*–appreciation of the church building.

I do not give many concrete solutions to the problems. Instead I prefer to call attention to passages from the Church's documents in order that the reader may consider them carefully. Nor have I given many examples of recent churches showing successful fonts, stained glass, sanctuary furnishings, and the like. I am not interested in suggesting that any one particular form was somehow the "ideal" or the "right way" to do something. My concern for design is not only in the end result but in the process. Therefore I have given the Church's guidelines so the architect and the community together may carefully consider them to find their own inspiration. And this method is much the same as that used by the Church in guiding all creative activity, whether by artists, liturgists, or theologians. By setting limits, the Church protects not only her mission and the deposit of faith entrusted to her but the work of the individual. The Church gives the individual these limits or guidelines not as rules to be blindly obeyed. Rather, they are safeguards. To use G. K. Chesterton's analogy, the Church builds a "corral of orthodoxy" in which the believer is safe to run freely. One ventures outside the corral at one's own risk. Church architecture is very much "built theology", and so the forms of the building must strive to "speak" the truths they represent. The risk for the theologian leaving the corral is heresy. The risk for the artist or architect is, at best, idiosyncratic isolation from the continuum of sacred art and architecture or, at worst, meaninglessness.

No aspect of building requires more ingenuity, care, industry, and diligence than the establishment and adornment of the temple. I need not mention that a well-maintained and well-adorned temple is obviously the greatest and most important ornament of a city; for the gods surely take up their abode in the temple. And if we decorate and splendidly furnish the houses of kings and visiting notables, what should we not do for the immortal gods, if we wish them to attend our sacrifices, and hear our prayers and supplications? But although men value them so highly, the gods have little concern for such perishables—they are moved solely by purity of mind and divine worship. There is no doubt that a temple that delights the mind wonderfully, captivates it with grace and admiration, will greatly encourage piety.

This is why I would wish the temple so beautiful that nothing more decorous could ever be devised; I would deck it out in every part so that anyone who entered it would start with awe for his admiration at all the noble things, and could scarcely restrain himself from exclaiming that what he saw was a place undoubtedly worthy of God.

—LEON BATTISTA ALBERTI

CHAPTER ONE

An Architectural Response to Vatican II

When Christ the Lord was about to celebrate the passover meal with his disciples and institute the sacrifice of his body and blood, he directed them to prepare a large room, arranged for the supper (Luke 22:12).

General Instruction of the Roman Missal, no. 1

It was our Lord who first instructed the apostles in the arrangement of the proto-church, in an "upper room", somewhere in Jerusalem. There Jesus instituted the Eucharist, in which we partake to this day. It may be difficult to see today's Church[1] as being *the* Church our Lord instituted; so much has changed with the passage of two thousand years. Her ecclesial structure, the liturgical form of the Eucharist, and its architectural surroundings all have developed since the apostolic age.[2] Nevertheless, the words of Saint Augustine are still valid: "The Church of today, of the present, is the Kingdom of Christ and the Kingdom of Heaven."[3]

Because the Church eternally is the "Church of today", she continually responds to the daily demands of the gospel with all the wisdom, insight, and resources at her disposal. The Church must be understood as a growing organism—meeting the demands of each age. "Thus, as the centuries go by, the Church is always advancing towards the plenitude of divine truth, until eventually the words of God are fulfilled in her."[4] This path toward her consummation can be traced from the apostolic age to the present through the documents she has produced. As Pope Saint Clement I's *Letter to the Corinthians* and the *Didache* encouraged the faithful in the early Church amid the prevalent paganism, as the councils of the patristic age responded to the questions of Christ's nature, as the Council of Trent sought to repair the breach caused by the Reformation, and as Pope Leo XIII's encyclical *Rerum novarum* answered the challenges of the changing industrial, commercial, and political structures in the nineteenth century, so the documents of the Second Vatican Council and the writings of Popes Paul VI and John Paul II are to be read as the Church's responses to the challenges of our own era.[5]

At Vatican II the Church not only responded to present concerns but opened the way for

---

[1] Throughout this book, *Church* (capitalized) refers to the apostolic institution, and *church* (lower case) to the building or to the particular church, being one part of the apostolic Church.

[2] For brief historical overviews of the development of the liturgy and of the church building, see Fr. Louis Bouyer, *Liturgy and Architecture* (South Bend, Ind.: University of Notre Dame Press, 1967), and Joseph Rykwert, *Church Building* (London: Sheed and Ward, 1966).

[3] St. Augustine, *De Civ. Dei* xx, 9, I; quoted in Karl Adam, *The Spirit of Catholicism* (London: Sheed and Ward, 1929), 14.

[4] Vatican II, *Dei Verbum* (Nov. 18, 1965), no. 8.

[5] See, for example, Vatican II, *Gaudium et spes* (Dec. 7, 1965), no. 10 [= GS].

15

1.1 The Second Vatican Council convening at St. Peter's.

tremendous advancement "toward the plentitude of divine truth" by critically examining her mission, direction, and components, and also the surrounding world. The most significant result of this inquiry has been a deliberate reform at her very heart, the liturgy. And since the church building exists primarily to support the liturgy, it would follow that there should also be corresponding developments in the design of her churches.

No one doubts that there have been significant and widespread changes to church buildings since the last Council. Some of these developments have been officially mandated or recommended by the Church through her various commissions, congregations, and episcopal conferences. Other changes have been unofficially implemented as developments of the twentieth-century Liturgical Movement. There have also been aberrations as the result of unapproved liturgical experimentation "in the spirit of Vatican II". To complicate things even more, in the tumult since the Council, several significant changes have been widely implemented—and are now concretized by common practice—that are thoroughly detrimental to the vision and mission of the Second Vatican Council: changes that will have to be reconsidered and redirected if the genius of

the Council is to bear the fruits desired in the hearts and minds of the laity and in the renewal of the temporal order. Today there is considerable confusion and a decided lack of direction in contemporary Catholic church architecture, and the church architect and local parish and priest may well be at a loss as to how to proceed. This book examines the current issues of church architecture and liturgy with the goal of pointing out an architectural direction that reflects the authentic teachings of the Catholic Church.

The context and intention of the Second Vatican Council

The Second Vatican Council was summoned by Pope John XXIII at a time when the postwar Church, especially in America, was strong, vibrant, and growing. The Council was convened to answer the needs of the age and to give direction for the approaching third Christian millennium. This represented a distinct difference from previous councils, which had been called to respond to various crises within the Church. Therefore, the Vatican II promulgations were intended to be more pastoral than dogmatic. Unlike previous councils, Vatican II did not define matters of faith and moral doctrine. The first seven ecumenical councils were called in response to the various christological heresies, the Reformation brought about Trent, and Vatican I sought to rebuff the assaults of the pantheistic, atheistic, and materialistic philosophies of the eighteenth and nineteenth centuries. It is noteworthy, therefore, that the agenda of the Second Vatican Council was pastoral in nature. After almost two thousand years of existence, the Church finally had the quietude and time for self-examination.

The Second Vatican Council was "convened in order to adapt the Church to the contemporary requirements of its apostolic task".[6] The Fathers of the Council recognized that the world's systems were rapidly changing: the Second World War had brought about both greater world awareness and a certain cynicism arising from the enormity of the massacres, the pogroms, and the genocidal policies of the day. The postwar rebuilding of Europe spurred both hope and materialism, while the Cold War and the threat of nuclear weapons brought a tenuous peace. The development of atomic energy, computer technology, and satellite communication systems all promised a continually changing world. In the midst of this change, the Second Vatican Council was called to speak the same timeless truths of the gospel "to a far different age in the world's history" and "to bring forward proposals and measures of a pastoral nature that could not have been foreseen four centuries ago [at the Council of Trent]."[7]

The Council issued sixteen documents, through which the Fathers of the Council sought to "impart an ever-increasing vigor to the Christian life of the faithful". This was to occur primarily through "the reform and promotion of the liturgy", since "it is through the liturgy, especially, that the faithful are enabled to express in their lives and manifest to others the mystery of Christ and the real nature of the true Church."[8] Thus, the first document issued was *Sacrosanctum concilium*, in English titled "The Constitution on the Sacred Liturgy". At the heart of this reform is the promotion of the royal priesthood of Jesus, through which all of Christ's faithful are called to enter into the liturgy with a renewed and deepened awareness of their place and their sacrificial participation in the Mass. As we shall see, this message has been widely ignored; in its stead has been substituted a feeble and effete version of "active participation" that essentially remains at the external level and reduces the laity to performing certain practical functions.

The reform of the liturgy was the primary, but far from singular, concern of the Council. The Vatican Fathers also developed certain doctrines concerning the role of the episcopate, religious freedom, ecumenism, the lay apostolate, and so on. Other issues were the renewal of religious life, the place of the Church in the world, the use of modern technology for the advancement of the gospel, Christian education, divine revelation, relations with non-Christian religions, and support for the Eastern Catholic churches.

The goal common to all of these varied documents was, in the words of Pope John Paul II, "the enrichment of the faith".[9] This process of "enrichment" was to occur through two broad avenues of change: (1) the policy of *aggiornamento* (Italian noun meaning "an update"); and (2) an increasing awareness among the laity of their role in the Church and her liturgy, known as *participatio actuosa*, or "active participation". Since both of these policies have far-ranging effects on the Church's liturgy and architecture, it is worthwhile to analyze their true meanings before examining the architectural implications of Vatican II's teachings about church buildings.

Since the Church is a two-thousand-year-old institution of both temporal and eternal dimensions, it should not be surprising that the movement toward *aggiornamento* has a certain underlying tension. Within the Church and her liturgies, there are both "unchangeable elements divinely instituted, and ... elements subject to change".[10] That

---

[6] *General Instruction of the Roman Missal*, 4th ed. (Mar. 27, 1975), intro., no. 12 [= GIRM].

[7] GIRM, intro., no. 10.

[8] Vatican II, *Sacrosanctum concilium* (Dec. 4, 1963), nos. 1 and 2 [= SC].

[9] Karol Wojtyla, *Sources of Renewal* (London: Collins, 1980), 15.

[10] GS, no. 21.

which is only humanly instituted may—in fact *ought to*—change to accommodate the needs of the day. That, however, which is divinely given is *ipso facto* immutable. *Aggiornamento*, therefore, does not—nor can it—entail a radical restructuring. Because certain things are founded on Christ, notably the nature of the liturgy and the structure of the Church, it is not even within the authority of the Church to change them. As the *General Instruction of the Roman Missal* points out in another context, the Church must "embrace one and the same tradition"[11] because "beneath all that changes there is much that is unchanging, much that has its ultimate foundation in Christ, who is the same yesterday, and today, and forever."[12] The same principles may be applied architecturally. Certain changes may be permitted or even necessary, in matters such as general seating, the use of pulpits, reservation in a tabernacle, or the form of the confessionals. But other things, such as the sacrificial aspect of the Mass, the unique place of the ministerial priesthood in the eucharistic assembly, and the uses of water at baptism and bread and wine at Eucharist, have their foundation in Christ and cannot change essentially.

Encouragement for active participation of the laity at Mass is at the heart of liturgical reform. "Mother Church earnestly desires that all the faithful should be led to that full, conscious, and active participation . . . which is demanded by the very nature of the liturgy."[13] The laity are called to be more than mere "strangers or silent spectators" at Mass. Rather "they should take part in the sacred action, conscious of what they are doing, with devotion and full collaboration . . . drawn day by day into ever more perfect union with God and each other, so that finally God may be all in all."[14] Clearly, the Council Fathers understood that participation of the laity in the liturgy, which is first and foremost an interior process, is essential for the fulfillment of the Church's mission. Fleshing this out, however, has proved problematic, as the very nature of the laity's true role has been badly misunderstood. Thus, while there have been many positive and salutary developments in the liturgy, there is still

much to be done, and there are even some things to be undone.

Among the salutary liturgical changes implemented to enable fuller lay participation was the wider use of the vernacular language for parts of the Mass.[15] Because the pressing concerns of the Church have shifted since the time when Latin was widely implemented as the language of the liturgy, it was agreed that the use of the vernacular would be "of great advantage to the people . . . especially in readings, directives, . . . prayers and chants."[16] Also, the structure of the Mass was revised to give greater prominence to the Liturgy of the Word, at which time the faithful are nourished "at the table of God's word", and most especially to the homily, when they are to be instructed in "the guiding principles of the Christian life".[17] The "common prayer", or the "prayer of the faithful", was restored so that the laity might be better able to enter into the prayers of the Mass with their whole lives.[18] The laity were also invited to take more active and visible places in the assembly as servers, readers, commentators, and choir members and to "take part by means of acclamations, responses, psalms, antiphons, hymns, as well as by actions, gestures and bodily attitudes".[19]

Moreover, the lay faithful are encouraged not to look upon the Sunday Eucharist as the limit of their spiritual life but to develop lives of personal sanctity with private prayer, works of charity, and Scripture study.[20] This is to enable them to fulfill the work unique to the lay vocations, namely, to "seek the Kingdom of God by engaging in temporal affairs and ordering them according to the plan of God".[21] Throughout these directives the Vatican Coun-

---

[11] GIRM, intro., no. 6.
[12] GS, no. 10.
[13] SC, no. 14.
[14] SC, no. 48.
[15] Latin had, for centuries, been one of the "sacred languages", along with Greek and Syro-Aramaic, used to "veil the mysteries". See Joseph Jungmann, S.J., *The Mass*, trans. Julian Fernandes (Collegeville, Minn.: Liturgical Press, 1976), 242.
[16] SC, no. 36 (2).
[17] SC, nos. 51 and 52.
[18] SC, no. 53.
[19] SC, nos. 29 and 30.
[20] SC, no. 12.
[21] Vatican II, *Lumen Gentium* (Nov. 21, 1964), no. 31 [= LG].

cil seeks to imbue the people of God with new life through a deeper appreciation of the Mass and with new understanding of their place in the Church and of their evangelical role in the Kingdom of God.

The baptismal priesthood of the people of God

There have been two recent directions in modern liturgy seeking to encourage more participation by the laity: the first is, in accordance with the documents, to call forth the gifts of the laity in service as readers, singers, acolytes, and such. This has unfortunately tended toward a functional understanding of active participation. As long as one sings, responds, sits, kneels, and stands at the right time, holds hands at the Lord's Prayer, or is an usher, a greeter, a music minister, or a liturgical dancer, one is thought to be fulfilling one's place in the assembly and actively participating. While some of these roles may have their place and can beautifully contribute to the aesthetic and emotional experience of the liturgy, the modern tendency is to stop at the level of this external participation. The second tendency (not in accordance with the documents and fortunately less widespread) is to make the laity feel more a part of the liturgy by having them assume places reserved for ordained ministers: giving homilies, gathering in the sanctuary at the Consecration, and even holding the elements during Consecration. The now unfortunately ordinary and widespread use of "extraordinary ministers" to distribute Holy Communion falls into this category. Because the theological dynamics of the liturgy are not widely understood even by liturgists, there is a tendency to blur the distinction between priest and people and to lose entirely the sense of the uniqueness of their individual roles and the unique natures of their respective sacrifices.

And yet there is a more robust and more profound understanding to be gleaned from the Vatican documents, one that has been widely ignored and that has vital implications for the correct implementation of liturgical changes and the proper ordering and arrangement of the church building: the promotion of the people of God as members of the royal priesthood of Jesus Christ.

Founded in the scriptural understanding that we are "a royal priesthood, a holy nation" (1 Pet 2:9–10), the recovery of this idea in Vatican II gives us a powerful understanding of the liturgical dynamic and of our place in the assembly. What does a priest do but offer sacrifice (Heb 5:1)? And what do all priests do but offer sacrifice in union with the one sacrifice of our High Priest now in heaven and thus participate in the one priesthood of Jesus Christ? Each form of priesthood has its own form of sacrifice: Jesus, the eternal High Priest, offered himself to the Father for the salvation of the world and is still "a minister in the sanctuary" (Heb 8:2). In sacramental participation with Christ, the ministerial priesthood now offers the Body and Blood of the Lord; and we, the royal priesthood, are called to offer ourselves as living and spiritual sacrifices "acceptable to God" through Jesus Christ, as our "spiritual worship" (cf. 1 Pet 2:9 and Rom 12:1).

The absence of this vital idea has, I believe, impeded the full implementation of the Second Vatican Council. The Council's goal of renewing the temporal order can come about only if the hearts and minds of Christ's faithful are first renewed. This can happen only by our entering with our lives into the depths of Christ's death and Resurrection. Only as we offer ourselves in imitation of our Lord, as priests offering ourselves as victims, can the power of the Resurrection take hold of us, heal us, empower us, and strengthen us. Until then, being "a Resurrection people" will remain just so many words. For there is tremendous and limitless potency in this sacrifice of the laity. When the man and woman and child at worship truly enter into the sacrifice of the Mass—conjoining the sacrifice of not just their bodies, but also their broken hearts, their joys and sorrows, their struggles and frustrations and toils, their families and their professions, their wounded relationships, and their vocations and states of life with the sacrifice of the Body of Christ offered to the Father—and then approach the altar-table to eat of the sacrifice at the Lord's Supper, the infinite grace of

God's compassion and mercy and healing can be unleashed in their lives.

As Fr. Louis Bouyer points out, sacrifices generally involve eating the victim. In the Body of Christ this is a mutual event: as Christ offers himself in sacrifice that we may consume him, so does Christ subsume us into his Body when we offer ourselves as victims. This mutual "self-donation" is the process by which we the Church, as the Bride of Christ, consummate our union with and become "one flesh" with the Groom at the Lord's Supper, which is also the Wedding Feast of the Lamb and a foretaste of our eternal union in heaven. For the full act of Holy Communion requires that two persons, the Lamb and the Bride, offer themselves in sacrifice to each other and to the Heavenly Father. Then, having given themselves to each other, they become one flesh: as the Body of Christ is consumed by us, we are subsumed into him.

This is the true dynamic of active participation: an exchange of persons in sacrificial love, a true covenant in the fullest sense of the word. This dynamic is of the utmost importance, and because of its neglect the potential of the sacrifice of the "people of God" has hardly been tapped. When it is tapped, it will become the source not only of personal sanctification and healing but of the restoration of relationships and families as well as of the re-integration and evangelization of society at large. Only then will the Council's charge to "renew the temporal order" find fruition. But in its neglect, the prevalent misunderstandings and misemphases have made this vital issue remote from the average lay person's consciousness.

The recent past

This is the heroic vision of the Second Vatican Council. The Church calls the faithful to an ever more profound awareness of the work of Christ in their lives and in the liturgy. Given such a calling, we should expect the arts and architecture of the Church to be particularly robust and pertinent in response to this challenge. Yet today, ecclesial design is in a state of confusion. It is directionless, in torpor even.

Similarly, much modern sacred art fails to engage us, to aid and challenge and direct us on our path of sanctification. We must, therefore, examine why there is so great an incongruity between the Council's vibrant message and the spiritually sterile (if purportedly functional) modern liturgical environment.

Since the promulgation of *Sacrosanctum concilium* in 1963, there have been both widespread and obvious changes to the liturgy and consequent changes to the buildings in which the liturgy is celebrated. While the roots of these liturgical and architectural changes predate the Council by quite a few decades, the vast majority of Western Catholic churches built up to the time of *Sacrosanctum concilium* were rather traditional and formal [figs. 1.2, 1.3]. They typically had straight rows of wooden pews; a communion rail; the altar, against the east wall of the sanctuary, embedded into a monumental, elaborately carved, and richly ornamented reredos, in which was enshrined the golden tabernacle; a life-size and realistic crucifix; a grand pulpit; a statuary army of saints and angels; depictive stained glass; and a stone baptismal font. Stylistic differences aside, until 1963, Catholic churches on the whole looked very much as they had for hundreds of years previously.

The changes since Vatican II have been significant and almost universal [figs. 1.4, 1.5]. In many churches the altar was brought into the middle of the sanctuary—or even into the nave—and Mass was now celebrated facing the congregation (*versus populum*). Reredos and communion railings were unceremoniously torn out and discarded, and pews were now padded or replaced by movable chairs. The tabernacle was shunted off to a side chapel, and in its place of centrality now sat the celebrant's chair; side altars were removed, and with them went the statues of the saints; the stations of the Way of the Cross came to look more like exercises in abstract art [fig. 1.6]; and the once holy altar came to resemble little more than a dining table.

But, as mentioned, these changes began much earlier. In the middle of the nineteenth century, Dom Prosper Guéranger, O.S.B. (1805–1875), set up the first center for liturgical

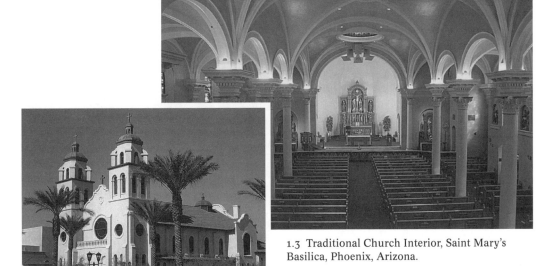

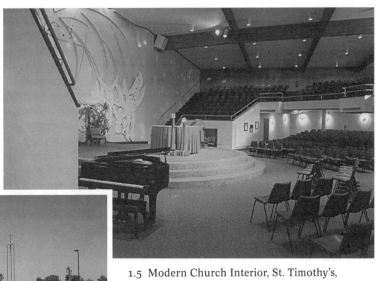

1.3 Traditional Church Interior, Saint Mary's Basilica, Phoenix, Arizona.

1.2 Traditional Church Exterior, Saint Mary's Basilica, Phoenix, Arizona.

1.5 Modern Church Interior, St. Timothy's, Mesa, Arizona.

1.4 Modern Church Exterior, St. Timothy's, Mesa, Arizona.

renewal at the abbey of Solesmes in France. Guéranger's efforts were seminal but hardly sweeping. His agenda was threefold: (1) the re-unification of the French churches under the Roman rite (as the Tridentine decrees had not been promulgated in France, many French bishops still authorized the various medieval and "neo-Gallican" rites); (2) a return to the Catholic mystical tradition largely swept away by the Enlightenment thinkers who deified Reason (hence, Guéranger was intent on main-taining Latin, in the tradition of "veiling the mysteries" from undue familiarity);[22] and (3) the need for renewed participation among all the faithful. "Guéranger advocated a return to the liturgy as the true source of spiritual life. He believed that people needed the liturgy and the liturgy needed the *whole* people of God to celebrate it."[23] He therefore saw a value in avoiding the mundanity of the vernacular lan-guage as allowing the faithful to enter into the liturgy in a nonlinear and nonanalytical par-ticipation.[24]

In 1905, with tremendous foresight and pro-found insight, Pope Pius X issued the decree *On Frequent and Even Daily Communion* to encourage the faithful to receive the Eucharist more often, as was the practice of the early Church. By 1909, Dom Lambert Beauduin, O.S.B. (1873–1960), a Belgian Benedictine who was following the tradition of liturgical study initiated at Solesmes, was promoting lay litur-gical activity. Beauduin also recognized that the liturgy was the true center of the Chris-tian's life and that it was necessary to combat the individualism of the age. For him, the lit-urgy united the faithful, one to the other, the gathered assembly to the universal Church, and the universal Church to Christ. Like many of the early liturgists in the movement, he was profoundly affected by the concept of the Mys-tical Body of Christ, recognizing that only in the Risen Lord could the people of God find true unity.[25]

Dom Odo Casel's influence at the German Benedictine monastery of Maria Laach and the German "Quickborn" movement (*Jung-brunnen*, literally "fountain of youth") in the 1920s under the influential theologian Ro-mano Guardini were other early forces in what

1.6 The Fourth Station, Chapel of the Red Rocks, Sedona, Arizona.

was rapidly becoming the international Litur-gical Movement.[26]

The general intention of the Liturgical Movement was to restructure the Mass so that it would no longer be perceived as essentially a clerical activity but would become fully com-munal. Fr. Josef Jungmann gives us the general schema of their work: "The offering to God in the sacrifice is the proper preparation for Holy Communion; the sacrificial meal belongs to the sacrifice, God invites us to it; all the prayers of the Mass lead up to it; and this meal is at the same time the meal of the Christian commu-nity."[27] Thus we see an attempt at a recovery of the integration between the meal as sacrifice and the sacrifice as meal in what Fr. Bouyer would call "the primitive implications" of the meal. Accordingly, their emphasis correctly spoke of the "priesthood of all believers".

The movement found its first architectural expressions in the works of two German

[22] Jungmann, *Mass*, 242.

[23] M. Kwatera, "Prosper Guéranger, Founder of the Modern Liturgical Movement", in *Leaders of the Liturgical Movement*, ed. R. Tuzik (Chicago: Liturgy Training Publications, 1990), 17–21.

[24] See Joseph Jungmann, S.J., *The Mass of the Roman Rite*, vol. 1 (New York: Benzinger, 1951), 159.

[25] R. Leggett, "Lambert Beauduin: The Vision Awaits Its Time", in Tuzik, *Leaders of the Liturgical Movement*, 27.

[26] See Austin Flannery, O.P., intro. to *Contemporary Irish Church Architecture*, by R. Hurley and W. Cantwell (Dublin: Gill and Macmillan, 1985), 9.

[27] Jungmann, *Mass of the Roman Rite*, 161.

Catholic architects: Dominikus Böhm, who worked with Fr. I. van Acken, and Rudolf Schwarz, who had come under the influence of Guardini while a member of Quickborn.[28] The modern architecture of the time was particularly well suited to the program of the modern liturgists. The idea of "universal space" as propagated by the German modernists worked well alongside the desire to replace the hierarchical model of the Church with an egalitarian, communal model. Moreover, the reductivist aesthetic then in vogue, a product of the de Stijl movement, worked hand in hand with the liturgists' ideas of simpler and less structured Masses in less fussy surroundings.

The movement was decidedly toward a "universal liturgical space", which can be seen in two of the most important churches of this era, Auguste Perret's church of Notre-Dame-le-Raincy near Paris and Schwarz's Corpus Christi in Aachen.[29] In both of these buildings the sanctuary is in the same space as the nave: gone is the chancel arch and with it the idea of a separation between heaven (the sanctuary) and the world (the nave) and between the priesthood and the laity. Gone, too, are images of saints in stained glass in favor of clear windows (Schwarz) or colored pattern glass with some symbolism incorporated (Perret). But, while it is important to note the innovations of the age, one must not ignore the continuity of traditional forms. Perret's church, while brilliantly exploiting the potential of concrete and stained glass curtain-walling, has the rather traditional basilican arrangement of a broad nave with side aisles [figs. 1.7 to 1.10]. Furthermore, the space retains a certain sense of sacrificial character and ministerial separation, since the sanctuary is raised quite high above the floor of the nave in the manner of the great Roman churches. Neither was Schwarz willing to abandon totally the traditional forms. So, at Corpus Christi, although there was a subdued differentiation of the sanctuary and the nave

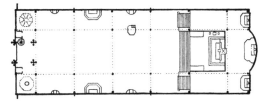

1.7 Notre-Dame-le-Raincy, by A. Perret, 1922, Plan.

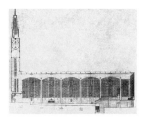

1.8 Notre-Dame-le-Raincy, by A. Perret, 1922, Section.

1.9 *right* Notre-Dame-le-Raincy, by A. Perret, 1922, Exterior.

1.10 *below* Notre-Dame-le-Raincy, by A. Perret, 1922, High Altar.

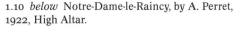

---

[28] S. Wormell, "Rudolf Schwarz and the Theology of Architecture", *Church Building*, autumn 1988, 22. See also Flannery, intro., 16.

[29] T. Gough, "Corpus Christi, Aachen", *Church Building*, autumn 1988, 23–24.

1.11 Corpus Christi, Aachen, by R. Schwarz, 1928–1930, Exterior.

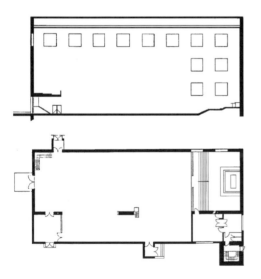

1.12 Corpus Christi, Aachen, Plan and Section.

by several series of broad steps in black marble—so that the nave "flows up" to the sanctuary—and by two tall columns of windows in the sanctuary as opposed to the clerestory windows of the nave, he still separated the two by the traditional, albeit slim and elegant, form of the altar rail [figs. 1.11 to 1.14].[30] Similarly, the pulpit is rendered in a sleek, planar manner, showing the traditional form in a stripped down, modernist vocabulary.

From 1920 through the 1950s, largely as the work of the Benedictines, the Liturgical Movement spread from France, Belgium, and Germany to Ireland, Austria, England, and the United States. After the Second World War the movement gained both ecclesial recognition and impetus from Pius XII's encyclical on the sacred liturgy, *Mediator Dei* (1947), the Holy Office's Instruction on Sacred Art (1952), and various other documents on liturgy and sacred music issued by the Sacred Congregation of Rites in the late 1950s.[31] These documents were not, however, complete approbations of the Liturgical Movement's agenda. It is important to note that the documents issued by Rome clearly spoke of maintaining the hierarchical and sacrificial aspects of the Eucharist and warned that "certain enthusiasts, over-eager in their search for novelty, are straying beyond the path of sound doctrine and prudence" and "sometimes even taint [the liturgy] with errors touching Catholic faith".[32] Specifically mentioned were the problems of making the altar into a primitive table, removing sacred images, and the denial of Christ's suffering by crucifixes that showed nothing of the Passion. It is further interesting to note, in light of the Liturgical Movement's emphasis on the amorphous "people of God", that Pius XII also clarifies that "priesthood" in the documents refers to the ministerial priest and reminds us of the need to maintain the separation of duties and sacrifices: "The people add something else, namely,

---

[30] This has now been "re-ordered": the rail has been removed, and an altar plinth—in awkwardly contrasting gray marble—has been built out from the chancel into the nave to allow Mass to be celebrated *versus populum*.

[31] Flannery, intro., 9–12.

[32] Pius XII, *Mediator Dei* (Nov. 20, 1947), no. 8 [= MD].

1.13 *above* Corpus Christi, Aachen, Ambo.

1.14 *left* Corpus Christi, Aachen, by R. Schwarz, 1928–1930, Nave.

the offering of themselves as a victim."[33] Here we see the beginnings of the recovery of the royal priesthood in Jesus Christ, through which, by virtue of their baptism, all men and women participate in the liturgy as priest and victim through the offering of themselves. It is, sadly, an agenda the Liturgical Movement has by and large ignored, and in many ways it is the unfinished business of both the Liturgical Movement and the Second Vatican Council.

Pius XII's admonition touches on growing problems in the thinking of the Liturgical Movement: first, a distortion of the idea of the "Body of Christ" into a "false mysticism" that did not uphold the distinction between Creator and creature; second, a gradual and growing emphasis on the "people of God" that was edging out of primacy the idea of the "Body of Christ". Certainly his magnificent document *Mystici Corporis* (1943) is to be seen as an attempt to correct this course. For in ways probably not envisaged by the founders of the Liturgical Movement—and certainly not by Guéranger, Beauduin, Guardini, or Parsch—the emphasis on the "people of God" (1 Pet 2:9–10) has led to a tacit rejection of the no-

tion of the "Body of Christ" (cf. Rom 12:4–5; 1 Cor 12:12–30) as a hierarchic and structured model. We shall see how explicit this becomes after the Council.

The implications of this point are sweeping, but there are other concerns as well. In reaction to the centuries-old emphasis on the "awesome mystery" of the Lord's sacrifice, the liturgists concerned themselves with the Eucharist as "the Lord's Supper" and thus promoted the communal "meal-aspect" of the Mass. As the call went out to the laity to "gather 'round the table of the Lord", these advocates sought justification in new methods of scriptural literary criticism, in archeology, and in the developing social sciences. It is unfortunate, as shall also be seen, that while their work has borne some good fruit in increasing lay participation, the whole sense of sacrifice—necessary and intrinsic to the Lord's Supper—has been widely lost. It is precisely the loss of this understanding of sacrifice—both as the re-presentation of the sacrifice of Christ and as the offering of oneself as victim—that has rendered much of the Liturgical

---

[33] MD, nos. 62 and 82–98.

Movement's agenda sterile. The process of again integrating the meal and the sacrifice as one reality for the modern consciousness is indeed the unfinished work of the Liturgical Movement.

The encyclicals of Pius XII should be read in the light of their day and are to be understood as voicing concerns regarding the integrity and appropriateness of some of the ideas then in vogue. One must note that such concerns went unheeded. In 1960 the Liturgical Movement gained great strength in the English-speaking world, especially in England and Ireland, with the publication of Peter Hammond's *Liturgy and Architecture*. Although written by an Anglican, *Liturgy and Architecture* had a great impact on Catholic church design. Until this time, nearly all new and rebuilt churches in Great Britain were still in the Victorian Gothic Revival style. Like any modernist of his day, Hammond took exception to this trend. He saw the failure to create a "living architecture" as a "theological rather than architectural" problem. Taking the rationale of the Liturgical Movement, he argued for the building to be a house for the church congregation, a "house of God's people", or *domus ecclesiae*, rather than a building dedicated primarily to the worship of God, a "house of God", or *domus Dei*. Hammond's "radical functionalist" approach to church design viewed the church as a building to house the congregation gathered around the altar, placing the emphasis on the community's action of gathering.[34] This is significantly different from the traditional Catholic emphasis, which is always on the Eucharist. It is the Eucharist around which the community gathers. Though Hammond does not appear to reject the hierarchical nature of the Church, his ecclesiological model does differ from the Catholic understanding. The central problem with this sort of demotic model, still prevalent today, is that by focusing the emphasis on the local community, it diminishes the importance of the universal and cosmic Church. It can easily lead to thinking that communities can form their own liturgies, that the liturgy can be "planned", and that the liturgy is somehow "made" by the gathered members: all prevalent ideas today. This model necessarily obscures

the fact that liturgy—a participation in the work of Christ—is *received* from his Church.

The problem of this one-sided ecclesiology, and its consequent architectural expression, was, oddly enough, compounded by the reception of the documents of the Second Vatican Council. Two of the key documents, *Sacrosanctum concilium* and *Lumen Gentium* (The Dogmatic Constitution on the Church), were selectively interpreted by many liturgists and theologians as defending the communitarian principles of the Liturgical Movement. These thinkers parboiled the documents to advance their original agenda and sold their ideas under the banner of "the spirit of the Council". It is my contention that such interpretations take conciliar texts out of context and were unintended by the Council. It should suffice to give one recent and clear demonstration of this.

The misinterpretation of Vatican II

In a recent book on Catholic church architecture, Austin Flannery, O.P., remarks that "an understanding of the Church primarily in terms of its hierarchical structure was well served by medieval church architecture." But he goes on to say that, in *Lumen Gentium*, "the main emphasis is placed not on the hierarchical structure of the Church . . . but on its members, 'the people of God,' to use the Constitution's terminology." Flannery argues, in effect, that Vatican II *replaced* the term "Body of Christ" (given its hierarchical implications), and that it is, therefore, this egalitarian idea of the "people of God" that is "most important to the architect's brief".[35] This is quite a stunning analysis, both for theological and for liturgical reasons. But can it be supported?

In comparing the document itself with the commentator's analysis, one does not find *Lumen Gentium* discarding the ideas of a hierarchical Church or the applicability of the "Body of Christ". Instead, this traditional expression and understanding are both regularly used and reaffirmed.[36] (Indeed, the entire third chapter

---

[34] Peter Hammond, *Liturgy and Architecture* (London: Barrie and Rockliff, 1960), 11, 28, 38.

[35] Flannery, intro., 26–28.

[36] LG, no. 7.

of *Lumen Gentium* is devoted to explaining the nature of the Church's hierarchy.) The document actually *emphasizes* the distinction between priests and lay people and upholds the hierarchical nature of the Church, stating that, while each "shares in the one priesthood of Christ", nevertheless, the two "*differ essentially* and not only in degree". The teaching remains constant: the ministerial priest "by the sacred power that he has . . . effects the eucharistic sacrifice and offers it to God in the name of all the people".[37] The laity enter into the liturgy with their own sacrifice, one of their lives, and by partaking in the Body and Blood in the Communion banquet.

This is not to say that the idea of the "people of God" is not a significant theme in *Lumen Gentium* and subsequent writings, but never does it supplant the idea of the "Body of Christ". The laity do truly participate in the offering of the Eucharist—as *Lumen Gentium* teaches, through the "reception of the sacraments, prayer and thanksgiving, the witness of a holy life, abnegation and active charity"[38]—however, their primary sacrifice is a personal one. The sacrifice of the laity is chiefly implemented by responding to the call to "present your bodies as a living sacrifice, holy and acceptable to God" (Rom 12:1).[39] To give but one example of the confusion in the modern liturgy, this is why it is absurd for the laity to hold or elevate the bread and wine at the Consecration (as some liturgists propose): it is only the ministerial priest, acting in the person of Christ the Head, who makes Christ's sacrificial offering present, and the people participate through the priest's action, not independent of or alongside it.

Many today still hold a false dichotomy between the "people of God" and "Body of Christ", through, one assumes, not understanding the terms or their implications. Both are important terms, but one does not stand in isolation from the other. The *Catechism* has made a profound integration of these two terms, along with another significant scriptural term, by describing the Church as "the People of God" . . . "the Body of Christ" . . . "the temple of the Holy Spirit".[40] This beautifully trinitarian formulation leads to a deeper

and richer understanding of the Church and, by extension, more opportunity for the church architect in expressing the unity and necessary relationship of these themes.

It is necessary for us to contemplate this new synthesis offered by the *Catechism* to find balance in our approach to liturgy and the liturgical environment. Why is this? On its own, the "people of God" risks becoming limited to a temporal and sociological concept. Its potential narrowness is seen when modern liturgists use the term in conjunction with the notions of the "gathered faithful" and the "local assembly". "People of God" may speak to the local community gathered in prayer, yet it does not necessarily suggest the greater community of saints and angels involved in the liturgy or the fact that the local sacramental liturgy is a participation in a far greater, transcendental reality.

The "Body of Christ", however, as the fulfillment of the "people of God", has theological implications that are a necessary complement to the "people of God", especially as a model for the liturgy (and therefore as a model for the church building).[41] It has, as Emile Mersch points out, been called upon throughout the ages to correct misunderstandings and to refute gnosticism, Arianism, Nestorianism, Pelagianism, Protestantism, and Modernism: "The very nature of the doctrine makes it both the center of resistance against error and the heart of the Church's positive teaching."[42] The reality of Jesus Christ contains the dual mysteries of his humanity and his divinity. In a similar fashion, the "Body of Christ" speaks simultaneously to the temporal and the eternal, the corporeal and the spiritual, the human and the divine. It is a transcendental term, since it speaks not only to the local assembly but to the visible, universal organization and hierarchical structure and includes the whole Church:

---

[37] LG, no. 10; italics added.

[38] LG, no. 10.

[39] John Paul II, *Christifideles laici* (Dec. 30, 1988), no. 14.

[40] See *Catechism of the Catholic Church* (San Francisco: Ignatius Press, 1994), nos. 782–98 [= CCC].

[41] Joseph Cardinal Ratzinger, *The Ratzinger Report* (San Francisco: Ignatius Press, 1985), 47.

[42] Emile Mersch, "The Whole Christ: On the Unity of the Church", *Communio* 14, no 1 (spring 1987): 76.

Militant, Suffering, and Triumphant. We shall see in chapter 8 how the idea of the Church as a great building, the "temple of the Holy Spirit", and as the heavenly Jerusalem has been effected throughout the ages.

It is unfortunate that modern liturgists have so exclusively adopted the one and discarded the others, for ultimately there cannot be any true opposition between these expressions. In the *Catechism*, the question is asked, "Who celebrates [the liturgy]?" and is answered thus:

> Liturgy is an "action" of the *whole Christ* (*Christus totus*). . . . [T]hese are the ones who take part in the service of the praise of God and the fulfillment of his plan: the heavenly powers, all creation (the four living beings), the servants of the Old and New Covenants (the twenty-four elders), the new People of God (the one hundred and forty-four thousand), especially the martyrs "slain for the word of God," and the all-holy Mother of God (the Woman), the Bride of the Lamb, and finally "a great multitude which no one could number, from every nation, from all tribes, and peoples and tongues." . . . It is the whole *community*, the Body of Christ united with its Head, that celebrates [the liturgy].[43]

Here we see clearly that the "people" are but one part of the heavenly liturgy, and this passage demonstrates the exclusionary problem of the "people of God" as a model for liturgy: it is but one aspect of the divine worship. The phrase can also ignore the reality of the heavenly liturgy, with which we unite ourselves through the sacramental expression of the one liturgy.[44]

It would be more profitable for modern liturgists to turn their attention to a key passage in *Lumen Gentium* that would help resolve the problems caused by isolating the term "people of God" from the "Body of Christ":

> The one mediator, Christ, established and ever sustains here on earth his holy Church, the community of faith, hope and charity, as a visible organization through which he communicates truth and grace to all men. But, the society structured with hierarchical organs and the mystical body of Christ, the visible society and the spiritual community, the earthly Church and the Church endowed with

heavenly riches, are not to be thought of as two realities. On the contrary, they form one complex reality which comes together from a human and a divine element. For this reason the Church is compared, not without significance, to the mystery of the incarnate Word. As the assumed nature, inseparably united to him, serves the divine Word as a living organ of salvation, so, in a somewhat similar way, does the social structure of the Church serve the Spirit of Christ who vivifies it, in the building up of his body.[45]

In this passage we can see again the limitations of using the "people of God" exclusively, especially if one uses it apart from an appreciation of the hierarchical structure of the Church. In focusing on the "people" as the gathered community, one ignores the greater spiritual community of the universal Church: angelic, Militant, Suffering, and Triumphant. This myopic focus on the "people of God" is no doubt a part of the reason that modern churches tend to be devoid of images of the saints (denying the Church Triumphant), just as modern theology avoids the issue of Purgatory (ignoring the Church Suffering), and modern piety no longer challenges us to "fight the good fight" (taking our place in the Church Militant). The false opposition between the "people of God" and the "Body of Christ" is clearly contrary to the message and intention of the Second Vatican Council. They must be understood as two facets of the one reality, integrally related. It is with this understanding that Pope Paul VI's *Credo of the People of God* explicitly defines the Church as "the Mystical Body of Christ, a visible society, hierarchically structured".[46]

Flannery also writes that, with the concept of the "people of God", nowadays "the architect does not have to choose between a conception of a church as the 'House of God' and as the 'House of God's People.' For God is present *in his people*; it is *in the assembly* that God is encountered."[47] In this statement (again presupposing the dichotomy while hoping to resolve it), he advances a third and all-

[43] CCC, nos. 1136, 1138, and 1140.
[44] CCC, no. 1326.
[45] LG, no. 8.
[46] Paul VI, *The* Credo *of the People of God* (June 30, 1968).
[47] Flannery, intro., 27; italics added.

too-common misconception: that the assembly is somehow a primary, and even sufficient, mode of encountering God. This confusion is found frequently among modern liturgists. For instance, in a pamphlet describing the reordering of their church, a particular community declared that "The assembly is the primary sign of the priesthood of Jesus Christ; the assembly is the primary minister; the assembly is the Church." They imply that "maximizing the collective sense of gathering . . . contemplating each other" is on par with attending to "the principal focal points of the action". (Although, as they fail to mention "sacrifice" as an option among "the sharing of our story . . . common reflection, song, processions, presentations, greetings, eating and drinking, movement and action", one is unsure of precisely *what* these principal focal points might be.)[48]

Simply put, this thinking is not in consonance with the teaching of Vatican II. While it is true that God is among his people because of Christ's promise in Matthew 18:20, this is neither the *only* way nor even the *primary* way in which God is encountered in the liturgy. *Sacrosanctum concilium* continues the ancient teaching that "Christ is always present in his Church, especially in her liturgical celebrations. He is present in the Sacrifice of the Mass, not only in the person of his minister, . . . but especially in the eucharistic species", in the word (Scripture), and "lastly" (*lastly* as least important in the series) in the assembly of the people.[49] Nor is the liturgy even primarily concerned with the gathering of the people. Vatican II continues the ancient teaching that "the sacred liturgy is principally the worship of the divine majesty."[50]

But what is most important, regardless of Flannery's attempts at clarification, the Second Vatican Council did not change the *purpose* of the church building. That building still exists primarily for the worship of the Lord. The Church sets aside a building—she creates a sacred place—that in it we may gather together in his presence and, through the holy liturgy, become "the people of God" by entering more deeply into the mystery of the Body of Christ. Here we speak not only of the gathered local community but of the worldwide Church Mili-

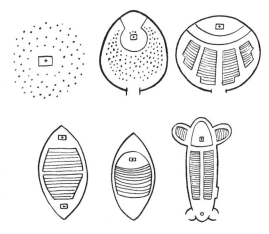

1.15 "Church as Amoebae (top) and Paramecia (bottom)" (after Hammond).

tant and of the Church Suffering and Triumphant, along with the choirs of angels, who join us in the eternal praises of God. One cannot design a building for "God's people" without first considering God. It is, nonetheless, interesting that Vatican II uses the term "house of God" for the church building.[51]

But what are the architectural implications of using "the people of God" as a primary or exclusive ecclesiological model? The main architectural problem is that "people of God" is an amorphous term—it evokes images of an unstructured crowd—and it says nothing of order, and nothing of structure, on which to base an architecture. To use this as a model for a church building, one would reasonably arrive at a "universal liturgical space". But the Body of Christ is not a one-celled amoeba or paramecium [fig. 1.15]. Rather it is a complex, multifarious, and organic reality. In short, "Body of Christ" and "temple of the Holy Spirit" lend themselves, in a way that "people of God" cannot, more easily to an articulated building, because they imply different roles and functions

---

[48] Congregation of the Sisters of the Holy Cross, *The Renewed Church of Our Lady of Loretto* (Notre Dame, Ind.: Saint Mary's College, n.d.).

[49] SC, no. 7. That there is a "hierarchy of presence" is made quite explicit in Sacred Congregation of Rites, *Eucharisticum mysterium* (May 25, 1967) [= EM].

[50] SC, no. 33. See also Paul VI, *Mysterium fidei*, which deals with errors about the various modalities of Christ's presence.

[51] SC, no. 124.

1.16 "Church as the Body of Christ" (after de Giorgio).

while preserving the senses of unity and integration [fig. 1.16]. Christ's head is at the apse, which is the seat of governance represented by the bishop's cathedra; the choir is his throat, from which the chants of the monks issue forth the praise of God; the transepts are his extended arms; his torso and legs form the nave, since the gathered faithful are his body; the narthex represents his feet, where the faithful enter the church; and at the crossing is the altar, which is the heart of the church. The power and clarity of this image of the crucified Lord is precisely why it was the predominant model for church design until the second half of the twentieth century.

Flannery's commentary is by no means unique; it only illustrates a much wider problem. There seems to be a certain bias in reading and interpreting the Council's documents that gives undue emphasis to the communal and social aspects of the church and the liturgy, while neglecting the necessary hierarchical and sacrificial aspects of the Lord's Supper. The above-outlined agenda has been given us in lieu of the vibrant and life-giving vision of the true *participatio actuosa* found in the sacrificial participation of the royal priesthood. Because of such overemphases and oversights, the full reform of the liturgy is still to come. And because these misconstructions affect architecture, the correct restructuring of churches to support the reformed

liturgy has likewise yet to come. Surely there is great progress to be made in the liturgy and its architectural environment. Any such advancements that make the liturgy more pertinent and vital to the life of the parish and the individual, however, can be made only if they are firmly rooted in the fullness of the Church's tradition, with which the Council is expressly in continuity.

The need for a reexamination and a fresh response

These problems in the interpretation of the Council's documents have undoubtedly contributed to the confusion in the architectural ordering of churches. Now, years after the Council, some prominent liturgists are beginning to realize that a number of the changes brought about by the Liturgical Movement have proven detrimental to genuine worship. Whether or not they would agree with my diagnosis and prescription, some would agree that, despite the millions of dollars spent in reordering churches and redirecting the liturgy, the laity have been brought into neither a more profound sense of active participation nor a deeper sense of community.

To correct these deficiencies, to build true eucharistic communities, and to aid the lay faithful in the understanding of their proper sacrificial place as members of the royal priesthood, it is now necessary to return to those documents and critically reexamine the changes made since Vatican II. We do not lack guidance in our tasks of examining the reform of the liturgy and finding a true architectural response to Vatican II. The Council, concerned with proper implementation, providentially set guidelines for the correct revision of the liturgy:

In order that sound tradition be retained, and yet the way remain open to legitimate progress, a careful investigation—theological, historical, and pastoral—should always be made into each part of the liturgy to be revised. Furthermore the general laws governing the structure and meaning of the liturgy must be studied in conjunction with the experience derived from recent liturgical reforms and from the indults granted to various places. Finally, there must be no innovations unless the good of the Church genuinely and certainly requires them, and care must be taken that any new forms adopted should in some way grow organically from forms already existing.[52]

In this citation we can find six criteria for the correct revision of the liturgy. There are three areas of investigation to be considered, viz., theology, history, and pastoral care. Along with these, there must be an appraisal of whether the good of the Church truly requires change in order to ensure that any change is for the enrichment of the faith. There must also be a concern for organic growth, growth from precedent, growth from the living reality of tradition, with the continuity of tradition in mind. Finally, we are called to evaluate the experiences gained from liturgical experiments and changes, to determine if they have contributed to the spiritual welfare of the faithful. And since liturgical changes inevitably find architectural expression, it would seem to be in keeping with the desires of the Council that we examine the church building and each of these components with these same criteria in mind in order to further these goals.

The full implementation of the Second Vatican Council is the theme of John Paul II's papacy. Even his pontifical name speaks to the memory and intentions of his predecessors, John XXIII and Paul VI (who respectively opened and closed Vatican II).[53] From his papal installation, John Paul II has repeatedly affirmed "the lasting importance of the Second Vatican Council" and regards it "our clear duty to devote our energies to putting it into effect".[54] The Council itself did not seek to make many changes—only those necessary to adapt to new circumstances.[55] But since so much has transpired in the name of the Council that was unintended by, and even foreign to the intentions of, the Council, the present Pope is now in the position of pulling in the reins of change, keeping the whole Church on "the narrow and difficult path" that the gospel demands (cf. Mt 7:14). And yet the Holy Father continues to explore new ways to bring about the true progress that is to be found in the authentic vision of the Council.

As the Pope's response to the demands of this age has been strong and forthright, so should the churches we build be strong architectural responses to our age. As the Pope seeks to bring Christ into the world, so should our architecture be *incarnational*. The banality and architectural impotence of churches of the recent past cannot be attributed only to an increasingly secularized modern society, for societies have always had tensions between the sacred and spiritual and the secular and material; there has always been a conflict between the City of God and the City of Man. I believe that it is rather a lack of conviction and direction, brought about by theological confusion, that has resulted in liturgical and architectural poverty. "The barrenness of the building reflects the barrenness of contemporary theology."[56]

When the Church has been strong and robust and sure of her vision, her architecture has likewise been rich and expressive. Historically, we can see noticeable connections between the Church's theology, her sense of mission, and the strength of her arts. The great ages of church building have all had strong architectural expressions to manifest the equally robust faith of the Church. The Constantinian basilican church, derived from the Roman judicial forum, was a statement that the Church brings forth the justice of Christ into the world [figs. 1.17, 1.18]. The Byzantine liturgy, architecture, and arts were forceful expressions of the contemporary patristic theology and spirituality [fig. 1.19]. The Gothic cathedral was an embodiment of Augustinian cosmology and theology, where the Church on earth was seen as a foreshadowing of the "heavenly Jerusalem" (cf. Rev 21:1) [fig. 1.20]. This was both contemporaneous and parallel to the work of

---

[52] SC, no. 23.

[53] John Paul II, *Redemptor Hominis* (March 4, 1979), no. 2.

[54] John Paul II, *First Message to the World* (Oct. 17, 1978); reiterated in his "Apostolic Letter on the 25th Anniversary of *Sacrosanctum concilium*" (Dec. 4, 1988); the latter published in English as *Love Your Mass* (London: Catholic Truth Society, 1989), 2.

[55] GIRM, intro., no. 10.

[56] C. Pickstone, "Creating Significant Space", *Church Building*, autumn 1988, 10.

1.17 Basilica of Maxentius, Rome, 307–312.

1.18 San Apollinare in Classe, Ravenna, 534–549, Nave.

the Scholastics (notably Saint Thomas Aquinas), who were deeply rooted in Saint Augustine. Later, the exuberance of the Baroque architecture during the Counter Reformation—with dual emphases on the cult of the Eucharist and the proclamation of the Word—was simultaneously an architectural affirmation of the Tridentine definitions and an implicit criticism of the austerities and iconoclasm of Calvinism [fig. 1.21].[57]

In the middle of the last century, the Gothic Revival, championed by A. W. N. Pugin, called for a "Christian architecture" to shore up the spiritual foundations of the increasingly materialistic and fragmented society brought about by the Renaissance, the Reformation, the Enlightenment, and the Industrial Revolution. The Middle Ages were seen by the English Romantics as a time when society was integrated, an age of great spirituality and faith. Men like Pugin reasoned that in order to restore the harmony of the Middle Ages one should reintroduce the Gothic style of the age. For Pugin it was more than a question of style, it was a matter of *principle*.[58] The Gothic Revivalists were interested in questions concerning the propriety of materials and the structural logic of the building, a return to the tradition of craftsmanship, and finding "honest" or "natural" expressions of design that respected the individual artisan and the created order. It was against the dehumanizing effects of the Industrial Revolution that the Gothic was employed to reconstruct a Christian society. The architectural implications of the arguments against materialism were also fostered by Pope Pius IX in his rejection of modern philosophical errors, as well as by the First Vatican Council, and later by Pope Leo XIII, who likewise decried the dehumanization that industrialized society can bring. That Gothic Revival churches were still being built until the time of Vatican II demonstrates the enduring ability that this style had in expressing the thoughts and attitudes of the Church at Vatican I [fig. 1.22].

1.19 San Apollinare in Classe, Dome mosaic.

1.20 Wells Cathedral, *c.* 1185–1239, Nave. Inkwash by Author.

---

[57] Paul Johnson, *Pope John Paul II and the Catholic Restoration* (London: Weidenfeld and Nicholson, 1982), 7.
[58] David Watkin, *Morality and Architecture* (Oxford: Clarendon Press, 1977), 13.

1.21 St. Nicholas Mala Strana, Prague, by C. and K. Dientzenhofer, 1703–1752, Nave.

Therefore, as Vatican II confidently and openly confronts and challenges the world with the demands of the gospel, so must our architecture follow. It is not a time for dogmatic architecture, which in today's architectural debates tends toward stylistic revivalism—be it Classical or modernistic. The bastions have been razed. We must forge a strong and vibrant architecture, rooted in the Church's traditional and enduring forms, that speaks to contemporary society and modern humanity of the source of our faith: the Incarnation. To accomplish this we must first reclaim and build upon the agenda of the Second Vatican Council, entering into "the true letter and the true spirit of the Council"[59] to find an architecture to support and manifest the vision. We must also, as did the Fathers at Trent and the Liturgical Movement, continue to engage in a profound *retour aux sources*, looking again at the Scriptures, at archeology, and at the patristic sources to find those essential elements that transcend the time and culture in which they first found expression. This will, no doubt, require significant educational efforts at both the diocesan and parish levels as well as in seminaries. With these goals in mind, we will now look at the relationship between the Church and the arts as well as at the effect of theology on architecture. We will then examine each of the main components of the church building in the light of the six criteria given for proper liturgical revision and end with an examination of the building as

1.22 Cathedral of the Madeleine, Salt Lake City, Exterior.

a whole, considering its architectural potential as an icon of the Kingdom of God in the modern world.

---

[59] Ratzinger, *Report*, 19.

CHAPTER TWO

Art, Architecture, and Theology

The Church and the arts

As *Mediator Dei* reminds us, the Church is a society, a civilization of relationships with structure, social patterns, language, and values.[1] As such, she has a culture through which these are expressed. This culture is not so much the body of works found in a society—which in the case of the Church would include such diverse products as the mosaics at Galla Placidia in Ravenna [fig 2.1], the Hagia Sophia [fig. 2.2], the *Divine Liturgy* of Saint John Chrysostom, the *Summa theologiae*, the tympanum at Chartres [fig. 2.3], Fra Angelico's *Christo deriso* [fig. 2.4], and Francis Thompson's "Hound of Heaven". It is, rather, the developed understanding of values that gives foundation to the production of such works. That is to say, although the seven above-mentioned masterpieces come from different ages, countries, and civilizations, are in different media, and serve different needs, they can all be considered part of the same culture because they are the products of the same mind: the mind of the Church. They are all products of the same Catholic institution, all rooted in a Catholic understanding of values and meaning, and they all serve the same end: the glory of God.

Josef Pieper, in his book *Leisure: The Basis of Culture*, demonstrates that culture is inextricably rooted in, and springs from, the act of public sacrifice or worship.[2] This connection becomes more obvious when we look at linguistic derivations. The word *culture* is derived from the Latin *cultus*, the worship of the deity. The word *liturgy* is from the Greek *leit-ourgia*;

it means literally the "work" of the people, or the public act of worship. Pieper shows us that *culture* and *liturgy* are fused in a society's public worship. It can be said of all civilizations and societies that what is *ultimately* valued, what is *worshipped*, is embodied in the products of the culture. In this sense, modern Western civilization is little different from the ancient Mayan, Egyptian, or Babylonian civilizations: all worshipped their gods in a public act, and their arts all expressed these values. The prevalent culture in western Europe and North America is likewise derived from the "public act", but, rather than sacrificial oblation, the public acts are commerce, consumption, work, and entertainment. Hence, the signifying products of Western culture are such things as high-rise commercial buildings and shopping malls, sports stadiums, television and motion pictures, and luxury automobiles.

This explanation is necessarily a simplification of the phenomenon of culture. Modern pluralistic societies have different and often opposing values (thus counter-cultures) as well as ethnic, religious, racial, and class subcultures. Furthermore, the Church herself exists in nations with disparate cultures and has her own subcultures, such as Melkite and Maronite, oriental and occidental, and North American and Latin American, as well as the

---

[1] Pius XII, *Mediator Dei* (Nov. 20, 1947), no. 42 [= MD].
[2] Josef Pieper, *Leisure: The Basis of Culture*, trans Alexander Dru. Mentor-Omega books (New York: New American Library, 1963).

2.1 *The Good Shepherd*, Mausoleum of Galla Placidia, Ravenna, *c.* 425.

recent rise of distinct and strong Afro-Catholic cultures. While these are all true and distinct cultures, they are also interdependent insofar as all are part of the one Church: the various rites and cultural expressions are commonly founded in the same act of divine worship, the Eucharist.

In the end, any civilization necessarily has a culture that springs from that which the people value ultimately, what they worship. A culture is shaped by the values held by the society. The products of the culture embody those values, and thus they both educate the society and help to continue those values. Its cultural products are primarily those that spring from the public act of worship. This is why we can

say that there is a true Catholic culture whose products are derived from the Church's public act of divine worship in the Eucharist. And, since the liturgy develops under the guidance of the Holy Spirit,[3] we can say that the valid expressions of the Church's culture develop under that same guidance: "Drawing their inspiration from heaven, these human arts will then shine with heaven's clear light and contribute not only to the progress of civilization but also to the glory of God and the salvation of souls."[4] Since the Church is in constant need of men and women to develop culture in

---

[3] MD, no. 65.
[4] MD, no. 209.

2.2 Hagia Sophia, Istanbul, 532–537, Exterior.

2.3 Tympanum, Chartres, 1220.

2.4 *Christo deriso*, by Bl. Fra Angelico.

art, music, and architecture, she has always been patroness to the arts.[5] The Church views the fine arts as among man's noblest activities because "the arts are directed toward expressing in some way the infinite beauty of God in works made by human hands." This is especially true of sacred art, when "dedication to the increase in God's praise and of his glory is more complete, the more exclusively they are devoted to turning men's minds devoutly toward God."[6] Since the gospel is the source of the Church's culture, it is primarily through the *sacred arts*, those dedicated to the promotion of the gospel, that the culture of the Church is advanced.

Artistic freedom and ecclesial control

In the promotion of culture the Church grants the artist wide latitude and great freedom of artistic expression. Since art is a human action—a *personal* act—the artist must be given due respect. Indeed, the Church must grant a certain freedom to the artist for conception and technique, innovation, materials, and design, for, as Jacques Maritain has noted, "There is no style *peculiar* to religious art, there is no *religious technique*."[7] Sacred art, however, is

---

[5] *General Instruction of the Roman Missal*, 4th ed. (Mar. 27, 1975), no. 254 [= GIRM].
[6] Vatican II, *Sacrosanctum concilium* (Dec. 4, 1963), no. 122, [= SC].
[7] Jacques Maritain, "Some Reflections upon Religious Art", in *Art and Scholasticism*, trans. J. F. Scanlan (London: Sheed and Ward, 1930), 143.

also a *public* act. It is ordered to support the public worship. Therefore, the Church does not give complete freedom—as Fr. J. O'Connell pointed out, to do so would not be true liberty but would only lead to license.[8] Obviously, the artist does not have the right to do anything profane, offensive, irreverent, theologically errant, or liturgically improper.

Historically, the Church has maintained a firm control over her artists: the Second Council of Nicaea (A.D. 787) cautioned that "the execution alone belongs to the painter, the selection and arrangement of subjects belong to the Fathers."[9] In the sixteenth century, Saint Charles Borromeo advised bishops to pay particular attention to the content of sacred images, warning that "a heavy punishment or penalty has been set for painters and sculptors so that they do not depart from the prescribed rules in their works" as well as for pastors who "have permitted an unusual and offensive image to be painted in their churches". In his *Instructiones*, Saint Charles catalogued the various kinds of inappropriate imagery, "whether in a church or in any other place". These include any image that "contains any false teaching, ... that suggests an occasion of dangerous error to the uneducated, ... that is contrary to Sacred Scriptures and Church tradition ... that is uncertain, apocryphal, and superstitious ... profane, base, or obscene, dishonest or provocative, whatever is merely curious, and what does not incite to piety, or that which can offend the minds and eyes of the faithful."[10]

While, no doubt, the intention remains the same, such stringent controls have been relaxed considerably, as *Mediator Dei* (1947) advised: "Modern art should be given free scope in the due and reverent service of the Church and the sacred rites, provided that they preserve a correct balance between styles tending neither to extreme realism nor to excessive 'symbolism,' and that the needs of the Christian community are taken into consideration rather than the particular taste or talent of the individual artist."[11] Vatican II reaffirms this principle in the document *Sacrosanctum concilium*, which gives art "free scope in the Church, provided it brings to the task the reverence and honors due to the sacred buildings

and rites." This same document, nonetheless, reaffirms the Church's authority to control sacred art as expressed in *Mediator Dei*, stating, "In fact the Church has, with good reason, always claimed the right to pass judgment on the arts, deciding which of the works of artists are in accordance with faith, piety, and the laws religiously handed down, and are to be considered suitable for sacred use."[12]

Jacques Maritain carefully examined the tension between the need for ecclesial control of sacred art and the necessary respect due the artist to allow him to bring to the task his own insight, aesthetic awareness, creative vision, and mode of expression. Looking first at the relationship between the secular and sacred art of an age, Maritain recognized that:

> Religious art is not a thing which can be isolated from art simply, from the general artistic movement of an age: confine it and it becomes corrupted, its expression a dead letter. On the other hand the art of a period carries with it all the intellectual and spiritual stuff which constitutes the life of a period; and in spite of whatever rare and superior qualities contemporary art may possess in the order of sensibility, virtue and innovation, the spirituality it conveys is not infrequently poor indeed and sometimes very corrupt.[13]

Since artists are products of their time and thus influenced by secular or temporal values, it is sometimes necessary for the Church to intervene in the production of sacred art to protect the spiritual welfare of the faithful. This protection is especially important because religious art seeks to convey theological truth:

> Sacred art is in a state of absolute dependence upon theological wisdom. There is manifested in the figures it sets before our eyes something far above all our human art, divine Truth it-

---

[8] Fr. J. O'Connell, *Church Building and Furnishing, the Church's Way* (London: Burns and Oates, 1955), 54.

[9] Quoted in Émile Mâle, *The Gothic Image* (London: Fontana, 1961), 392.

[10] St. Charles Borromeo, *Instructiones Fabricae et Supellectilis Ecclesiasticae* (Instructions on Ecclesiastical Buildings), trans. Evelyn Carol Voelker. Ph.D. diss., Syracuse University, 1977 (Ann Arbor, Mich.: University Microfilms International, n.d.), 228–29.

[11] MD, no. 195.

[12] SC, no. 123.

[13] Maritain, *Scholasticism*, 142.

self, the treasure of light purchased for us by the blood of Christ. For this reason chiefly, because the sovereign interests of the Faith are at stake in the matter, the Church exercises its authority and magistracy over sacred art.[14]

As Vatican II later noted, continuing in the path of Saint Charles Borromeo, this exercise of authority is properly the work of the bishop in his capacity as the shepherd of the diocese: "Bishops should be careful to ensure that works of art which are repugnant to faith, morals, and Christian piety, and which offend true religious sense either by depraved forms or through lack of artistic merit or because of mediocrity or pretense, should be removed from the house of God and from other sacred places."[15] This same directive is restated in the *Catechism*. "For this reason bishops, personally or through delegates, should see to the promotion of sacred art, old and new, in all its forms and, with the same religious care, remove from the liturgy and from places of worship everything which is not in conformity with the truth of faith and the authentic beauty of *sacred* art."[16]

We see that the Church does keep a watchful eye over the artist but, in a very real sense, no more than in any other client-provider arrangement. Ideally, she gives the artist guidelines for the qualities desired and then allows the artist the freedom to work within that framework. Because the purpose of sacred art is not just beauty but the glorification of God and the proper education of man, it will have significantly tighter requirements than secular art in order to achieve its goals. As *Sacrosanctum concilium* charges artists and architects: "All artists who, prompted by their talents, desire to serve God's glory in holy Church should ever remember that they are engaged in a kind of holy imitation of God the Creator: That they are concerned with works destined to be used in Catholic worship, for the edification of the faithful and to foster their piety and religious formation."[17]

The qualities of sacred art

We have seen some good reasons why the Church requires that the artist submit his work

to the proper authorities. But for a truly robust revival of the sacred arts, the Church must be willing to train her artists. While there are many gifted men and women of exceptional artistic skill, the production of sacred art demands more than this: it calls for spiritual and theological formation. The religious artist pursues a vocation by cooperating with God in the creation of sacred art. He must therefore strive for nothing less than perfection: both moral perfection (like any of us) and artistic perfection. The religious artist needs also to endeavor to be a true prophet: he needs to learn to hear the voice of God and to bring all his skill to bear in translating that message, whether through the medium of chisel, brush, glass, or building. He must strive for that perfection which transcends the work itself—beauty.

In his concern for beauty and the glorification of God, the artist is encouraged to look for "noble beauty rather than sumptuous display".[18] Underlying this statement, the Church recognizes not only that aesthetic tastes have changed since the Baroque age but that there is a responsibility to use Church funds wisely. Today especially, there needs to be a trilateral tension between beauty, simplicity, and appropriateness, without sacrificing the sense of the noble. Though Jesus himself lived the humble life of a carpenter's son, often warning the wealthy and proud, we cannot justify the "whitewashed barns" of modern iconoclasm. God's house ought not be impoverished.

This trilateral tension is difficult to state positively but is more easily understood in its negation. The whole atmosphere of the church must be dignified, avoiding the trivial or humorous, while allowing a certain natural drama without cheap theatrics.[19] To demand an underlying simplicity is not to accommodate the cheap or banal. "There is a banal simplism, and there is the simplicity which is the expression of maturity. It is this second,

[14] Ibid., 144.
[15] SC, no. 124.
[16] *Catechism of the Catholic Church*, no. 2503 (emphasis in original) [= CCC].
[17] SC, no. 127.
[18] Ibid., also GIRM, no. 279.
[19] O'Connell, *Church Building*, 59.

true simplicity which applies in the Church."[20] The art must be appropriate, both in content and execution. And the proper execution demands, as Maritain insists, that the work must be *finished*. "It is in the highest degree fitting that nothing shall enter the house of God but work which is done well, accomplished, clean, permanent and honest."[21] The artist must find that which is beautiful, suitable and worthy, educational, and proceeding from a true Christian spirit. Cardinal Ratzinger has written in this regard:

> The Church is to transform, improve, "humanize" the world—but how can she do that if at the same time she turns her back on beauty, which is so closely allied to love. For together, beauty and love form the true consolation in this world, bringing it as near as possible to the world of the resurrection. The Church must maintain high standards; she must be a place where beauty can be at home; she must lead the struggle for that "spiritualization" without which the world becomes the "first circle of hell".[22]

Sacred art, in addition to depicting beauty, is also meant to nourish faith and piety, taking on a didactic function. Though in modern Western society sacred art is no longer as necessary for a largely illiterate population as it once was, it can still serve both to educate the young and to remind people of their faith. The human imagination is informed by the senses, largely through auditory and visual imagery, and will generally conform to whatever input it receives. If the image is consumer-oriented or pornographic, the soul can be distorted to accept it as a reflection of reality. Conversely, the image can aid in the pursuit of holiness if it is meant to nourish the soul's faith and pursuit of the things of God. On a more practical note, since during the course of a Mass one's mind and eye may wander, it seems better to give the eye a sacred image on which to rest and contemplate—even if not directly pertinent to the Mass, it is still a part of the *communio sanctorum*—than to leave one wandering in an image-free wasteland where the mind could turn more easily to profane subjects.

To serve didactically, a work of sacred art must have several characteristics. The work must be both *social* and *universal*: social, because it is "art in the service of the community... not merely for a coterie of aesthetes, but for the public";[23] and universal, because of the *catholicity* of the Church. This is not a question of uniformity; rather, the art dedicated for the Church must strive to address all mankind. It requires a "universality which, while respecting legitimate local customs, manifests the unity of the Church."[24] It must also be both *orthodox* and *intelligible*, "for it is there above all for the instruction of the people, it is a theology in graphic representation."[25] The art must be in complete conformity with doctrine so that the people are correctly instructed, and it must readily express the primary message, avoiding the esoteric. It seems to me that, as a rule of thumb, any work that *requires* thematic explication (at least to the faithful) fails to be didactic. The work may have deeper and more extended meanings or subtleties, such as the multivalent nuances found in the Gothic stained glass at Chartres, but its subject should also be comprehensible at face value.

Since Vatican II we have moved from what in some instances may have been a fussy sentimentality to a sophisticated, church-as-art-gallery mentality. But much modern art tends to be devoid of symbolism, preferring geometric abstraction, emotional response, social criticism, or "artistic expression". The desire for abstraction is often at odds with the real need for sacred art to communicate a matter of faith. Over fifty years ago, Jacques Maritain was decrying the sentimentalist "repository art" of plaster Madonnas and saccharine Sacred Heart statues [figs. 2.5 to 2.7]. Most churches today are too "sophisticated" for such kitsch, but these have often been replaced with abstractions or bizarre figurative art that fails to communicate the subject on any intellectual or spiritual level. Thus we can reread

---

[20] Joseph Cardinal Ratzinger, *The Feast of Faith* (San Francisco: Ignatius Press, 1986), 122.
[21] Maritain, *Scholasticism*, 144.
[22] Ratzinger, *Feast*, 124–25.
[23] O'Connell, *Church Building*, 35.
[24] MD, no. 199.
[25] Ibid.

2.5 Holy Family Church, Jerome, Arizona, High Altar.

2.6 Holy Family Church, Jerome, Arizona, Detail.

2.7 Coronation Shrine, Orvieto, Italy.

Maritain's analysis and still find profound meaning for our present situation:

> This is the reason why Christian artists are faced by very grave difficulties. They must on the one hand reaccustom the faithful to beauty, whose taste has been spoiled for more than a century past . . . and so it is a question of destroying bad aesthetic habits while re-establishing good ones–no easy task. On the other hand, to recover a really live religious art, it is the whole of modern art that they have to elevate, spiritualize, and lead to the feet of God–and that is not an easy task.[26]

The Christian artist today has much the same challenge: to reaccustom the people to beauty (although the "bad habit" today is a sort of iconoclasm, or at least iconophobia, rather than superfluous ornamentalism) and to use his art to elevate, spiritualize, and lead them to the feet of God–still not an easy task. Sacred art has a multiplicity of functions, so it provides special challenges to the artist. Perhaps as a goal we can recall the challenge given to artists by Pope Saint Pius X, simply, "to make their people pray upon beauty".[27]

The role of the architect and of architecture

The reeducation and redirection of artists engaged in service to the Church are vital for restoring the traditions of the sacred arts. The

---

[26] Maritain, *Scholasticism*, 142.
[27] Quoted in ibid., 141.

same holds true for architects. If the goal of Vatican II is, in Pope John Paul II's phrasing, "the enrichment of faith", the architect must learn what this means for the buildings he designs. We are reminded that "churches and other places of worship should . . . be suited to celebrating the liturgy and to ensuring the active participation of the faithful. Further, the places and requisites for worship should be truly worthy and beautiful signs and symbols of heavenly realities." [28]

This commissions the architect to work simultaneously on several different levels: the functional, the social, the symbolic, the qualitative, and the aesthetic. They are all necessary for the enrichment of faith. It is because the Eucharist is a *sacrament*–a visible sign instituted by Christ to confer grace to his Church by means of words and liturgical gestures–that the environment in which these actions are presented is of great importance. Thus it is of equally great importance that the architect follow the Church's direction when designing for the liturgy:

> The celebration of the eucharist, like the entire liturgy, involves the use of outward signs that foster, strengthen, and express faith. There must be the utmost care therefore to choose and to make wise use of those forms and elements provided by the Church which, in view of the circumstances of the people and the place, will best foster active and full participation and serve the spiritual well-being of the faithful. [29]

The whole building must be a superlative effort–down to the last detail the work should be clean, simple, and of the highest quality available–as befits a building dedicated to God. [30] In addition to the usual technical proficiencies that the profession requires, the architect must come to understand the nature of the liturgy and its dynamics, the historical forms and precedents, the tradition of architectural meaning and iconic symbolism, and the liturgical laws that affect the design. The architect must have "both the skill and the will to find in religion the inspiration of methods and plans best adapted to the exigencies of divine worship". [31]

As the architect is to serve the Church, so architecture is to serve the liturgy, as is written

in *Mediator Dei*, "like a noble handmaid entering the service of divine worship". [32] Everything in the church, including decoration, should refer back to the liturgy. [33] Nothing in the design can be superfluous or carelessly considered; nothing should exist as an end in itself: for if it does, it has nothing to offer, nothing to teach, nothing with which to draw the soul closer to God.

The question of style

Even as "a noble handmaid" serving the Church, architecture is not limited by way of style, theory, or expression. There is no "religious technique" to art, and there is no single "Catholic style" to churches. The history of Western civilization shows the development and acceptance of many styles throughout the ages within Catholic church architecture. Vatican II asserts that the Church does not claim any particular style exclusively and that the Church is open to any style, including the modern, asking only that it "bring to the task the reverence and honor due to the sacred building". [34] In accordance with the qualities of art previously listed, a few of the concerns that are applicable directly to the architecture of the church are the qualities of universality, social nature, and appropriateness. Because there is a certain reverence and honor due to churches, church design is not the arena for inordinate architectonic experimentalism, nor for bizarre or idiosyncratic architecture. Above all, a Catholic church ought to look like a Catholic church. What this means, and the question of "how", shall be addressed in the last chapter.

In *Christifideles laici*, Pope John Paul II writes of the necessary relationship between the universal Church and the local parish. The Church "finds its most immediate and visible

---

[28] GIRM, no. 253.
[29] GIRM, no. 5.
[30] MD, no. 200; GIRM, no. 312.
[31] MD, no. 209.
[32] Ibid.
[33] Peter Hammond, *Liturgy and Architecture* (London: Barrie and Rockliff, 1960), 38.
[34] SC, no. 123.
[35] John Paul II, *Christifideles laici* (Dec. 30, 1988), no. 26 [= CL].

expression in the parish. It is there that the Church is seen locally."[35] Because of this intrinsic relationship, with the local parish building being an expression of the whole apostolic institution, the architect should remember that the church building is not just for *this* parish at *this* time. In a very real sense, it is for the *whole* body of Christ. Therefore, the architect must work to express those universal values that the Church holds. This, at least in part, means designing a building that is truly beautiful, well reasoned, carefully detailed, and properly constructed. It also involves using the best materials and techniques available and affordable, as the dignity of a church and true economy demand.[36] Furthermore, it means that the forms of the building should in some way express the existential nature of the Church. That is to say, the building should suggest in some way the image of the Church, the Bride, and the body of Christ and express the unity of the people of God. Everything in the design should work to foster prayer, create a sense of the sacred, and reflect the holiness of the mysteries for which it is the setting.[37] As Pope John Paul II has written, "Holy things must always be treated in a holy manner."[38]

This need to express the universal principles held by the Church ought in no way to inhibit or limit but rather should empower and direct the designer. There is great latitude granted in taking into account local piety, vernacular architecture, indigenous building systems, the context of the site, and other typical architectural determinants. Furthermore, the converse of the Holy Father's comment concerning the relationship between the universal Church and the local parish is that the church building is not only an expression of the universal Church, it is also an expression of the presence of Christ in the local community. It is not only an expression of the unity of the local community with the universal Church, it is also an expression of the local Church. In this, the church building is also an icon of the community. This can have important implications: "An entire parish set-up, its structure, and its setting in the neighborhood or the village, visibly expressed the . . . fundamental conception of the spiritual life of the community within society."[39] Hence, for the sensitive and proficient designer, there should be no conflict between designing for the universal Church and designing for the particular church; rather, the complexity should be an opportunity to develop a richer and more satisfying architectural expression.

Theology and architecture

Peter Hammond, in his influential book *Liturgy and Architecture*, made the point that architects should work hand in hand with theologians and liturgists to create better churches.[40] As we have seen, this was done in the early days of the Liturgical Movement, notably in the relationships of Dominikus Böhm with Fr. van Acken and between Rudolf Schwarz and Romano Guardini. Now, several decades after Hammond's book appeared, a period that includes the Second Vatican Council, we can again affirm his basic premise that church architects need to work closely with theologians and liturgists—the question today being: *Which* theologians and *which* liturgists?

If church architecture is, or should be, "built theology", then in order to have good church architecture one must have good theology. Conversely, it is easy to see why the theological confusion of the recent past has brought about as a consequence a great deal of architectural confusion. The theological confusions have been primarily in three areas of study: Christology, which deals with the Person of Jesus; sacramental theology, which is concerned with the general nature and specific characteristics of the sacraments; and ecclesiology, which is the theology of the nature, form, structure, and operation of the Church. Let us consider a few examples of how theological errors in these areas have had detrimental effects upon church architecture.

---

[36] O'Connell, *Church Building*, 50.
[37] GIRM, no. 257.
[38] John Paul II, *First Message to the World* (Oct. 17, 1978); reiterated in *Love Your Mass* (London: Catholic Truth Society, 1989), 13.
[39] André Biéler, *Architecture in Worship*, trans. Donald and Odette Elliot (Philadelphia: Westminster Press, 1965), 1.
[40] Hammond, *Liturgy and Architecture*, 31.

Christological errors take many forms. Some deny the complete divinity of Jesus; others deny his full humanity; and many others fail to show the union of the two natures in the divine person of the Word. The history of theology has largely centered on the christological question: "Who do you say that I am?" The Chalcedonian definition—that the Lord is one Person in two natures, the divine and human—is to be maintained intact. Yet it has also been subject to reinterpretation in a way more understandable to the modern consciousness. The purported difficulty for the modern Christian is that we, at the advent of the third millennium, generally no longer understand such technical patristic terms as "physis", "hypostasis", "homoousios", or even the metaphysical sense of English words such as nature, person, substance, and accident. Yet the movement toward accommodating the doctrinal definition to the modern consciousness is fraught with difficulty. Dermot Lane, for instance, argues that the Aristotelian-Thomistic framework is no longer meaningful, because "what was formerly called person now approximates to what we call nature and what was known as nature in the past is understood today as person."[41] Yet to invert Chalcedon and define the second Person of the Trinity as "two persons in one nature" is heretical. And so he, among many others, must try to resolve the problem of definition while avoiding both the monophysite position and the dualism of Nestorius.

But our immediate concerns are architecture and art in the liturgical environment. Without getting into nuances of technical theological terms, we can see certain similarities in current patterns. Even if the theological argument is different, the effects are surprisingly similar. For instance, the first-century Ebionites denied the divinity of Jesus and believed that Christians were still under the Mosaic law: in short, they denied the reality of the New Covenant. Consequently, they emphasized temporal works for the Church's goal. We can sense this materialistic concern in their modern-day equivalents: those who ignore Christ's divinity and substitute a political or social agenda for the eschatological mission of the Church. Still at the core of this thinking is

a denial of the divinity in Jesus. There is a lack of understanding of the comprehensiveness of the Incarnation: that he who was *fully God* became *fully man*. In its milder forms, there is often the tendency to do away with sacred space, making the church multifunctional to serve the needs of the social programs of the parish, often at the expense of its liturgical function. In the more radical forms, such as Marxist liberation theology, Jesus is seen as a political figure, often as a "martyr" killed for political reasons in the class struggle. The iconography is then distorted to depict him as such. Paul Johnson cites the Church of Mercy in Managua, Nicaragua, where Christ is depicted in the stations of the Cross as a left-wing revolutionary being beaten and crucified by soldiers of the National Guard. The "altar" in the church is in the form of a sand-bagged barricade.[42]

Today we live in an age of religious iconoclasm. Graphic images have little place in our modern churches, while our consumerist culture barrages us with materialistic, glossy, and pornographic imagery. Yet where the iconoclasm of the eighth century was based on protecting the divinity of Christ—that is, to portray the Person of Jesus would be to try to "circumscribe his uncircumscribable Godhead"—our current iconophobia does not seem to be christological in nature. We, nevertheless, can still see certain similarities. No one in the modern debate seems to deny that God can be represented, but there does seem to be in Christian art a certain underlying avoidance of Christ's suffering. This may be because the modern consciousness excludes the possibility that suffering can be redemptive. Thus we see the proliferation of "Resurrection crosses" replacing crucifixes and of stations of the Cross abstracted to irrelevant compositional exercises.

It is also highly ironic that in this age of "low Christology", when so much emphasis is being placed on understanding the human aspect of "the Jesus of history", portrayals of the Lord

---

[41] Dermot Lane, *The Reality of Jesus* (New York: Paulist Press, 1975), 113–14.
[42] Paul Johnson, *Pope John Paul II and the Catholic Restoration* (London: Weidenfeld and Nicolson, 1982), 103.

Jesus are so abstract that frequently they fail to capture his humanity. Despite the charge that the "high Christology" of past times overly emphasized the divinity of the Christ, at least the art it produced had a Jesus with a real and fleshy appearance.

The iconoclast council of Hieria forbade images of our Lord, along with images of our Lady, the saints, and the angels. Consistent with this, the emperor, Constantine V, denied the communion of the saints and their intercessory value for us. Ironically, with the recent removal of visual representations of the saints and angels, the iconoclastic goals of Constantine V have finally been achieved. Twelve hundred years ago, in response to Constantine, Pope Saint Gregory II demanded the graphic representation of the Lord because of the demands of the Incarnation.[43] An orthodox Christology will ask no less today. It will also lead to a proper emphasis being placed on the veneration of images, as our present Pope asks.[44]

Sacramental theology, which affects the expression of the liturgy, is a vital issue in the Church: "The question of liturgy is not peripheral: the Council itself reminded us that we are dealing here with the very core of Christian faith."[45] An error in sacramental theology, such as the idea that the Eucharist is only (or even *primarily*) a meal, rather than first and foremost a sacrifice, will affect the form of the altar as well as its relationship to the nave. Pope Paul VI has been accused, quite unjustly, I think, of turning "the altar into little more than a communion table".[46] But people gather around a table to eat: we are comfortable with the ideas of eating, tables, and social gathering—whereas few in today's society are comfortable with the notions of priests offering expiation with blood sacrifices, fiery immolations, and altars. The reality of the Lord's sacrifice is jarring to modern sensibilities. Thus many prefer simply to ignore it. The fact that it occurs in the context of a meal leads many to overemphasize the meal and ignore that it is a *sacrificial* meal. This misemphasis has probably had the single greatest impact on recent church design, just as the isolation of the sacrifice from its intrinsic meal context had caused

an undue sense of separation in the medieval church.

Because the sacrificial aspect of the eucharistic meal has largely been lost, altar rails have been removed, altars have been pulled into the nave, the distinction between sanctuary and nave has been blurred, and kneelers are often no longer provided. In order to make the congregation more "comfortable", we have even seen glass-topped tables with wooden bases: materials better suited for a coffee table in a contemporary middle-class living room than for that most sacred place where our redemption is being effected.

Modern notions of ecclesiology have also had wide-ranging impact on the design of churches, and with good reason: church buildings are necessarily representations of the Church.[47] Since the relationships within the building are meant to support the function, the structured space will reflect characteristics of the model they represent. A demotic model for a church will be shown primarily in the relationship of the sanctuary to the nave by blurring the distinction between them—which is really blurring the distinction between the priest and the laity. Whereas a hierarchic model would suggest an ordered sequence of spaces from the earthly or profane to the heavenly or sacred, the demotic model will tend toward a "universal liturgical space". The advocate of a demotic model wants all parts of life to be "sacred". Would that our modern consciousness allowed us truly to enter into the wondrous creation of God as something wholly sacred! This is the path of the mystic, the saint, the one who practices true religion. Certainly a worthy journey, but does it speak to modern man? Can one deny the profane without recognizing that to make all things "sacred" is to allow nothing to be truly sacred?

Having seen a few unfortunate examples of the potential impact of poor theology on the

---

[43] John Saward, "Christ, Our Lady, and the Church", *Chrysostom* 8, no. 1 (spring 1988): 4 and 10.

[44] John Paul II, *Duodecimum saeculum* (Dec. 4, 1987), no. 11.

[45] Joseph Cardinal Ratzinger, *The Ratzinger Report* (San Francisco: Ignatius Press, 1985), 120.

[46] Johnson, *Catholic Restoration*, 53.

[47] CL, no. 25.

arrangement of churches, we can now better understand the pressing need for working with solid and critical theologians and liturgists. Architecture is affected by theology because the church building *does* represent the values of the culture. These values are, in large part, determined by how we think of God and his work in the Church and by our concept of what the Church is and of our place within it. Therefore, we must be both discerning and deliberate about which values we choose to express, and in what proportion. In the end, the church building will be only as good as the ideas represented are true.

Transcendence in architecture

Perhaps the greatest challenge for the contemporary church architect is to create a place that *evokes* the sacred; a space that allows for and encourages transcendence; a building that, quoting Pope John Paul II, appreciates in mankind "an essential dimension of his being, his search for the infinite".[48] Mankind is both body and soul, with temporal and eternal dimensions, and the churches we build should respect this. The goal therefore should be a building that speaks to the whole human being—body and soul, will and intellect, head and heart, rational, emotional, and aesthetic faculties—as well as to the parish community and civic community at large. What is needed is an architecture of transcendence, an architecture that provides the human soul with an environment that encourages both corporate and private prayer.

The chasm between matter and spirit is too great for most Western thinkers. It is a common error today to deny the existence of the spiritual; or to deny the possibility of objectively knowing that which is metaphysical, that which is not demonstrable scientifically; or else to resolve the question in a facile expression, whether New Age or fundamentalist, that ignores the full mystery of our existence: What is the purpose of our human existence; what is true human worth; why is there human suffering; where do I belong in creation?

It is only in the Incarnation—because God became man—that the problem of matter and spirit, the finite and the infinite, is resolved. To transcend (Lat.: *trans* = across + *scandere* = to climb) is to move across or beyond limits. The process of religion is one of transcendence: in the Eucharist the Church transcends space and time to partake in both the sacrifice of the Cross and the Wedding Feast of the Lamb. This happens at the altar "where heaven and earth touch and where time and eternity meet". In private prayer we also transcend space and time, going beyond ourselves, as we become "partakers of the divine nature" (2 Pet 1:4). In union with Christ's sacrifice, our temporal, physical, emotional, and spiritual sufferings can become transcendental as we seek to find the redemptive value of our pain. And, above all, our final resolution in death and judgment is our final transcendence when "we shall be like him, for we shall see him as he is" (1 Jn 3:2).

Transcendence is at the heart of Christianity: as Saint John tells us, "The Word became flesh" (Jn 1:14), that is, it is the wholly transcendent Word who enters our world. Ecclesial architecture should seek to transcend space and time, seeking timelessness rather than temporality. A church should strive to be "otherworldly", to allow the person to leave behind the anxieties and cares of the world and enter into the heavenly Jerusalem. At Mass the people are called to "lift up [their] hearts". The architecture should allow this to happen, so that the congregation may lift up their hearts to God in divine worship. The people are called to go beyond themselves, to transcend the world and enter into the eternal worship, which is centered on the Eucharist. How this can best be done, whether through liturgical ordering, the manipulation of space, lighting, focus, or scale, is for the architect to determine. However it is accomplished, it is an important aspect of the architecture to aid in the prayer life of the community.

The problem many modern thinkers have with all this is that they have been taught to see a fundamental incompatibility—even an opposition—between matter and spirit. For the Christian this is resolved not only in the hypostatic union, the doctrine that Jesus is "fully

---

[48] Quoted in Johnson, *Catholic Restoration*, 95.

God and fully man", but also within our own persons, being both body and soul. As Eric Gill was fond of reminding us, "Man is composed of both matter and spirit, both real and both good." [49] The Church has continually held to the intrinsic goodness of the material world, most notably against the Manicheans in the third and fourth centuries. Since the "age of Enlightenment", with its empiricism, skepticism, and positivism, the problem has been more the rejection of the spiritual realities. So today the Church continues to hold that the material can be a vehicle of spiritual good:

> Thus, for well-disposed members of the faithful the liturgy of the sacraments and sacramentals sanctifies almost every event of their lives with the divine grace which flows from the paschal mystery of the Passion, Death and Resurrection of Christ. From this source all sacraments and sacramentals draw their power. *There is scarcely any proper use of material things which cannot thus be directed toward the sanctification of men and the praise of God.*[50]

This idea follows the tradition of Saint John Damascene, pseudo-Dionysius (hereafter, for simplicity, Dionysius), John Scotus Erigena, and Saint Thomas Aquinas, who held that the mind was raised to contemplation through material objects. Hence, the whole basis for icons. As with icons, in architecture this happens on the level of the *sacramental*. A sacramental is like a sacrament in that it may bestow grace to the recipient by way of an action or a thing used, such as making the sign of the cross, using holy water, or blessing a house. But, unlike a sacrament, (a) it has not "been instituted by Christ in order to be perpetuated within the Church as divinely established means of conferring grace"; (b) its "efficacy does not come from the ritual performed but partly from the dispositions of the person who uses them and partly from the intercessory prayer of the whole Church"; and (c) "they do not confer sanctifying grace directly but merely dispose a person to its reception." [51] As Pope John XXIII has said, "Christian art is of such a character we should almost call it sacramental . . . as the vehicle and instrument which God uses to dispose his creatures to the

wonders of grace." [52] Church buildings are sacramentals because they are blessed objects given for our sanctification. Sacramentals always include a prayer, which is effected in the dedication rite.[53] Thus the church building itself, a sign and symbol of heavenly things, which is consecrated and dedicated exclusively for liturgical use, may become a sacramental vehicle for those faithful who wish to enter into it.[54] It is in this way that, to recall Mr. Hammond's aim, "the whole structure, no less than the altar, the font or the chalice, is an instrument of worship." [55]

One significant obstacle to this process happening is that today we do not generally "read" buildings. Modern art has largely replaced representation with abstraction or disjointed imagery. Modern architecture has tried to reduce building to first principles. The issues concern function, economics, and utilitarian values instead of beauty and delight. Although buildings can still communicate to those who learn the language, our society today has become architectonically illiterate. Thus, the Gothic idea of light breathing life into stone [fig. 2.8], or the Palladian ideal that architecture should reflect the perfection of God's order [fig. 2.9], is widely lost today. And yet, the church building has much to offer to the edification of man and is a rich opportunity for a contemplative experience. The scriptural notions of Church—the heavenly mansion of the Father, the Body of Christ, the true vine or the mustard tree, the temple, the city, or the imagery of Revelation, to name but a few—are all full of structural metaphors with which we can enrich our faith through architectonic means. In the final chapter we shall look at just what is needed to regain the idea of the church as a symbol of

---

[49] Eric Gill, *Beauty Looks after Herself* (London: Sheed and Ward, 1933), 53.

[50] SC, no. 61; italics added.

[51] John A. Hardon, S.J., *The Catholic Catechism* (New York: Doubleday, 1975), 548–49.

[52] M. Chinigo, ed.: *The Teachings of Pope John XXIII*, trans. A. A. Coppotelli (London: George G. Harrap and Co., 1967), 106. Note that the Pope uses "sacramental" as the adjective of sacrament, and not as a noun.

[53] Cf. CCC, nos. 1667–1672.

[54] K. Rahner and H. Vorgrimler, *Concise Theological Dictionary* (London: Burns and Oates, 1965), s.v. "opus operatum", "sacrament", and "sacramental".

[55] Hammond, *Liturgy and Architecture*, 29.

2.8 Nantes Cathedral, Chancel.

heavenly things, but the first step is to regain the awareness that churches *can* be transcendent. The building itself *can* help lead the community to the worship of God and thus transcend the world. It can also transcend the mere material constraints as well as time and continue to speak to mankind through mute stone of the eternal truths of God.

For a church building to serve the whole human being, the architect must work on several levels simultaneously. The Church is a complex reality; mankind is a complex reality; so must our churches be. Of all buildings, the church should speak most clearly to our senses, our intellect, emotions, memory and imagination, our aesthetic sensibility, and our desire for transcendence or "search for the infinite". It must speak to us not only as individuals but as social persons, living in a historical community with a common tradition and communal responsibilities, and as participants in the liturgy from which Christian life flows. Only when church buildings serve the complete human person, and the social community of persons, will architecture contribute to that enrichment of faith which the Second Vatican Council sought to impart:

> What the faithful have received by faith and sacrament in the celebration of the Eucharist should have its effect on their way of life. And so everyone who has participated in the Mass should be eager to do good works, to please God, and to live honestly, devoted to the Church, putting into practice what he has learnt, and growing in piety. He will seek to fill the world with the Spirit of Christ and in all things, in the very midst of human affairs to become a witness of Christ.[56]

---

[56] Sacred Congregation of Rites, *Eucharisticum mysterium* (May 25, 1967), no. 13.

2.9 San Giorgio Maggiore, by A. Palladio, 1565, Nave.

CHAPTER THREE

An Architecture for the Mass

The nature of the holy liturgy

The Second Vatican Council's primary vehicle for liturgical renewal was the document *Sacrosanctum concilium*. These general principles, as they regard the Mass, were elaborated upon and codified in the document *General Instruction of the Roman Missal*, first published in 1970. In it, we read a succinct account of the meaning, the nature, and the purpose of the Mass:

> The celebration of Mass, the action of Christ and the people of God arrayed hierarchically, is for the universal and the local church as well as for each person the center of the whole Christian life. In the Mass we have the high point of the work that in Christ God accomplishes to sanctify us and the high point of the worship that in adoring God through Christ, his Son, we offer to the Father. During the cycle of the year, moreover, the mysteries of redemption are recalled in the Mass in such a way that they are somehow made present. All other liturgical rites and all the works of the Christian life are linked with the eucharistic celebration, flow from it, and have it as their end.
>
> Therefore, it is of the greatest importance that the celebration of the Mass, the Lord's Supper, be so arranged that the ministers and the faithful who take their own proper part in it may more fully receive its good effects. This is the reason why Christ the Lord instituted the eucharistic sacrifice of his body and blood and entrusted it to the Church, his beloved Bride, as the memorial of his passion and resurrection.[1]

In this statement we find a wealth of information to help us understand the Mass properly so as to design for the liturgy properly. One ought first to keep in mind that the Mass is *a profoundly sacred and august action of God*. It is primarily the action of our Lord Jesus Christ, in union with his gathered faithful, worshipping the Father. Through this action God sanctifies the Church as we enter into the *sacrifice* of the Lord's Body and Blood, which we are then called to *consume*. Thus we see the twofold integrated reality of the sacrificial meal. We eat what we sacrifice; so, to approach the *table* properly, we must first participate at the *altar*; and they are one and the same. It is the sacrifice of the Lord, and it is the Supper of the Lord. The Mass is one unified reality.

The Church enters into worship as a community, a local expression of the universal Church, and does so as a hierarchically ordered body. Each person, cleric and lay, has a proper place and particular part. Significantly, we read that the liturgy is *central* to the life of the Church, both corporately and in the life of each member, and foundational to every other work of the Church. This is why every aspect in the design of the building that affects the liturgy demands the greatest consideration so that the environment can fully contribute to the celebration.

Since the Mass is *sacred* and *august*, indeed "a sacred action surpassing all others",[2] the Church has always held that normally it is to be celebrated in a special, reserved place: that is, a building set aside exclusively for liturgical

---

[1] *General Instruction of the Roman Missal*, 4th ed. (Mar. 27, 1975), nos. 1 and 2 [= GIRM].

[2] Vatican II, *Sacrosanctum concilium* (Dec. 4, 1963), no. 7 [= SC].

worship, and one that is worthy of the Eucharistic Sacrifice.[3] This building needs to account for both the *communal* and the *hierarchical* aspects of the congregation. Because there are two forms of participation in the one priesthood of Christ—a ministerial priesthood of the clergy and a royal priesthood of the laity—there are certain things reserved for the clergy and others entrusted to the laity.[4] The Church teaches that the ministerial priesthood "forms and rules the priestly people" and "effects the eucharistic sacrifice and offers it to God in the name of all the people".[5] But the Church also teaches that there is an "organic" unity between the two priesthoods as "each in its own proper way shares in the one priesthood of Christ."[6] Thus, there is great need for design sensitivity, to avoid expressing the importance of one to the neglect of the other. Finally, because the liturgy is *central* to every aspect of the Church—Vatican II calls the Eucharist "the source and summit of the Church's life"[7]—the liturgical requirements of the sanctuary and nave must necessarily take precedence over every other architectural consideration.

An architecture for the sacrificial meal

In his book *The Early Liturgy*,[8] Fr. Joseph Jungmann mentions that, around the turn of this century, a debate arose among German theologians as to the early Church's understanding of the nature of the eucharistic celebration. Was it a true sacrifice? Was it primarily a communal meal with a "sacrifice of thanksgiving"? Was there any real understanding that the elements on the Lord's table (*mensa dominica*) were truly the sacrifice of the Lord's Body and Blood?

Looking to apologists such as Minucius Felix, who wrote, "Do you think that we hide the objects of our worship because we have no shrines and altars?"[9] and Saint Justin Martyr, who wrote, "Prayers and thanksgivings performed by worthy men are the only perfect sacrifices pleasing to God",[10] some argued that before Saint Irenaeus (*c.* A.D. 203) the only sacrifice in the Church was the prayer of thanksgiving. Therefore, they concluded, the

gifts of bread and wine received at Communion were probably not thought sacrificial; much less would they have been considered the true and permanent sacrifice of the Body and Blood of the Lord. As Jungmann summarizes, this debate was resolved, for the time being, by Emil Dorsch, who showed that "the very authors cited as stressing the spirituality of the Christian service also saw in the Christian Eucharist the fulfillment of Malachy's prophecy of the clean oblation which is offered everywhere from the rising of the sun to its setting." By pointing to other sources, such as the *Didache* and Saint Clement of Rome, "it was not difficult [for Dorsch] to show, therefore, that the thanksgiving prayer recited over the gifts was at the same time an offering of the gifts, and that theologically, therefore, the Eucharist was considered during the first centuries, as now, a unique but real sacrifice."[11]

While this debate has ended, its vestiges continue. The idea that the church is a place of sacrifice is all but lost today. The "meal aspect" has been so emphasized that we even now speak of the "priesthood of believers" without the necessary conclusion that, by virtue of being a *priest*, one offers *sacrifice*! As Saint John Chrysostom observed, "Nobody can be a priest without the sacrifice."[12] With the loss of the necessary and intrinsic understanding of sacrificial participation in the Eucharist, much of the architectural language of sacrifice—with its connotations of procession, ceremony, solemnity, and formality—has also been lost. Recently there has been a renewed emphasis in

---

[3] GIRM, no. 253; also *Code of Canon Law* (1983), can. 932, sec. 1.

[4] Paul VI, *Ministeria quaedam* (Aug. 15, 1972).

[5] Vatican II, *Lumen Gentium* (Nov. 21, 1964), no. 10 [= LG].

[6] Ibid., and John Paul II, *Christifideles laici* (Dec. 30, 1988), no. 20 [= CL]; also cf. Vatican II, *Presbyterorum ordinis* (Dec. 7, 1965), no. 9 [= PO].

[7] SC, no. 10.

[8] Josef [Joseph] A. Jungmann, S.J., *The Early Liturgy*, trans Francis A. Brunner (South Bend, Ind.: University of Notre Dame Press, 1959), 45ff.

[9] Minucius Felix, *Octavius*, chap. 32; quoted in Jungmann, *Early Liturgy*, 45.

[10] St. Justin Martyr, *Dialogue with Trypho*, 117; quoted in Jungmann, *Early Liturgy*, 45.

[11] Jungmann, *Early Liturgy*, 46.

[12] From PG 63:111; quoted in Msgr. Klaus Gamber, *The Reform of the Roman Liturgy* (San Juan Capistrano: Una Voce, 1993), 117.

the Church's post–Vatican II promulgations concerning the sacrificial aspect of the Mass. This has been done, no doubt, as part of the continuing effort to regain the ancient awareness lost in the recent past.

That the Eucharist is the sacrifice both of and by the Lord is an ancient doctrine rooted in the Scriptures and found in the earliest writings of the apostolic Fathers. Even as early as A.D. 107, Saint Ignatius of Antioch wrote, "Make certain, therefore, that you all observe one common Eucharist; for there is but one Body of our Lord Jesus Christ, and but one cup of union with His Blood, and one single altar of sacrifice—even as also there is but one bishop." [13]

And again, the *Didache* makes the connection: "Assemble on the Lord's Day, and break bread and offer the Eucharist; but first make confession of your faults, so that your sacrifice may be a pure one." [14] The Fathers of the Church continued to develop this idea, seeing the Eucharist as the perfection of the various types of Old Testament sacrifices, with Jesus as the Priest of priests found in the Old Testament (e.g., Abel, who first offered the lamb; Melchizedek, who offered the bread and wine; and Abraham, who offered his own son, Isaac). Throughout the history of the Church this idea has continued in the writings of popes, doctors, and councils. [15] Vatican II addresses the issue several times:

At the Last Supper, on the night he was betrayed, our Savior instituted the eucharistic sacrifice of his Body and Blood. This he did in order to perpetuate the sacrifice of the Cross throughout the ages (SC, no. 47).

As often as the sacrifice of the cross by which "Christ our Pasch is sacrificed" (1 Cor 5:7) is celebrated on the altar, the work of our redemption is carried out (LG, no. 3).

In the eucharistic assembly of the faithful . . . [priests] exercise in a supreme degree their sacred function; there, acting in the person of Christ and proclaiming his mystery, they unite the votive offerings of the faithful to the sacrifice of Christ their head, and in the sacrifice of the Mass they make present again and apply, until the coming of the Lord (cf. 1 Cor 11:26), the unique sacrifice of the New Testament, that namely of Christ offering himself once and for all a spotless victim to the Father (cf. Heb 9:11–28) (LG, no. 28).

Through the ministry of priests the spiritual sacrifice of the faithful is completed in union with the sacrifice of Christ the only mediator, which in the Eucharist is offered through the priests' hands in the name of the whole Church in an unbloody and sacramental manner until the Lord himself come (PO, no. 2).

Hence priests teach the faithful to offer the divine victim to God the Father in the sacrifice of the Mass and with the victim to make an offering of their whole life (PO, no. 5).

Pope John Paul II stated the position thus: "The Eucharist is above all else a sacrifice. It is the sacrifice of the Redemption and also the sacrifice of the New Covenant, as we believe and as the Eastern Churches clearly profess: 'Today's sacrifice,' the Greek Church stated centuries ago, 'is like that offered once by the Only-begotten Incarnate Word; it is offered by him (now as then), since it is one and the same sacrifice.'" [16] As is evidenced in the above passages, the Church continues to teach the integrated realities of meal and sacrifice in the Eucharist, for the two cannot be separated. Although the Church is very clear about the sacrificial nature of the Mass, many modern theologians and liturgists prefer to continue to dwell primarily on the "meal aspect" of the Lord's Supper. Cardinal Joseph Ratzinger confronts this issue directly in his book *The Feast of Faith*, building on the foundation laid by Fr. Jungmann. The common argument is that since the Eucharist was instituted at the Last Supper, the meal is the "true form" for the Mass. Thus, to appreciate this, the eucharistic celebration should have the *character* of a meal. One does not need to contest that the meal aspect is, of

---

[13] St. Ignatius of Antioch, *Phil. 4*, in *Early Christian Writings*, ed. Maxwell Staniforth (Harmondsworth, England: Penguin, 1968), 112.

[14] *Didache*, pt. 2, no. 14, in Staniforth, *Early Christian Writings*, 234.

[15] Although it is the predominant model in the writings of the saints, the sacrifice of the Mass was dogmatically defined only at the Council of Trent, because of the attacks on the Eucharist by Protestant critics.

[16] John Paul II, *Dominicae cenae*, (Feb. 24, 1980), no. 9, [= DC].

course, important. But it is not a particularly recent rediscovery of a scriptural theme; Bishop Durand, for instance, writing in the thirteenth century, notes that the altar "signifies the table at which Christ did feast with his disciples".[17] Ceremonial meals are important human and social experiences. But in the light of the recent past, we must now seek to integrate the meal symbolism into the larger whole.[18] What makes the meal religious in the Judeo-Christian tradition is that it involves a sacrifice; what makes it specifically Christian is that Jesus is both the Priest and the Victim.

While due regard must be given to the Eucharist as meal, we must be careful to avoid overstating the case, especially in consideration of the historical evidence. From the evidence of early Christian liturgies, we can read in the description of the Eucharist by Saint Justin Martyr (d. c. 165) that after the readings and the homily the faithful stood for prayers and the Consecration. This is hardly the posture at a meal. The importance of the meal is made appropriately manifest in the use of the elements of bread and wine, which are consumed. However, it is an oversimplification to reduce the Lord's Supper to only, or even primarily, a meal.[19] Moreover, it is also theologically dangerous, for, as the Holy Father points out, "if separated from its distinctive sacrificial and sacramental nature, the Eucharistic mystery simply ceases to be." [20]

The Pope's statement is meant to defend the true importance of the Eucharist in the Church. The Eucharist is first and foremost a sacrifice, and this understanding is vital to designing churches that are intelligent and faithful responses to the Second Vatican Council. The Lord's Supper as a meal also has necessary signficance, which is represented by the action of communication when we eat and drink of the Lord's sacrifice. Fr. Louis Bouyer contends that all religious sacrifices, through the ages, involve meals. For him, a religious sacrifice without a meal (consuming the victim) is as meaningless and self-contradictory as a religious meal without a sacrifice. There is as great a problem in deemphasizing the meal as there is in ignoring the sacrifice. We must therefore seek to reintegrate these two dimen-

sions. Only in this way can the legitimate work of the Liturgical Movement find its fulfillment and thus mature in a stronger synthesis of meal and sacrifice so as to restore the original understanding of the Eucharist.

The meaning of the sanctuary

The essential division of space within the Catholic church building is that between the sanctuary and the nave. This reflects the differentiation of the ministerial priesthood from the lay priesthood; or those "ministries which are derived from the Sacrament of Order" from those "that find their foundation in the Sacraments of Baptism and Confirmation".[21] The previously quoted passages from *Lumen Gentium*, no. 28, and *Presbyterorum ordinis*, no. 2, show clearly the differences in the nature of each sacrifice. The ministerial priesthood, in offering the Body and Blood of Christ, acts to sanctify and unite the laity's "votive offerings", the "spiritual sacrifice" that is the "offering of their whole life", at the representation of the one sacrifice of Christ the Lord. Each offers true sacrifice. The two priesthoods, each in its own proper way, share in the one priesthood of Christ. However, the two differ *essentially* and are called to be ordered one to the other.[22]

The Church teaches that the priest, when administering the sacraments (such as penance or the sacrifice of the Mass), is acting in the person of Christ, *in persona Christi*, which means that Christ acts through him. Because there is only one High Priest (cf. Heb 4:14) and one perfect sacrifice to take away the sins of

---

[17] Guillaume Durand, *The Symbolism of Churches and Church Ornaments: A Translation of the First Book of the* Rationale divinorum officiorum, trans. J. M. Neale and B. Webb (Leeds: T. W. Green 1843; reprint New York: AMS Press, 1973), bk. 1, chap. 2, no. 4. (Throughout this book, I have taken the liberty of recasting the work of Messrs. Neale and Webb into more contemporary English.) Interestingly, Bishop Durand gives no fewer than twelve interpretations of the spiritual meaning of the altar, including this fifth meaning, the actual table of the Last Supper.

[18] Joseph Cardinal Ratzinger, *The Feast of Faith* (San Francisco: Ignatius Press, 1986), 38.

[19] Ibid., 48–49.

[20] DC, no. 8.

[21] CL, nos. 22 and 23.

[22] LG, no. 10.

the world (cf. Heb 10:12), the ministerial priest sharing in Christ's eternal Priesthood offers the Body and Blood, yet it is Jesus who is both the High Priest and the Victim. The priest is *alter Christus*, and it is Christ who administers the sacraments through the priest. "Christ is present at the august sacrifice of the altar ... in the person of His minister."[23] As Pope John Paul II has written:

> The priest offers the Holy Sacrifice *in persona Christi*; this means more than offering "in the name of" or "in the place of" Christ. *In persona* means in specific sacramental identification with "the eternal High Priest" who is the Author and principal Subject of this Sacrifice of his, a Sacrifice in which, in truth, nobody can take his place. ... Awareness of this reality throws a certain light on the character and significance of the priest celebrant who, *by confecting the Holy Sacrifice and acting "in persona Christi"*, is sacramentally (and ineffably) brought into that most profound *sacredness*, and made part of it, spiritually linking with it in turn all those participating in the Eucharistic assembly.[24]

The architectural significance of this is found in the idea of the *sacredness* of the priest's position in the assembly: what he does is *supremely and intrinsically holy*. Even apart from his personal disposition, the action of offering the Sacrifice of the Lord is that which sets the ministerial priest apart from the community. And yet what he does is for the whole community, even for the whole Church. Thus the position of the priest demands, in some manner, to be set apart from the rest of the assembly, yet also be obviously and organically linked with that assembly. Therefore, the architectural relationship must express both differentiation and union. While the days of erecting chancel screens are long gone, the sanctuary is still to be marked off from the nave by some means, e.g., by a higher floor level, altar rail or balustrade, distinctive structure, or some such architectural device.[25] This separation is not warranted merely by the title or office of the priest but is an imperative derived from the nature of the priest's role.

Sacrifice takes place in a sacred space. The place is first *designated* as sacred, that is, set aside for the Holy. It is furthermore *made* sacred by the sacrifice and by the presence of the Holy. Throughout the ages, man has set aside sacred ground made holy by the Divine Presence. From St. Catherine's Monastery at Mount Sinai to the Holy Sepulcher where Jesus rose from the dead, Christianity has traditionally revered what it considers *terra sancta*. As Yahweh commanded Moses, "Do not come near; put off your shoes from your feet, for the place on which you are standing is holy ground" (Ex 3:5). This idea of holy ground, a truly sacred place, also needs to find expression in the design of the sanctuary.

This hierarchic separation of the sacred and the profane, indeed a procession from the profane (the world) to the sacred (the altar, being heaven), is found from Christian antiquity onward. In fact, in almost every ancient culture we can see deeply rooted expressions of this separation. Evidence is scanty and subject to interpretation when studying the earliest Christian churches. It is, however, thought that by the end of the third century the basilica plan had been established. This plan expressed a transition from the profane to the sacred via an entry courtyard, a narthex, and a longitudinal nave leading to the sanctuary, such as is seen at the excavations in Mérida, Spain.[26] This arrangement, of course, is derived from the contemporaneous Mediterranean culture, the Jewish synagogue, and pagan temples and law courts, in an age that was familiar with the notions of both sacrality and profanity.

Among the most ancient of Christian churches is the Syrian, which was derived from the synagogues of the time and thus shows a similar hierarchic separation. There was normally a raised bema for the clergy and a chancel screen separating the nave from the sanctuary. The altar was usually found in an apse at the east end behind a veil, an arrangement derived from the veil in the Holy of Holies in Jerusalem.[27]

---

[23] Pius XII, *Mediator Dei* (Nov. 20, 1947), no. 20.

[24] DC, no. 8.

[25] GIRM, no. 258.

[26] R. Milburn, *Early Christian Art and Architecture* (London: Scolar, 1988), 14.

[27] Fr. Louis Bouyer, *Liturgy and Architecture* (South Bend, Ind.: University of Notre Dame Press, 1967), 26.

The Christian Church took two Old Testament forms in particular as models for the church building: the Tabernacle of Moses [figs. 3.1 to 3.3], and the Temple in Jerusalem [fig. 3.4]. In taking these forms they gave analogous and extended meanings to the various parts to express symbolically the *cosmos*: all of creation, both heaven and earth. The narthex is, for the Fathers, a symbol of the unredeemed world. It is analogous to the Court of the Gentiles in the Temple of Jerusalem. The narthex is not a sacramental part of the church, but neither is it completely outside the church. Hence, it is a place for those who are either catechumens and not yet part of the Church or the penitents and unreconciled who are not admitted to the eucharistic mysteries. The nave is the next stage in the transition between the world and the Kingdom. The nave probably takes its name from the Greek word *naos* (ναος), which refers to the cella, or the innermost part of the pagan temple. In this we see the great Christian innovation that all the baptized, men, women, and children, were admitted into the inner sanctum, to witness for themselves the mysteries of the Faith. The word also may be derived from the Greek *naus* (ναυς), meaning "boat". The Fathers saw Noah's ark as a typological precedent for the Church: the faithful are saved from the final destruction of the Last Judgment only by being "on board". The nave is derived from the "Holy" of the Tabernacle and the Court of the Priests at the Temple and is therefore the place for the royal priesthood. It symbolizes the sanctified and redeemed created world, the "new heavens and a new earth" (2 Pet 3:13). Finally, the sanctuary is heaven itself, expressing the Tabernacle and the "Holy of Holies".[28] For the Fathers, this series of relationships gives meaning to the whole building and sets it firmly within the created order of the universe, and even within the ecclesiological order of Christ's Church: "In a church, the sanctuary and the nave communicate: the sanctuary enlightens and guides the nave, which becomes its visible expression. Such a relationship

[28] L. Ouspensky, *The Theology of the Icon* (Crestwood, N.Y.: St. Vladimir's Seminary Press, 1978), 24–31.

3.1 The Tent of Dwelling (after Orlinsky).

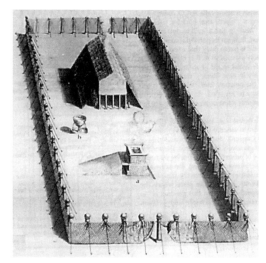

3.2 The Tent of Dwelling (after Ritz, S.J.).

3.3 Plan of the Tabernacle (after Arthur and Klein).

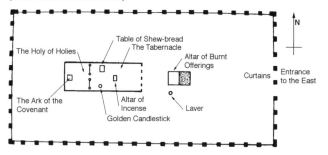

restores the normal order of the universe, which has been destroyed by the fall of man. Thus it reestablishes what had been in paradise and what will be in the Kingdom of God." [29]

This understanding that the nave is the Court of the Priests, as well as the redeemed earth, and that the sanctuary is the Holy of Holies, and even heaven itself, is seminal to understanding the proper places for the assembly. For within this model the priest as *alter Christus*—in place of Christ, who is now our High Priest—is the proper one to go into the Holy of Holies, just as it is Christ who penetrated the veil separating heaven and earth by his sacrifice to the Father. Simply put, in the light of this understanding, one must ask what place the laity can have in the sanctuary! Traditionally and theologically, it is the ordained, the anointed, who enter the sanctuary on behalf of the people of God to make expiation. Our modern tendency to allow one and all into the sanctuary denies this expression. However, while denying it, modernist liturgists offer no new paradigm to help us understand the liturgy. Some radically demotic liturgists would do away with all sacred ministerial orders, empowering each and every person to be priest and priestess, thus doing away with the sanctuary, but this could only lead to chaos. The Body of Christ requires an organic order, which the church building must somehow express—that is the challenge to modern liturgists who are trying to rework the ancient traditions of the assembly.

With all sorts of variations throughout the ages, and to greater or lesser degrees, churches showed similar patterns of both hierarchic separation and transition from the profane to the sacred. Some liturgists have argued that many important early Christian churches were centralized (pointing to Santa Costanza, San Stefano Rotondo, San Vitale, San Lorenzo, and the Holy Sepulcher, for instance) and that the liturgies held within were more "communal" than "hierarchic". Therefore, so they argue, since the centralized model is found within the earliest tradition of Christian building, it is appropriate to use such an arrangement today for typical parish life. However, this assertion is now known to carry no historical weight, be-

cause the centralized churches were certainly centralized for nonliturgical reasons. Very few early Christian churches were truly centralized; one perhaps was the "Golden Octagon", the cathedral of Antioch (A.D. 330), of which little is known. The early circular or centralized church buildings were generally either baptisteries, such as at St. John Lateran in Rome; martyr-shrines and mausoleums, such as the magnificent basilica of San Lorenzo in Milan and the Church of Santa Costanza, which adjoins the Santa Agnese basilica in Rome [fig. 3.5]; or buildings commemorating sacred sites, such as the original Constantinian rotunda of the Holy Sepulcher in Jerusalem.[30] These buildings were centralized for specific, nonliturgical reasons and in no way argue for a primitive "liturgy in the round". In fact, the early centralized churches generally had a prominent axis to the east where the sanctuary opened into the centralized nave (e.g., the cathedral at Bosra; SS. Sergius and Bacchus, Constantinople; the Round Church at Tel Beth-shean; St. Mary's on Mount Gerizim).[31] We shall see this arrangement in the octagonal Church of San Vitale in Ravenna (to be discussed at length in chapter 8), which shows a profound sense of hierarchical separation via an immense triumphal arch between the east-facing longitudinal sanctuary and the octagonal nave. Another interesting example is the triple church complex of St. George, St. John the Baptist, and SS. Cosmas and Damianus at Gerasa (529–533) [fig. 3.6]. Here a large, axially oriented, centralized church is flanked by two typically linear basilicas. In all three churches the altar is in the apse, toward the east, which gives us nothing on which to base an argument for "liturgy in the round".

The other oft-mentioned church, San Stefano Rotondo, has its foundations deep in antiquity [fig. 3.7]. In spite of its circular form and its title dedicated to the proto-martyr, the

[29] St. Maximus the Confessor, *Mystagogia*, 8.21; quoted in Ouspensky, *Theology of the Icon*, 30.

[30] Milburn, *Early Christian Art and Architecture*, 101; also Joseph Rykwert, *Church Building* (London: Sheed and Ward, 1966), 34.

[31] Cyril Mango, *Byzantine Architecture* (New York: Harry N. Abrams, 1976), passim; Yoram Tsafrir, ed., *Ancient Churches Revealed* (Jerusalem: Israel Exploration Society, 1993), passim.

3.4 Model of the Temple in Jerusalem, Holy Land Hotel, Jerusalem.

3.5 Santa Costanza, Rome, 4th cent., Interior.

3.6 St. George, St. John the Baptist, SS. Cosmas and Damianus, Gerasa, 529–533.

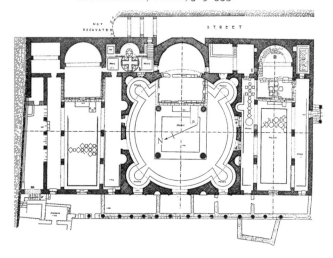

building probably never was a *martyrium* and rather was used only as a parish church. Its extant circular form has now been demonstrated by archeological evidence to be the remaining structure heavily modified from what was originally a larger, complex circle-in-Greek-cross plan [fig. 3.8]. San Stefano is certainly an anomaly, at any rate. As one writer conjectures of San Stefano, "Its effective use must have presented considerable problems, and the lack of any follow-up suggests that it was acknowl-

edged to have been a mistaken experiment." [32] Sandor Ritz, S.J., has done extensive analysis of this building and shows that the program of the building involves a complex iconographic statement. It is, in fact, a patristic era architectural exegesis of the heavenly Jerusalem, with layered radial geometries, none of which have to do with any sort of "liturgy in the round" [figs. 3.9 and 3.10]. [33]

In a similar vein, many liturgical authors advocate "multifunctional" spaces, and some attempt to use historical data to advance their points. J. G. Davies, for instance, went to the great length of writing an entire book, *The Secular Use of Church Buildings*, to show historically how churches were used for eating, sleeping, selling, dancing, legal sanctuary, and so forth. Some authors contend that in the Gothic age cathedrals were used for such profane purposes as law courts, markets, fairs, and the like. So they argue that because churches were "social centers" where, in an integrated society, Masses would be said near vendors hawking their wares, the recent importance given to separation is ahistorical. Churches nowadays, they say, should also be multifunctional, where the sacred and profane can likewise intermingle.

This argument does not entirely stand up to historical scrutiny. It is, of course, fairly well documented that the great medieval fairs often took place in part in the cathedrals. Otto von Simson relates how, at the great fairs at Chartres, food and fuels were sold by the south transept and textiles at the north one, while the wine merchants set up shop in the crypt. There were, however, many ordinances passed by the cathedral chapter to prevent the activity from invading, disrupting, and profaning the sanctuary—a point that Davies ignores. [34] Similarly, Abbot Suger recounts how, in the upper choir at Saint-Denis, the "chamber of divine

---

[32] Sir Banister Fletcher, *A History of Architecture*, ed. J. Musgrove, 19th ed. (London: Butterworths, 1987), 270.

[33] Sandor Ritz, S.J., *L'insuperabile creazione del passato, presente e futuro; Il tempio perenne di Santo Stefano Rotondo in Roma; La nuova Gerusalemme dell'Apocalisse* (Rome: Edizione speciale riservata all'autore, undated).

[34] Otto von Simson, *The Gothic Cathedral*, 2d ed. (New York: Pantheon Books, 1962), 167. J. G. Davies, *The Secular Use of Church Buildings* (New York: Seabury, 1968), 56.

3.7 San Stefano Rotondo, Rome, 468–483, Interior.

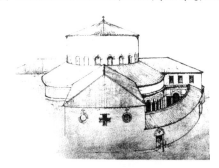

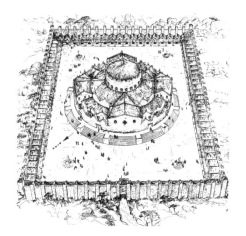

3.8 *above left* San Stefano Rotondo, Rome, 468–483 (after Corbett).

3.10 *above* San Stefano Rotondo, Rome, 468–483 (after Ritz, S.J.).

3.9 *left* San Stefano Rotondo, Rome, 468–483, Interior.

atonement" was constructed so that the Mass might be offered "without disturbance by the crowds".[35] Furthermore, it is often not mentioned that the cathedrals usually had huge chancel screens that effectively created barriers between the sacred and profane activities. In effect, the chancel screen defined "a church within the church": there was a holy and sacred space reserved exclusively for the sacramental life of the community; it was the sanctuary *of* the *entire community*.[36]

While efforts such as Davies' book are worthy and scholarly contributions to our understanding of the social complexities of church buildings through the ages, clearly more research needs to be done in this area. We must be especially careful about interpreting such information polemically. The issues of hierarchic separation and "sacred progression" can-

not be easily dismissed under the banners of relevance. The argument for maintaining a clear differentiation between the sanctuary and the nave is made on both theological and historical grounds. Recent rejection of this separation has been a rejection of the previously established form, without true need and with dubious pastoral benefit. The need for the sacred, though dulled by society, is still a very real need.[37] In a world that tends to avoid the distinction between "sacred" and "profane" and therefore desacralizes everything, this distinction must be revived for the preservation of the sacred.[38] A clear separation of the sanctuary from the nave would also speak to the distinctive nature of the ministerial priest by giving prominence to his place both in offering sacrifice and in presiding over the assembly.[39]

---

[35] Abbot Suger, *De Administratione*, in *Abbot Suger on the Abbey Church of St.-Denis and Its Art Treasures*, ed. and trans. E. Panofsky, 2d ed. (Princeton, N.J.: Princeton University Press, 1979), xxviii.

[36] Rykwert, *Church Building*, 84.

[37] J. Kelly, S.J., "The Sense of the Holy", *The Way*, 13, no. 4 (Oct. 1973): 249–58.

[38] DC, no. 8.

[39] GIRM, intro., no. 4.

CHAPTER FOUR

Furnishing the Sanctuary

You saw me celebrate holy Mass on a plain altar without any decoration behind it. The crucifix was large, the candlesticks heavy, with thick candles of graded height, sloping up toward the cross. The frontal, the liturgical color of the day; a sweeping chasuble; the chalice, rich, simple in its lines, with a broad cup. We had no electric light, nor did we miss it.

And you found it difficult to leave the oratory. You felt at home there. Do you see how we are led to God, brought close to him, by the liturgy of the Catholic Church?

Blessed Josemaría Escrivá, The Way

The sanctuary furnishings

There are seven traditional elements of furnishing to be considered in planning the sanctuary. Four of these express particular aspects of Christ's presence at Mass: (1) the altar, (2) the celebrant's chair, (3) the crucifix, and (4) the ambo [fig. 4.1]. The fifth, (5) the tabernacle in which the consecrated Eucharist is reserved, is intrinsically related to the sacrifice of the Mass and is in many ways the focus of Catholic devotional life. Although the tabernacle is not necessary for Mass, nor need it be in the sanctuary proper, its location demands the utmost consideration when planning the church. Finally, (6) the lectern and (7) the communion rail, though not liturgically required, are traditional elements for very practical reasons.

The Church teaches that the furnishings for the sanctuary, along with the sacred vessels and garments, demand special care and attention. Since they are instruments used in the Eucharistic Sacrifice, they should be of the highest-grade materials, as is worthy of the worship of God. The scriptural principle to keep in mind is Saint Paul's admonition to Saint Timothy that

4.1 Typical sanctuary furnishings, Saint Mary's Basilica, Phoenix, Arizona.

"there are not only vessels of gold and silver but also of wood and earthenware" (2 Tim 2:20): the precious ones are held in honor, the cheap ones are for base uses. The traditional teaching on this is eloquently summarized by Abbot Suger of Saint-Denis, who wrote in the twelfth century:

To me, I confess, one thing has always seemed preeminently fitting: that every costlier or

61

costliest thing should serve, first and foremost, for the administration of the Holy Eucharist. *If* golden pouring vessels, golden vials, golden mortars used to serve, by word of God or the command of the Prophets, to collect *the blood of goats or calves or the red heifer, how much more* must golden vessels, precious stones, and whatever is most valued among all created things, be laid out, with continual reverence and full devotion, for the reception of *the Blood of Christ*.[1]

This attitude of profound reverence for the liturgy is what brought about the opulent and, by today's standards, even ostentatious displays of finery in the design of churches, reliquaries, monstrances, tabernacles, chasubles, and altarpieces throughout the centuries. Traditionally, only the finest materials affordable were used: gold, silver, marble, silk, linen, and precious jewels. This was never, however, a question only of worthiness, but always of appropriateness as well. Bishop Durand writes that Pope Urban and the Council of Rheims (874) decreed that gold or silver should be used for patens and chalices, but, if these are too costly, tin should be used because it doesn't rust. Glass is too fragile for chalices, wood is too absorbent for the Precious Blood, and brass and bronze both oxidize.

Today the emphasis is more on practicality, but still with a concern for appropriateness. Sacred furnishings "must always be durable, of good quality according to contemporary taste, and well adapted to sacred use". Within this proviso commonplace, profane, or shoddy materials are to be rejected.[2] The Church has continued to be realistic about economics, always looking for the best affordable. In today's economies, however, these vessels need not be made just of the "traditional materials", such as marble, gold, silver, or lacquered brass.

The local episcopal conferences are also permitted to approve other materials, a power that grants wider scope to artistic expression: "If greater freedom is given for their [i.e., sacred vessels, vestments, and church furnishings] material and design, it is to give different nations and different artists the widest possible scope for applying their talents to divine worship." This decision also provides for

the expression of indigenous cultures: "The Church welcomes the artistic style of every region for all sacred furnishings and accepts adaptations in keeping with the genius and traditions of each people provided they fit the purpose for which the furnishings are intended."[3]

Sanctuary furnishings should also be simple, reflecting a "noble simplicity". In recognizing that styles and aesthetic sensibilities change, today it is all the more appropriate to call for a profound simplicity in church furnishings. The days are past when ornate reredos and pulpits were fashionable; but, what is more important, our present awareness of impoverished humanity calls for a just and well-reasoned response to be made manifest in the liturgical environment. As Bishop Helder Camara has written, "In a world where two-thirds of the people are in the state of underdevelopment and hunger, how can we squander huge sums on the construction of temples of stone, forgetting the living Christ, who is present in the person of the poor? And when shall we come to understand that in too sumptuous churches the poor have not the courage to enter and do not feel at home?"[4]

This is not to say that the materials or their employment should be mean or miserly, nor should churches and furnishings be artificially impoverished. Even less should we fall into the trap of Judas, who castigated the penitential woman, saying, "Why this waste? For this ointment might have been sold for a large sum and given to the poor" (Mt 26:8–9).[5] The Church calls for a "noble simplicity that is the perfect companion of genuine art"

[1] Abbot Suger, *De Administratione*, in *Abbot Suger on the Abbey Church of St.-Denis and Its Art Treasures*, ed. and trans. E. Panofsky, Abbot Suger, 2d ed. (Princeton, N.J.: Princeton University Press, 1979), xxxiii.

[2] Sacred Congregation for Divine Worship, *Liturgiae instaurationes* (Sept. 5, 1970), no. 8.

[3] *General Instruction of the Roman Missal*, 4th ed. (Mar. 27, 1975), no. 287 [= GIRM].

[4] Dom Helder Camara, *Race against Time*, trans. Della Couling (London: Sheed and Ward, 1971), 63.

[5] Bishop Guillaume Durand, *The Symbolism of Churches and Church Ornaments: A Translation of the First Book of the Rationale divinorum officiorum*, trans. J. M. Neale and B. Webb (Leeds: T. W. Green, 1843; reprint New York: AMS Press, 1973), bk. 1, chap. 3, no. 46.

when selecting furnishings and designing the environment.[6] Again we see a delicate and trilateral balance to be maintained between the beautiful, the simple, and the appropriate. Lastly, the various furnishings should relate in some way, being harmonious one to another. How this is best done—through whatever combination of form, material, proportion, detail, and stylistic expression—is left to the designer. The Church simply asks that there be a strong visual unity within the sanctuary, in order to create an integrated and balanced liturgical environment as the proper focal point of the church building.

The altar: Symbolism, history, and form

The main altar of the church is rightly seen as the focus of the Church's liturgical life,[7] for it is "the sign of Christ himself, the place at which the saving mysteries are carried out, and the center of the assembly, to which the greatest reverence is due".[8] In a very real sense, the church is not just a building to contain—among other things—an altar. Rather, the building is to be planned around the altar. The altar is the center of the church, it is the *raison d'être* of the building. This understanding is the basis of the prohibition found in the rite of *Dedication of a Church and an Altar*, where it is expressly forbidden "both by custom and liturgical law to dedicate a church without dedicating the altar, for the dedication of the altar is the principal part of the whole rite".[9]

The altar is truly sacred, made so by the precious sacrifice offered upon it as well as by its consecration and symbolic value. It is a symbol of Christ, who is the true altar of the Eucharist.[10] As Saint John Chrysostom wrote, "This altar is an object of wonder: by nature it is stone, but it is made holy when it receives the body of Christ."[11] Because of the nature of this sacrifice, the eternal sacrifice of Christ now in heaven, the altar is a particularly sacred place where Christ comes to meet, to nourish, and to sanctify his Church.

Historically, we see that the idea of sacrifice to the Deity has been common to all ancient religions, hence the idea of a special altar of sacrifice was often found within these religions. Indeed, the Latin word *altare* means just that, a place of sacrifice. The first Christian altars were probably small, square, and wooden. Wood, of course, has a certain significance for the Church, since the table of the Last Supper was probably of wood, but, more importantly, so was the Cross. Saint Cyril of Jerusalem wrote, "Life ever comes from wood. In the time of Noah, the preservation of life came from a wooden ark. In Moses' time the sea, on beholding the figurative rod, gave way before him who struck it; could the rod of Moses be so mighty, and the cross of the Savior powerless?"[12] Thus the early Church easily adopted the idea of wooden altars, a practice that lasted into the eleventh century. That said, throughout the first several centuries Christian altars were also made of bronze, silver, gold, ivory, and stone.[13] There is even a legend of an earthen altar erected by Saints Lazarus and Mary Magdalen at the Castle of St. Mary in Provence.[14]

As the Church developed her liturgy, stone became the predominant material for altars, and with good reason. The ancient Jewish altars were often of stone, and in one instance Yahweh explicitly commanded that they not be of "hewn stones" (Ex 20:25).[15] Stone also has a particular symbolism for Christianity, as Jesus

---

[6] GIRM, no. 287.

[7] Sacred Congregation of Rites, *Inter oecumenici* (Sept. 26, 1964), no. 91 [= IO].

[8] Sacred Congregation of Rites, *Eucharisticum mysterium* (May 25, 1967), no. 24 [= EM].

[9] Sacred Congregation for the Sacraments and Divine Worship, *Dedication of a Church and an Altar* (May 29, 1977), chap. 3, no. 1 [= DOCA].

[10] Heb 4:14 and 13:10. For the varied symbolism of the altar, cf. DOCA, chap. 4, nos. 1–4.

[11] St. John Chrysostom, *Homilia XX in II Cor.*, 3; quoted in DOCA, chap. 4, no. 23.

[12] St. Cyril of Jerusalem, *Cat.* xiii, 20, in *The Works of St. Cyril of Jerusalem*, ed. L. P. McCauley, S.J., and A. A. Stephenson (Washington, D.C.: Catholic University of America Press, 1969–1970).

[13] Joseph Rykwert, *Church Building* (London: Sheed and Ward, 1966), 18.

[14] Durand, *Rationale*, bk. 1, chap. 7, no. 28.

[15] Cf. 1 Sam 6:14, 14:33. The Mosaic altar of burnt offering was of acacia wood and bronze (Ex 27:1–6), the altar of incense was acacia and gold (Ex 30:1–5), and the altars in Solomon's Temple were also bronze (2 Chron 4:1) and gold (1 Kings 7:48 and 2 Chron 4:19), though this may have been the covering over stone. Presumably, the postexilic altar in the rebuilt temple was of stone.

4.2 Arcosolium in Catacombs, Rome.

identifies himself with "the stone which the builders rejected", which "has become the cornerstone" (Ps 118:22–23, Mt 21:42).

Many authorities also examine the historical development of the stone altar, suggesting that the Christian stone altar is an adaptation of the *cartibulum*, the altar used to offer sacrifice to the Roman household god, or that it developed from the *arcosolium*, from the days when Masses were offered in the catacombs over the sarcophagi of the martyrs [fig. 4.2].[16] However, there is much debate as to these historical developments. Current scholarship generally supports the thesis that the catacombs were frequently used liturgically by the early Church, even after the Edict of Milan in 313. Pope Saint Damasus sponsored a building program through which the catacombs were enlarged and underground chapels were created to allow larger groups to celebrate anniversary Masses. Hence we find sanctuary alcoves separated by low stone railings (*cancelli*), cathedra and bap-

tisteries even cut out of the soft tufa stone, and walls decorated with elaborate paintings (many of which are dated before the Edict).[17]

But rather than look to the *cartibulum* or the *arcosolium*, it seems we should first consider the message of the stone slab in the Anastasis in Jerusalem. We know that the early Church revered the stone in the Holy Sepulcher from which Jesus rose, and, in fact, the Orthodox continue to use it as an altar to this day. Its form is roughly similar to the *arcosolium*, but the vitality of its message must have had an incalculable impact on the early Church. It should be noted that some important altars were built of porphyry, a purplish feldspar often used for the royal funeral sarcophagus. It is certainly significant that Constantine had the altar over the tomb of Peter at the Vatican cemetery built of porphyry: it spoke of Peter's place as the Prince of the Apostles. Porphyry was also later used for the high altar at Saint-Denis, the funeral basilica of the kings and queens of France.

By whatever precise series of events, as the Church developed in her liturgy and theology, stone altars gradually began to replace wooden ones. Saint John Chrysostom seems to have been the first to recommend their use.[18] By the sixth century local legislation began to require stone altars, but, although stone altars were practically universal by the twelfth century, it was only in 1596 that the Church decided to make all altars of stone.[19] This requirement, normatively still in force, has largely been ignored for the past twenty-five years. Since the Second Vatican Council there has been an

[16] *A New Dictionary of Liturgy and Worship*, ed. J. G. Davies (London: SCM, 1988), s.v. "altar" [= NDLW]; also Fr. J. O'Connell, *Church Building and Furnishing, the Church's Way* (London: Burns and Oates, 1955), 127, 134, and 136.

[17] Much has been written on the liturgical use of catacombs. See, for instance, Fr. Louis Bouyer, *Liturgy and Architecture* (South Bend, Ind.: University of Notre Dame Press, 1967), 40–41; Frs. Stephen and Cuthbert Johnson, *Planning for Liturgy* (Farnborough, England: St. Michael's, 1983), 13; R. Milburn, *Early Christian Art and Architecture* (London: Scolar, 1988), 22 and 25; O'Connell, *Church Building*, 90; Émile Mâle, *The Early Churches of Rome*, trans. David Buxton (London: Benn, 1960), 47; and L. Ouspensky, *The Theology of the Icon* (Crestwood, N.Y.: St. Vladimir's Seminary Press, 1978), 82.

[18] St. John Chrysostom, *Homilia XX in II Cor.*, 3; cited in R. Kevin Seasoltz, *The House of God* (New York: Herder and Herder, 1963), 159.

[19] O'Connell, *Church Building*, 136.

undue proliferation of wooden tables, despite the fact that Vatican II documents do not recommend wood as a desirable material. The modern use of wooden tables, which is intended to connote a gathering for a common meal, thus replacing the *mensa*, which is proper for a sacrificial meal, is a by-product of the Liturgical Movement. However, only fifteen years before the Council, Pope Pius XII wrote, "Thus . . . one would be straying from the straight path were he to wish the altar restored to its primitive table-form." [20] And it would seem that the overtly sacrificial emphasis of John Paul II's encyclical *Dominicae cenae* seeks to redress this problem, especially as he cites the danger of viewing the Mass "as *only* a banquet".[21] In the light of all this, it is certainly time for architects and liturgists to reevaluate the symbolism of the altar, to incorporate the dually integrated realities of meal and sacrifice. For unless the appropriate materials and forms are revived, how can the message be restored?

Postconciliar Church documents call for the ancient idea of the altar as a symbol of Christ to be respected and continued. The main altar should be made of stone,[22] in fact, "of a single natural stone", without crack or fissure, to symbolize the personal unity of the Lord.[23] Although the documents of Vatican II allow for the altar to be either fixed or movable, it is preferred that altars be fixed, as a sign of Christ's permanent sacrifice.[24] Finally, the main altar (and only the main altar) should be consecrated.[25] As the rite of consecration requires the altar to be anointed with chrism, five crosses should be incised in the top surface—one in the center and one at each of the four corners—representing the Lord's five wounds.[26]

The altar should be freestanding, enabling it to be incensed on all sides. The altar should remain clear of anything not needed for the sacrifice, having only the elements of bread and wine, the sacramentary, and a missal stand or cushion. Candles are permitted on the altar, or near it, but these must not obstruct the view of the people. Since the altar is to be kept clear, a small table, called a *credence table*, is used to keep the cruets and other items needed for the

Mass. The credence table is utilitarian and not liturgical, so it need only be a simple, portable table of some becoming material, such as wood, usually covered with white linen. The table should be high enough to be convenient for the standing priest and servers and large enough for chalices, decanters, cruets, patens, and such, as well as hymnals and notes (hence a second shelf may be useful).

Movable altars are permitted and have their rightful place, often in eucharistic chapels for daily Mass, in interdenominational chapels, such as those at hospitals and schools, and in temporary church facilities. But even a movable altar should look substantial, stable, and dignified.[27] It may be built out of any material suitable for liturgical use.[28] A movable altar should also "be treated with religious respect because it is a table destined solely and permanently for the eucharistic banquet". Canonically, it is to be blessed, if it cannot be solemnly dedicated, though it is not permissible to deposit relics in a movable altar.[29]

This association of relics and altars goes back even to the first century, as is obvious in the visionary language of Saint John's Revelation: "When he opened the fifth seal, I saw under the altar the souls of those who had been slain for the word of God and for the witness they had borne" (Rev 6:9). Later, in the same vein, Saint Ambrose wrote, "Let the triumphant victims occupy the place where Christ is victim: he, however, who suffered for all, upon the altar; they, who have been redeemed by his

---

[20] Pius XII, *Mediator Dei*, (Nov. 20, 1947), no. 66 [= MD].

[21] John Paul II, *Dominicae cenae* (Feb. 24, 1980), no. 11 [= DC].

[22] GIRM, no. 263.

[23] Ibid.; also *Code of Canon Law* (1983), can. 1236 [= CIC]. The local bishops' conferences may authorize other generally accepted and solid, worthy materials. From the American Appendix to GIRM, no. 263: "Materials other than natural stone may be used for fixed altars provided these are worthy, solid and properly constructed, subject to the further judgment of the local ordinary in doubtful cases."

[24] GIRM, nos. 260, 262; CIC, can. 1235, sec. 2; O'Connell, *Church Building*, 134.

[25] GIRM, no. 262; CIC, can. 1237: movable altars are either consecrated or blessed.

[26] DOCA, chap. 4, no. 49; also Durand, *Rationale*, bk. 1, chap. 7, nos. 29–32.

[27] The Bishops' Conference of England and Wales, *The Parish Church* (London: Catholic Truth Society, 1984), 19 [= PC].

[28] CIC, can. 1236, sec. 2.

[29] DOCA, chap. 6, nos. 1–3.

4.3 Saint Catherine Reliquary Altar, Santa Maria-sopra-Minerva, Rome.

4.4 Reliquary Altar, Santa Maria della Vittoria, Rome.

4.5 Confessio, Santa Cecilia, Rome, by S. Maderno, 1599.

suffering, beneath the altar."[30] The tradition of placing relics of martyrs beneath or within the altars arose from the earliest days of the Church. The bodies, bones, and even ashes of the Christian martyrs have always been treasured. In the second-century account of the martyrdom of Polycarp, we read that after his execution and subsequent cremation:

> We did gather up his bones—more precious to us than jewels, and finer than pure gold—and we laid them to rest in a spot suitable for the purpose. There we shall assemble, as occasion allows, with glad rejoicings; and with the Lord's permission we shall celebrate the birthday of his martyrdom. It will serve both as a commemoration of all who have triumphed before, and as a training and a preparation for any whose crown may be still to come.[31]

This celebration of "the birthday of his martyrdom" seems to be an early reference to the continuing practice of honoring the saints with anniversary Masses. This ancient passage also brings to mind the threefold purpose of the relic-altar. First, it is a way of honoring the faithful who have died and have been given the crown of eternal life (cf. Rev 2:10). Second, the association of the altar with a particular saint is an expression of belief in the communion of saints. And third, it is also an expression of belief in the Resurrection of the Lord and of his people (cf. 2 Tim 2:11). Properly speaking, the altar is not dedicated to a saint but to God, as is made clear at the rite of dedication. As Saint Augustine expressed it, "It is not to any of the martyrs, but to the God of the martyrs, though in memory of the martyrs, that we raise our altars."[32]

This association of relics with altars has perhaps unduly influenced the form of the altar. Early on, altars were commonly built over tombs, such as Constantine's porphyry altar that has been found over Saint Peter's tomb. Later this developed into the *confessio*, where it was possible to look beneath the raised altar platform into the crypt containing the tombs of saints. By the seventh century relics were sometimes actually contained within the altar as a tomb, and by the eighth century the practice began of putting small relics within the table of the altar. Later, from the ninth to the fourteenth century, relics were placed *on* the altar as well as *over* and *behind* it. This change was brought about not by legislation but by the demands of popular piety: the reliquaries of the saints began invading the table, the stone of sacrifice. Even the high altar thus often became also a relic shrine, with the body of a saint, or else an effigy, encased in a glass casket beneath the stone table, as is the case with Saint Catherine of Siena beneath the high altar of Santa Maria-sopra-Minerva [figs. 4.3 to 4.5]. The table, which had traditionally been freestanding and often square, was made oblong in imitation of the sarcophagus [figs 4.6, 4.7] and was subsumed into the larger composition of the medieval and Baroque reredos [figs. 4.8, 4.9]. The *confessio* and the civory or

---

[30] St. Ambrose, *Epistula*, 22:13; quoted in DOCA, chap. 2, no. 14.

[31] *The Martyrdom of Polycarp*, in *Early Christian Writings*, ed. Maxwell Staniforth (Harmondsworth, England: Penguin, 1968), 162.

[32] St. Augustine, *Contra Faustum*, XX, 21; quoted in DOCA, chap. 4, no. 10.

4.6 Sarcophagus Altar, Brno Cathedral.

4.7 Sarcophagus Altar, Karlskirche, Vienna.

4.8 Gothic Reredos, Winchester Cathedral.

4.9 Baroque Reredos, Convento de Tepotzotlan, Mexico.

baldacchino were abandoned when the altar was integrated into the rear wall, often as little more than a shelf.[33]

Today, with the return of the freestanding altar, the ancient practice of enclosing the relics of a martyr or other saint within the altar has been retained.[34] It is a fitting and salutary practice, but not mandated. When relics are deposited beneath the altar, they "should be of such a size that they can be recognized as parts of human bodies". Therefore very small relics should not be deposited. The authenticity of the relics should be verified, as it "is better for an altar to be dedicated without relics than to have relics of doubtful credibility placed beneath it". Lastly, the reliquary must not be placed (as it once was) in the *mensa*, or the altar proper, but beneath it, either in the supporting base or in a floor vault (though obviously, in the latter case, the altar must be truly permanent).[35]

In one of the liturgical changes of Vatican II, the altar was disengaged from the reredos and returned to its former and rightful place in the center of the sanctuary. This was done to emphasize its place as the center of the assembly, to make it the natural focus in the sanctuary, and to enable it to be freestanding so that it could be incensed.[36] Later, this gave the priest the option of celebrating Mass facing the people. It is interesting to note that while this option was almost completely adopted in the Catholic West, it is not even implicitly found in the original Second Vatican Council documents. We will, therefore, examine this issue in due course. Several documents issued by various episcopal conferences or other committees call for modern altars to be square or slightly rectangular, rather than like the elongated altar that was attached to the reredos.[37] This emphasis, of course, diminishes the Resurrection symbolism of the stone slab from which the Lord rose again. It does, nonetheless, have the merit of returning the attention of the assembly back to the sacrifice at the altar, as the square shape is historically more closely associated with the act of sacrifice.[38]

There are, however, two problems encountered with the return to the smaller, square altar. The first difficulty is that the altar loses its power as a visual terminus to the nave, even becoming less prominent as the focus of the sanctuary. Second, it makes concelebration somewhat awkward. Some liturgists consider this last point an asset—in fact, it seems actually to be part of the reason for using the square altar—in accordance with the dubious teaching that "the altar is designed and constructed for the action of a community and the functioning of a single priest."[39] While such an altar may answer the general needs of most parish churches, it is not universally satisfactory. Quite to the contrary, *Eucharisticum mysterium* clearly considers concelebration to be an asset, because "it demonstrates the unity of the sacrifice and the priesthood", and "it both symbolizes and strengthens the brotherly bond of the priesthood." Therefore, "it is *desirable that priests should celebrate the Eucharist in this eminent manner.*" This instruction, in fact, insists that the proper authorities should "facilitate, and indeed positively encourage concelebration".[40] Hence, there are many situations where the small, square altar would be decidedly *inappropriate*. For instance, at a cathedral church, where the "principal manifestation of the Church . . . [is in the liturgy] . . . at which the bishop presides, surrounded by his college of priests and by his ministers",[41] the altar should be quite large to accommodate a number of priests, so that they do not seem to be crowding the altar. Also, at places such as pilgrimage sites, monasteries, seminaries, religious houses, and secular clerical communities,

---

[33] O'Connell, *Church Building*, 128–29.

[34] CIC, can. 1237, 2; GIRM, no. 266.

[35] DOCA, chap. 2, no. 5, a–c; chap. 4, no. 5.

[36] EM, no. 24; GIRM, no. 262.

[37] United States Catholic Conference, *Environment and Art in Catholic Worship* (Washington, D.C.: USCC, 1978), 72 [= EACW]. Also PC, 70.

[38] The altars of Moses (cf. Ex 27:1; 30:1; 37:25; 38:1) and Solomon (2 Chron 4:1) were square, as probably were the early Christian altars (cf. O'Connell, *Church Building*, 127). In Augustinian cosmology, the square particularly symbolizes Christ: as the square is a "magnitude multiplied by magnitude", so does the second Person of the Trinity perfectly proceed from the first. Cf. Otto von Simson, *The Gothic Cathedral*, 2d ed. (New York: Pantheon Books, 1962), 27.

[39] EACW, 72.

[40] EM, no. 47, italics added.

[41] Vatican II, *Sacrosanctum concilium* (Dec. 4, 1963), no. 41 [= SC].

altars large enough for concelebration should positively be provided.[42]

The altar: Direction and liturgical dynamics

Almost universally since Vatican II, priests have celebrated the Roman Rite of the Mass *versus populum*–facing the people in a sort of "dialogue Mass"–although this was done entirely without the direct mandate of the Council Fathers.[43] There is, in fact, no mention of rearranging the altar in the actual documents of Vatican II. It seems to be mentioned first in number 91 of *Inter Oecumenici* (1964), a document of the Sacred Congregation of Rites, and much later in number 262 of the *General Instruction of the Roman Missal*, where the general sense is that the altar should be freestanding so that the priest may have the *option* of celebrating facing the people.

The change of direction, however, came about almost instantaneously–not so much because the Vatican Fathers had the altar moved away from the rear wall so that Mass *might* be said facing the congregation, but more likely because the first internationally televised papal Mass was from St. Peter's during the Council. Since the telecast showed Pope Paul VI celebrating *ad orientem* in the Roman basilican arrangement, ostensibly facing the people, the common conclusion seems to have been that this was now the new norm.[44] While perhaps this *versus populum* orientation is now almost taken for granted, it is an issue certainly worth examining, as it has great impact both on architecture and on the goal of realizing Christian community.

Before venturing into this discussion, however, it is important to understand the dynamic of the liturgy. Our modern and revisionist explanation is usually that the pre–Vatican II priest, "with his back to the people", was doing something secretive, elitist, and quite separate from the laity. Whether or not this was actually the commonplace attitude, what the posture suggests is something quite different. When the priest and the people are facing the same direction, they are, in fact, doing the same thing: offering the sacrifice of the Mass together "in a common act of trinitarian worship".[45] The priest is simply leading the people in worship. The arrangement calls to mind the fact that the priest, who is somewhat anonymous in that his face cannot be seen, is truly *alter Christus*, properly mediating between man and God.[46] As *Sacrosanctum concilium* explains, "The liturgy, then, is rightly seen as an exercise of the priestly office of Jesus Christ. . . . In it full public worship is performed by the Mystical Body of Christ, that is, by the Head and his members."[47] With this arrangement the whole Church is then doing the same thing in total union with herself, not against or *versus* herself. This can be understood by opposing it to a performance where actors on stage are acting and facing the audience, who are doing something quite different, namely, observing. As Fr. Louis Bouyer points out in this regard: "Either you look at somebody doing something for you, instead of you, or you do it with him. You can't do both at the same time."[48]

Western society has so embraced the entertainment media that we are very comfortable watching performances. So it becomes very easy to go to Mass, sing the songs, give the proper responses at the proper time, and watch the priest perform his duties, without ever entering into the worship. The parish community may well become complacent. This then raises a very interesting pastoral question: Does the position of the priest facing the congregation to offer the Eucharist truly help the laity to enter into the celebration, or does it actually hinder the *participatio actuosa* so earnestly sought? I am not convinced that average, conscientious laymen believe themselves to be any more a part of the liturgy with the priest facing them than they do when he does not.

---

[42] EM, no. 47.

[43] Joseph Cardinal Ratzinger, *The Feast of Faith* (San Francisco: Ignatius Press, 1986), 142.

[44] Bouyer, *Liturgy and Architecture*, 105–6.

[45] Ratzinger, *Feast*, 140.

[46] The symbolic purpose of the alb and chasuble is, similarly, to remove the priest's personal identity as he "puts on Jesus Christ", thus reinforcing the idea that the agent of sacrifice is Jesus Christ, through the ministry of the priest *in persona Christi*.

[47] SC, no. 7.

[48] Bouyer, *Liturgy and Architecture*, 59.

4.10 "Da Vinci Model" of Last Supper (artist unknown).

And on another and perhaps simpler level, the symbolism is all wrong. Now there is an altar *between* the priest and the congregation, the priest is *versus populum*, or "against the people", and the body of Christ is divided; now the priest is truly "doing something different", doing something for the people, who are watching.[49]

Historically there is a strong, and practically conclusive, argument for preferring the priest and people to face the same direction. It may not be entirely conclusive, but clearly when the celebrant "faced the people", he did so for other reasons than to "include" the laity. In fact, in the first millennium of Christianity it is clear from archeological evidence that *versus populum* was definitely *not* the norm. Where the smaller churches tended to have the sanctuary in the east, so that the priest and people all faced the same direction, a large number of cathedrals and major basilicas were ordered with the apse in the west, so that the liturgy was celebrated to the east. The great eastern doors were opened so that the sunlight streaming in would remind the people of the Lord's promised Second Coming. It is significant, and

rarely mentioned, that the laity were not in the central nave but rather in the side aisles. During this time, in both the East and the West, the deacon would summon the congregation to "Turn to the east", or "Turn toward the Lord", in directing the laity to worship toward the rising sun as a symbol of the Lord. At the Consecration the central nave, with its view to the sanctuary, was veiled by curtains that the deacons drew back only after the eucharistic prayers. Hence, the people would not even be in "dialogue" relationship with the priest. This arrangement, even with the use of veils, was in practice throughout the late Middle Ages, as Durand attests, and was finally lost in the West only in the Baroque age.[50] The question of direction toward the people has never been a concern in the Christian East, where the concern has always been one of correct liturgical orientation.[51] In fact, the vast majority of

---

[49] Ibid., 110–11.

[50] Msgr. Klaus Gamber, *The Reform of the Roman Liturgy* (San Juan Capistrano: Una Voce, 1993), 126ff.

[51] By *orientation* we mean the altar placed so Mass is said to the east; by *direction*, the relationship between the priest and the congregation; and by *position*, the place of the altar within the church.

churches built up to the Counter Reformation, both oriental and occidental, were intentionally oriented to the east.

Even if one based the decision regarding direction on the notion that the Last Supper was a prototype of the Christian liturgy (something that would need serious qualification), this would suggest that all should be facing the same direction: the Lord and his apostles were all on one side of a table, which was served from the other—assuming that this was the common arrangement for banquets in the Mediterranean cultures.[52] However, the best research discredits the "da Vinci" model of the Lord surrounded by his apostles [fig. 4.10]. In Mediterranean cultures, both at the time of Christ and for centuries afterward, banquets were held around semicircular or crescent-shaped tables, with all the guests on the outside being served from the inside. The place of honor was the right-most seat, hence this was the place Jesus would likely have occupied [fig. 4.11].[52] With such an arrangement it would be difficult to order a modern church. The anniversary Masses said over a martyr's sarcophagus in the catacombs were probably likewise celebrated with everyone facing the same direction, since the sarcophagus in the arcosolium sat against the wall.[54]

As for orientation, it is interesting that one of the many reasons that Bishop Durand gives for the medieval liturgy to be oriented eastward, citing Saint John Damascene, is that "our Lord, at his Crucifixion, looked toward the east: and also when he ascended into heaven, he ascended toward the east: and thus the apostles adored him: and thus 'he shall come again *in like manner as they saw him go into heaven.*'" Bishop Durand also quotes Saint Augustine, who says, "No Scripture has taught us to pray toward the east", and "Though I find not a thing on record in Scripture, yet I receive it as proceeding from the apostles if the universal Church embrace it."[55] From these quotes we can deduce that an eastward orientation must have been the prevalent practice in Augustine's times "if the universal Church embrace it", and that its origins are distant enough to be considered apostolic.

4.11 "Historical Arrangement" of Last Supper (after Gamber).

In the early Syrian churches, there seems to have been great room for flexibility in placing the altar. While it perhaps most frequently stood against the rear wall of the apse, it could also be placed on the chord of the apse, in the nave at the chancel steps, or even in the middle of the nave. Regardless of the position of the altar, the Eucharist was always celebrated toward the east, by both priest and people, as part of the cosmic liturgy.[56] Interestingly, in the early Egyptian churches where the priest was "facing the people", the people were called to "Turn to the east!" at the eucharistic prayer. They were expected to turn their backs to the altar for the entire canon of the Mass, includ-

---

[52] Gamber, *Reform*, 53–54 and 83.

[53] Ibid., 139ff.

[54] O'Connell, *Church Building*, 154.

[55] Durand, *Rationale*, bk. 5, chap. 2, no. 57.

[56] Cf. Cyril of Jerusalem, *Works*, 192, n. 5.

ing the Consecration, which shows the immense value given to liturgical orientation.[57]

The practice in the major Roman basilicas from the fourth to the seventh century is instructive, since it appears to give a liturgical basis for the celebration of the Mass facing the people. The old church of St. Peter's, pulled down in the sixteenth century to build the present one, had the altar on the west end of the transept, just east of the apse, and facing the east. It is important to note that the building was "occidented", with the apse in the west end—thus when Mass was said toward the east it was done toward the people, who were east of the altar.[58] The emphasis, again, was on the orientation of the liturgy toward the *east*, not toward the *congregation*. As we have noted, in those basilicas the people were not in the center of the nave; they were themselves turned toward the east, and the sanctuary itself was veiled. Since canon law required Mass to be celebrated toward the east, the priest had to face the people in churches where the sanctuary was to the west.[59] Later, with the growth of the monasteries and the subsequent multiplication of Masses, side altars were more or less oriented toward the east. The position of the priest at the side altar was such that priest and people faced the same way, and this was gradually adopted for the high altar as well. By the tenth century the predominant position was of the priest facing an altar that was against the wall. So whether Mass was celebrated in the Roman basilican style or against the monastic reredos, the primary concern was proper orientation: the offering of the Eucharist toward the east. Gradually this concern for orientation died away, so that most Baroque churches were built without regard for this ancient practice.

During the Enlightenment there was a liturgical movement that was greatly influenced by the rationalists of the day. Ignoring the sacrificial essence of the liturgy, some liturgists were at work to reduce the divine worship to matters of "instruction and moral admonition". Others were interested in, among other agenda, "the turning of the altars towards the people [and] greater restraint in the exposition of the Blessed Sacrament".[60] It is interesting

(even if entirely coincidental) that it took several hundred years for these Enlightenment agenda to reappear in the Liturgical Movement of our time.

As we have seen, the main concern throughout most of the history of the Church was for the proper orientation of the liturgy rather than whether or not the priest faced the people. Therefore it seems to be a false archeologism that calls for the altar to be "turned around". To return to the concerns of Vatican II, namely, a true and profoundly spiritual *participatio actuosa*, it is necessary to rethink the questions of orientation, direction, and position. While it was unquestionably good to return the altar to the center of the sanctuary and restore it to its ancient square form, it may well have been a fundamental error to turn the celebration of the Lord's sacrifice toward the congregation. This was done without regard for orientation, and thus the idea of our participation in the cosmic liturgy—of Christ and his Church offering sacrifice to the heavenly Father—was lost. In retrospect, it has also diminished the idea of the priest as *alter Christus*, making the priest more of a discussion moderator than a sacrificial mediator, and has brought the people inevitably into a posture of observing. As Fr. Joseph Jungmann summarizes, "The rule which grew ever more important, that at prayer all should look to the East—and naturally this included the celebrant first of all—led even in the Middle Ages to the priest's assuming a place almost without exception . . . on the side of the altar nearest the people, for he is the leader of the people in their prayer and at their head offers up to God their prayer and sacrifice."[61]

To correct these problems, we must reconsider the relationship of the sanctuary and altar to the nave. Just as Fr. Louis Bouyer argued against adopting the late-nineteenth-century church as the definitive model for a church, so

---

[57] Bouyer, *Liturgy and Architecture*, 56.
[58] Milburn, *Early Christian Art and Architecture*, 96–97. Also Josef [Joseph] A. Jungmann, S.J., *The Mass of the Roman Rite*, trans. Francis A. Brunner, C.SS.R., vol. 1 (New York: Benziger Brothers, 1948), 72.
[59] Jungmann, *Roman Rite*, vol. 1, 255, n. 13.
[60] Ibid., 153.
[61] Ibid., 255.

must we not tacitly accept the current post–Vatican II form, especially given its pastoral, theological, and historical weaknesses.[62] There are four things to be considered: first, an arrangement that allows for true participation of the laity in the sacrifice of the Mass without the danger of lapsing into a spectator's role; second, an arrangement that respects the due differentiation of the ministerial and lay priesthoods; third, one that gives the altar its due prominence; and fourth, one that recovers the truly ancient and profoundly Christian practice of the whole Church—both clergy and laity—praying toward the east.[63]

There is no doubt that this fourth consideration is by far the most controversial and difficult. Many priests trained since Vatican II have no real concept of the value of liturgical orientation or of their true role as leader and mediator rather than as moderator and "presider". Most lay people, while perhaps still feeling detached and uninvolved at Mass, might see eastward orientation as a throwback to pre–Vatican II clericalism. Furthermore, we have generally lost our Christian cosmology and therefore our respect for the significance of the east. No doubt, many individual dioceses and parishes, liturgical commissions, and episcopal conferences would consider it more prudent and less difficult to maintain the status quo, even given its obvious weaknesses, than to work to reeducate her royal priesthood in their true place as active participants in the sacrifice of the liturgy. Even Cardinal Joseph Ratzinger, while impressively articulating the value of liturgical orientation, suggests that, rather than implement further external changes, efforts would be better spent to "promote the kind of liturgical education which will enable people to participate in a proper inward manner".[64] Nevertheless, as it is the goal of this book to propose architectural considerations that further the vision of the Second Vatican Council, without respect to politics and liturgical agenda, I will briefly continue with what seems consonant with that goal.

For those churches, both new and reordered, where the congregations wish to enter into an oriented liturgy, it is not enough simply to place the priest on the west side of the altar. Traditionally there has been a definite cleft between the sanctuary and nave, often accentuated by a balustrade, a rood screen, or a chancel arch, which clearly defined two separate zones—one for the clergy and one for the laity. If it be objected that such an arrangement overemphasized the hierarchical character of the Church at the expense of the people of God, it may be possible to seek an architectural arrangement that respects both the "hierarchic" body of Christ and the "demotic" people of God without rejecting either. For they cannot be diametrically opposed, as each expresses the mystery of the Church. Recently this "opposition" of nave to sanctuary has been diminished somewhat, yet in many churches there remains a strong lateral separation, a neat division akin to a stage in an auditorium. This lateral division makes the altar psychologically remote from the people and thus reinforces the notion of observing the Mass.

Rather than having a straight, lateral separation of the nave and sanctuary, it may make sense to bring the altar and sanctuary back into the nave, so the congregation can be wrapped around the altar, all facing east. By bringing the altar toward the congregation, as in the ancient Syrian practice, a sense of intimacy and union could be fostered. The line of distinction between the sanctuary and nave would thus be softened and would give a sense of the "organic" nature of the assembly. The altar should still have both prominence and protection, and this could be achieved by raising the platform several steps and by covering it with a civory or other such architectural device. It seems necessary to restore the civory (*ciborium*) as the proper "crowning glory" of the altar, so that it does not get lost as an "altar island", so commonplace today. The architectural expression would still be of the priestly people gathered around the ministerial priest. Then the Church would be gathered together in a common act of worship. And then the

---

[62] Bouyer, *Liturgy and Architecture*, 86.
[63] Ratzinger, *Feast*, 143.
[64] Ibid., 139.

most profound vision of the Second Vatican Council might be realized:

> The Church, therefore, earnestly desires that Christ's faithful, when present at this mystery of faith, should not be there as strangers or silent spectators. On the contrary, through a good understanding of the rites and prayers they should take part in the sacred action, conscious of what they are doing, with devotion and full collaboration. They should be instructed by God's word, and be nourished at the table of the Lord's Body. They should give thanks to God. *Offering the immaculate victim, not only through the priest but also together with him, they should learn to offer themselves.* Through Christ, the Mediator, they should be drawn day by day into ever more perfect union with God and each other, so that finally God may be all in all.[65]

The altar: Prominence and emphasis

The question of orientation aside, with a return to a small square altar there remains the architectural problem of the altar's prominence. In previous times an altar canopy was often used to define the altar within the sanctuary. This canopy generally took one of two forms, the *civory* (also called a *ciborium*, *baldaquin*, or *baldacchino*), which is a columned edifice in stone, metal, or wood over the altar, such as the great baldacchino by Bernini in St. Peter's [figs. 4.12 to 4.14]; and the *tester*, which is a smaller, lighter structure, usually suspended from above. In the early Syrian churches, when the altar was in the middle of the nave and the Eucharist was offered among the people, the altar was raised on steps and covered by a canopy to protect it and to enhance its sacrality. The reredos of the medieval and Baroque ages served to give a visual terminus to the sanctuary. Even the wide altars common to churches since Vatican II help to define the altar's prominence. The language of the Church's documents suggests that the altar deserves special architectural consideration, stating that "the mystery of the Eucharist is the true center of the sacred liturgy and indeed of the whole Christian life"[66] and calling for the altar to "be so placed as to be a focal

4.12 Baldacchino, St. Peter's, Vatican, by Bernini.

point on which the attention of the whole congregation naturally centers".[67]

There is a danger that a small square altar will lose its place of primacy among the other furnishings, as well as amidst a wide sanctuary. This loss may be prevented through various means, including the ancient and symbolic canopy. The idea of a tent covering a sacred item or place is Mosaic—the Israelites were commanded by Yahweh to construct a tent in which the Ark of the Covenant was to be kept (cf. Ex 26:1–27) [see figs. 3.1, 3.2]. The canopy has also been a mark of distinction and honor over the throne of the king. The use of the canopy over the high altar goes back to at least the fourth century—as is evidenced by a similar device over the tomb of Saint Peter in the archeological excavations beneath the Vatican—and was most common from the seventh to tenth centuries. Its use generally declined after relic altars became popular, although canopies have continued to be used in the great Roman basilicas. Up to the time of Vatican II, a canopy was required for high altars in cathedrals and especially for altars where the Blessed Sacrament was reserved.[68]

While the canopy is no longer required, it is an idea that deserves reconsideration. It is not only a traditional mark of respect for the altar, but it also helps to define and give prominence

---

[65] SC, no. 48, italics added.
[66] EM, no. 1.
[67] GIRM, no. 262.
[68] O'Connell, *Church Building*, 186. Cf. *Caeremoniale Episcoporum*, I, xii, 13; xiii, 3; xiv, 1; and S.R.C. documents nos. 1966 and 2912.

4.13 Baldacchino, Santa Maria Maggiore, Rome.

to the altar within the sanctuary. If one is used, the pillars should be placed so as not to hinder free movement around the altar or to obstruct the view from the nave. The ornamentation need not be "classical"; the definition of the altar might even be implied by a dramatic, well-placed skylight [fig. 4.15]. However it is achieved, the main concern is to give the altar

4.14 Baldacchino, St. Louis Cathedral, Missouri.

4.15 Mount Claret Chapel, Phoenix, Arizona, Interior.

4.16 Cancelli, San Clemente, Rome.

4.17 SS. Peter and Paul, Gerasa, (by F. Crowfoot).

the architectural prominence that it is liturgically due.

The altar rail

The use of the altar rail has gone by the wayside since the Second Vatican Council. Especially in America, many beautiful marble balustrades were unceremoniously torn out of churches and discarded in the years immediately following the Council. The sentiment of the day saw the altar rail as an icon of clericalism that expressed a divided body of Christ and as an obstacle to "the gathering of the faithful around the table of the Lord". Another justification offered for its removal was to decrease the distance between the congregation and the altar, which admittedly it has done by some twelve feet or so. It is perfectly clear that the altar rail is not a liturgical requirement. But, using the six criteria outlined in *Sacrosanctum concilium*, we would do well to examine the value of the altar rail to determine whether or not it was rightfully discarded.

The use of an architectural barrier to separate the nave from the sanctuary and choir dates at least to the fourth century, with some archeological evidence of earlier chapels in the catacombs arranged with a low railing separating the nave from the apse.[69] In the early basilicas the *cancelli* (also called *septum* or *transenna*) was a balustraded wall to protect the altar from irreverence [figs. 4.16, 4.17].[70] Eusebius, the court historian of Emperor Constantine, writes of the cathedral at Tyre as having a "wooden trellis-work wrought by the craftsmen with exquisite artistry" that protected the altar from undue familiarity.[71] In the Byzantine church this protective barrier developed into the *iconostasis*, an elaborate screen, pierced by three doors, that separates the nave from the sanctuary [fig. 4.18].[72] Originally, the iconostasis was simply a series of columns surmounted by a parapet and coping that separated the nave from the sanctuary. The icons were added (thus giving it the name) to express

[69] Ouspensky, *Theology of the Icon*, 87.
[70] O'Connell, *Church Building*, 12.
[71] Eusebius, *History of the Church*, trans. G. A. Williamson (New York: Dorset Press, 1965), x and 4.
[72] N. Pevsner, J. Fleming, and H. Honour, *A Dictionary of Architecture* (Woodstock, N.Y.: Overlook Press, 1976), s.v. "iconostasis" [= DA].

4.18 Iconostasis, Monastery of the Cross, Jerusalem.

the sanctuary as a symbol of heaven. From the middle of the sixth century, we have an eye-witness description of the iconostasis at Hagia Sophia by Justinian's court poet, Paul the Silentiary:

For as much of the great church by the eastern arch as was set apart for the bloodless sacrifice, no ivory, no stone, no bronze distinguishes, but it is all fenced with the silver metal. Not only upon the walls, which separate the holy priests from the crowd of singers, he has placed mere plates of silver, but he has covered all the columns themselves with the silver metal, even six sets of twain; and the rays of light glitter far and wide. Upon them the tool has formed dazzling circles, beautifully wrought in skilled symmetry by the craftsman's hand, in the centre of which is carved the symbol of the Immaculate God, who took upon Himself the form of man. In parts stand up an army of winged angels in pairs, with bent necks and downcast mien (for they could not gaze upon the glory of the Godhead, though hidden in the form of man to clear man's flesh from sin). And elsewhere the tool has fashioned the heralds of the way of God, even those whose words were noised abroad, before He took flesh upon Him, the divine tidings of the Anointed One. Nor had the craftsman forgotten the forms of the others, whose childhood was with the fishing-baskets and the net; but who left the mean labors of life and unholy cares to bear witness at the bidding of the heavenly king, fishing even for men, and forsaking the skill of casting nets to weave the beauteous seine of eternal life. In other parts [art] has limned the Mother of Christ, the vessel of eternal light, whose womb brought Him forth in holy travail.[73]

With the rise of militant Islam attacking the Christian East in the seventh century, the iconostasis sometimes became more of a defensive barrier, protecting the altar from violation by creating a sort of "strong room". Gradually the iconostasis grew ever more grand, sometimes even to three or four stories high, with rows of icons depicting the saints and angels in strict iconographic order: Christ on the right and the Virgin and Child on the

---

[73] Paulus Silentiarius, "Ode", from W. R. Lethaby and H. Swainson, *The Church of Sancta Sophia, Constantinople: A Study of Byzantine Building* (New York: Macmillan, 1894), 46–47.

4.19 Chancel Screen, Winchester Cathedral, 1079–1093.

4.20 *right* Jube, Chapelle Saint-Fiacre, Le Faquet, Bretagne.

left, with the patron saints of the church and the altar flanking them.

Likewise, in the Christian West, by the twelfth century there was often a similar disposition of the *cancelli*. This effectively created a sort of "church within a church", although in general the altar was more open to the nave than with the iconostasis.[74] In the late Romanesque period, with the widespread use of unleavened bread, the *cancelli* began to evolve into a communion rail. Up to this time, Communion under both species had been received standing up. Now, as the practice of reception from the chalice died out, the Eucharist was regularly distributed in small wafers placed directly on the communicant's tongue, and the ancient devotional practice of kneeling became the common posture at Holy Communion: thus a low communion rail was used to

facilitate reception while retaining the traditional idea of hierarchic separation found in the *cancelli* and the iconostasis.[75]

This notion of hierarchic separation is found throughout the Church and across the ages. From the *cancelli* to the iconostasis to the immense chancel screens [fig. 4.19] and delicate *jubes* of the Middle Ages [fig. 4.20], this

[74] Bouyer, *Liturgy and Architecture*, 79–80.
[75] O'Connell, *Church Building*, 13; also Seasoltz, *The House of God*, 106.

4.21 Altar Rail, San Girolamo della Carita, Rome, by F. Borromini, 1660.

4.22 Detail, San Girolamo della Carita, Rome.

idea has been prevalent and persuasive. It is interesting that Bishop Durand, for instance, taught that the rail "by which the altar is divided from the choir teaches the separation of things celestial from things terrestrial".[76] This idea is expressed in the beautiful altar rail at San Girolamo della Carita in Rome, where two angels support the rail as intermediaries between earth and heaven, unveiling the sanctuary for us to see [figs. 4.21, 4.22]. In light of the bishop's quote, we must necessarily ask what the removal of the rail teaches us.

We have already considered in chapter 3 the reasons for the hierarchic separation of the nave and the sanctuary. We will now consider the liturgical and pastoral implications of the altar rail as a device toward that end. The Second Eucharistic Prayer includes the phrase "as we receive from this altar", for it is true and proper that the people *do* receive from the al-

tar. Fr. J. O'Connell makes this point in writing (in 1955, before the removal of the rail): "Although lay folk normally receive Holy Communion at the Communion rail, they are supposed to be receiving the Body of Christ *from* the altar of sacrifice, and so it is preferable to think of the Communion rail rather as a prolongation of the altar. . . . Hence the ideal is to construct the rail to resemble somewhat the altar (the same material, style, decoration, etc.)."[77] While I do not find his reasoning entirely convincing, the removal of the rail, with no symbolic architectural device to replace it, has probably weakened the individual consciousness of the idea.

There is no doubt that receiving Holy Communion on one's knees at the altar rail provides a greater opportunity for recollection and prayer. Kneeling at reception is still to be preferred, as *Eucharisticum mysterium* states: "When the faithful communicate kneeling, no other sign of reverence towards the Blessed Sacrament is required, since kneeling is itself a sign of adoration."[78] Since the Church suggests that the faithful revere the Eucharist by communicating in this posture, it seems inadvisable to remove the opportunity for doing so. There is also a dimension of community provided by kneeling together to receive Communion. A diversity of people—mayor, housewife, teacher, pupil, worker, socialite, child—kneel side by side in a silent profession of faith as they come to receive the Sacred Host. The communion rail also provides an opportunity, if only for a few moments, to compose one's thoughts before the crucifix and to reflect on the great mystery of the Sacrament. Today, with reception standing and in a line, it is more difficult to focus on the meaning of the Sacrament when communicating. It has also become impossible to pray or meditate (if again only for a few moments) before the crucifix after communicating, since the communicant must immediately make way for the next person.

The inefficiencies of standing reception have also made it seem necessary to resort to

---

[76] Durand, *Rationale*, bk. 1, chap. 1, no. 31.

[77] O'Connell, *Church Building*, 13.

[78] EM, no. 34.b.

the use of many extraordinary ministers of communion. Whereas previously, given a sufficiently long altar rail, two or three priests could quickly communicate a large congregation, now there are sometimes ten or more "lay ministers" for a church of equal size. The problem is not in the use of extraordinary ministers, for they are permitted by canon law,[79] but—and this is the Pope's concern—the elevation of *extraordinary* ministers to the status of ordinary ministers. In fact, this is clarified quite strongly in *Inaestimabile donum*: "The faithful, whether religious or lay, who are authorized as extraordinary ministers of the Eucharist can distribute Communion only when there is no priest, deacon or acolyte, when the priest is impeded by illness or advanced age, or when the number of the faithful going to communion is so large as to make the celebration of Mass excessively long."[80]

Clearly, then, the permission for extraordinary ministers does not mean that priests have a carte blanche in their deployment. In fact, the clear historical pattern, as summarized at Trent, is that "it has always been the custom of the Church of God that the laity receive communion from the priests . . . which custom ought with justice and reason to be retained as coming from Apostolic tradition."[81] Moreover, extraordinary ministers are largely needed only because of the inherent inefficiency of standing reception. So some of the problems resulting from the removal of the rail may have been resolved, but certainly in a less than satisfactory way. It is interesting to note that in this regard Pope John Paul II writes: "It is also necessary that pastors guard against a facile yet abusive recourse to a presumed 'situation of emergency' or to 'supply by necessity', where objectively this does not exist or where alternative possibilities could exist through better pastoral planning."[82] Clearly, the use of the rail could qualify as an area of "better pastoral planning".

The last pastoral issue concerns the innately human recognition of the need for separation between oneself and that which is truly holy. As the centurion said to Jesus, "Lord, I am not worthy to have you come under my roof" (Mt 8:8), so these words are repeated in the communion rite of the Mass. It is a fairly common

human experience to be uncomfortable when made unduly familiar with that which we intuitively sense should be more formally approached. And yet, the hew and cry of modern liturgists is for a "barrier-free" design. Their agenda is to remove all obstacles from us, insisting that we belong right up at the altar, where we can "participate actively". In a glaring way, this shows a lack of sensitivity to the human issues of the heart. It has been suggested that when a sense of "sacred distance" or "sacred separation" is not provided, as with the recently encouraged familiarity of the nave to sanctuary, the congregation may create its own comfort zone.[83] Sometimes the heart needs a quiet corner, out of the harsh glare of the lights, to find solace. Sometimes we need a sense of distance, especially as we become profoundly aware of our own brokenness, our sinfulness, our lack of holiness and wholeness. The architect and priest alike should respect the fully human, emotional response to the *mysterium tremendum et fascinans*. For it is a love-fear response that both calls us to the sacred and yet keeps us from a facile comfort.

Given the significant historical, liturgical, and pastoral considerations of the altar rail, we need to question the received wisdom that had the altar rail expelled from existing churches and banished from new ones. Was its abandonment either a product of or a stimulus for "organic growth"? Was this innovation promoted for "the genuine and certainly required good of the Church"? Were the theological, historical, and pastoral considerations examined prior to its removal?[84] Has the experiment proved successful over the past quarter-century in promoting the true vision of the Second Vatican Council, that the faithful "may more certainly derive an abundance of grace from the sacred liturgy"?[85] These are more

---

[79] CIC, can. 230, sec. 3, and can. 910, sec. 2.

[80] Sacred Congregation for the Sacraments and Divine Worship, *Inaestimabile donum* (April 3, 1980), no. 10 [= ID].

[81] Trent, session 13, chap. 8; quoted in *The Canons and Decrees of the Council of Trent*, trans. Rev H. J. Schroeder (St. Louis: Herder, 1941), 78.

[82] John Paul II, *Christifideles laici* (Dec. 30, 1988), no. 23.

[83] C. Pickstone, "Creating Significant Space", *Church Building*, autumn 1988, 9.

[84] SC, no. 23.

[85] SC, no. 21.

than rhetorical questions. Today more than ever they need to be asked, especially in the light of the time since the Council. It would be good for priests, architects, parish councils, and building committees to confront this issue directly. It will help them to define for themselves what sort of relationship the parish wants between the nave and the sanctuary and how they want the architectural arrangement of the church to support the community's understanding of itself and of its place in the universal Church.

The crucifix

> They shall look on him whom they have pierced (Jn 19:37).

Since the Mass is intrinsically and inseparably connected to the Crucifixion, the main icon of the liturgy, apart from the altar, is the crucifix [fig. 4.23]. As Pius XII explicates:

> The august sacrifice of the altar is therefore no mere simple commemoration of the Passion and Death of Jesus Christ; it is truly and properly the offering of a sacrifice, wherein by an unbloody immolation the High Priest does what he has already done on the Cross, offering Himself to the eternal Father as a most acceptable victim. "One ... and the same is the victim, one and the same is He who now offers by the ministry of His priests and who then offered Himself on the Cross; the difference is only in the manner of offering."[86]

The crucifix, a representation of the Lord's Body upon the Cross, directly symbolizes the whole meaning of the Mass. It calls to mind the various facets of the Lord's act of sacrifice—becoming man and taking the form of a slave (cf. Phil 2:7), taking away the sins of the world (cf. Jn 1:29), his Passion and Death—and further serves to remind the faithful of their obligation to share in Christ's suffering. It also calls to mind the Resurrection, as well as the Parousia, and with it our personal triumph over death (cf. Eph 5:14).[87] Given these understandings, the connection between the Cross and the Mass cannot be overstated.[88]

From the earliest days of Christianity the Cross was seen as central to the Faith: Saint

4.23 Crucifix, San Luis Potosi, Mexico, by Sra. Maria Elena Salazar.

Paul preached "Jesus Christ and him crucified" (1 Cor 2:2). Saint Paul also rather harshly reminded the people of Galatia that they were people "before whose eyes Jesus Christ was publicly portrayed as crucified" (Gal 3:1). In this regard, there is an interesting passage in *The Golden Legend* about an eighth-century Syrian Christian who owned a beautiful and miraculous image of the crucified Christ that had been in his family since apostolic times. As he testified before the bishop: "Nicodemus painted it and at his death bequeathed it to Gamaliel; Gamaliel left it to Zacheus, Zacheus to James, and James to Simon. So it remained in Jerusalem till the fall of the city. Then the faithful took it into Agrippa's kingdom. From there it was brought into my country by my

---

[86] MD, no. 68. Cf. Trent, session 22, chap. 2, in *Canons and Decrees*, 145–46.

[87] Ratzinger, *Feast*, 143.

[88] Bouyer, *Liturgy and Architecture*, 117.

ancestors and came to me by right of inheritance."[89] While some authorities believe the first Christians avoided the symbol of the Cross because of its association with pagan torture and humiliation, there is sufficient literary and archeological evidence to suggest otherwise.[90] The very earliest known crucifix is found on a second-century carnelian from Constanza, Romania, which shows the crucifixion with the Greek letters ΙΚΘΥΣ to indicate Christ.[91] There is also a fourth-century depiction of the Crucifixion on an ivory casket [fig. 4.24], now found in the British Museum.[92]

More often, though, the cross was implied. One explanation of the "Sator Square" found in Pompeii—an acrostic of the Latin words ROTAS, OPERA, TENET, AREPO, and SATOR,[93] which can be read from top, bottom, left, or right—is of an anagram that can be reworked to form a cross reading in both directions A–PATERNOSTER–Ω: "Our Father" bracketed by the Greek letters Alpha and Omega.

The cross was also commonly implied on funerary containers found in Christian cemeteries through such devices as the anchor, the tree, the plow, and the ladder. These and other implied cross-symbols are found decorating ossuaries in the first-century cemetery of Dominus Flevit on the Mount of Olives in Jerusalem, as well as in the paintings in the Roman catacombs.[94]

Though sometimes concealed in iconography, the cross was understood by the early Church as a natural symbol of hope and victory. For instance, Justin Martyr saw the mast of the ship as a cross, writing, "The sea cannot be traversed unless this sign of victory, the sail outspread, is firm set in the midst of the ship." He also saw the plow as a type of cross, since

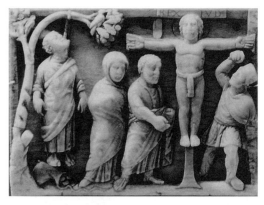

4.24 Crucifixion Scene, Ivory Casket, 4th cent., British Museum.

"without the cross, the earth is not tilled."[95] Many of the early Fathers elaborated on these two ideas. Maximus of Turin, for instance, remarked, "When sailors plough the sea, first they set up a mast and they stretch the sail, so that after the cross of the Lord has been made, they may break through flowing waters . . . [and] seek the harbor of salvation and escape the danger of death."[96]

Other authorities point to the very early custom of placing a cross on the east wall of Christian meeting rooms, first as a sign of the Parousia and later as a reminder of the Passion.[97] The crucifix was likewise implied by the *Orans*, or "Pray-er", a painted figure shown standing with arms outstretched horizontally

[89] Jacobus de Voragine, *The Golden Legend*, trans. William Granger Ryan, vol. 2 (Princeton, N.J.: Princeton University Press, 1993), 171.

[90] O'Connell, *Church Building*, 101.

[91] Ouspensky, *Theology of the Icon*, 110.

[92] G. Frere-Cook, *Decorative Arts of the Christian Church* (London: Cassell, 1972), 11 and 21.

[93] This roughly translates to "The sower, with his eye on the plough, holds its wheels with care." This can be seen as an allusion to the parable of the sower as well as to Jesus' warning that "He who puts his hand to the plough and looks back is not fit for the Kingdom of God." AREPO might also be the acronym Alpha-Rex-et-Pater-Omega, thus alluding to God. This would then render it "The God who sows the seed [of the Gospel] holds the spheres [of the universe] with care." Cf. Michael Green, *Evangelism in the Early Church* (London: Hodder and Stoughton, 1970), 339–400.

[94] Milburn, *Early Christian Art and Architecture*, 1–5 and 30.

[95] Quoted in ibid., 3 and 5.

[96] *Serm.* 38: 11–17; quoted in M. C. Conroy, *Imagery in the Sermones of Maximus, Bishop of Turin* (Washington, D.C.: Catholic University of America Press, 1965), 46, 164, and 194.

[97] Ratzinger, *Feast*, 141, citing E. Peterson.

4.25 *Orans*, Domitilla Catacombs, Rome.

[fig. 4.25]. The *Orans* has a particularly poignant message, as it is usually a woman, hence the Bride of Christ, the Church. Through this symbol of a person imitating the posture of the Crucified, faithful believers were called to offer their lives in imitation of their Lord: to share in his suffering so as to share in his glory. The *Orans* is, therefore, a type of Eucharist figure that speaks of the Church as both corporately and individually participating in the sacrificial thanksgiving by which God is glorified [fig. 4.26].

After the victory of Constantine and the finding of the True Cross by Saint Helena (326), the cross came to be seen as a "glorious emblem".[98] It was several hundred years, however, before the crucifix came into common use, and even then in a more decorative role, such as the wood-cut Crucifixion scene in a door panel at the fifth-century church of Santa Sabina in Rome. Still, it was most common even in this age to depict the cross with either a lamb, a chi-rho symbol (X-P), or the head of

4.26 Daniel in *orans* posture, Sarcophagus, San Vitale, Ravenna, 5th cent.

---

[98] O'Connell, *Church Building*, 102.

4.27 Apse Mosaic, San Apollinare in Classe, Ravenna, 534–549.

4.28 Detail, San Apollinare in Classe, Ravenna, 534–549.

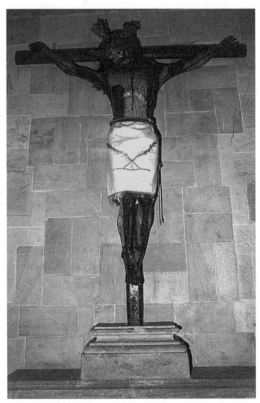

4.29 Crucifix, Templo de San Francisco, Mexico City, 18th cent.

Christ superimposed, such as in the apse mosaic at San Apollinare in Classe, which shows a large jeweled cross with the head of the Lord in a central medallion [figs. 4.27, 4.28]. From the sixth to the thirteenth centuries, Christ was generally shown nailed to the cross, but usually as a triumphant Redeemer and sometimes garbed as a priest.[99] The first realistic crucifixes date from the eleventh century and gradually became increasingly popular and increasingly realistic. From the thirteenth century Christ is usually shown in death—eyes

[99] Thanks to John Saward for pointing out that even in the early "triumphant crucifixes" our Lord is shown *nailed* to the cross; unlike most modern "Resurrection crosses", which show the Lord's body detached from the cross, thus not fully expressing the reality of the Crucifixion. One really ought to look to see if the artist depicts the wounds of the Lord's crucifixion on the corpus.

closed, head dropped, beaten and bloody, crowned with thorns, and wearing only a loin cloth [fig. 4.29]. Today there has been an unfortunate proliferation of Resurrection crosses—images that often fail to show even the marks of the Passion; and modern Western crucifixes depicting the Lord either in death or in anguish tend to be less realistic and more stylized.

The liturgical use of the crucifix is to set the Mass within the context of the Lord's sacrifice, perfected as at Calvary. Hence, as a reference point, it should be positively related to the altar, either on it or near it.[100] Traditionally, as we have seen, the cross was on the east wall, with the priest and people facing it for the eucharistic prayer. Thus the crucifix was the common focus of the Mass. Nowadays, with the priest *versus populum*, this symbolism is largely lost. In some churches, particularly in Great Britain, a second crucifix is placed on the back wall of the nave so the priest may offer Mass toward this icon. Today, with the priest facing the people, the crucifix would best be placed *between* the priest and people, perhaps in what Cardinal Ratzinger sees as a sort of "open iconostasis": "Even now, when the priest faces the people, the cross could be placed on the altar in such a way that both priest and people can see it. At the eucharistic prayer they should not look at one another; together they ought to behold him, the Pierced Savior (Zech 12:10, Rev 1:7)."[101]

The cross thus placed on the altar "is not obstructing the view; it is a common point of reference . . . which, far from hindering unity, actually facilitates it: it is the image which draws and unites the attention of everyone." To give this common focus to the whole congregation is "actually a necessary precondition for celebrating toward the people". This arrangement might also be used to sharpen the distinction between the Liturgy of the Word and the Liturgy of the Eucharist, because the former would be proclaimed to the congregation and the latter addressed to the image of the Lord.[102]

The size of the crucifix will depend on the size of the church and proximity of the seating to the altar. The Church's directives call for it

4.30 Detail, Crucifix by Sra. Maria Elena Salazar.

to be large enough to be "clearly visible to the congregation".[103] This bears directly upon the question of the processional cross. While allowed by the instructions,[104] the processional cross is necessarily rather small and thus might not be easily and clearly seen in even moderate-size churches. And since the crucifix also serves as a contemplative device, one should be able to appreciate some level of

---

[100] GIRM, no. 270.
[101] Ratzinger, *Feast*, 144.
[102] Ibid., 145.
[103] GIRM, no. 270.
[104] GIRM, no. 79.

detail. A large, if not life-size, crucifix speaks well to the various concerns.

The detail is important as well. The use of "a Resurrection cross" should not be a denial of the Passion. This is cautioned against by Pope Pius XII: "Thus . . . one would be straying from the straight path were he . . . to order the crucifix so designed that the Divine Redeemer's Body showed no trace of His cruel suffering."[105] But neither should the crucifix be grossly realistic, "as it tends to obscure the divinity of Christ and the victory of the cross. . . . The ideal crucifix expresses the resignation, nobility and serenity of the Crucified, inviting sorrow, confidence and love" [fig. 4.30].[106] "In other words, the humility of God the Word must be represented in such a way that, when looking at the image, we contemplate also His divine glory, the human image of God the Word, and that, in this way, we come to understand the saving nature of His death and the resulting deliverance of the world."[107] Again, the Church commissions her artists to strike a careful balance while working "for the edification of the faithful to foster piety and religious formation".[108]

The chair

The fourth item of furnishing in the sanctuary is the celebrant's chair, which here is considered along with the supplementary seating for altar servers and lectors. The use of a special chair for the celebrant dates to the early Church, when the celebrant was the local bishop. The chair (Gk. *cathedra*, "a seat") is the oldest symbol of the episcopal office, predating the miter and crosier by centuries [fig. 4.31].[109] Reference is made to the apostles setting up episcopal chairs in the dioceses they founded. Both Antioch and Rome still commemorate the Feast of the Chair of Peter, as he was the founding bishop of each diocese. The symbol of the chair was taken from the *cathedra* of the Hellenic schools of philosophy and thus is primarily a symbol of the episcopal teaching office. Hence the bishop would teach from the *cathedra*, which was often elevated on a small platform, such as is found at Dura-Europus.[110] That said, there are also obvious

4.31 Cathedra, Ravenna, mid-6th cent.

references to the judge's seat found in the Roman basilica and even to the king's throne, which speak to the fact that the bishop rules in the diocese.[111]

Throughout the ages the *cathedra* has been reserved for the bishop alone. Its earliest form was the faldstool (*faldistorium*), a simple, folding, backless armchair used by the ancient Romans. Early episcopal seats were generally made of stone or wood, though sometimes they were even carved out of the

---

[105] MD, no. 66.

[106] O'Connell, *Church Building*, 102.

[107] Ouspensky, *Theology of the Icon*, 119.

[108] SC, no. 127.

[109] The word *cathedral*, which is used to designate the bishop's main church, is from *cathedra*, meaning "where the episcopal seat is". Cf. NDLW, s.v. "cathedra".

[110] Milburn, *Early Christian Art and Architecture*, 10.

[111] Rykwert, *Church Building*, 13 and 19; Bouyer, *Liturgy and Architecture*, 43.

rock in the catacombs. After the emancipation under Constantine, when the Church took on a more juridical role, the bishop's chair became increasingly elaborate, bejeweled, and thronelike. By the time of Saint Augustine (fifth century), the *cathedra* was often elevated on a dais and covered by a canopy or draped.[112]

In the Christian West the *cathedra* was normally in the center of the east apse, behind the altar, where the bishop would be surrounded by his priests and deacons. It was from this seat that he would preach the homily. In the East, notably Syria, the *cathedra* was in the chancel, in the middle of the nave, so the bishop sat facing east with his back to the congregation. At the offertory he would then go to the altar, which was in the east apse, to celebrate the sacrifice. Fr. Bouyer points out that this was also the arrangement in Rome for the pope's seat at Santa Maria Maggiore up to the time of Pope Pascal I (817–824). Citing the *Liber pontificalis*, Bouyer tells us that Pascal moved the chair to the apse behind the altar to distance himself from the chattering women in the rear of the church![113]

The *cathedra* is important symbolically because the bishop is a direct successor of the apostles, having "the fullness of the Sacrament of Orders" and being "the steward of the grace of the supreme priesthood".[114] This means that the bishop is most perfectly Christ's representative to the local Church, and the authority of his priests is derived from and granted by the bishop. The norm for the early liturgies had the bishop surrounded by his priests and deacons, and the early Church understood the relationship of the bishops to his priests as reflecting Christ and his apostles. This is why Saint Ignatius, who was probably the third bishop of Antioch, could commend the Trallians for obeying their bishop "as though he were Jesus Christ", and why he wrote to the Church at Smyrna: "Follow your bishop, every one of you, as obediently as Jesus Christ followed the Father. Obey your clergy too, as you would the Apostles."[115]

This idea is reaffirmed by Vatican II, which teaches that "the bishops have by divine institution taken the place of the apostles as pastors

4.32 Sedilia, St. Mary-on-Tyne, Prague, 14th cent.

of the Church, in such wise that whoever listens to them is listening to Christ and whoever despises them despises Christ and him who sent Christ."[116] Because the local bishop is the successor of the apostles and bears the fullness of the sacrament of holy orders, the Mass "celebrated by the bishop has a quite special significance as an expression of the Church gathered around the altar, with the one who represents Christ, the Good Shepherd and Head of his

---

[112] O'Connell, *Church Building*, 90 and 249.

[113] Bouyer, *Liturgy and Architecture*, 52.

[114] Vatican II, *Lumen Gentium* (Nov. 21, 1964), nos. 24 and 26 [= LG].

[115] St. Ignatius of Antioch: *Tral.* 2; *Smyr.* 8; Staniforth, *Early Christian Writings*, 95, 121.

[116] LG, no. 20, citing Lk 10:16.

Church, presiding."[117] So the bishop's chair is seen as a symbol of the governance of Christ, and it deserves particular attention as a piece of furniture. Since it is still seen as a "place of proclamation" from which the bishop instructs the faithful, the *cathedra* should be placed so that it is easily seen from the nave. While most bishops today do not preach from their chairs, the *cathedra* is a rich, powerful, and ancient symbol that can be easily revived.

Before the Second Vatican Council, only the bishop would have a special type of seat, and the lower clergy would sit on a movable bench called a *sedilla* or *sedile*.[118] Often a medieval church had a three-seated niche on the south wall of the chancel. This niche, called a *sedille* (plural: *sedelia*), provided seats for the priest, the deacon, and the subdeacon [fig. 4.32].[119] Recently, the importance of the celebrant's chair has been emphasized, perhaps to clarify the distinction between the ministerial priesthood and the lay priesthood expressed in the idea of the people of God. The priest's chair is derived from the *cathedra* and likewise is given a place of importance so that "the celebrant when seated should appear as truly presiding over the whole gathering."[120] Thus, the instructions recommend that the chair be in the apex or center of the sanctuary, behind the altar and facing the people, though this is not a strict requirement. In cases when older churches are reordered, the chair may be placed opposite the ambo if it cannot be behind the altar.[121] On each side of the celebrant's chair are usually found smaller, armless chairs for altar servers. Other seating may be required for lectors and cantors and the like, in places convenient to their functions.[122]

It is clear from the *General Instruction* that it is most important that the position of the celebrant's chair draw attention to the priest's office as presiding over the assembly and leading the Church in prayer.[123] It is recommended that the celebrant's chair avoid the appearance of a throne, since such reverence is due only to the bishop of the diocese. Rather, the priest's chair should speak to the fact that he *serves*, not *rules*, the assembly.[124] To state this architecturally, however, one would not normally consider placing the chair centered in the apex of

the sanctuary, which is the place of primary importance. This position is traditionally very much a place of glory, as in the basilican apse. While this is appropriate for a *cathedra*, in the normal parish it would seem to diminish the importance of the altar (to say nothing of the tabernacle, which has traditionally occupied this place). There is still much work to be done in considering the seating for the ordained ministers, and, while the present guidelines are to be respected and followed, the issue deserves further consideration by the appropriate authorities so that the symbolic statement can more accurately reflect the intended message.

The ambo

> And Christ is still proclaiming his Gospel (*Sacrosanctum concilium*, no. 33).

In *Dominicae cenae*, Pope John Paul II writes of "the two tables of the Lord" at which God feeds the Church. Having looked at the requirements for the altar, the table of the Lord's sacrifice, we now turn our attention to the table of the Word of God, the ambo. In his encyclical the Holy Father gratefully notes that, in response to the directives of the Second Vatican Council, there is an increasingly active participation in the Liturgy of the Word. By way of readers, cantors, and choirs, "the word of God, the Sacred Scripture, is beginning to take on new life in many Christian communities." The Pope notes that this activity requires "a new sense of responsibility towards the word of God". The proclamation of the Word at the liturgy is to be done with "capacity, simplicity and dignity [so] as to highlight the special character of the sacred text".[125] Under-

---

[117] *Catechism of the Catholic Church* (San Francisco: Ignatius Press, 1994), no. 1561.
[118] O'Connell, *Church Building*, 66.
[119] DA, s.v. "sedilia".
[120] IO, no. 92; GIRM, no. 271.
[121] PC, no. 174.
[122] Ibid.
[123] GIRM, no. 271.
[124] Johnson, *Planning for Liturgy*, 23.
[125] DC, no. 10.

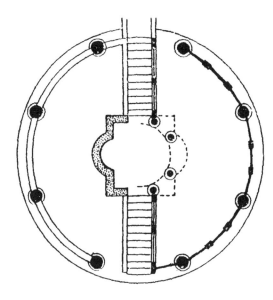

4.33 Ambo, Hagia Sophia, Plan (after Lethaby).

standing this "special character" will help us to understand better what sort of accommodation we should make for "the table of the Word of God" in the church.

The Liturgy of the Word, which culminates in the proclamation of the Gospel, is an integral and necessary part of the whole Mass. The two Liturgies, that of the Word and that of the Eucharist, "are so closely connected with each other that they form but one single act of worship".[126] In the Liturgy of the Word we find a distinct manifestation of Christ's presence, "for it is he who speaks when the Scriptures are read in the Church".[127] Indeed, the Gospel and homily are reserved only for ordained priests and deacons because "Christ, present in his own word, is proclaiming the Gospel."[128] As the *General Instruction* recalls: "The liturgy itself inculcates the great reverence to be shown toward the reading of the gospel, setting it off from the other readings by special marks of honor. A special minister is appointed to proclaim it and prepares himself by a blessing or prayer. The people, who by their acclamations acknowledge and confess Christ present and speaking to them, stand as they listen to it."[129]

In the early Church the Gospel was usually read by an ordained priest. The bishop would give the homily, teaching from either his *cathe-*

dra or a faldstool placed at the footpace of the altar. As churches became larger, especially after the Edict of Milan, a raised speaking platform, or *ambo*, was used for addressing the congregation. "Ambo" in fact seems to be derived from the Greek word *anabainein*, meaning "to mount to a high place".[130] The Christian use of the idea may have been inspired by the references to such a form in the Old Testament[131] and was certainly taken from the contemporaneous Jewish synagogue. Typically ornamented and built of wood or stone, through the years the ambo became larger, more prominent, and more ornate. Milburn cites the fourth-century Syrian church at Qirk Bizza as having a large horseshoe-shaped ambo, big enough for a bench for the deacons and a small throne for the bishop.[132] Not surprisingly, one of the most elaborate ambos was found at Hagia Sophia. Paul the Silentiary, a sixth-century court official, went into lavish detail in describing the ambo. Here I quote parts to indicate its configuration [fig. 4.33]:

Now in the central space of the wide temple, yet tending towards the east, rises a tower (*purgos*), fair to look upon, set apart for the reading of the sacred books. Upright it stands on steps, reached by two flights, one of which stretches towards the west, but the other towards the dawn. . . .

And up to the height of a man's girdle our godlike king has formed, with the help of silver, beauteous walls curving like crescents. He has not bent silver right around the stone, but a silver plaque (*plax*) is spread out in the centre, to adorn the circling walls. Thus has the skilful workman spread out two sure crescents and opened on either side a flight of steps.

Nor does fear seize those descending the sacred steps, because the sides are unfenced; for hedge walls of glittering marble have been reared there; and they are high above the steps for the hand of a man to hold as he mounts, grasping them to ease his way; so on each side

---

126 SC, no. 56.
127 EM, no. 9.
128 GIRM, no. 9.
129 GIRM, no. 35.
130 Seasoltz, *House of God*, 190.
131 Cf. Neh 8:3 and the apocryphal 3 Esdras 9:42.
132 Milburn, *Early Christian Art and Architecture*, 125.

4.34 Ambo, San Marco, Venice.

4.35 Ambo, Pisa Cathedral, by G. Pisano, 1302–1310.

they grow upwards in a rising line, and stop at length with the steps which are between them. . . .

Now near a rocky hill stands the sacred city—Hierapolis—which gives its name to a well-known marble; and of this is made all the fair floor of the place where they read the holy books; and it is fitted by the craftsmen's skill on eight cunningly wrought columns. Two of these are towards the north, two towards the southern wind, two towards the east, and two towards the home of the evening. Thus is the floor raised up. And beneath there is as it were another space, where the priests continue their sacred song. And the underside the mason (*laotomos*) has cut out and hollowed, so that, by the craftsmen's skill, it rises from the capitals, curving over like the hollow shell-back of a tortoise, or some oxhide shield held up over the helmet, when the warrior leaps in the mazes of the Pyrrhic dance. . . .

But with all its steps and floor and the columns as well, the artificers have formed for it a fixed foundation, and raised a base (*krepsis*), the height of a man's foot, above the floor of the church; and in order that they might widen the foundation of the space they have placed on either side, round the belly (*gaster*) in the middle, half circles in stone, and have surrounded the space with separate columns arranged in semicircles. Thus the whole belly is widened by means of four rich columns on either side, to north and to south; and the cave space (*speos*), like a house, is surrounded on all sides by a fence of circling stones. . . .

In this manner is the shining ambo made; thus have they called it "the place ascended" (*ambatos*), by holy paths, and here the people direct their eyes, as they gaze on the divine gospel.[133]

Though this ambo was probably destroyed in the October 975 earthquake, a vestige of such a grand ambo can be found in the Cathedral of San Marco, in Venice [fig. 4.34]. Although some churches would have a single ambo—these were often quite ornate, as seen in the famous ambos by Nicola and Giovanni Pisano in Pisa [fig. 4.35]—more commonly two ambos were to be found. Typically the Gospel

[133] This is excerpted from an ode written by Paulus Silentiarius for the opening ceremonies at the rededication of Hagia Sophia on December 24, 563. It is published in Lethaby and Swainson, *Church of Sancta Sophia, Constantinople*, 54ff.

4.36 Gospel Ambo, San Clemente, Rome.

ambo, the larger and more ornate, was found on the north side, and the smaller and simpler epistle ambo on the south side [fig. 4.36]. This symbolic arrangement was to express that the Gospel was to be preached to the pagan Vikings and Goths who lived to the north. The Gospel ambo would usually be large enough to accommodate not only the reader but also two candle bearers (*taperers*), one at each side.[134] Sometimes the epistle ambo was divided into an upper platform for the chanting of the epistle and a lower dais for the lector of the

---

[134] NDLW, s.v. "ambo".

4.37 Epistle Ambo, San Clemente, Rome.

Old Testament readings, an arrangement that may still be seen at San Clemente in Rome [fig. 4.37]. The ambo was widely used in the eighth through tenth centuries, when it was used for the chanting of the scriptural readings, but fell into disuse by the thirteenth century.[135]

As the culture changed and the emphasis shifted from the Byzantine and medieval chanting to the preaching of the Word, so did the pulpit gradually replace the ambo. First found in the twelfth century, the pulpit was originally a simple platform surrounded by a parapet and corbeled out from a pier of the chancel arch. Like the ambo a thousand years before, the pulpit gradually grew larger, higher, more prominent, and more ornate. By the fifteenth and sixteenth centuries, especially in the Counter

Reformation churches when the Word was strongly emphasized, the pulpit was often quite grand and elaborate and surmounted by a canopy or sounding board [fig. 4.38].

Today the pulpit has fallen into disuse. With modern electronics and acoustic systems, it is hardly necessary in all but the largest churches. The use of the ambo, however, has had a growing resurgence since Vatican II. *Sacrosanctum concilium* sought to promote "that sweet and living love for the sacred Scripture", seeing the place of Scripture as having "the greatest importance in the celebration of the liturgy".[136] Following on this, *Dei Verbum* restated and re-

---

[135] O'Connell, *Church Building*, 77–78.
[136] SC, no. 24.

emphasized the place of the Scriptures in the life of the Church, "particularly in the sacred liturgy".[137] And as the *General Instruction* states, "The dignity of the word of God requires the church to have a place that is suitable for proclamation of the word and is a natural focal point for the people during the liturgy of the word." So it calls for the ambo to be fixed, not a simple movable stand, and "so placed that the ministers may be easily seen and heard by the faithful".[138]

Like the altar, the ambo should ordinarily be fixed and elevated, because it represents Christ's presence in the Word "which stands forever"[139]—it would be unseemly to have a temporary or movable ambo.[140] It should be sufficiently large to accommodate the minister and taperers and should be equipped with a reading light and sound amplification equipment if necessary.[141] There should be a strong architectonic relationship between the altar and the ambo, as the "liturgy of the Word and the celebration of the Lord's Supper . . . constitute a single act of worship."[142] The Church, therefore, demands that "careful attention should be given to the structural harmony and spatial relationship between the ambo and altar" to express the oneness of Christ presenting himself to the Church under different aspects. This does not mean, however, that the ambo should vie for attention with the altar. The altar is central to the Eucharist and thus demands centrality and prominence. The ambo should be positively related to the altar but remain subordinate. Such an arrangement is necessary to respect the Church's teaching that Christ is present "above all under the species of the Eucharist".[143]

The emphasis on lay participation has commonly brought about the use of lay readers for the Old Testament reading, the responsorial psalm, the epistle, and the prayers of the faithful. This raises the question of whether there should be one ambo or two, having separate places for the lesser readings and for the proclamation of the Gospel. The *General Instruction* does permit all the Scripture readings, the responsorial psalm, the homily, the prayers of the faithful, and the paschal *Exsultet* to be read from the ambo.[144] But, while it is clear

4.38 Pulpit, Templo de Santa Veracruz, Mexico City, *c.* 1730.

that the Scriptures are all one, and all inspired by the Holy Spirit (which could suggest having one place of proclamation), the notion of a hierarchy of readings is also an ancient and important consideration. Today it is still emphasized that, "when the Scriptures are read in the Church, God himself is speaking to his people, and Christ, present in his own word, is proclaiming the Gospel."[145] Because of this,

[137] Vatican II, *Dei Verbum* (Nov. 18, 1965), no. 21 [= DV].
[138] GIRM, no. 272.
[139] DV, no. 26; citing Is 40:8 and 1 Pet 1:23–25.
[140] Sacred Congregation for the Sacraments and Divine Worship, *De verbi Dei*, or *General Introduction to the Lectionary for Mass* (Jan. 21, 1981), no. 32 [= GILM].
[141] GILM, no. 34.
[142] EM, no. 10; following on SC, no. 56.
[143] EM, no. 9; following on SC, no. 7.
[144] GIRM, no. 272.
[145] GIRM, no. 9.

the Gospel is to be proclaimed in the liturgy only by those ordained to do so (viz., bishops, priests, and deacons), whereas the other reading can be read or sung by those who hold the office of "reader", as well as by unordained religious or laymen. This distinction between the Gospel and the other readings is further emphasized by the people standing for the proclamation of the Gospel, and in the reminder that "the liturgy itself inculcates the great reverence to be shown toward the reading of the gospel, setting it off from the other readings by special marks of honor." [146] This distinction could be clearly expressed by having a special place of proclamation for the Gospel apart from the other readings, with the lectern serving for the other readings and the nonliturgical announcements, or even a third place, perhaps a movable stand, for the announcements.

The lectern

Since the Liturgy of the Word demands a separate and special place of proclamation, it is proper to have a separate lectern for nonliturgical announcements and instruction. It is a question of strict propriety whether there should be three separate places for addressing the congregation: an ambo for the Gospel and homily; another ambo for the lesser readings, the responsorial psalm, and the prayers of the faithful; and a lectern for everything else. There is no question, however, that there should be both an ambo and a lectern, since it is inappropriate for the commentator, cantor, or choirmaster to use the ambo.[147] The lectern should be harmonious with the other pieces of liturgical furnishing, though obviously smaller, simpler, and less prominent.

A place of reservation: The tabernacle

Ecce tabernaculum Dei cum hominibus
(Rev 21:3)

In order to meet the needs of the liturgical reform implemented by the Second Vatican Council, many existing churches have been reordered, and further guidelines have been

drawn for new buildings. With this reordering, perhaps the most perplexing issues facing the parish and architect alike are the questions of reservation and placement of the tabernacle. Liturgists and episcopal conferences have offered different explanations as to why the tabernacle should be in one place or another, what the relationship of the tabernacle to the altar is, how the supposedly "active and static aspects" of the Eucharist should affect placement, and so on.[148] And while in several documents the Holy See has made statements concerning the placement of the tabernacle, not much has been stated definitively. The impression one gets in reading the directives is an attitude of some uncertainty within certain clear guidelines and strong suggestions, giving due consideration to local custom and the church's internal arrangement.[149]

The laws regarding the tabernacle itself are simple and straightforward. There is to be one and only one tabernacle in a church or oratory for permanent and regular reservation, and this tabernacle is to be constructed so it is solid, opaque, unbreakable, fireproof, and inviolable.[150] In keeping with the ancient custom of showing highest respect, a veil (conopaeum) should completely cover the tabernacle, recalling the veil that covered the Ark of the Covenant.[151] "A lamp must burn perpetually before it, as a sign of the honor paid to the Lord",[152] and this lamp announces Christ's presence [fig. 4.39]. The laws regarding the placement of the tabernacle, however, are less clear and are open to wide interpretation.

The reservation of the Eucharist in the tabernacle of every church or oratory is mandated. The Blessed Sacrament is to be "kept in churches and oratories as the spiritual center of the religious community and the parish community, indeed as the spiritual center of the universal Church and the whole of human-

---

[146] GIRM, no. 35.
[147] GIRM, no. 272, also GILM, no. 33.
[148] EACW, 40.
[149] GIRM, no. 276.
[150] EM, no. 52; GIRM, no. 277; ID, no. 25; Johnson, *Planning for Liturgy*, 35.
[151] O'Connell, *Church Building*, 172; Ex 40; also ID, no. 25. This is not necessary if the tabernacle has artistic merit.
[152] ID, no. 25. This seems to clarify EM, no. 57, by replacing "should" with "must".

4.39 Tabernacle, Orvieto Cathedral.

and teaches that at the Consecration the elements of bread and wine are changed into the Body and Blood of Christ. The Church teaches this in order to be faithful to Christ's words, "This is my body." In the early second century, Saint Ignatius of Antioch reproved those who "will not admit that the Eucharist is the self-same body of our Savior Jesus Christ which suffered for our sins, and which the Father in His goodness afterwards raised up again".[156] Following this apostolic-era teaching, *Eucharisticum mysterium* teaches: "For in this sacrament Christ is present in a unique way, whole and entire, God and man, substantially and permanently. This presence of Christ under the species is called 'real' not in an exclusive sense, as if the other kinds of presence were not real, but *par excellence*."[157] So the consequent place of the Eucharist is at the very center of the spiritual life of the Church, the parish, and the individual. The question for us is "What is the consequent place of the tabernacle within the church?"

The tabernacle: Its history

Historically, the Eucharist was reserved for a variety of reasons, though not at first in churches. In the earliest days of the Church, the bishop would be the first to celebrate the Sunday Eucharist. Then, throughout the day, his deacons would carry the Eucharist to each of the priests in the diocese to add to the chalice at the Fraction (when the priest breaks the Host at the *Agnus Dei*). This practice, in Rome called *fermentum*, was an expression of the unity found in Holy Communion between the bishop and his entire flock. The Eucharist was also kept to communicate the infirm or dying and for clandestine distribution during the height of the persecutions. The Eucharist was occasionally kept in private houses when communal celebrations were not possible. Saint Basil of Caesarea cites the practices of the fourth-century Church when the desert hermits

ity".[153] So while "the primary and original purpose of reserving the sacred species in church outside Mass is the administration of Viaticum", the reserved Eucharist is also understood as being integral to the spiritual life of both the individual and the parish community, "especially since belief in the real presence of the Lord has as its natural consequence the external and public manifestation of that belief." [154] In fact, "public and private devotion to the Holy Eucharist outside Mass also is highly recommended: for the presence of Christ, who is adored by the faithful in the Sacrament, derives from the Sacrifice and is directed towards sacramental and spiritual communion." [155]

In order to appreciate what precisely are the natural consequences of the belief in the Real Presence, it is necessary to understand first what the belief is. By participating in the sacrifice Christ commanded, the Church believes

[153] Paul VI, *Mysterium fidei* (Sept. 3, 1965), no. 68 [= MF].
[154] EM, no. 49.
[155] ID, no. 20.
[156] *Smyr.* 7, in Staniforth, *Early Christian Writings*, 121.
[157] EM, no. 9.

reserved the Eucharist to communicate when there were no priests available and the general practices in Alexandria, where "each member of the laity [would] keep the Communion at his own house."[158] We know that by this time the Eucharist was reserved in churches, sometimes on altars, where it was an object for adoration and personal devotion. Saint Gregory of Nazianzus tells the story of his sister, Gorgonia, who when seriously ill "went before the altar" and reverenced the Eucharist for her healing.[159] From this time until the sixteenth century, there were as many different forms of reservation as there were cultures and eras.

Commonly at first, and widely until the twelfth century, the Eucharist was kept in a cupboard in the *sacrarium*, a room adjoining the sanctuary of the church. In the Christian East the room in which the Sacred Species is kept is called the *prothesis*.[160] The *aumbry* (or ambry), a cupboard built into the wall of the sanctuary near the altar, became common during the early Middle Ages in Germany, Spain, and parts of Italy. After the tenth century, perhaps slightly earlier, the Eucharist was often suspended over the altar from the civory. The container took a variety of forms and names. This was sometimes called a *dove*, being in the form of a dove over the altar to recall the Holy Spirit descending upon Jesus at his baptism, or a *pyx* or a *casket*. The pyx was common in England until the Reformation and in France until the Revolution. The late-medieval bishop Guillaume Durand uses the terms *pyx* and *portfolio* as two methods of reservation. For him, the various materials used in the container's construction (gold, silver, ivory, wood, or crystal) speak to different attributes of the Body of Christ. He also mentions that unconsecrated hosts, as well as relics, could be contained in the pyx.[161] From the fourteenth century, in Germany and the Low Countries, the *sacrament house* or *sacrament tower*, which was a large and elaborate, freestanding structure, was built in the church [fig. 4.40]. In some towers, the Sacrament was visible for adoration within a transparent container [fig. 4.41]. Sometimes the Blessed Sacrament was temporarily reserved *on* the altar, in either a movable tabernacle or a pyx, though there is no evidence of permanent reservation *on* the altar before the ninth century. This practice became more prominent in the Renaissance.[162]

Toward the end of the twelfth century the tabernacle began to be used and slowly gained prominence until it was universally legislated in the nineteenth century. The word *tabernacle*, which is from *tabernaculum*, the Latin word for "tent", was used to recall the tentlike structure in which the Ark of the Covenant was kept [see figs. 3.1 and 3.2]. In the Middle Ages "tabernacle" referred to a variety of things: an altar covered by a civory; a monstrance, reliquary, or sacrament tower; the veil over a casket containing the Eucharist or covering the pyx; canopied niches for statues of saints; a type of medieval altarpiece; and, finally, the safe in which the Blessed Sacrament was kept.[163] Bishop Durand writes about the tabernacle as a particularly appropriate symbol of the Church Militant:

> "God", said the Prophet, "is in his tabernacle":[164] God is in this world, as in a temple dyed scarlet by the Blood of Christ. The tabernacle is, however, more especially symbolical of the Church Militant, which has "here no continuing city, but seeks one to come."[165] Therefore, it is called a tabernacle, for tabernacles or tents belong to soldiers: and this saying, "God is in his tabernacle", means God is among the faithful collected together in his Name. . . . The tabernacle gives place to the temple: because after warfare comes the triumph.[166]

In 1198 Archbishop Eudes de Sully of Paris first ordered all reservation within his diocese to be in a locked tabernacle on the altar. His

---

[158] St. Basil of Caesarea, *Epistolae*, 93; quoted in Henry Bettenson, *The Later Christian Fathers* (London: Oxford University Press, 1970), 89. For other early references to reservation, see Tertullian, *Ad Uxorem*, ii, 5, and *De Oratione*, 19, in Henry Bettenson, *The Early Christian Fathers* (London: Oxford University Press, 1956), 148–49.

[159] St. Gregory Nazianzus, *Orationes*, 8; quoted in Bettenson, *Later Christian Fathers*, 123.

[160] Richard Krautheimer, *Early Christian and Byzantine Architecture* (Harmondsworth, England: Penguin, 1979), 244.

[161] Durand, *Rationale*, bk. 1, chap. 3, 25.

[162] O'Connell, *Church Building*, 165–66.

[163] NDLW, s.v. "tabernacle"; also O'Connell, *Church Building*, 167.

[164] Ps 11:4.

[165] Heb 13:14.

[166] Durand, *Rationale*, bk. 1, chap. 1, no. 6.

4.41 Detail, Sacrament Tower.

4.40 Sacrament Tower, Cathedral of the Madeleine, Salt Lake City.

order, however, was widely resisted in favor of the hanging pyx. Shortly thereafter, the Fourth Lateran Council (1215), Pope Innocent III (1198-1216), and his successor, Honorius III (1216-1227), ordered that the Blessed Sacrament be kept under lock and key in all churches.[167] The Council of Trent retained this "salutary and necessary" custom of reserving the Eucharist in a sacred place, even charging *anathema* "if anyone says that it is not lawful that the Holy Eucharist be reserved in a sacred place".[168] Several years later, the *Rituale Romanum* of 1614 ordered the use of the taber-

nacle, and in 1863 the Sacred Congregation of Rites formally ended the use of all other methods of reservation [fig. 4.42].[169]

At least since the time of Archbishop de Sully it has been considered proper to place the tabernacle on the altar, although universal use of the tabernacle was not until much later. After the Reformation, the Bishop of Milan,

[167] Johnson, *Planning for Liturgy*, 30; also O'Connell, *Church Building*, 167.

[168] Trent, session 13, chap. 6 and canon 7. Cf. *Canons and Decrees*, 77 and 80.

[169] O'Connell, *Church Building*, 167-68.

4.42 Tabernacle, Chapel of Sixtus V, Santa Maria Maggiore, Rome.

regular part of the reredos, though without any sort of standard. "Sometimes it was an elaborate structure—in keeping with the altar itself over-sized and over-ornate; at other times it was a mere cubbyhole lost in the great structure in which it was embedded." [170] As the practice of eucharistic adoration and benediction became more widespread during the seventeenth through nineteenth centuries, the altar came to be seen as the "home of the Blessed Sacrament", where the sense of "presence" overshadowed the expression of the altar as a place of sacrifice. Thus the tabernacle followed the path of the cathedra, ambo, iconostasis, reredos, and pulpit. The tabernacle grew bigger, more elaborate, and more ornate, finally overshadowing the altar and becoming the focus of the church.

The tabernacle: The question of placement

> They have taken the Lord out of the tomb, and we do not know where they have laid him (Jn 20:2).

Now that the tabernacle is in general use, the architect and priest must find the proper place for it. Since Vatican II, with the altar moved to emphasize its prominence, there has been a subsequent separation of the tabernacle from the altar. Properly speaking, of course, the tabernacle was not on the altar itself, the *mensa*, but behind the altar on the *gradine* or within the reredos. The relationship of altar and tabernacle, therefore, was similar to that of the suspended pyx of the early Middle Ages. The location of the tabernacle may well have wrongly overshadowed the altar, but the proximity served to express the close relationship between the two.

Today, the overriding concern of all the documents that consider the placement of the tabernacle is that it be "*in a truly prominent place*", or "in a part of the church that is *worthy* and properly adorned". [171] With all this in mind, there are three locations to consider for

Saint Charles Borromeo, to implement the reforms of Trent, ordered that the tabernacle be placed on the high altar of the churches in his diocese. Only then did its use come into common practice. The association, however, between the altar and reservation, commonly by the hanging pyx over the altar, has been widely accepted from at least the eleventh century, and perhaps as early as the ninth. The association of the tabernacle with the altar grew with the development of the reredos, the sculptural altarpiece behind the altar. From the late fifteenth century the tabernacle became a

---

[170] Ibid., 130.
[171] EM, no. 53; ID, no. 24; GIRM, no. 276. Italics added.

the placement of the tabernacle: on the altar, elsewhere in the sanctuary, and in a separate chapel.

Having the tabernacle on the altar is, for good reason, not optimal. It is permitted, but it has poor symbolic value:

> In the celebration of Mass the principal modes of worship by which Christ is present to his Church are gradually revealed. . . . Consequently, by reason of the symbolism, it is more in keeping with the nature of the celebration that the eucharistic presence of Christ, which is the fruit of the consecration and should be seen as such, should not be *on the altar* from the very beginning of the Mass through the reservation of the sacred species in the tabernacle.[172]

It is clear from the above passage that the tabernacle does not belong on the altar of sacrifice. The dignity of the tabernacle demands its prominence; it can be either in the sanctuary or in a separate chapel for reservation.[173] There have been many confusing and unsound arguments made for not placing the tabernacle in the sanctuary. These require comment.

The first commonly advanced argument is that the tabernacle needs to be placed elsewhere to avoid the possible "confusion" between "the celebration of the Eucharist and its reservation", or to avoid competition for our attention between "active and static aspects of the same reality".[174] Having never heard anyone mention being confused as to why the priest would confect the Eucharist when he already had it reserved, I find this to be more polemical rhetoric than a true pastoral issue. Furthermore, the phrase "active and static aspects of the same reality", used in *Environment and Art in Catholic Worship*, is an unfortunate and poor description of the spiritual reality. As John Saward points out, "The One who is really present under the sacramental species is not 'static' or 'inactive,' but the dynamic Risen Lord."[175] Furthermore, this distinction between the two manifestations of the Lord is not made in most Church documents.

Rather, throughout the Church's documents, the idea that *the Eucharist is the center of the Church* is applied when speaking of both the eucharistic liturgy and the reserved eucha-ristic species. In *Eucharisticum mysterium* it is said that "the celebration of the Eucharist is the true center of the whole Christian life."[176] But as we have already seen, *Mysterium fidei* states that the *reserved* Eucharist is "kept in churches and oratories *as the spiritual center* of the religious community and the parish community, *indeed as the spiritual center of the universal Church and the whole of humanity.*"[177] Similarly, *Evangelica testificatio* states:

> Your communities, since they are united in Christ's name, *naturally have as their center the Eucharist*, "the Sacrament of love, the sign of unity and the bond of charity." It is therefore normal that these communities should be visibly united around an oratory, in *which the presence of the Holy Eucharist expresses* and at the same time makes real that which must be the principal mission of every religious family, as also of every Christian assembly.[178]

Finally, Pope Paul VI, in *The* Credo *of the People of God*, calls the tabernacle "the living heart of our churches".[179] The fact is that they are both "centers" because they are but two facets of the same thing. As such, there is no division; recall Saint Paul's admonishment, "Is Christ divided?" (1 Cor 1:13). This integrated understanding is expressed well by Pope John Paul II, who writes in *Redemptor Hominis*, "It is at one and the same time a Sacrifice-Sacrament, a Communion-Sacrament, and a Presence-Sacrament."[180] And if it is to be expressed as the center of the life of the parish or religious community, then where better than in the sanctuary, the heart of the church building?

The sort of reasoning that opposes different aspects of Christ's manifestation in the Church —which would exclude the tabernacle from the sanctuary—raises some questions. Is one truly ignoring Christ in the tabernacle when partaking in his sacrifice? If so, then when thinking about how Christ presents himself in the

---

[172] EM no. 55; italics added.
[173] GIRM, no. 276.
[174] Cf. EACW, 39–40.
[175] From personal correspondence.
[176] EM, no. 6.
[177] MF, no. 68; italics added.
[178] Paul VI, *Evangelica testificatio* (June 29, 1971), no. 48.
[179] Paul VI, *The* Credo *of the People of God* (June 30, 1968).
[180] John Paul II, *Redemptor Hominis* (Mar. 4, 1979), no. 20.

Eucharistic Sacrifice, is one neglectful in not thinking about how he presents himself in one's neighbor? If there ought to be a separation of the tabernacle from the sanctuary, is it still proper to have daily Mass in a Blessed Sacrament chapel? Would we not then have the same problem? These questions need to be asked only as consequences of the original premise. In fact, there is neither confusion nor a true conflict in need of resolution. Therefore, it does not seem that a supposed opposition between reservation and celebration is a justifiable reason for removing the tabernacle from the sanctuary. (There is, however, a definite difference between *adoration* and celebration. It is quite improper, and in fact liturgically forbidden, to celebrate Mass before the *exposed* Eucharist.)[181]

The second reason commonly given for removing the tabernacle from the sanctuary is that eucharistic adoration is essentially a private devotion, whereas the celebration is a public work. Therefore, the tabernacle should be kept in a private chapel so as not to conflict with the public nature of the sanctuary. However, the adoration to which the tabernacle speaks is not just a matter of "individual devotion", but, as we read in *Evangelica testificatio*, a communal activity. Indeed, adoration of the Eucharist is inextricably related to the sacrifice. The relationship should not be understated or dismissed. As Saint Augustine wrote, "No one, however, eats this flesh without first adoring it . . . and not only is our adoration no sin but we sin if we fail to adore it."[182] This adoration is necessarily a communal activity, as Cardinal Ratzinger points out: "It is an intensification of communion. It is not a case of 'individualistic' piety: it is a prolonging of, or a preparation for, the community element."[183] Since the tabernacle has not only a strong connection to the altar but is an icon of community activity as well, it again does not seem unreasonable to place it within the bounds of the sanctuary.

The common objection to this is the third argument: that the altar is the true icon of the liturgy, that the sanctuary space is set aside to contain the altar, and that nothing within the sanctuary should detract from the altar.[184] In-

deed, the importance of the altar as an icon of Christ has been largely lost, at first to the grand reredos that sometimes obscured it, but more recently to the idea of the "communion table". The altar has historically been reverenced: in the early Church only the priest was allowed even to touch the altar and "only then with the greatest reverence", wrote Saint Gregory of Nyssa.[185] And throughout the Middle Ages devotion to the altar was a common popular piety, dying away only with the advent of the reredos.

This argument, however, also leads to several questions. Again we must ask: Does the tabernacle really compete with the altar? For if the tabernacle does detract from the altar, there is the same problem if daily Mass is said in the Blessed Sacrament chapel. But the vital question is *whether the altar is truly more important than the Eucharist* contained in the tabernacle? The altar is *a symbol* of Christ, but the tabernacle contains the Eucharist which *is* Christ. "The Eucharist is neither icon nor figure, but the body and blood of Christ really and truly present under the appearances of bread and wine." However highly we esteem the altar as an icon of Christ, it must be subordinated to the infinitely greater gift of his Body.[186]

Msgr. Peter Elliott's sound analysis of the postconciliar documents shows that it was a false effort from the start to try to find "theological" reasons for removing the tabernacle from the sanctuary proper.[187] Simply put, the mind of the Church does not call for its removal. Whereas the *General Instruction of the Roman Missal* [GIRM], no. 276, favored placing the tabernacle in a "chapel suited to the faithful's private adoration and prayer", the

---

[181] EM, no. 61.

[182] *In Ps.* 98, 9; cited in MF, no. 55.

[183] Joseph Cardinal Ratzinger, *The Ratzinger Report* (San Francisco: Ignatius Press, 1985), 133.

[184] M. Migliorino, "The Real Presence of Christ and Placement of the Tabernacle", *Christian Order* 29, no. 2 (Feb. 1988): 118-26.

[185] Johnson, *Planning for Liturgy*, 14.

[186] John Saward, "Christ, Our Lady, and the Church", *Chrysostom* 8, no. 1 (spring 1988): 16–17; citing St. Nicephorus and Nicaea II.

[187] Msgr. Peter Elliott, *Ceremonies of the Modern Roman Rite* (San Francisco: Ignatius Press, 1995), 323–24.

later *Inaestimabile Donum* favors its location in the sanctuary, suggesting that the tabernacle "can be located on an altar, or away from it, in a place in the church which is very prominent, truly noble and duly decorated, or in a chapel suitable for private prayer and devotion". Canon 938 § 2 reflects this developed understanding, ruling out neither the placement of the tabernacle in the sanctuary nor the placement on the altar: "The tabernacle in which the Most Holy Eucharist is reserved should be placed in a part of the church that is prominent, conspicuous, beautifully decorated, and suitable for prayer."

So, rather than removing the tabernacle from the sanctuary, it seems better to give both the tabernacle and the altar their due prominence and respect with canopies, niches, aedicules, or other such architectural devices. If the altar is centralized in the sanctuary, it will naturally be the liturgical focus, and if the tabernacle is against the wall in a handsome niche or some other significant aedicular structure, it will naturally speak to the state of repose. In traditional cruciform churches that have been reordered to bring the altar to a freestanding position, the altar of sacrifice can be placed at the crossing, with a sort of roodscreen behind to separate the sanctuary from the apse and thus create a chapel of reservation. The tabernacle could also be placed in a large freestanding cupboard, similar both in form and purpose to the modern Jewish ark in which the Torah is kept in a place of esteem in the synagogue. The doors could be closed during the liturgy and opened for personal or communal adoration.

In some instances, however, there are real and pressing concerns for maintaining a separate Blessed Sacrament chapel. It is recommended that in places of heavy secular traffic a separate place be reserved for the Eucharist.[188] This is the case in cathedrals or other places of historic or architectural interest where tourists frequently visit and in places of pilgrimage, where throngs often gather and Mass may be almost continually celebrated. This happens at St. Peter's in Rome, although it is interesting to note that there the tabernacle is ensconced in a great Baroque reredos in the chapel in which

daily Mass is celebrated. It is effectively "a church within a church", which again calls into question the real need for separation.

If the tabernacle is to be placed apart from the sanctuary, there are several considerations that need to be addressed. The first concern is one of suitability. *Eucharisticum mysterium* calls for the following: "The Blessed Sacrament should be reserved in a solid, inviolable tabernacle in the middle of the main altar or on a side altar, *but in a truly prominent place*. Alternatively, according to legitimate customs and in individual cases to be decided by the local ordinary, it may be placed in some other part of the church *which is really worthy and properly equipped*." [189]

The second concern is for the sense of orientation that the tabernacle provides. The tabernacle is very much an icon of Catholicism, and one may immediately know one is in a Catholic church upon seeing the familiar red lamp burning before the tabernacle. Conversely, if the tabernacle is not obvious, one may feel uneasy or disoriented. Imagine being invited to an acquaintance's home for dinner and, upon arriving, finding the door ajar and no one home. You might cautiously enter the house, calling out to see if anyone was inside, and finally take a seat in the parlor to wait uneasily for your host's arrival. Conversely, the clear view of the presence of the tabernacle very much says: "Welcome. Come in. Be at peace."

Furthermore, a clear view to the tabernacle also gives orientation for entering into the liturgy. When we enter the church, we follow a series of age-old rituals through which we prepare to come into the presence of the Holy. We symbolically wash and anoint ourselves with the sign of the cross, using holy water. We see the tabernacle and genuflect to acknowledge the Lord residing therein. Before the Mass begins we kneel in prayer to put ourselves in the correct frame of mind. And so on. To prepare oneself to enter into the divine worship is a human need, and reverencing the Blessed Sacrament, the Lord present in the tabernacle, is a part of this process for Catholics. If the taber-

---

[188] EM, no. 53.
[189] EM, no. 54; italics added.

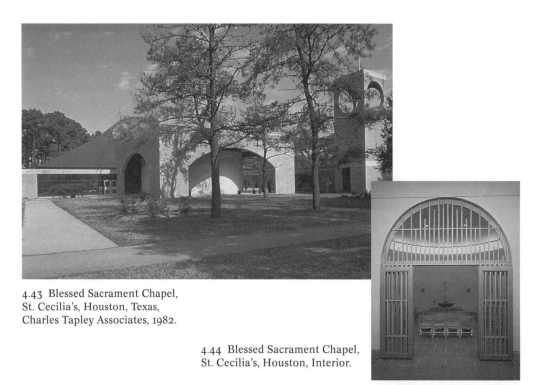

4.43 Blessed Sacrament Chapel,
St. Cecilia's, Houston, Texas,
Charles Tapley Associates, 1982.

4.44 Blessed Sacrament Chapel,
St. Cecilia's, Houston, Interior.

4.45 Mount Claret Chapel, Phoenix, Arizona, Interior.

4.46 Mount Claret Chapel, Phoenix, Arizona, Tabernacle.

nacle is not where one expects it, if there is no sign of the Host present, it may well be harder to enter into the ritual, harder to leave behind the world, and harder to feel at home within the house of God. This is the human, and therefore pastoral, concern for orienting the faithful to the Lord's presence in the church.

The tabernacle: Making a suitable place of reservation

This leads us to the question of how best to create a truly prominent and visually orienting Blessed Sacrament chapel, in a location that accounts for both the communal and individual aspects of eucharistic adoration. Several locations suggest themselves: off the narthex; behind the sanctuary, in a clearly defined yet visually related space; or to one side of the sanctuary, well within the main liturgical space, yet a room within a room.

Placing the chapel off the narthex has been done recently, and done well. At St. Cecilia's in Houston, Texas, the church is ordered so that the Blessed Sacrament chapel is expressed as its own structure [fig. 4.43]. It is convenient for daily use yet removed from the main circulation. The chapel is on-axis with the sanctuary to express the relationship between the altar and the tabernacle. The relationship of the tabernacle to the altar is strengthened by the stone paving that cuts across the narthex, and through the nave, to form the sanctuary floor. This relationship allows easy access to the chapel for daily Mass and private devotion, while allowing the main church to be closed during the week to reduce maintenance costs.

The chapel may also successfully be placed behind the sanctuary, as seen at the chapel at Mount Claret, Phoenix, Arizona. The Blessed Sacrament chapel can be closed off from the sanctuary with broad folding doors [figs. 4.45, 4.46]. With this arrangement, a multitude of problems are resolved simultaneously. The tabernacle is housed in a space separated from, yet visually related to, the sanctuary. The tabernacle is central and visible and thus serves both its iconographic and orienting functions,

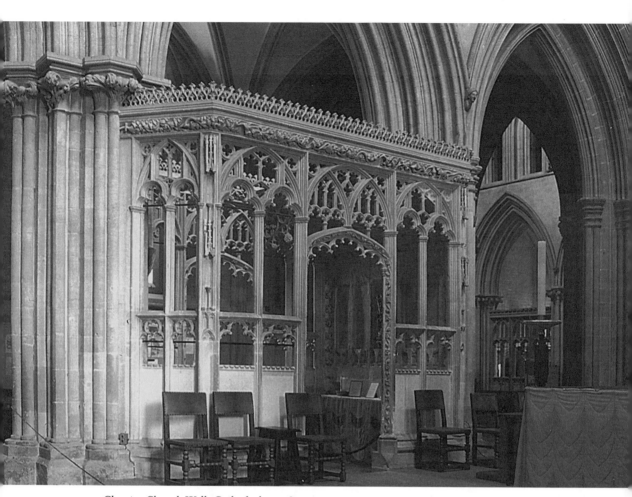

4.47 Chantry Chapel, Wells Cathedral, *c.* 1185–1239.

yet within its own intimate space, which serves the needs of personal devotion, and the folding doors can be opened for communal devotion [fig. 4.46].

A third possibility is to place the tabernacle in a room, even a distinct freestanding edifice, within the larger liturgical space. This would be done to convey simultaneously the idea of separation and relationship. Similar forms are found throughout Christian tradition, notably in the Byzantine altar, which is, in fact, not just the table but the entire room behind the iconostasis. This idea is also found in the freestanding Gothic chantry chapels, such as are seen at Wells, in which an intimate and reserved space is defined within the vast nave by

a distinct architectural form [fig. 4.47]. It is also similar to Christ's tomb in the Holy Sepulcher Church in Jerusalem [fig. 4.48]. Here, in a feat of Roman engineering and brutality, Constantine's architect Dracilianus cut away the entire hillside in which the tomb was found, leaving only a freestanding stone chapel sitting inside the church where the floor had been cut down to the level of the floor in the tomb [fig. 4.49]. In 1009, this edifice, called the "Aedicule", was smashed by Caliph al-Hākim, and around 1048 Emperor Constantine Monomachus had it rebuilt. By the sixteenth century this was in bad repair due to the heavy volume of graffiti-inscribing and souvenir-chipping pilgrims. In 1555, the Franciscans rebuilt the

Aedicule, but it was severely damaged in the fire of 1808 [fig. 4.50]. The present-day structure, of dubious architectural merit, was built by the Greek Orthodox according to the plans of a Greek architect named Calpha Comninos. Something more akin to the eleventh-century form can be seen at the Church of the Holy Sepulcher at San Stefano, Bologna [fig. 4.51]. This brief review of its checkered history aside, the Holy Sepulcher in Jerusalem gives us a typological model for creating a special place within a larger volume that can be used for a Blessed Sacrament chapel. Another instance of this arrangement is Saint Francis' Portiuncula near Assisi [fig. 4.52].

In such a scheme the chapel could be architecturally distinct from the rest of the church, again, as a sort of "church within the church", such as the one Jean Rouquet designed for l'Église du Rosaire, in Rezé, France (1960) [figs. 4.53 to 4.55]. The tabernacle would then have a place that is truly prominent: a sacred precinct for private devotion and small daily Masses. Such a space could be intimate, perhaps recalling the profound intimacy of the Holy Sepulcher or the small gatherings of the faithful in the early domus ecclesiae or the catacombs. The tabernacle would then be fittingly enshrined in a "Holy of Holies", seen for its contemplative (rather than "static") qualities, and still be easily accessed from the sanctuary for the functional needs of the holy liturgy. The wall facing the nave could be translucent, obscured glass or stained glass, so the faithful would be aware of the Lord's abiding presence. A small oil lamp burning outside the doorway should remind the faithful of the tabernacle and thus give a point of orientation.

On a smaller scale, this sense of separation was achieved by the author in the Blessed Sacrament Chapel at St. Anthony's Church in Phoenix, Arizona [fig. 4.56]. The parish's needs for a daily Mass chapel and for adoration were solved by the large, free-standing Sacrament tower: a ten-foot diameter, stone-clad form housing the monstrance set in a Gothic arch niche [fig. 4.57], and with a small sacristy inside. The tower expresses the centrality of the Eucharist in the comunity's prayer life, while the "containing" sense of the tower al-

4.48 Holy Sepulcher, Jerusalem.

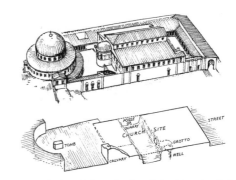

4.49 Holy Sepulcher, Study of the Constantinian Basilica.

4.50 *below* Holy Sepulcher, *c.* 1555 (after da Ragusa).

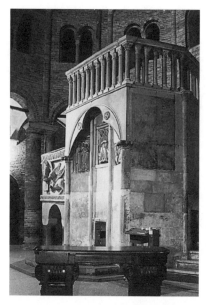

4.51 Holy Sepulcher, San Stefano, Bologna.

4.52 Portiuncula, Santa Maria degli Angeli, near Assisi.

lows the liturgy to be celebrated without conflict, for the monstrance is removed during the Mass.

These are but a few ideas in an attempt to solve the manifold problems incurred in separating the tabernacle from the sanctuary. As we have seen, there is no need to separate the tabernacle from the sanctuary, and there are numerous architectural difficulties in creating a place that is "truly prominent" apart from the sanctuary, which is the natural focal point of the church building. Clearly, more attention needs to be given to this issue. The Church gives certain guidelines but also allows great flexibility in determining the placement of the tabernacle. The main points that should be considered when planning the place for reservation are:

1. The Eucharist is the true center of the Christian life, both corporate and individual, while the altar is the main focus of the liturgy. Both these ideas need to be expressed and protected. The functional demands of the liturgy must be accounted for, which include convenient access to the tabernacle. The relationship between the altar and the tabernacle should not be ignored.

2. The place of reservation must be fully suitable: a truly prominent place that is worthy of the Lord and properly equipped. One should hardly be concerned about making a place "too prominent".

3. The tabernacle should be placed so that it serves to orient the faithful to the Lord's presence in the church.

4. The chapel should be so situated, arranged, and sized as to serve both the communal and personal needs of devotion.

With these points in mind, the architect will need to use great ingenuity to solve this delicate problem. The history of the Church's building activity has seen great variety and innovation in solving the needs of the day. Today, no less than ever before, architects and priests still need to work together to find solutions to the problems at hand. And the problem of "what to do with the tabernacle" is one such question of paramount importance that deserves continued consideration.

4.53 Église du Rosaire, Rezé, France, by
Jean Rouquet, 1965, Exterior.

4.54 Église du Rosaire, Rezé, France, by Jean Rouquet, 1965, Interior.

4.55 Église du Rosaire, Rezé, France, by Jean Rouquet, 1965,
Blessed Sacrament Chapel.

4.56 Blessed Sacrament Chapel, St. Anthony's, Phoenix, Arizona, by S. Schloeder, 1996.

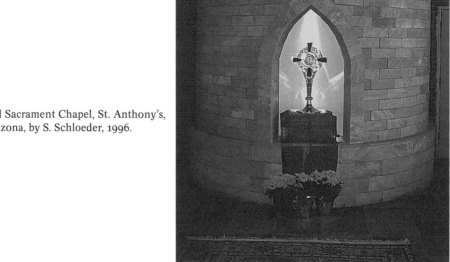

4.57 Blessed Sacrament Chapel, St. Anthony's, Phoenix, Arizona, by S. Schloeder, 1996.

The sacristy

One further topic to be considered in planning for the needs of the ministerial priesthood, before examining the place of the faithful in the nave, is the sacristy. The sacristy supports the liturgy by providing the place for the ministers to assemble and robe as well as storage for all the items used in the liturgy. Its requirements are strictly functional, as there are no liturgical laws about the sacristy. As it is a place of preparation for the celebration of the liturgy, it should be very well ordered to aid reverence and quiet. Today, the sacristy is not considered a "sacred place"—it is neither consecrated nor blessed with the church. In the past the significance of the sacristy was clearly understood otherwise. Bishop Durand gives us a beautifully poetical medieval statement on the dignity of the sacristy: "The sacristy, or place where the holy vessels are deposited, or where the priest puts on his robes, is the womb of the Blessed Mary, where Christ put on his robes of humanity. The priest, having robed himself, comes forth into the public view, because Christ, having come from the womb of the Virgin, proceeded forth into the world." [190] How much we have lost today.

The architect needs to consider the sacristy carefully to ensure adequate storage for a myriad of items, for ease of movement in cumbersome vestments, and for orderly upkeep of the church. The sacristy is best divided into two distinct rooms: a "vestry", where the clergy and acoltyes robe and assemble for the procession, and a "working sacristy", which supports the liturgy and provides for common storage needs. They should both be well lighted, well heated, and well ventilated, with easy access to a lavatory. The key to a well ordered vestry and sacristy is in having sufficient storage facilities, and O'Connell recommends making the sacristy "as large as possible . . . it can scarcely be too large."

The vestry should be convenient to the narthex and should be large enough to facilitate grand processions. Its doors should be wide enough for easy movement in a chasuble and high enough to allow for a prelate wearing his miter or for a processional cross to pass eas-

4.58 Vesting Table, Iglesia de San Pedro de Tlalpan, Mexico City.

ily. In the past, most vestments were kept in a "vesting table", which is a high chest of deep drawers. This served both as storage space for chasubles, albs, surplices, stoles, and the like and as a vesting table for dressing and for caring for the vestments. Today, while most vestments are hung in closets, a vesting table is still a convenience if the garments are precious or to be laid out [fig. 4.58]. It should be covered with a felt cloth to prevent garments from slipping off. Since vesting is part of the priest's preparation for the Eucharist, a crucifix should hang on the wall over the vesting table as a focus for prayer. A full-length mirror should be provided so ministers can see that they are properly vested. One deep wardrobe closet should be provided to hang chasubles and copes (if valuable, these are best preserved when laid flat in a vesting table drawer) and another for albs.

The working sacristy should be convenient to the sanctuary and have access from both the outside (or the presbytery) and the nave, so that entrance to it does not require passing through the sanctuary. In the sacristy, a large chest is needed for altar cloths and linen storage. The *sacrarium*, a basin with the drain leading to the earth, is needed for washing the sacred vessels and disposing of holy water. For

---

[190] Durand, *Rationale*, bk. 1, chap. 1, no. 38.

other uses, a utility sink is also necessary. If the sacrarium is next to the utility sink, the sacrarium should have a lid so that it is not inadvertently used for regular washing. A high-security, fireproof safe is needed for the sacred vessels, registers, and other precious items. Within the vestry there should be a chart listing the name of the titular saint of the church; the day, month, and year of dedication; and the name of the consecrating bishop.[191] At the door there should be a holy water stoup. It is convenient to have a phone or intercom to the parish office or presbytery, an electric signal to the organist or music leader, and a sanctuary bell to signal the beginning of the liturgy. The control panels for the church—audio, lighting, air conditioning, etc.—should be easily accessible from the vestry or the sacristy.

The working sacristy provides much of the church equipment storage, so it is wise to plan for a large storage room next to it. Among the sundry items usually stored are processional crosses, prie-dieux, banners and poles, candlesticks, candle lighters and snuffers, thuribles and incense boats, bells, cruets, hosts and altar wine, the crèche set, flower vases, the ewer and basin, and cleaning supplies. The working sacristy should have the holy water vat, a notice board, a working table and chairs, a sink, drainboard, and drying rack.

The more generous the space and the more varied the storage, the better. A very large church, such as a cathedral or a pilgrimage church, will require a large vestry, where many priests can comfortably assemble and robe, and a lot of storage space. When planning the sacristy, it is best to have an itemized inventory of the church's goods to determine how big it should be and what sort of storage need is anticipated.

---

[191] DOCA, chap. 2, no. 25.

CHAPTER FIVE

Designing for the Other Sacraments and Rites

Architectural requirements of the other sacraments

The only three sacraments that demand major specific architectural consideration are the Eucharist, baptism, and penance. Of the others, holy orders, which is normally conferred in a cathedral,[1] requires a wide area in front of the altar at the bottom of the altar steps for the prostration of the candidates. Matrimony, in addition to the requirement of the bridal room (see chapter 6), usually requires an area in front of the altar for the bridal party's kneelers. The anointing of the sick usually occurs outside the church, either in a hospital or private house, and requires only an aumbry in the sanctuary or baptistery in which to keep the holy oil. Confirmation is usually administered within the Eucharist and requires no other considerations.[2] Finally, provisions must be made for the funeral Mass. There should be sufficient space at the top of the nave, but outside the sanctuary, for the coffin to rest while not obstructing the processions or Communion. If necessary, several removable seats on each side of the main aisle in the front few rows can accommodate this. Some churches hold wakes in a chapel inside the church. In a cathedral, pilgrimage place, or other important church, a mortuary chapel should be provided to allow a reserved and respectful place for the coffin. Busy parishes should also consider mor-

tuary chapels, since funerals can overlap each other, and a body should be kept in a place of honor.

The baptistery: History and symbolism

Apart from the Eucharist, the sacrament of baptism demands the most architectural consideration. Whereas the Eucharist is "the source and summit" of the Christian life,[3] baptism is "the first and fundamental sacrament";[4] thus the baptistery should be a focal point in the church. Although there has never been any uniformity in the design, decoration, or placement of the baptistery and its font, the font and baptistery have always been important iconographic elements in the church. Their form, location, and decoration were all used to explain and symbolize the meaning of baptism.

---

[1] *Code of Canon Law* (1983), can. 1011, sec. 1 [= CIC].

[2] Though it seems that in the early patristic age special anointing rooms, called *chrismaria*, were used for confirmation; rooms such as these were found at Dura-Europus. Also, the presence of the apse for a *cathedra* in some baptisteries and other archeological evidence suggest that in the days when adult baptism was normative and thus the sacraments of baptism and confirmation were more closely linked, sometimes confirmation also took place in the baptisteries. Cf. Joseph Rykwert, *Church Building* (London: Sheed and Ward, 1966), 22; also J. G. Davies, *The Architectural Setting of Baptism* (London: Barrie and Rockliff, 1962), 30.

[3] *Inter oecumenici* (Sept. 26, 1964), no. 5.

[4] K. Rahner and H. Vorgrimler, *Concise Theological Dictionary* (London: Burns and Oates, 1965), s.v. "baptism".

The early Church saw baptism as full of rich and complex meaning. The baptism of John was a baptism of repentance (cf. Mt 3:11) and was understood as a prefiguration of the sacrament of baptism. As water baptism marked the beginning of Jesus' ministry (cf. Mt 3:13–17, Mk 1:9–11, Lk 3:21–22), so the early Church saw the washing in baptismal waters as the proper entrance into the Church. For the early Church, then, baptism had three main effects: the removal of original sin and the forgiveness of personal sin; incorporation into Christ and his Church through participation in Christ's death and resurrection; and rebirth as an adopted son of God and sanctification as a temple of the Holy Spirit. Through baptism the Christian becomes a partaker of the life of the Blessed Trinity. We can see such concurrent themes in the Church's early writings, in the form of the baptismal ceremony, and in the forms and decorations of the baptistery and fonts.

Because baptism was an entrance into the Church, baptisteries were often placed at the entrance to the church, either inside or outside the building. The baptistery at Orvieto makes this point by having the font cover in the form of a great church building, surmounted by the Lord, to teach that we are baptized into the Church and into Jesus Christ [fig. 5.1]. This placement also served to help *discipla arcani*. In the early Church (and still in the Christian East), the liturgy was divided into three parts: the Prothesis; the Liturgy of the Catechumens, which is known today as the Liturgy of the Word; and the Liturgy of the Faithful, when the Eucharistic Sacrifice was offered. Typically, the laity would gather only after the Prothesis, which was when the priests and deacons prepared the elements in the room that still bears the name *prothesis*. The catechumens would stay in the narthex throughout the Liturgy of the Catechumens and would be dismissed with a blessing before the Credo and the Eucharistic Sacrifice to attend instruction in the Faith. It was only after baptism that the neophytes would be allowed into the nave of the church and initiated into the sacred mysteries of the Lord's Supper. Thus, the placement of the baptistery at the entry to the

5.1 Baptismal Font, Orvieto Cathedral.

church was a very poignant symbol of entering the Church.

This entrance into the life of the Church has always been seen as the individual's participation in the death and Resurrection of the Lord. Jesus referred to his impending death as a type of baptism, in Luke 12:50, and this theme was taken up by Saint Paul to associate baptism with the process of death and rebirth:

> Do you not know that all of us who have been baptized into Christ Jesus were baptized into his death? We were buried therefore with him by baptism into death, so that as Christ was raised from the dead by the glory of the Father, we too might walk in newness of life (Rom 6:3–4).

> . . . [Y]ou were buried with him in baptism, in which you were also raised with him through faith in the working of God (Col 2:12).

There is a similar theme running through Saint Mark's account of the Lord's Passion and Resurrection, which perhaps even alludes to the proto-Christian baptismal ceremony. In Mark 14:51–52, when Jesus was arrested at

Gethsemane, we read that a "young man followed him with nothing but a linen cloth" about his body. A possible translation of the original Greek gives a much more interesting understanding. The young man (νεανίσκος) is said to be "wrapped up in a burial shroud over his nakedness" (περιβεβλημένος σινδόνα ἐπὶ γυμνοῦ). When the soldiers seized him, he slipped out of his robe and ran off naked into the night to avoid capture. After the account of the Crucifixion, we next find this same "young man" in Mark 16:5. He is now at the tomb, and again dressed, but this time he is "wrapped in a white robe" (περιβεβλημένον στολὴν λευκήν). This phrase "wrapped in a white robe" carries with it immense hope, for we also see the same words in Saint John's Revelation (7:9): the saints in heaven are likewise "dressed in white robes" (περιβεβλημένους στολὰς λευκὰς). In these texts it is not difficult to see the "young man" as an allegorical figure representing the baptismal candidate who was baptized naked and wrapped in a white robe. The personal sense of death evoked through such images as the burial shroud and running fearfully into the night, the account of Christ's Passion, the candidate's experience of the Resurrection made manifest through the images of the empty tomb and the white robe, all speak to the early Church's understanding of baptism. These passages also clearly parallel the early Church's practice of nude baptisms, as several sources indicate:

And let a deacon receive the man, and a deaconess receive the woman, so that the conferring of this inviolable seal may take place with a becoming decency.[5]

So now, though the church doors are barred and you are all inside, let distinctions be kept: men with men, women with women. Let not the principle of salvation be made a pretext for spiritual ruin.[6]

Immediately, then, upon entering, you removed your tunics. This was a figure of the "stripping off of the old man with his deeds." Having stripped, you were naked, in this also imitating Christ who was naked on the cross . . . you were naked in the sight of all and were not ashamed! Truly you bore the image of the first-formed Adam, who was naked in the garden and "was not ashamed."[7]

In the full darkness of the night, he strips off . . . your robe . . .[8]

After stripping you of your robe, the priest himself leads you into the flowing water. But why naked? He reminds you of your former nakedness, when you were naked in Paradise and you were not ashamed.[9]

As the burial shroud would symbolize the dead life of the pagan, so the candidate would leave his old clothes behind and enter into the waters, which were commonly understood, as we shall see, as a type of tomb. The newly baptized Christian was then dressed in the white baptismal garment mentioned by Saint John as belonging to those who "have washed their robes and made them white in the blood of the Lamb" (Rev 7:14). As Saint Cyril of Jerusalem instructs the newly baptized: "Now that you have put off your old garments and put on those which are spiritually white, you must go clad in white all your days. I do not, of course, mean that your ordinary clothes must always be white, but that you must be clad in those true, spiritual garments which are white and shining."[10]

Before going on to look at the architectural symbolism of the baptistery, a few more comments about the baptismal ceremony are in order. In the early Church baptism was by one of four methods: complete submersion of the entire body, immersion of the head, affusion or pouring, or aspersion or sprinkling. The *Didache* prefers running water, suggestive of rivers in the age before baptisteries, although immersion in still water and even sprinkling were also permitted.[11]

---

[5] *Apostolic Constitutions*, III, 16.
[6] St. Cyril of Jerusalem, *Protocat.*, 14, in *The Works of St. Cyril of Jerusalem*, ed. L. P. McCauley, S.J., and A. A. Stephenson, (Washington, D.C.: Catholic University Press, 1969–1970), 1:80.
[7] St. Cyril of Jerusalem, *Catech. Mystag.*, II, 2, in *Works*, 2:161–62.
[8] St. John Chrysostom, *Baptismal Instructions*, II, 24.
[9] Ibid., XI, 28.
[10] St. Cyril of Jerusalem, *Catech. Mystag.*, IV, 8, in *Works*, *2:184.*
[11] *Didache*, II, 7, in Maxwell Staniforth, *Early Christian Writings* (Harmondsworth, England: Penguin, 1968), 230–31.

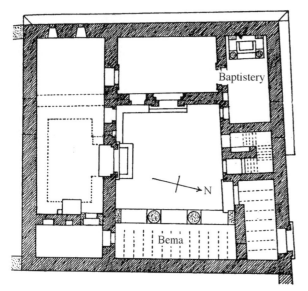

5.2 Baptistery, Dura-Europus, *c.* 232
(after Gamber).

At first, baptisms and confirmations were generally performed by the bishop. Hence, the early baptisteries were normally found inside or near the cathedral. Husband and wife, children, infants, and slaves would be baptized as households as the husband embraced the Faith. The *disciplina arcani* was observed, whereby the catechumens would be dismissed from the church after the Liturgy of the Word and before the profession of the Creed, to undergo catechesis. On Palm Sunday the catechumens became neophytes by staying to profess the Creed. But it was only after being baptized at Easter that the neophytes were allowed to partake in the Liturgy of the Eucharist and thus enter into full communion with the Church. Because of these requirements, some ancient baptisteries had ancillary rooms to accommodate the various functions. Since people were baptized nude, sometimes there were changing rooms. When the candidates were dismissed after the Liturgy of the Catechumens, they were sometimes sent to the *catechumenon*, an adjacent room, for instruction. In some ancient baptisteries there was a *pistikon*, which is thought to have been a special room in which the candidates would make their profession of faith.

The early fonts were often large enough to stand in, although many were not deep enough for full submersion.[12] The neophyte would either immerse his head in the water, or water would be poured over his head and whole body. Some ancient fonts would have allowed only for the neophyte to lean over the font and have water poured over his head. The fonts were usually sunken into the ground from one to four steps to symbolize the act of *descent* to death, as Saint Cyril of Jerusalem wrote: "And then you dipped thrice under the water and thrice rose up again, therein mystically signifying Christ's three days' burial. For as our Savior passed three days and three nights in the bowels of the earth, so by your first rising out of the water represented Christ's first day in the earth, and by your descent the night."[13]

Following the Pauline idea that baptism is a burial with Christ, submersion became the common form, and so the fonts were fairly large tubs in which to submerge the babies. This idea of death and rebirth through washing in the baptismal waters became expressed in the design of baptisteries. As the Church did with the basilica, taking a pagan architectural form and giving it analogous Christian meaning, so she took the public baths, symbolizing washing, and the mausoleum, symbolizing death, as architectural forms for the baptistery.[14] One of the earliest known baptisteries is at Dura-Europus (*c.* A.D. 232) [fig. 5.2]. Here the baptistery is a room at the entrance of the house-church with an elaborate civory surmounting the font. It alludes both to the *frigidarium* (cold pool) of the public baths by its arrangement and to a tomb by its sarcophagus-shaped quadrilateral font. J. G. Davies takes a quote from Saint Ambrose, "the font, whose appearance is somewhat like that of a tomb in shape", to illustrate this connection.[15] This

---

[12] Davies, *Baptism*, 24–26.
[13] St. Cyril of Jerusalem, *Catech. Mystag.*, II, 4, in *Works*, 2:164.
[14] Krautheimer extensively examines the formal precedents of the baptistery and concludes that it has significantly more in common with the mausoleum than with the thermae and hence was of more symbolic importance in relationship to death than to cleansing. See R. Krautheimer, "An Introduction to an 'Iconography of Mediaeval Architecture'", *The Journal of the Warburg and Courtauld Institutes* 5 (1942): 21ff.
[15] Davies, *Baptism*, 14 and 19.

5.3 San Giovanni in Fonte, Rome, 432–440.

5.4 Cruciform Baptistery, Sbaita (after Crowfoot).

5.5 Cruciform Baptistery, Leptis Magna.

idea is made even more explicit by Saint Basil, who writes, "How then are we made in the likeness of His death? In that we are buried with Him by baptism."[16] The understanding of the baptistery as a type of sepulcher certainly adds depth to Saint Mark's account of the "young man" at the Resurrection tomb. And this symbolism was dramatically driven home to the early Christians in Jerusalem, where, as Etheria witnessed, the bishop brought the neophytes into the actual Anastasis tomb to explain the mysteries of baptism.[17] This association with death is undoubtedly the explanation for baptismal fonts found in the catacombs, cut into the soft tufa, as can be seen in the catacombs of Saint Priscilla and Saint Pontianus.[18]

After the Edict of Milan in the fourth century, when the Church began widespread building, the baptistery usually became a separate building. This fact shows the indisputable importance of the sacrament. It was often sited to the northwest of the church: to the west so as to place it at the church entrance, to signify entrance into the Kingdom of God, and to the north, to symbolize the fact that the catechumens were coming from the darkness of paganism into the light of Christ.[19] Again, we read in Saint Cyril of Jerusalem:

I want to tell you why you stand facing west. This is necessary because the west is in the region of visible darkness, and Satan is darkness and has his dominion in darkness. . . . Then, when you renounce Satan, utterly cancelling every covenant with him, the ancient alliance with hell, there is opened to you the paradise of God, which he planted towards the east, whence our first ancestor was expelled. To symbolize this, you turned from the west to the east, the region of light.[20]

For both liturgical and symbolic reasons, the baptistery was usually a compact and centralized building [fig. 5.3]. Since baptisteries recalled the River Jordan, where Jesus was baptized, the plan was similar to other centralized churches that commemorated sites. There was also an undoubtedly intentional similarity with the mausoleum and martyrion, to express the death of the old self into the new life in Christ. These centralized arrangements gave rise to the use of several concentric geometries, all of which had Christian significance. The earliest baptisteries and fonts were almost all square or rectangular, but by the fourth century they were also constructed in octagons, hexagons, circles, trefoils, and crosses [figs. 5.4, 5.5]. The square, as we saw in the case of the altar, represents Christ as the second Person of the Trinity, as

[16] St. Basil, *Book on the Spirit*; quoted in Krautheimer, "An Introduction", 27.

[17] Krautheimer, "An Introduction", 31.

[18] Émile Mâle, *The Early Churches of Rome*, trans. David Buxton (London: Benn, 1960), 47; also Krautheimer, "An Introduction", 28.

[19] Fr. J. O'Connell, *Church Building and Furnishing, the Church's Way* (London: Burns and Oates, 1955), 118–19.

[20] St. Cyril of Jerusalem, *Catecheses*, 19; quoted in Henry Bettenson, *The Later Christian Fathers* (London: Oxford University Press, 1970), 42–43.

5.6 *Baptism of Christ*, Neonian Baptistery, Ravenna, Dome mosaic.

5.7 *As a deer yearns . . .*, San Clemente, Rome, Mosaic.

"magnitude multiplied by magnitude".[21] The circular font expresses the unity of the Trinity, as well as the rebirth or regeneration spoken of in John 3:3.[22] In this sense, the round font can also be seen as a kind of womb that, according to Saint Ephrem, "daily and without pain gives birth to the children of the kingdom of heaven".[23] The hexagon represents Friday, the sixth day of the week. For the sixth day was the day on which Adam was created, hence it symbolizes the death of the old self; and it is also the day on which Christ died and was entombed, thus to remind the neophyte that he must die with Christ and that if he "loses his life for my sake, he will save it" (Lk 9:24). Similarly, the octagon represents the eighth day of the week. This is the day of both the Old Covenant—the day on which Jewish males were to be circumcised—as well as that of the New Covenant—the day of the Resurrection, which has become the first day of the new week and the day of rebirth. This symbol would have expressed to the neophyte that he would share in Christ's Resurrection because he had shared in his baptism. The trefoil is an overtly trinitarian symbol, for the Christian is to be baptized "in the name of the Father and of the Son and of the Holy Spirit" (Mt 28:19). In many cases two forms were juxtaposed; commonly with a hexagonal font in an octagonal building or vice versa, but also squares in octagons, circles in hexagons, and so on. Later fonts were sometimes cruciform or quatrefoil, to associate more directly the idea of baptism with the Crucifixion. J. G. Davies quotes both the Eastern and Western Fathers to demonstrate this connection: "Baptism is a cross. What the Cross was to Christ and what His burial was, that baptism was to us" (Saint John Chrysostom); and "When thou dippest, thou takest on the likeness of death and burial; thou receivest the sacrament of the Cross" (Saint Ambrose).[24]

[21] Otto von Simson, *The Gothic Cathedral*, 2d ed. (New York: Pantheon Books, 1962), 27.

[22] *New Dictionary of Liturgy and Worship*, ed. J. G. Davies (London: SCM, 1988), s.v. "font".

[23] *Hymni de virg.*, 7, 7; quoted in Davies, *Baptism*, 22.

[24] Davies, *Baptism*, 22. Cf. St. John Chrysostom, *Baptismal Instructions*, XI, 12, and X, 8–11.

The importance of baptism in the early Church is further evidenced by the amount and type of ornamentation in the baptistery. Where the form of the font or building could subtly suggest some aspect of the sacrament, the ornamentation became an opportunity for powerful and lavish pictorial statements symbolizing the meaning of baptism. And images were drawn not only from Scripture but from nature and even pagan mythology as well. While there were dozens of allegorical symbols used from Scripture, most common are the baptism of Jesus by John [fig. 5.6], the women at the tomb, the Samaritan woman at the well, the Good Shepherd, and the deer that recalls Psalm 42: "As a hart longs for flowing streams, so longs my soul for thee, O God" [fig. 5.7]. From nature, the peacock, the palm tree, and the fruit tree are all symbols of paradise, and the stars, often shown in a vaulted dome, refer to heaven. In some places the dome was covered with vines, recalling that the Lord is "the true vine" and his people are the "branches" (cf. Jn 15:1–5). The dove, a symbol of the Holy Spirit, is often found above the font.[25] The fish recalls that Jesus made the Church "fishers of men" (Mt 4:19); it also refers to the ΙΧΘΥΣ, an ancient acronym of the Greek word for *fish*, composed of the first letters of each of the words in the phrase "Jesus Christ, God's Son, Savior" (Ἰησοῦς Χριστός Θεοῦ Υἱός Σωτήρ). The patristic theologian Tertullian tied this into baptism with his statement, "We, little fishes, after the example of our Fish (ΙΧΘΥΣ), Jesus Christ, are born in water."[26] Similarly, Saint Cyril of Jerusalem wrote, "You are a fish, caught in the net of the Church", no doubt with the same intent. Even from pagan mythology, the symbols of the phoenix and the unicorn were used to represent immortal regeneration.[27]

As Christianity spread and paganism died out, the number of adult baptisms declined. By the seventh century infant baptism was the general case, so large baptisteries, separate buildings, and sunken fonts were no longer needed. Infant baptism was already an ancient practice. Both Origen and Saint Augustine considered it a "tradition received from the apostles". In the second century, Saint Irenaeus considered it a matter of course that "in-

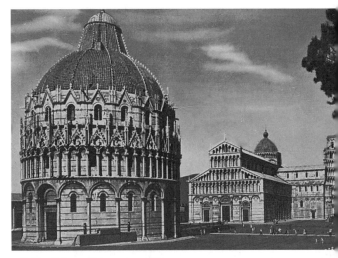

5.8 Baptistery, Pisa, 1153–1265.

fants and small children" should be baptized. Similarly, the third-century *Apostolic Tradition* states: "First baptize the children. Those of them who can speak for themselves should do so. The parents or someone of their family should speak for the others."[28] As this practice became the norm, the fonts were accordingly raised to facilitate it. Moreover, as Christianity became more well established and society more commonly Christian, the notion of leaving the pagan world and entering a new life in the Church lost its meaning. As the catechumenate and the *disciplina arcani* became unnecessary, so did the need for a changing room, a *catechumenon*, and a *pistikon*. The baptistery had first become smaller, then attached to the church, and finally subsumed within it. This trend, however, was not universal, as detached baptisteries continued to be built and, often, rebuilt on the site of ancient ones in Italy, France, Germany, England, and Russia until the later Middle Ages [fig. 5.8].[29]

---

[25] Davies, *Baptism*, 32–38.

[26] *De Bapt.*, 1; quoted in Davies, *Baptism*, 36.

[27] Cf. St. Cyril of Jerusalem, *Catech. Mystag.*, xviii, 8; St. Clement of Rome, *First Epistle to the Corinthians* 1:25; and St. Ambrose, *On His Brother Satyrus*, 2:59.

[28] Quoted in Sacred Congregation for the Doctrine of the Faith, *Pastoralis actio* (Oct. 20, 1980), no. 4, [=PA].

[29] O'Connell, *Church Building*, 118; also Davies, *Baptism*, 43.

5.9 Stone Font, Iglesia de San Jerónimo, Mexico City.

From the sixth century, when bishops began to have priests administer baptism, baptisteries were permitted in rural parishes and monasteries. Because each church had to administer baptism, it was common simply to dedicate one corner of the church, typically at the north side of the west entrance, to the baptistery. Often the baptistery was a chapel dedicated to Saint John the Baptist, with an altar and sometimes even a pulpit.[30] The font itself might be under an elaborate civory (ciborium) as a mark of respect. The medieval font took many different forms, with legs or a pedestal base, sometimes taking the shape of a chalice, and using the same patristic symbolism for the shapes of circles, octagons, hexagons, and so forth. The fonts were commonly made of stone, symbolizing Christ as the Rock and Cornerstone as well as alluding to the rock from which Moses drew water (cf. Ex 17:5–6) [fig. 5.9], but fonts were also made of wood, bronze, and lead [fig. 5.10].[31]

In addition to the standard scriptural references for ornamentation on the font—i.e., the baptism of Christ, the Crucifixion, the Resurrection, or the four creatures of Revelation (cf. Rev 4:7),[32] or the depiction of various saints— the comprehensive medieval mind also imparted more complex symbols to baptism, showing the demonic struggle for souls with dragons, griffins, hydras, and snakes attacking souls, battling angels, or being conquered by the Lamb of God. Abbot Suger of Saint-Denis, for instance, had a window installed in the baptistery depicting the Pharaoh and his army submerged by the sea, with the verse, "What baptism does to the good, that it does to the soldiery of the Pharaoh. A like form [*forma facit similis*] but an unlike cause [*causaque dissimilis*]." That is to say, the same means can bring about different ends: death to the enemy of God and life to the friend of God. In a different vein, Hugh of Saint-Victor, Suger's contemporary, considered the Red Sea to be a prefiguration of baptism, "where the waters proclaimed baptism, and the redness blood".[33] Such nuancing of interpretations is alluded to by J. G. Davies as he aptly sums up the medieval symbolism by writing:

> The iconography of baptism in the Middle Ages was far more extensive than that of the early Christian period. Most of its elements, however, cannot be considered inappropriate, but then, since baptism is the actualization of Christ's saving work, there can be few Christian themes that cannot be associated with it more or less closely. Perhaps a greater emphasis was placed upon the struggle with the devil than is congenial to the modern mind, but it resulted in the production of some of the finest examples of mediaeval sculpture and served to render the font a handsome and imposing instrument of the first Gospel sacrament.[34]

[30] Davies, *Baptism*, 52–53 and 69.

[31] Ibid., 65–68.

[32] The Fathers understood these as symbols of the four Gospels, in which each Gospel emphasizes a different aspect of Christ: the lion of St. Mark representing Christ the King, the ox of St. Luke alluding to Jesus as the Sacrificial Victim, the man of St. Matthew depicting Christ's humanity, and the eagle representing the divine wisdom of the Logos in St. John's Gospel.

[33] Hugh of Saint-Victor, *De Sacramentis*, bk. 2, pt. 6, XV. Cf. *Hugh of St.-Victor on the Sacraments of the Christian Faith*, trans. R. J. Deferrari (Cambridge, Mass.: Mediaeval Academy, 1951).

[34] Davies, *Baptism*, 78 and 80–84.

5.10 Medieval Bronze Font, Winchester Cathedral.

During the Counter Reformation, Saint Charles Borromeo recommended returning to the ancient practice of building detached baptisteries, especially for cathedrals and other large or important churches. They were to be either round, hexagonal, or octagonal, with a vestibule and altar, and dedicated to Saint John the Baptist. In smaller parish churches that could not have a separate baptistery, Saint Charles prescribed a side chapel on the north side of the entrance, enclosed by an iron or wood gate, and sunken several steps beneath the floor of the nave so that it "should bear some resemblance to a sepulcher".[35] Saint Charles' directives were to influence the layout of baptisteries until the Second Vatican Council.

The baptistery today

In the past thirty years or so the baptistery has been the subject of much architectural experimentation. The idea of baptism as initiation and entrance into the Church has been explored by bringing the font into the narthex or by creating a separate and architecturally distinct chapel attached to the west end of the church. Some liturgists, arguing for a closer relationship between baptism and the Eucharist or favoring more communal participation, suggest that the font might be placed at the east end, near the sanctuary, yet in a clearly defined area so as to be seen as autonomous from the sanctuary.[36] Other authors emphatically insist that the baptistery must be at the entrance to the church.[37] Rather than examining the complexities of these nuanced arguments, perhaps it would be of greater value to determine principles for the design and placement of baptisteries from what the Church has written.

The design of the baptistery has always been determined more by tradition than by liturgical law; nonetheless, there are certain

---

[35] Ibid., 106–7 and 148.

[36] Frs. Stephen and Cuthbert Johnson, *Planning for Liturgy* (Farnborough, England: St. Michael's, 1983), 38–40. These are not the authors' recommendations, merely their critique of others' ideas.

5.11 Baptismal Font, Parroquia de la Santa Cruz del Pedregal, Mexico City.

5.12 Baptismal Font,
St. Paul's-outside-the-Walls,
Rome.

requirements given. Since the parish church is the proper place for baptism, all parishes should have a baptistery. "It must be reserved for the sacrament of baptism and should be entirely worthy, as befits the place where Christians are reborn from water and the Holy Spirit."[38] Because baptism is a part of the paschal mystery of the Church, provision should be made in the baptistery for placing the paschal candle in a place of honor after the Easter season: "Thus it can be lit during the celebration of baptism and the candles of the candidates for baptism may be easily lit from it" [fig. 5.11].[39] And, since the Scriptures are read as part of the rite, a small ambo or other suitable place of proclamation should be provided.[40] The font may incorporate running water (which is blessed at the beginning of the baptismal rite as it flows), and the water may be heated for cold weather.[41] There should be a place, perhaps a wide and level part of the font rim, where the priest can keep the requisites during the rite [fig. 5.12]; and an aumbry should be nearby to keep the holy oil.[42]

The font itself should be both "scrupulously clean and decorative",[43] and the water should be "natural and clean to ensure the authenticity of the symbolism and in the interest of hygiene."[44] Canon law states that baptism is "validly conferred only by washing with true water".[45] This follows the teachings of the Council of Trent that invoke anathema "if anyone says that true and natural water [*aqua vera et naturalis*] is not necessary for baptism".[46] But why water? Hugh of Saint-Victor, the twelfth-century theologian, writes that water "alone has full and perfect cleanness. All other liquids indeed are purified by water. And if anything has been touched by any other liquid it is washed off by water so that it be cleansed. Therefore, in water alone is the sacrament of cleanness established, as it is written, 'Unless a man be born again of water and the Holy Ghost, he cannot enter into the Kingdom of God' (cf. Jn 3:5)."[47]

The Church continues to affirm the primary meanings of baptism: that it is an entry and initiation into the body of Christ and that it cleanses the soul of both original and personal sin by sacramentally sharing in Christ's paschal death and Resurrection. Throughout the history of the Church, baptism has primarily been understood as a sacrament of initiation, our incorporation into the body of Christ: it is "the gate to the sacraments".[48] *Lumen Gentium* states that Jesus himself "explicitly asserted the necessity of faith and baptism (cf. Mk 16:16; Jn 3:5) and thereby affirmed at the same time the necessity of the Church which men enter through baptism as through a door."[49] As we have seen, this idea of baptismal entering "as through a door" is both ancient and important in determining the location of the baptistery.

Baptism is also still understood as a personal cleansing of the soul, where the "washing with water accompanied by the living word cleanses men and women of all stain of sin, original and personal."[50] This cleansing is still seen as a death, where men "are grafted into the paschal mystery of Christ; they die with him, are buried with him, and rise with him."[51]

Baptism, much more effective than the purifications of the old law, produces these effects by the power of the mystery of the Passion and resurrection of the Lord. When people are baptised, they share sacramentally in Christ's death, they are buried with him and

---

[37] Fr. Louis Bouyer, *Liturgy and Architecture* (South Bend, Ind.: University of Notre Dame Press, 1967), 121.

[38] Sacred Congregation for Doctrine and Worship, *Per initiationis Christianae*, 2d ed. (June 24, 1973), no. 25 [= PIC]; also CIC, can. 857, sec. 1.

[39] The Bishops' Conference of England and Wales, *The Parish Church* (London: Catholic Truth Society, 1984), no. 28 [= PC].

[40] PIC, nos. 5 and 24.

[41] PIC, nos. 20–21; also United States Catholic Conference, *Environment and Art in Catholic Worship* (Washington, D.C.: USCC, 1978), 77 [= EACW]. It is interesting that the author of the *Didache* actually prefers cold water, stating, "This should be cold if possible; otherwise warm" (*Didache*, II, 7, in Staniforth, *Early Christian Writings*, 231).

[42] PC, 107.

[43] PIC, no. 19.

[44] PIC, no. 18.

[45] CIC, can. 849.

[46] The Council of Trent, session 7, "Canons on the Sacrament of Baptism", 2. Cf. *The Canons and Decrees of the Council of Trent*, ed. Rev. H. J. Schroeder (St. Louis: Herder, 1941).

[47] Hugh of St.-Victor, *Sacraments*, bk. 2, pt. 6, XIV.

[48] CIC, can. 849.

[49] Vatican II, *Lumen Gentium* (Nov. 21, 1964), no. 14 [= LG].

[50] PIC, no. 5.

[51] Vatican II, *Sacrosanctum concilium* (Dec. 4, 1963), no. 6 [= SC]; see also LG, no. 7.

lie dead, they are brought back to life with him and rise with him. For baptism recalls and actualises the very paschal mystery itself, since by its means men and women pass from the death of sin to life.[52]

The mystery of this participation in Christ's paschal sacrifice is meant to be made evident through the ancient practice of celebrating baptisms at the Easter Vigil or on Sunday, when the Church commemorates the Resurrection, and by the placement of the paschal candle in the baptistery.[53] This symbolism can be furthered by creating a sepulchral space alluding to the tomb and by reviving the patristic forms of the font and baptistery.

The Church has also called for a new emphasis on the relationships between baptism and community life, and baptism and the Eucharist. Baptism is necessarily a social event, for, as Saint Paul wrote, "by one Spirit we were all baptized into one body" (1 Cor 12:13). The Church has begun to emphasize this communal aspect, writing that in baptism "priests introduce men into the People of God"[54] and: "Baptism, further, is the sacrament by which men and women are incorporated into the Church, assembled together into the house of God in the Spirit, into a royal priesthood and a holy nation. It is the sacramental bond of unity between all those who have received it."[55]

The implications of this, architecturally, call for the baptistery to have more of a communal character [fig. 5.13]. This is expressed in different documents in various ways with varying emphases. At their simplest, the guidelines call for the baptistery to be a clearly defined space apart from the sanctuary, where it should be "capable of accommodating a large number of people" and in a prominent place where it is clearly visible.[56] If the baptistery is within the church itself, it should be "in clear view of the faithful".[57] The U.S. Bishops' Committee on the Liturgy calls for the placement of the font to "facilitate full congregational participation, regularly at Easter Vigil".[58]

In the *Introduction to the Rite of Infant Baptism* (*Nomine Parvulorum*, June 24, 1973), the Sacred Congregation for Divine Worship permitted infant baptism during Mass on Sunday, "so that the entire community may be able to attend and so that the link between Baptism and Eucharist may be seen more clearly", though with the proviso that this not be done too often.[59] In this statement we see that, in addition to the emphasis on community participation, there is now a desire to emphasize the connection between baptism and the Eucharist. Although one can argue that all sacraments are intertwined, it would seem that the desired connection is weakened by the fact that the baptized infants are not communicated. This practice only serves to demonstrate the difference between the two sacraments. Nevertheless, there is a current trend to try to connect these two sacraments. In this spirit, the Bishops' Conference of England and Wales calls for an architectural integration, or design harmony, between the font and the altar to show "the link between the life-giving and the life-sustaining sacraments".[60]

These various guidelines can raise some problems in implementation. As baptism is an entrance into the Church, the font should probably be near the entry. That its placement should "facilitate full congregational participation" suggests perhaps that it be placed in the nave, or an open area, near the sanctuary, so that the congregation can witness. Yet that the sacrament "should always manifest its paschal character"[61] suggests that the environment should perhaps have a somewhat closed, intimate, and sepulchral character. This, however, may be at odds with the desire that the font be "in clear view of the faithful".[62]

To address these problems, one allowable (though not recommended) solution is to use a portable font placed in front of the congregation for "maximum visibility and audibility". Where the U.S. bishops seem to allow the font to be in the sanctuary, providing only that it

[52] PIC, no. 6.
[53] CIC, can. 856; PIC, no. 6; also Sacred Congregation for Doctrine and Worship, *Nomine parvulorum*, 2d ed. (June 24, 1973) [= NP].
[54] Vatican II, *Presbyterorum ordinis* (Dec. 7, 1965), no. 5.
[55] PIC, no. 4.
[56] PIC, no. 25; PC, 103.
[57] PIC, no. 25.
[58] EACW, 77.
[59] NP, no. 9.
[60] NP, no. 9; PC, 108.
[61] PIC, no. 28.
[62] EACW, 77.

5.13 Baptismal Font, Cathedral of the Madeleine, Salt Lake City.

not crowd or obscure the altar, ambo, or chair,[63] the English and Welsh bishops explicitly prohibit the font from being *in* the sanctuary, preferring it, rather, to be "placed where it does not conflict with the altar, ambo or chair". They furthermore suggest that the permanent font have a removable inner lining that can be used in a specially designed base for a portable font, providing that it "be in keeping with the solemnity of the sacrament".[64]

There are, however, significant objections to the use of a portable font. Each place in which the Lord sacramentally nurtures his people deserves special consideration. Hence, the Eucharist is normatively to be celebrated on an altar in a church; weddings, ordinations, and funerals take place in churches; and the reconciliation chapel is an appropriate setting to repair our relationship with God. A portable font necessarily diminishes the baptistery as *a worthy place specially reserved* for the sacrament.[65] The idea of a separate baptistery is to give due honor to the sacrament. Hence, it seems contradictory to ignore this by using a portable font: "The use of basins or movable fonts cannot be condoned; neither the importance of baptism nor its meaning can be adequately expressed by these expedients."[66] Moreover, the idea of a portable font wheeled out for special occasions seems only to reinforce the idea of a static community. Should a portable font be required (for some truly overriding concern), it is still up to the designer to provide for the feeling of permanence that speaks of the reverence due to the sacrament.

There are, however, other solutions to the problem. Many liturgists today are arguing for dynamic movement in the liturgy, appreciating the value of procession in active participation, and this can become a part of the communal celebration of baptism. The entire rite does not have to happen in one place, and the Church allows a great deal of latitude:

> The portions of the baptismal rite which are to be celebrated outside the baptistery should be performed in whatever parts of the church best facilitate the numbers taking part and best suit the stages of the celebration. If the baptistery is not able to accommodate all the catechumens and the congregation, the parts of the rite which ordinarily take place there can be moved to some other suitable area in the church.[67]

Once we get beyond this constraining "pew mentality"—which only encourages the

[63] Ibid.
[64] PC, 103 and 106.
[65] PIC, no. 25.
[66] Davies, *Baptism*, 176.
[67] PIC, no. 26.

spectator posture with such expedient devices as portable fonts—and begin to explore the advantages of liturgical movement and flexibility, we can find new appreciation for the practices of the early Church. For instance, Saint Justin Martyr recorded the second-century practice: "After we have thus washed him who has been convinced and assented to our teaching, [we] bring him to the place where those who are called brethren are assembled."[68] In this citation we can read of the obvious separation between the place of baptism and the place of assembly (undoubtedly the altar). And not only was this separation important for the *disciplina arcani*, but the procession between the two was no doubt an important statement of entering the fold and of being welcomed and embraced by the Church. The restoration of the catechumenate called for in *Sacrosanctum concilium*[69] has widely seen the reintroduction of the *disciplina arcani*. Often nowadays, the catechumens are dismissed with a blessing after the prayers of the faithful to go for instructions in the Faith. Within this revived context, the procession from the font to the altar for the newly baptized can take on a whole new richness.

Taking all this into account, it seems reasonable to continue placing the baptistery at the entrance to the church, either inside the church in the back of the nave or in an open narthex or even outside the church in a freestanding baptistery, where it speaks to the initiative aspect of the sacrament and reminds the faithful of their baptismal promises as they enter the church. The baptistery can be somewhat below grade, with a sepulchral character, perhaps as an architecturally distinct chapel akin to a mausoleum within the entry hall. By recessing the baptistery even three or four feet below grade, with a solid parapet or balustrade another three feet or so above, quite a strong sense of enclosure can be achieved, while still allowing the congregation gathered above to witness the celebration. Thus in a very striking way the ideas of dying with Christ and rising again can be resolved with the full participation of the congregation. For the act of baptism is the beginning of the neophytes' full participation in the community. It is also the

beginning and continuation of the real challenge for the parish community:

> The parish community... should play a part in the pastoral practices regarding baptism. "Christian instruction and the preparation for baptism are a vital concern of God's people, the Church which hands on and nourishes the faith it has received from the Apostles." This active participation by the Christian people, which has already come into use in the case of adults, is also required for the baptism of infants, in which the people of God, that is the Church, made present in the local community, has an important part to play. In addition, the community itself will as a rule draw great profit, both spiritual and apostolic, from the baptism ceremony. Finally, the community's work will continue, after the liturgical celebration, through the contribution of the adults to the education of the young in faith, both by the witness of their own Christian lives and by their participation in various catechetical activities.[70]

Designing for the sacrament of penance

The sacrament of penance has had an architectural setting, properly speaking, only since the sixteenth century, when a partition between the penitent and confessor was first ordered by Saint Charles Borromeo at the Council of Milan. Before that time the confessor would usually sit in the nave or narthex of the church, with the penitent kneeling beside him.[71] In his *Instructiones*, Saint Charles gives minute details as to the construction, size, and location of the confessionals: he effectively developed the traditional wooden confessional box, explicitly to ensure the dignity of the sacrament by assigning it a special place within the church [fig. 5.14].[72] In the first several centu-

---

[68] *Apol.*, I, 65. Davies italicized this quote to express the corporate nature of baptism; however, the whole context seems to speak more directly of the process than of the community. Davies, *Baptism*, 164.

[69] SC, no. 64.

[70] PA, no. 33.

[71] O'Connell, *Church Building*, 72.

[72] St. Charles Borromeo, *Instructiones Fabricae et Supellectillis Ecclesiasticae* (Instructions on Ecclesiastical buildings), trans. Evelyn Carol Voelker. Ph.D. diss., Syracuse University, 1977 (Ann Arbor, Mich.: University Microfilms International, n.d.), 297ff.

5.14 Confessional, San Carlo alle Quattro Fontane, Rome, by F. Borromini.

ries of Christianity, before the advent of private and frequent confessions, the penitent would openly confess his sins on the steps of the church before the bishop, who would then impose the penance. The penitent might then be relegated to the narthex until the satisfaction was accomplished. As absolution was usually granted only once in a person's life, as penance was so public, and as the disciplines imposed might be severe and last for years, often people tried to wait until their deathbeds to confess. In the sixth century, largely through the influence of the Irish monks, penance evolved into a private and repeatable sacrament—showing that although the Church's understanding of the nature of sacrament had not changed, her pastoral strategy thankfully had.

In the Eastern Church the sacrament is aptly named "metanoia", for the emphasis is on change of heart, change of direction, and continuing conversion. In the Christian West, the emphases have traditionally been placed on personal acknowledgment and reparation for our sins, hence the terms "confession" and "penance". Today the emphases are on mercy and healing, and so we also use the term "rite of reconciliation". The rite is the prayer form used to bring about our reconciliation with the Father through Jesus and the Holy Spirit. With this emphasis on reconciliation, *Lumen Gentium* recalls: "Those who approach the sacrament of Penance obtain pardon from God's mercy for the offense committed against him, and are, at the same time, reconciled with the Church which they have wounded by their sins." [73]

Therefore, the architectural setting for penance should be "seen as inviting and a reminder of the Church's healing ministry".[74] The proper place for conferring the sacrament, which should normally take place in a confessional, is a church or oratory;[75] and the ordinary means today is still private and individual confession and absolution.[76]

The penitent may be given the option between anonymous confession, such as in the traditional confessional, or "open confession", face-to-face with the priest [fig. 5.15]. Whether the church has traditional confessionals adapted for open confession or reconciliation rooms, the penitent should always be given the option of anonymous confession [fig. 5.16].[77] "In whichever way the confessional is designed, the penitent should not be immediately confronted by the priest, but be at liberty to adopt a kneeling position behind a screen or to kneel or sit within the sight of the priest." [78]

In order to preserve the dignity of the sacrament (and of the penitent), a separate room, or "reconciliation chapel", can be incorporated in new buildings and in remodeling projects. The room should be well lighted and ventilated, with either an obscured glass door or a signal light to indicate occupancy. The interior

[73] LG, no. 11.
[74] PC, 111.
[75] CIC, can. 964. secs. 1 and 3.
[76] CIC, can. 960.
[77] CIC, can. 964, sec. 2.
[78] PC, 111.

5.15 Confessional, San Stefano, Assisi.

5.16 Reconciliation Chapel, Cathedral of the Madeleine, Salt Lake City.

should be without a step and large enough for the disabled in a wheelchair.[79] An amplifying loop system for the deaf, whether priest or penitent, should be furnished, with resistors to limit the system to the confessional.[80] A kneeler with a fixed grille should shield the priest from the door, and a chair to the side facing behind the screen will give the penitent the option to choose. The room should be light, airy, comfortable, and simple. The only furnishings needed, apart from the kneeler and screen, are chairs for the priest and the penitent, a small table for a Bible and the priest's stole, and a crucifix or other appropriate image on the wall. The room can be carpeted, which helps both to absorb sound and to create a comfortable atmosphere.[81]

The confessionals can be in any suitable place in the church, provided they are in an open area, such as the nave or narthex [figs. 5.17, 5.18].[82] Many authorities are recommending placing the confessionals in the narthex or entry hall, especially if they can be near the baptistery or the Blessed Sacrament chapel, to place the sacrament in its symbolic and traditional context.[83] In the early Church the narthex was not just the entrance to the church but was also reserved for those not admitted to the sacraments, be they pagans, penitents, or the unreconciled. Since the Church forbids reception of the Eucharist by those conscious of grave sin, and since by penance one reenters the sacramental life, the latter sacrament is seen as a sort of "second baptism", whereby the tears of repentance become the waters of cleansing. Therefore, placing the reconciliation chapels at the entry to the nave delivers the same message that placing the baptistery there does. The placement of the confessionals in the narthex would also serve as a reminder to the faithful of the importance of the sacrament for a healthy Christian life: "The practice of the virtue of Penance and the Sacrament of Penance are essential for sus-

---

[79] Fr. J. Hargreen, "Confessionals for the New Rite", *Clergy Review*, 67, no. 9 (Sept. 1982): 323.

[80] PC, 112.

[81] Hargreen, "Confessionals", 323–24.

[82] CIC, can. 964, sec. 2.

[83] EACW, 81.

5.17 Reconciliation Chapel, Parroquia de Ia Santa Cruz del Pedregal, Mexico City.

5.18 Confessional, Parroquia de Ia Santa Cruz del Pedregal, Mexico City.

taining in us and continually deepening that spirit of veneration which man owes to God himself and to his love so marvelously revealed."[84] As Saint Paul wrote: "Whoever, therefore, eats the bread or drinks the cup of the Lord in an unworthy manner will be guilty of profaning the body and blood of the Lord. Let a man examine himself, and so eat of the bread and drink of the cup" (1 Cor 11:27–28). So the confessional in the narthex, seen upon entering the church, invites the faithful to repentance to prepare for the Eucharist. If the tabernacle is nearby, before which the penitent can contritely pray, the connection between the Eucharist and penance can be made even apart from Mass. In this way, to quote Pope John Paul II, "It is not only that Penance leads to the Eucharist, but that the Eucharist also leads to Penance."[85] For the Pope this connection is intrinsically linked not only to the "enrichment of the faith" as set forth by Vatican II but to the very mission of the Church: "It is certain that the Church of the New Advent, the Church that is continually preparing for the new coming of the Lord, must be the Church of the Eucharist and of Penance. Only when viewed in this spiritual aspect of her life and activity is she seen to be the Church of the divine mission, the Church *in statu missionis*, as the Second Vatican Council has shown her to be."[86]

---

[84] John Paul II, *Dominicae cenae* (Feb. 24, 1980), no. 7.
[85] Ibid.
[86] John Paul II, *Redemptor Hominis* (Mar. 4, 1979), no. 20.

CHAPTER SIX

Domus Ecclesiae:
The Parish Community

The essential division of space within the church is between the sanctuary and the nave. This division expresses the twofold priesthood of the clergy and the laity, giving each a proper place in which to perform its ministry. Having examined the sanctuary and its elements—the place and furnishings for the ministerial priesthood—we now turn our attention to the places for the laity, the royal priesthood of the people of God.

Today the term *domus ecclesiae* ("house of the church" or "house-church") is often used by liturgical writers to describe the church building [fig. 6.1]. It is an ancient term, used as early as the fourth century by Eusebius, who was Constantine the Great's historian.[1] To understand it, we should remember that the Greek word ἐκκλησία, of which *ecclesia* is the Latin form, is derived from the verb meaning "to call" and refers to the assembly of those who have been called together. As Saint Cyril of Jerusalem wrote, "It is appropriately called the Church (ἐκκλησία), because it calls out (ἐκκαλεῖσθαι) all men and assembles them together."[2] *Domus ecclesiae*, then, means "the house of those who are called [by God or by the Church]". This is very similar to the Jewish term *synagogue*, also a Greek word, which means "brought or called together [for teaching or leading]".

The use of *domus ecclesiae* is a fitting reminder that the church is "the house of God's people gathered together by his call". It is un-

fortunate and inappropriate that this term is often used by liturgical writers in contrast or opposition to the term *domus Dei*—an even more ancient term, used by Tertullian in the second century—meaning "the house of God". *Domus Dei*, for some, implies a remote God, known only through his ministers, the priests, and thus it speaks of clericalism, structure, and ritual formality. This they contrast with *domus ecclesiae*, which emphasizes the people gathered and is thus a more "social" and "community-oriented" phrase. There is a similarity here to the false distinction between the "people of God" and the "body of Christ" discussed in the first chapter. The problem with this thinking, of course, is that without *Deus* there can be no *ecclesia*. The Church is not primarily a gathering of people, but rather, as Saint Paul instructs us, the Church is the body of Christ, "the fulness of him who fills all in all" (Eph 1:23). It is Christ, the Head and Bridegroom, who gives the Church, his body and bride, her identity. It is he who calls us into his body (and hence into profound relationship with one another) through our participation in the Eucharist.

The two terms do have valid use, not in opposition to one another, but in expressing two

---

[1] Eusebius, *The History of the Church*, 7:30; 8:13; 9:9; cited in R. Kevin Seasoltz, *The House of God* (New York: Herder and Herder, 1963), 84.

[2] St. Cyril of Jerusalem, *Catecheses*, 18:24; quoted in Henry Bettenson, *The Later Christian Fathers* (London: Oxford University Press, 1970), 39.

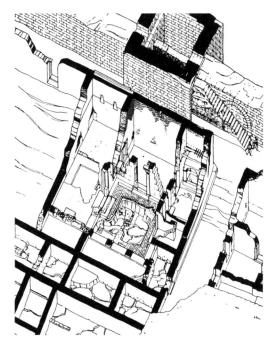

6.1 *Domus Ecclesiae*, Dura-Europus, *c.* 232 (after Hopkins).

Dei also reminds us of the Blessed Sacrament, where Christ sacramentally dwells within the church, making it truly "the house of God". That these two phrases, *domus ecclesiae* and *domus Dei*, express different facets of the same reality becomes apparent when one considers that they are two expressions of the idea of "Church". The word "church" is derived from the Greek κῡριακός, meaning "the Lord's" or "belonging to the Lord". Since all belongs to the Lord and only the term "church" expresses this totality, we should understand the two other phrases in relationship to this.[4] It is with these understandings that I will use the two terms, first looking at the *domus ecclesiae* and all that supports it and then concluding by examining the *domus Dei*, the church as a sacred building in society, as an icon of the Heavenly Jerusalem, and as an epiphany of the God who loves mankind.

Liturgy, community, and active participation

It is God alone who gathers the parish community to participate in the liturgy, the "public work" of worship. The community does not meet on its own initiative or spontaneously, but rather it is called into being by the Word of God.[5] The liturgy is the Church's great work. "Liturgy has a cosmic and universal dimension. The community does not become a community by mutual interaction. It receives its being as a gift from an already existing completeness, totality, and in return it gives itself back to this totality. . . . This is why liturgy cannot be 'made.'"[6] Likewise, the parish community is not "made" but comes into being by individuals responding to the call of God to offer the sacrifice of the Eucharist:

> For no Christian community can be built up unless it has as its basis and pivot the celebration of the holy Eucharist. It is from this

facets of the one reality. The *ecclesia* incorporates both clerics and laity, for both respond to God's call, albeit in different ways. The term expresses the whole community gathered as one, and with the two priesthoods "ordered to one another; each in its own proper way shares in the one priesthood of Christ."[3] For our purposes, let us use *domus ecclesiae* to address the horizontal relationships within the body of Christ: brother to sister, cleric to lay, and prayer community to both the diocese and the universal Church. The phrase *domus Dei*, which speaks of the "house of God", can appropriately be applied to the vertical relationships of the Body: God to the person and the assembly, the assembly and the individual to God. The Judeo-Christian concept of God is one of revelation: God desires to make himself known to us so that we can love him in return. Since God reveals his presence to man primarily by signs (the wind of Ezekiel, the Ark, the Eucharist), the term *domus Dei* also can apply to the symbolic, or the iconic, as well as to the sacred aspects of the church building. *Domus*

---

[3] Vatican II, *Lumen Gentium* (Nov. 21, 1964), no. 10 [= LG].

[4] Clement of Alexandria used the term Ο᾿κον κυριακόν, or "The Lord's house", to describe the place where the church met. Cf. *Stromata*, 3,18 in PG, VIII, 32.

[5] Fr. Louis Bouyer, *Life and Liturgy* (London: Sheed and Ward, 1956), 32.

[6] Joseph Cardinal Ratzinger, *The Feast of Faith* (San Francisco: Ignatius Press, 1986), 66.

therefore that any attempt to form a community must begin.[7]

Plainly and simply, the parish is founded on a theological reality because it is a Eucharistic community. This means that the parish is a community properly suited for celebrating the Eucharist, the living source for its upbuilding and the sacramental bond of its being in full communion with the whole Church.[8]

This is why the altar and the crucifix are the proper *foci* of the liturgy: they are signs of Christ's presence and action among his people. So we must understand, before designing a place for the people of God, that the primary sacramental community is called into being by God, and it is from this that the community of persons is built.

"In the celebration of the Eucharist, a sense of community should be encouraged."[9] Hence, the architect must work to create a sense of *place* for this community, to augment the individual's awareness that it is God who has called the Church together to be present among them. This individual awareness of God's action is at the heart of *participatio actuosa*, the active participation of the laity in the Mass, which is so earnestly desired by the Church: "This purpose [that the participating ministers and faithful may more fully receive the good effects of the Eucharist] will be best accomplished if . . . the celebration is planned in such a way that it brings about in the faithful a participation in body and spirit that is conscious, active, full, and motivated by faith, hope, and charity. The Church desires this kind of participation, the nature of the celebration demands it, and for the Christian people it is a right and duty they have by reason of their baptism."[10]

There is, however, another dimension of active participation within the liturgy. In *Christifideles laici*, Pope John Paul II writes of the growing awareness among the laity that they have certain tasks to perform within the liturgy and for its preparation. The Pope has permitted more lay service in the Mass, writing: "It is, therefore, natural that the tasks not proper to the ordained ministers be fulfilled by the lay faithful. In this way there is a natural transition from an effective involvement of the lay

faithful in the liturgical action to that of announcing the word of God and pastoral care." The Pope, however, goes on to warn against a "clericalization" of the laity and the creation of a parallel ecclesial structure of lay "ministers". The differentiation must be maintained "between the ministerial priesthood and the common priesthood, and the difference between the ministries derived from the Sacrament of Orders and those derived from the Sacraments of Baptism and Confirmation."[11] The main task of the priestly people grows from "their specific lay vocation", that is, the work of bringing the gospel into the world through "evangelizing activities" in politics, economics, the sciences, the arts, media, education, and so on.[12]

It is unfortunate that many modern liturgists have equated "active participation" primarily with external activities[13]—such as being a lector, extraordinary minister of Communion, or sacred dancer—or with physical proximity to the altar as in "gathering 'round the table of Lord". Some liturgists are now beginning to question this whole approach to the liturgy: "The faithful do at times play a part in the liturgy by answering, singing and reading, but all this remains at the level of external formalism. There is no corresponding authentic commitment to the community outside the celebration."[14] And even less have these concepts of active participation truly allowed the lay faithful to enter into the sacrificial aspects of the Mass.

True liturgical participation is not so much a question of singing, dancing, reading, or being close to the altar. It is, rather, an inner process,

[7] Sacred Congregation of Rites, *Eucharisticum mysterium* (May 25, 1967), no. 13 [= EM]. Also Vatican II, *Presbyterorum ordinis* (Dec. 7, 1965), no. 9.

[8] John Paul II, *Christifideles laici* (Dec. 30, 1988), no. 26 [= CL]. Emphasis in original.

[9] EM, no. 18.

[10] *General Instruction of the Roman Missal*, 4th ed. (Mar. 27, 1975), no. 3 [= GIRM].

[11] CL, no. 23.

[12] Ibid., quoting Paul VI, *Evangelii nuntiandi* (Dec. 8, 1975), no. 70.

[13] Ratzinger, *Feast*, 123.

[14] L. Maldonado, "Liturgy as Communal Enterprise", in *The Reception of Vatican II*, ed. G. Alberigo, trans. Matthew J. O'Connell (Washington, D.C.: Catholic University Press, 1987), 310.

a conversion, an offering of one's self in the sacrifice. As Pope Pius XII wrote in *Mediator Dei*, "But the chief element of divine worship must be interior. For we must always live in Christ and give ourselves to Him completely, so that in Him, with Him, and through Him the heavenly Father may be duly glorified." [15] Similarly, *Sacrosanctum concilium* warns that "it is necessary that the faithful come to [the Mass] with proper dispositions, that their minds be attuned to their voices, and that they cooperate with heavenly grace lest they receive it in vain." [16] It is only from this interior process that full participation in the liturgy can truly happen. Only then can the faithful, "by virtue of their royal priesthood, participate in the offering of the Eucharist. They exercise that priesthood, too, by the reception of the sacraments, prayer and thanksgiving, the witness of a holy life, abnegation and active charity." [17] *Lumen Gentium* expresses the depth and breadth of the true priestly sacrifice of the lay faithful:

> For all their works, prayers and apostolic undertakings, family and married life, daily work, relaxation of mind and body, if they are accomplished in the Spirit—indeed even the hardships of life if patiently borne—all these become spiritual sacrifices acceptable to God through Jesus Christ (cf. 1 Pet 2:5). In the celebration of the Eucharist these may most fittingly be offered to the Father along with the body of the Lord. And so, worshipping everywhere by their holy actions, the laity consecrate the world itself to God. [18]

In *Christifideles laici*, Pope John Paul II amplifies this by stating, "Incorporated in Jesus Christ, the baptized are united to him and to his sacrifice in the offering they make of themselves and their daily activity." [19] Again, the emphasis is placed on the interior disposition of the faithful. The main architectural problem, then, is to create a place where, unimpeded, the laity can best enter into the liturgy:

> The role of the faithful in the Eucharist is to recall the passion, resurrection, and glorification of the Lord, to give thanks to God, and to offer the immaculate victim not only through the hands of the priest, but also together with him; and finally, by receiving the

6.2 "Church as Theater", St. Timothy's, Mesa, Arizona.

Body of the Lord, to perfect that communion with God and among themselves which should be the product of participation in the sacrifice of the Mass. For the faithful achieve a more perfect participation in the Mass when, with proper dispositions, they receive the Body of the Lord sacramentally in the Mass itself, in obedience to his words "take and eat." [20]

Too often we have settled for facile solutions to the problem of community and active participation; e.g., "liturgy in the round", church-qua-dining room or lounge. One author innocently comments that "following the example of the theatre, the Church now offers 'communion in the round' and encourages audience participation" [fig. 6.2]. [21] As if Christ's gathered faithful were an "audience"!

The problem with these approaches is that they fail to reach the heart of the matter. What is needed is "an architecture of conversion", a building in which people can pray, a place where the individual and the community can enter into God's presence and find true union

---

[15] Pius XII, *Mediator Dei* (Nov. 20, 1947), no. 26 [= MD].
[16] Vatican II, *Sacrosanctum concilium* (Dec. 4, 1963), no. 11 [= SC].
[17] LG, no. 10.
[18] LG, no. 34.
[19] CL, no. 14.
[20] EM, no. 12.
[21] G. Frere-Cook, ed., *Decorative Arts of the Christian Church* (London: Cassell, 1972), 286.

with one another in the Eucharist. The primary goal in church design is to create a space in which the faithful can enter unhindered into the sacrifice of the Mass both body and soul, for "the worship rendered by the Church to God must be, in its entirety, interior as well as exterior. It is exterior because the nature of man as a composite body and soul requires it to be so."[22]

Designing the nave

In planning the nave there are several complex and subtle relationships to facilitate. There are delicate balances to be struck between the sacrificial and communal aspects of the liturgy, between the need for sacred space and the desire for intimacy and proximity, and between expressing the differentiation of the clerical from the lay priesthoods and expressing the unity of the body of Christ. These concerns show that great care is required in shaping the seating in relationship to the sanctuary and the whole of the church. The principles for this balance can be derived from some of the key passages in the *General Instruction of the Roman Missal*:

> The people of God assembled at Mass possess an organic and hierarchical structure, expressed by the various ministries and actions for each part of the celebration. The general plan of the sacred edifice should be such that it conveys the image in some way of the gathered assembly. It should also allow the participants to take the place most appropriate to them and assist all to carry out their individual functions properly.
> The congregation and the choir should have a place that facilitates their active participation. . . .[23]

> The places for the faithful should be arranged with care so that the people are able to take their rightful part in the celebration visually and mentally. . . . Chairs or benches should be set up in such a way that the people can easily take the positions required during various celebrations and have unimpeded access to receive communion.[24]

From these passages we can see several things. First, the assembly is "organic", organized as a living system of related parts. Second, the hierarchical structure is essential, and the arrangement of the nave and sanctuary should express this relationship. Third, the places for the faithful, including the choir (about which more shall be said later), should be carefully planned to allow full participation. This includes provision for sitting, kneeling, and standing with good visibility and audibility, and with reasonable proximity. Fourth, the arrangement must facilitate and express the true unity of the Church, found in praying together, sharing in the sacrifice with a union of mind, heart, purpose and posture: "The uniformity in standing, kneeling, or sitting to be observed by all taking part is a sign of the community and the unity of the assembly; it both expresses and fosters the spiritual attitude of those taking part."[25]

Fifth, since during the course of the liturgy practically everyone moves around to receive Communion, easy traffic circulation should be planned. This should allow for liturgical processions as well. The main circulation in the church should be by way of a wide, formal, processional aisle down the center of the nave.[26] During the entrance procession the congregation stands to honor Christ, who is entering the church in the person of the celebrant: "For it is he who, represented by the celebrant, makes his entrance into the sanctuary and proclaims his Gospel."[27] Likewise, other occasions, such as Palm Sunday, Holy Thursday, Easter Vigil, Corpus Christi, weddings, and funerals, call for formal processions. If the church symbolizes "the heavenly Jerusalem", the designer must account for traffic patterns inside the city. Hence, there should be loop routes so communicants can return to their seats without crossing the paths of those going to receive. There should be no dead ends in the aisles, nor should the routes be unduly circuitous. If possible, all rows of seats should offer

---

[22] MD, no. 23.
[23] GIRM, no. 257.
[24] GIRM, no. 273.
[25] GIRM, no. 20.
[26] While the aisle does not *demand* to be centered, the church is traditionally symmetrical, and it seems that there ought to be some truly overriding reason for having an asymmetrical or skewed nave.
[27] John Paul II, *Dominicae cenae* (Feb. 24, 1980), no. 8 [= DC].

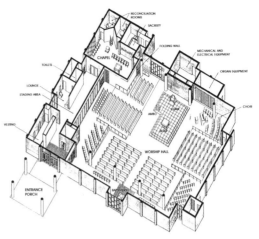

6.5 Patchwork Quilt Seating, St. Patrick's, Baton Rouge, La., by William C. Burks, AIA.

6.3 *top* Traditional Pew Arrangement, Madonna della Strada, Chicago.

6.4 *bottom* Theater Seating Arrangement, Madonna della Strada, Chicago.

free passage without columns blocking the path. Perimeter circulation facilitates loop routes and makes for a processional route for the stations of the Cross, as well as allowing the priest to cover the entire congregation at the asperges.

The architect's primary task is to arrive at a suitable arrangement that respects both the hierarchical and organic qualities of the assembly. The arrangement of rows of parallel pews with a definite cleft between the nave and sanctuary emphasizes the hierarchical issue quite clearly [fig. 6.3]. Conversely, the "theater in the round" model ignores the complexity of the church as an ordered body with a multiplicity of functions [fig. 6.4]. Other recent experiments have developed "patchwork quilt" plans [fig. 6.5], and a return to the monastic choir assembly, sometimes called "antiphonal seating", with the ambo and altar at opposite ends of a central space dividing the assembly [fig. 6.6], much like the opposition arrangement of the British House of Commons [fig. 6.7].

To resolve this vital question of the seating arrangement, it is important again to recall exactly what it is that the lay people "do" at Mass. Only then will we be able to determine where

6.6 Antiphonal Choir Arrangement, Madonna della Strada, Chicago.

6.7 British House of Commons, London.

the lay people should be. I would refer the reader, especially if he is part of the planning process for a new or reordered building, to chapters 1 and 3 to meditate on the action of the individuals and the assembly at the Eucharist.

Seating for the assembly

The Mass is dynamic, with a rhythm and cadence all its own. The community rises to greet the celebrant at the entrance and stands for the penitential rite, sits for the lesser readings but rises again to acknowledge Christ in the Gospel, kneels for the Consecration only to arise victoriously in the joy of the Great Amen, and so on.

Historically, the pew is a fairly late arrival, first appearing during the late Middle Ages. Before that time the laity stood or knelt as required, as seating was not generally provided. Up to this time, it is interesting to note, men and women were often separated during the liturgy. In the Christian East, women sometimes stood in a gallery above the nave called the *gynaikon.* In the Christian West, in what Bishop Durand explains as an ancient tradition, citing Saint Bede as a reference, the women were often placed to the north and west and the men to the south and east. Modern women need not resent this separation, since, as Durand explicates, "the saints who are most advanced in holiness should stand against the greater temptations of this world: and they who are less advanced, against the less."[28] For the medievals, who placed Hades in the west and thought the north to be the land of paganism, this arrangement gave the women of the community the role of protecting the less holy and less strong from the greater temptation! As is seen in Saint Charles Borromeo's *Instructiones*, this arrangement was still found in the sixteenth century. Saint Charles recommended a demountable wall (or partition), about six feet ten inches high (five Milanese cubits), "going in a straight line through the middle of the nave from the main chapel entrance to the main door . . . so as to divide it in half, and so divided it will facilitate a distinct entrance into the Church for the men and for the women." This necessitated both oc-

casional doors in the boarding, which were to be opened only when it was necessary to pass from one side to the other, and horizontally hinged upper panels that could be dropped so that the entire congregation could see the preacher and the celebrant.[29]

From the thirteenth century, some churches had backless benches. Pews as such were adopted first by the Protestants, enabling them to sit during the hours-long sermons. These, likewise, became more common among Catholics with the Counter Reformation liturgical emphasis on the proclamation of the Word. By the late sixteenth century the benches became bigger and fixed, with kneelers and high backs, and often with elaborately carved end panels. This was not the universal case, however. Saint Charles allowed for low seating and kneeling benches, called *predelle*, on the women's side of the nave. He insisted, however, that, "on the side of the Church reserved for men, there should be no benches to kneel upon."[30]

With the recent reordering of churches, many churches have removed the pews in favor of interlocking separate chairs. These have both advantages and disadvantages. Separate seating goes a long way toward breaking down the rigidity of the nave and can offer a more organic expression of the assembly. Though chairs better express the individual person in the congregation, they also diminish the family aspect of the pew. Perhaps the poorest argument is that they also allow for the church to be easily rearranged: a rather dubious symbolism, as churches should speak to the "eternal" rather than the "temporary". The other problem with chairs is that individual seats can remind us of theater seating. They can suggest a spectator relationship and hence may not encourage true participation.

Chairs, if used, should be very sturdy. If they

---

[28] Bishop Guillaume Durand, *The Symbolism of Churches and Church Ornaments: A Translation of the First Book of the* Rationale divinorum officiorum, trans. J. M. Neale and B. Webb (Leeds: T. W. Green, 1843; reprint New York: AMS Press, 1973), bk. 1, chap. 1, no. 46.

[29] St. Charles Borromeo, *Instructiones Fabricae et Supellectillis Ecclesiasticae* (Instructions on ecclesiastical buildings), trans. Evelyn Carol Voelker. Ph.D. diss., Syracuse University, 1977 (Ann Arbor, Mich.: University Microfilms International, n.d.), 318.

[30] Ibid., 324.

are to be regularly moved, they should be light as well. Stacking chairs generally do not work well, as they have no provision for kneeling or for missal storage. Some styles of chairs have hinged kneelers, others have simple movable cushions, which store beneath the chair to the front. The chairs should be comfortably padded, but without the "artificially plush" seating of a theater.[31] Above all, the chairs must be of high quality. Cheap plastic or metal folding chairs give the church "the sense of a lecture hall, and the feel of impermanence and lack of concern for beauty".[32]

In some instances, depending on the local culture, permanent seating may not be necessary. Portable "kneeling benches", similar to Saint Charles' *predelle*, are sometimes used in monasteries, convents, university chaplaincies, Newman Centers, and Blessed Sacrament chapels. The laity might also be given kneeling cushions for the Consecration and Communion meditation, and they could stand for the remainder of Mass. Either built-in perimeter seating or a few dozen movable chairs could easily accommodate the elderly or the infirm. This is the common arrangement in much of the Christian East. The structure of the community would then perhaps more suggest the quality of the "people of God", amorphously gathered around the altar, focused but unregimented, evoking the crowds that gathered to hear Jesus as he taught on the hillside or from the boat.

It is lamentable that the removal of pews in many churches, especially in America, has led to the discarding of kneelers and even of the practice of kneeling. The Church calls the faithful to kneel at the Consecration,[33] and not without reason, for at this moment the bread and wine are changed into the Body and Blood of Christ. Kneeling is the traditional and central posture for worship and one that is found throughout Scripture: the Lord knelt to pray (Lk 22:41), as did Stephen (Acts 7:60), Peter (Acts 9:40), and Paul (Acts 20:36). Furthermore, "the hymn to Christ in Philippians 2:6–11 speaks of the cosmic liturgy as a bending of the knee at the name of Jesus. . . . In bending the knee at the name of Jesus, the Church is acting in all truth; she is entering into the cos-

mic gesture."[34] This is no small point, and we should not be quick to discard this bodily gesture. As the *General Instruction of the Roman Missal* insists, "the faithful should kneel at the consecration unless prevented by the lack of space, the number of people present, or some other good reason."[35] So, in the normal parish situation, some accommodation for the faithful to kneel during the liturgy should be made, regardless of the type of seating used.

Thought must be given also to provisions for the disabled. The Americans with Disabilities Act of 1990 (ADA) now sets accessibility requirements for all public buildings.[36] Although churches are explicitly exempted from ADA compliance, there are, nonetheless, special provisions to be considered for the church community. Inviting entrances with ample disabled parking, curb cuts, and wheelchair ramps will help the disabled enter more easily. We should take our cue from the paralytic in Luke 5:18–19 and make provision so that the disabled do not need to cut holes in the church roof in order to approach the sacraments. "Pew cuts" on the ends will allow the chair-bound to sit with their families. In numerous parishes, areas are set aside for the deaf and hearing impaired in clear sight of a signing interpreter. We should do all we can to encourage the disabled to participate fully in the sacramental and mission life of the community. We must, therefore, remove all obstacles in the buildings that hinder them from coming to the Lord.[37]

The last general consideration is whether or not to provide a cry room for nursing mothers

---

[31] Fr. J. O'Connell, *Church Building and Furnishing, the Church's Way* (London: Burns and Oates, 1955), 68–71; also Frs. Stephen and Cuthbert Johnson, *Planning for Liturgy* (Farnborough, England: St. Michael's, 1983), 27-29.

[32] Personal correspondence with Gregory Tatum, O.P.

[33] And in some countries, such as the U.S., during the entire Eucharistic Prayer. Cf. the American Appendix to GIRM, no. 21: "At its meeting in November, 1969, the National Conference of Catholic Bishops voted that . . . the *General Instruction* should be adapted so the people kneel beginning after the singing or recitation of the Sanctus until after the Amen of the Eucharistic prayer."

[34] Ratzinger, *Feast*, 74.

[35] GIRM, no. 21.

[36] While religious institutions are legally exempted from this regulation, the higher law suggests that we set the example to open our churches to the suffering members of the Body.

[37] Cf. Kelly Norton Humphrey, "Let Us in the Church!" *Catholic Digest*, January 1994, 111–16.

and babies. Some see the cry room as segregating and penalizing young families and showing "a disheartening contempt for new life", arguing quite rightly that families with young children "should have seats of honor in our churches, welcomed for the sacrifices they make and the example they give".[38] Even so, some parents would appreciate a place where they could participate in the Mass with their infants close at hand for nursing or changing and yet not have their crying baby disturb the congregation. If a cry room is to be provided, it should be designed as an integral part of the assembly, looking into the nave, with a good view to the sanctuary. It should be acoustically isolated with double glazing, door seals, and other such measures. As such, the room should have a monitor speaker with a volume control connected to the sound system so the parents can hear the Mass in progress.[39] If possible, it should be located near the washrooms and have changing facilities. Some churches have adapted side chapels near the sanctuary as cry rooms; such an arrangement can be easily accommodated in a new project.

The choir

Liturgical music today is in some ways more complex than the organ and choir music before the Second Vatican Council, with the introduction of modern instruments into the liturgy (viz., acoustic and electric guitars, pianos and keyboards, drum sets, and so on). The pipe organ, which has been used liturgically since the eighth or ninth century,[40] is still considered "the traditional musical instrument" in the Latin Church and "is to be held in high esteem".[41] Other instruments deemed worthy by competent local authorities may be used "only on the condition that the instruments are suitable, or can be made suitable, for sacred use; that they accord with the dignity of the temple, and that they truly contribute to the edification of the faithful".[42] The Instruction *Musicam sacram* does allow that "the culture and traditions of individual peoples must be taken into account" and thus gives scope to differing musical expressions and instrumentation, as long as they are used appropriately:

"Any musical instrument permitted in divine worship should be used in such a way that it meets the needs of the liturgical celebration, and is in the interests both of the beauty of worship and the edification of the faithful."[43]

As this is not a paper on sacred music, it is not the place to discuss whether or not electric guitar, synthesizers, and drum sets fulfill the above-mentioned requirements. In some ways music has become a more active part of the Mass, especially in America, where parishes now hire "music ministers" who not only lead the congregation in worship but compose as well. This is certainly in keeping with the effect sought in *Liturgiae instaurationes*: "All means must be used to promote singing by the people. New forms of music suited to different mentalities and to modern tastes should also be approved by episcopal conferences." Within this proviso, however, is the significant caveat: "Though the Church does not exclude any kind of sacred music from the liturgy, not every type of music, song or instrument is equally capable of stimulating prayer or expressing the mystery of Christ." The passage, which may be of interest to the reader, goes on to give guidelines for what is considered to be appropriate liturgical music.[44]

Music, especially in the American parish, has changed markedly since the close of the Second Vatican Council. Nevertheless, the pipe organ still holds an esteemed place in the divine worship, and traditional choirs still have their due place. These require consideration and planning. If a pipe organ is not financially feasible in the initial budget, a pipe organ specialist should be consulted to make plans for the future addition of an organ. Since a pipe organ is a very expensive piece of furnishing and one that requires truly expert specialization, a specialist should be consulted beforehand to site, size, and design the organ

---

[38] Personal correspondence from Gregory Tatum, O.P.

[39] The Bishops' Conference of England and Wales, *The Parish Church* (London: Catholic Truth Society, 1984), 122.

[40] O'Connell, *Church Building*, 87.

[41] SC, no. 120.

[42] Ibid.

[43] Sacred Congregation of Rites, *Musicam sacram* (Mar. 5, 1967), no. 63 [= MS].

[44] Sacred Congregation for Divine Worship, *Liturgiae instaurationes* (Sept. 5, 1970), no. 3.a.

properly for the particular space, so it is not added as an afterthought.[45]

The choir area should be large enough for an organ console and a large choir. The location must allow the choir to lead the congregation in musical worship and must be in a suitable place so that the instruments "can sustain the singing of the choir and congregation and be heard with ease when they are played alone".[46] Since the choir is part of the assembly of the faithful, the location needs to function for both the exercise of the choir's role and the participation of the members in the liturgy.

In monasteries, when the choir or *schola cantorum* was composed of religious, it was usually within the *cancelli* in front of the sanctuary [fig. 6.8]. The liturgical movement of the Baroque age removed it to a choir loft at the back of the church, thus enabling the sanctuary to be more integrated with the nave. Most recently the choir is often placed to one side of the sanctuary so that the members may be clearly seen and may easily participate in the Mass. As in many design considerations involving the liturgy, there is necessarily a certain tension in arriving at an arrangement that adequately and appropriately addresses the diverse concerns. The purpose of the choir, or "music ministry", is to *support* the liturgy; therefore its place should not be overstated. By virtue of its operation, the choir can naturally draw the congregation's attention and even unintentionally compete with activities in the sanctuary. In the past, this had been mitigated against in several ways. For one, when the *cancelli* or the *schola cantorum* was placed between the nave and the high altar, the choir sat on either side, parallel to the nave, with members facing one another. The congregation had an unobstructed view to the sanctuary, and the choir was organically integrated in both the liturgy and the architectural arrangement. In other situations, particularly in monasteries, the choirs of monks were arranged in the apse around the rear half of the sanctuary to form a backdrop to the liturgy. It should also be noted that within these traditions, with monks wearing robes, deacons in dalmatics, and minor clerics and lay and religious choristers wearing surplices or habits, the choir retained a sense

6.8 Cancelli, San Clemente, Rome.

of corporate identity harmonious with the requirements of the Mass.

If the choir is to be located near the sanctuary, it should be done so judiciously. Modern music is often more "performance oriented" than traditional ecclesial music. Hence, due care must be taken to avoid the appearance of a performance, perhaps by placing the musicians well to the side of the sanctuary. The choir can also be placed at the rear of the church, or even in a gallery. Some suggest that the sound of the choir from behind the congregation better fills the church and helps the faithful to sing along, so the cantor or music minister can be placed in front and the choir in a loft to the rear. If the nave is shallow and broad, the choir can be placed in a loft that wraps around the congregation from behind, thus both giving a degree of intimacy and aiding participation.

How best to position the choir is left to the ingenuity and judgment of the design team. The most important considerations are that the choir be placed so as to lead the musical worship effectively; second, that the choir can operate and be seen as a distinctive but integral part of the assembly; and third, that the choir may participate easily in the liturgy, both corporately and individually.[47] The choir or

[45] Cf. Johnson, *Planning for Liturgy*, 47–49.
[46] GIRM, no. 275.
[47] MS, no. 23, and GIRM, no. 274.

music group will also require a room for robing choristers, a practice room for the musicians, and storage space for instruments and music.

The narthex

> The Church is . . . a sheepfold, the sole and necessary gateway to which is Christ (Jn 10:1-10) (*Lumen Gentium*, no. 6).

The church's main door means more than just an entrance to the building; it is a symbol of a whole process of transition and conversion. Entering the church means leaving the world behind and entering the Kingdom of God; it allows us to cast off the workday cares and troubles to find solace, healing, and sanctuary. It is even a foretaste of entering the very gates of heaven, in that "the earthly liturgy is a foretaste of the heavenly liturgy." [48] In the Middle Ages, Abbot Suger explicitly tells us that he modeled the western façade of Saint-Denis on the idea of a great city gate, complete with towers, to call this entrance to mind [fig. 6.9]. [49] During the Renaissance, Alberti, for instance, expressed this same idea with a Roman triumphal arch, suggesting that the worshipper entered the glory of heaven through the doors of the church [figs. 6.10, 6.11]. [50]

The narthex, a large entrance hall or porch, is the traditional entrance to the church: it functions as a place of welcome into the House of the Father. This sense of refuge, of invitation, historically was extended to all mankind, even to those who could not or would not participate in the liturgy. Symbolically, it expressed the unredeemed world: hence it was the place in the early Church for catechumens when the *disciplina arcani* was enforced, as well as the place for penitents, the excommunicated, and pagans. Here they could hear the Gospel and the instructions without participating in the eucharistic mysteries. Today these subtle understandings have been all but lost; the narthex now provides for the secular needs of the church—notice boards, parish bulletins, book and newspaper racks, bake sales, men's and women's washrooms, and so forth.

6.9 Saint-Denis, Paris, by Abbot Suger, 1140, Exterior.

Yet it is still a transitional space between the secular and the sacred and serves to buffer the nave from the hustle and bustle of the city street. This is part of the transition in the hierarchical procession from the secular to the sacred. Mircea Eliade writes of this process in his discussion of the difference between sacred and profane spaces:

> For a believer, the church shares in a different space from the street in which it stands. The door that opens on the interior of a church actually signifies a solution of continuity. The threshold that separates the two spaces also indicates the distance between the two modes of being, the profane and the religious. The threshold is the limit, the boundary, the frontier that distinguishes and opposes two worlds—and at the same time the paradoxical

---

[48] SC, no. 8.
[49] Otto von Simson, *The Gothic Cathedral*, 2d ed. (New York: Pantheon Books, 1962), 108–9.
[50] R. Wittkower, *Architectural Principles in the Age of Humanism*, 3d ed. (London: Alec Tiranti, 1962), 37–38; also Joseph Rykwert, *Church Building* (London: Sheed and Ward, 1966), 101.

6.10 San Francesco Rimini, by L. Alberti, 1450– , Exterior.

6.11 Arch of Constantine, Rome, 312–315.

place where those worlds communicate, where passage from the profane to the sacred world becomes possible.[51]

6.12 Old St. Peter's, Plan and Isometric.

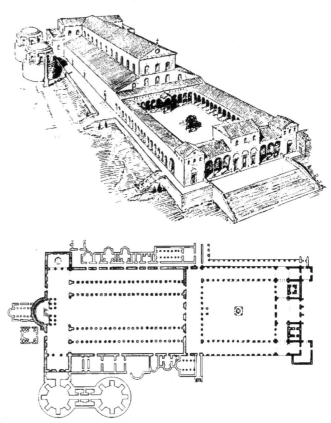

This process has been architecturally expressed throughout the history of church building [fig. 6.12]. It begins at the entrance to the courtyard, passes through the narthex and the nave to the sanctuary, and culminates at the altar or at the tabernacle. In this model, the narthex, as a transitional space, allows time and space for personal preparation, in order that the faithful may better prepare for the liturgy.

The narthex is also a place of welcome for those preparing to be received into the Church either through baptism or with confirmation. Thus the proper place for the baptistery is traditionally, liturgically, and symbolically either in or directly off the narthex. This idea of preparation and entrance has had varied expressions throughout the ages. One of the more remarkable cases is seen at the great Romanesque pilgrimage church in Vézelay, France. Here, at the doors between the narthex and nave, the floor steps down a few inches to create large shallow recesses at each portal. It is thought that they were probably filled with

---

[51] Mircea Eliade, *The Sacred and the Profane: The Nature of Religion*, trans. Willard R. Trask (New York: Harcourt, Brace, 1959), 25.

6.13 Holy Water Stoup,
St. Paul's-outside-the-Walls.

6.14 Detail, Holy Water Stoup,
St. Paul's-outside-the-Walls, Rome.

water to create pools through which the pilgrims would walk when entering the church to remind them of their baptism. Such an experience would have surely also called to mind the Israelites passing through the Red Sea, as well as such places as the Pool of Siloam, where Jesus cured the ill. Today most parishes are satisfied with holy water stoups placed in the narthex to remind the faithful, as they enter the church, of their baptismal vows.

The stoup frequently found exuberant expression, especially in the Baroque age. At Saint Paul's Outside the Walls in Rome, we find a wonderfully sculpted stoup showing a young boy casting away a demon by the power of the holy water [figs. 6.13, 6.14]. In another vein, at the church of Sant' Agostino near the Piazza Navona, in Rome, there is a large stoup borne by Saint Raphael, the archangel and healer [fig. 6.15]. These sorts of didactic statement remind us of the need to continue to immerse ourselves in Christ's power to overcome evil, to find healing, and to make spiritual progress.

Another aspect of personal preparation is the need for repentance. If the church is fairly quiet, the narthex is a good place for the confessionals, where the penitent can be recon-

6.15 Holy Water Stoup, Archangel Raphael, Sant' Agostino, Rome.

ciled before entering the nave. This can work especially well if the Blessed Sacrament must be reserved in a separate chapel. If the Blessed Sacrament chapel is adjacent to the narthex, and near the confessionals, the architect can create a processional relationship between the sacrament of penance and the reserved Species, thus giving architectural expression to the words of Pope John Paul II: "It is not only that Penance leads to the Eucharist, but that the Eucharist also leads to Penance."[52]

The narthex also serves as a gathering place and assembly area for processions. As such, the main doors of the church need to be quite large to allow enough room for a prelate with miter or for pallbearers carrying a casket. Because the entrance procession begins in the narthex, it is advantageous to have the vestry adjacent to the narthex. As it is also a staging area for wedding processions, a bride's room should be provided off the narthex and near the women's washroom. The bride's room should be large enough to accommodate a number of women (often in large dresses) and should be cheerful, well lighted, and well ventilated, with mirrored vanities and full-length mirrors.

Social activities and their provisions

The Church is a community. The early Church worshipped and served together, fed the poor, cared for those in need, and even held material possessions in common. As the Church grew, dioceses were formed to unite the local congregation to the universal Church through the local bishop. As these dioceses grew, parishes were created to unite the faithful under a pastor who was the bishop's representative.[53] The parish church was the spiritual home and often the social center of the community. This sense of community is being lost today, partly due to our increasingly transient and mobile Western society. Because of the strong forces in our society that work to isolate us, the parish must strive to remain (or, in most cases, become) the center of a Catholic's life.

Vatican II calls us to make the parish the center of our community life again. *Christifideles laici* reminds us that the parish "is not principally a structure, a territory, or a building, but rather, 'the family of God, a fellowship afire with a unifying spirit,' 'a familial and welcoming home,' the 'community of the faithful.'"[54] Pope John Paul II, following the lead of his predecessor Paul VI, has called for a renewed emphasis on the parish community "to create the basic community of the Christian people; to initiate and gather the people in the accustomed expression of liturgical life; to conserve and renew the faith in the people of today; to serve as the school for teaching the

---

[52] DC, no. 7.
[53] SC, no. 42. Cf. St. Ignatius of Antioch: "Let that be considered a valid Eucharist which is under the bishop or one whom he has delegated" (*Smyr.* 8); quoted in Henry Bettenson, *The Early Christian Fathers* (London: Oxford University Press, 1956), 67.
[54] CL, no. 26.

salvific message of Christ; to put solidarity in practice and work the humble charity of good and brotherly works."[55] This renewed emphasis on the social aspects of the "living" Christian community—viz., education, evangelization, and working to restore the temporal order, which are rooted in and spring forth from the communal liturgy—is very much an integral part of the Second Vatican Council's agenda for renewing the whole Church.

For this to happen, we need to see the parish as more than just a Sunday facility. New churches should be designed with the expectation that they will be active all week long. Churches, therefore, need to be planned to accommodate social functions, group apostolates, and works of service and to be centers for education and evangelization. In *Apostolicam actuositatem*, the Vatican II Decree on the Apostolic Activities of the Laity, the Church calls the laity "to a deeper and deeper awareness of their responsibility and urges them on everywhere to the service of Christ and the Church".[56] Many lay apostolates properly revolve around the parish community.[57] These works, whether they be evangelization, catechetics, or running soup kitchens, clothing banks, or homeless shelters for the needy, require an investment in space and facilities for their success.

In an attempt to foster community spirit, in the 1970s many parishes and architects experimented with "multifunctional" churches. The nave was freed for secular events either by keeping the tabernacle in a separate chapel or by partitioning off the entire sanctuary with a movable wall. Some dioceses also adopted a policy of first constructing a multifunctional building in which to celebrate the liturgy until the new parish was financially able to build a permanent church. This may make some economic sense as a stopgap measure. Unfortunately, it is rare to find a multifunctional building that functions optimally both as a church and as a meeting hall. The first reason, of course, is the lack of an appropriate sense of separation between the profane and the sacred. But the church and the meeting hall have different functions, different needs, and different design constraints that logically should be resolved in different buildings. A church that functions well as a reception room or gymnasium is probably an impoverished church. Therefore, the investment in a social hall is simultaneously an investment that safeguards the sanctity of the church proper.

The social hall needs to serve a multiplicity of functions, and the better equipped it is, the more of service it will be. It should be large enough to hold receptions and dances; it should have a stage, a catering kitchen, separate washrooms, and plenty of storage for chairs and tables. Smaller meeting rooms and classrooms should be provided for religious education and various apostolic groups. Given the current renewal of consciousness toward the social demands of the gospel, the parish should carefully consider what sorts of facilities may be reasonably needed to respond to the various works to which the laity are called.

For an architectural model of a parish as the center of community life, we can look to the ancient Christian basilica, such as San Clemente or Old St. Peter's in Rome, where the buildings were arranged around a central courtyard [figs. 6.12 and 6.16]. This is architecturally derived from both the Jewish and pagan temples, in which an entrance courtyard created a temple precinct. The word *temple* is derived from the Greek verb τέμνω, meaning "to cut" or "to divide". The τέμενος was a piece of land marked off from common uses and dedicated as a sacred precinct to a god. The word *temple*, then, refers not only to the building itself but to the whole of the sacred precinct, including the τέμενος, the semipublic courtyard in front of the building.[58] In the pre-Christian Mediterranean religions, the sacrifice occurred in this courtyard. The temple building was where the statue of the god (or, in the Hebraic instance, the Ark of the Covenant) was housed [fig. 6.17]. This form was adapted to the Christian assembly, with the significant reinterpretation that, as members of the body of Christ, all the faithful could now enter into the sacrifice

---

[55] Ibid., quoting Paul VI, *Discourse to the Roman Clergy* (June 24, 1963).

[56] Vatican II, *Apostolicam actuositatem* (Nov. 18, 1965), no. 1 [= AA].

[57] Cf. AA, nos. 5 and 10.

[58] Rykwert, *Church Building*, 27.

6.16 Courtyard, San Clemente, Rome.

6.17 Forecourt, Model of the Temple in Jerusalem, Holyland Hotel, Jerusalem.

inside the *domus Dei*, because they themselves expressed the presence of the Divine, and their sacrifices in union with the sacrifice of the ministerial priests perfected what was before only hinted at by the idol or the Ark.

Eusebius, in one of the earliest known descriptions of a Christian church, gives us an account of such a building:

> The whole area that he [i.e., the architect] took in was much larger [than just the church building], and he gave the outer enclosure the protection[59] of a wall surrounding the whole, to provide maximum safety for the entire structure. Then he opened up a gateway, wide and towering high, to receive the rays of the rising sun.[60] . . . He does not permit a man who has passed inside the gates to go at once with unhallowed and unwashed feet into the holy places within; he has left a very wide space between the church proper and the first entrances, adorning it all around with four colonnades at right angles, so that the outer walls turn the site into a quadrangle and pillars rise on every side. The space between these he has filled with wooden screens of trellis work. . . . In the middle he left a clear space where the sky can be seen, so that the air is bright and open to the sun's rays. There he placed symbols of sacred purification, constructing the fountains exactly in front of the

cathedral: these with their ample flow of fresh water enable those who are proceeding towards the centre of the sacred precincts to purify themselves.[61]

Eusebius describes the traditional basilican arrangement that has been used throughout history. Saint Charles Borromeo recommends it when ordering the site for a new church: "An atrium should be built in front of the sacred edifice, proportioned to the space and in harmony with the structure of the ecclesiastical building. Porticos should surround the atrium on the inside and decorative work should be architecturally suitable." Citing the Council of Carthage, he advises that the clergy's housing should be grouped around this courtyard.[62]

This historical form can be used effectively today: by adapting this arrangement, by creating a precinct within the city, by creating a forecourt as a semipublic zone, and by then flanking the courtyard with the other facilities,

---

[59] Protection, presumably, from fire.

[60] According to this account, it would seem that the entrance was toward the east. As this was a cathedral church, the liturgy would then have probably been celebrated toward the east, as in the Roman basilica.

[61] Eusebius, *The History of the Church*, trans. G. A. Williamson (New York: Dorset Press, 1965), bk. 10, 4:42ff., 393.

[62] St. Charles Borromeo, *Instructiones*, 75 and 36.

6.18 Courtyard, Esperanza, Mexico.

the modern parish can create a sense of place for activities throughout the week.[63] The courtyard would allow a sense of enclosure for social functions such as bazaars, parish festivals, and wedding receptions [fig. 6.18]. It would also allow for an intermediate transitional area between the street and the church. The church building, then, would be seen, not as an isolated object, but rather as a part of a cluster of activities. Even in a suburban or rural area, this urban planning approach would allow the community to have its own *piazza*, which not only brings together the various facets of parish life but allows for outdoor activities as well. Such a model would express the Church within the larger urban framework as a microcosmic city, the *Civitas Dei*, and give architectural form to what Saint John experienced when he wrote: "I saw the holy city, the new Jerusalem, coming down out of heaven from God, prepared as a bride adorned for her husband; and I heard a great voice from the throne saying, 'Behold, the dwelling of God is with men. He will dwell with them, and they shall be his people, and God himself will be with them'" (Rev 21:2–3).

---

[63] Cf. The German Liturgical Commission, *Guiding Principles for the Design of Churches according to the Spirit of the Roman Liturgy* (1947); conclusion, nos. 1–2.

CHAPTER SEVEN

Sacred Images in the Church

We have considered the functional requirements of the church building, that which is recommended or required to accommodate the liturgy and other aspects of parish life. But the church building needs to satisfy more than just functional requirements: it also has important value as a symbol. That is to say, the forms of the building itself should address the idea of "church" both to the parish community and as a part of the urban fabric. It should in some way speak of what it is: not a secular building surmounted by a cross, but a sacred building: a place set aside for God and his people. Furthermore, it should speak to us of the Body of Christ, the Kingdom of God, or the heavenly Jerusalem. To some degree, a church may begin to take on this character if it is truly well ordered for the liturgy and for parish life. However, we must look beyond the functional arrangements so that even the language and grammar of the building might contribute to our understanding of the things of God. To give direction to this inquiry of the symbolic aspects of the building, it may be helpful to look first at the sacred image, or *icon*, on the small scale, considering its theological value, its historical treatment, and its place in the church today. Then we may turn our attention to the whole building and consider the idea of the church as an icon, what it has meant historically, and what it means today.

The theology and history of the icon

Throughout the history of Christianity, the sacred image has been an important part of the church's furnishing. Through frescoes, mosaics, stone and wood carving, painted icons, and stained glass, artisans have contributed significantly to the environmental quality of the building by filling them (and our minds) with images depicting the Lord Jesus, our Lady, the angels and the saints, and stories from Scripture and hagiography. The early Christians illustrated their meeting and burial places with signs of their faith: images and symbols of Christ, portraits of martyrs, and murals of biblical events or of heaven. This they did for several reasons: to commemorate people and events, to help focus prayer and meditation, and to teach both children and catechumens about the Faith. Most important, however, was to depict the truths of the gospel in material media. From her earliest days, the Church recognized a unity and harmony in the ways in which God reveals himself: in the person of Christ, in the words of the Gospels, and in their emblemization in the symbolic, graphic language of icons.

It is difficult for modern Western thinkers to penetrate the idea of the icon. The modern understanding of a symbol is that it gives physical reality a poetical meaning. But for the iconodule, and medieval man in general, the physical itself was but a symbol of the reality. What is "true" in today's culture are facts, data, quantifiable information—ultimately what is material and therefore scientifically or mathematically demonstrable. This consciousness often traps us in the position of being detached observers of reality. But what was ultimately true for the pre-Cartesian man, as well as for many today who have rejected the Enlightenment, is that which is spiritual, that which is of God: the One who created and therefore defines material reality. The Augustinian and Scholastic tradition sees that all created things reflect, or resemble, their Creator by way of *vestigium*, that is, by "vestige" or by "trace". Rational creatures resemble the Creator by *imago*, we are images of the divine, we are "made in his image". Thus what is to be known through the symbol, the icon, is not the knowledge gained through abstraction or detached analysis. It is, rather, a deep and vibrant knowledge acquired through participation, as lovers know each other. And through this fully human participation in the created world, we can come to know God in the type of profound and holistic relationship for which he created us. All things lead us to God. Hence, all things are symbolic of the reality behind the symbol. This is why for the medieval man the symbol is "the only objectively valid definition of reality".[1]

Throughout both Eastern and Western Christianity, validation and explanation of the sacred image are traced to the same source: Dionysius the Areopagite.[2] This mysterious sixth-century theologian wrote that the whole of creation is a "theophany", or a manifestation of God. Because the finite human mind is incapable of apprehending the infinity of God, God reveals himself to man through Scripture, creation, and images.[3] This idea, of course, is a development of what Saint Paul wrote: "For what can be known about God is plain to them, because God has shown it to them. Ever since the creation of the world his invisible nature, namely, his eternal power and deity, has been clearly perceived in the things that have been made" (Rom 1:19–20). What we know about God and his creation is revealed through the image or, to use the Greek word, *eikon*. First and foremost, God gave us the great revelation of his son Jesus Christ as the "image of the invisible God" (Col 1:15). There are numerous other scriptural references that speak to the christological basis of the icon (cf. Jn 1:18, 12:45, 14:9; 2 Cor 4:4). It is significant that theologians consider the second Person of the Trinity—the "Word made flesh"—to be "the Pri-

mordial Icon".[4] It is because of the Incarnation that there is now a restored relationship between the spiritual and the material. Thus a material image can validly represent true spiritual reality. It is a divinely ordained link with God. This is hardly a Christian "innovation". Despite the general iconoclastic sense of Jewish art, the Church Fathers recognized that this possibility of expressing a spiritual reality through material art was, surprisingly, first *commanded* by God, who ordered Moses to construct the Tabernacle with gilt figures of the cherubim (cf. Ex 25:18, 26:1 and 31) [see fig. 3.1].[5]

This insight is important because it safeguards our understanding of the Incarnation and also of the icon. On the one hand, it shows that the relationship between the spiritual and material worlds as ordered by the Creator allows for such an event as the Incarnation. On the other hand, it also shows a christological basis for the icon. All points of orthodoxy, whether Marian, ecclesiological, sacramental, or eschatological, have their foundation in Christology. They either protect orthodox Christology, clarify it, or proceed reasonably from it. Thus the icon, like the doctrine of the Immaculate Conception or the ministerial priest as *alter Christus*, finds its authority in the Person of Christ.

The earliest tradition of icons tells the story of a certain King Abgar of Edessa, who, during the time of Christ's earthly ministry, was afflicted by leprosy. Having heard of the miracles of Jesus, Abgar sent his emissary Hannan (or Ananias) to Jerusalem to bid Jesus to visit him for his healing. Hannan was unable to get near to Jesus because of the crowds, but, as he was an archivist and painter in Abgar's court, he

---

[1] Otto von Simson, *The Gothic Cathedral*, 2d ed. (New York: Pantheon Books, 1962), xix.

[2] For an understanding of the place of Dionysius in Orthodox thought, see V. Lossky, *The Mystical Theology of the Eastern Church* (Crestwood, N.Y.: St. Vladimir's Seminary Press, 1976).

[3] Von Simson, *Gothic Cathedral*, 53.

[4] Bishop Kallistos Ware, lecture, "Praying with Icons" (London, Nov. 28, 1990).

[5] L. Ouspensky, *The Theology of the Icon* (Crestwood, N.Y.: St. Vladimir's Seminary Press, 1978), 59–64. Written by an Orthodox theologian. Despite his unrelenting anti-Western and anti-Roman Catholic bias, this is a very fine book on the theology and history of icons.

attempted to paint the face of the Lord. He found himself unable to paint the portrait because "of the indescribable glory of His face which was changing through grace". When the Lord saw what Hannan was attempting to do, he asked for some water and a cloth to wash his face. The image of his face miraculously transfixed to the linen. He gave this to Hannan for the healing of Abgar with the message that, while he was himself unable to go because of his mission to Israel, he would send one of his disciples. After the Ascension, Saint Thaddeus visited Edessa and evangelized Abgar and his nation. This miraculous image, which came to be known as "the icon made by God" (θεότευκτος εἰκών), is the source of the Mandylion, or the Holy Face icon [fig. 7.1]. The image was well known throughout the Church, and there are many texts, including eyewitness accounts, that mention it. It was last known of during the Crusades, when it was either hidden by the Eastern Church, destroyed by the Moslems, or lost in transit back to Europe by a crusader.[6] The Mandylion was evidently known, and perhaps revered, in Winchester during the late Middle Ages, as evinced by vault bosses and corbel brackets showing the Holy Face Icon [figs. 7.2, 7.3].

Other significant early icons of Christ include the Shroud of Turin [fig. 7.4], Veronica's Veil,[7] and images of the Virgin and Child supposedly painted by Saint Luke in various areas around the Mediterranean. Those that "were not made by human hands", viz., the Mandylion, the Shroud, and Veronica's Veil, held particular importance for Christians, as they testified as "irrefutable witness[es] of the divine incarnation".[8]

7.1 Holy Face Icon.

7.2 *left* Holy Face Metope, San Lorenzo Maggiore, Milan.
7.3 *right* Holy Face Corbel, Winchester Cathedral.

7.4 The Shroud of Turin.

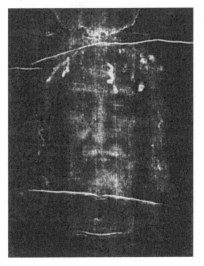

---

[6] Many scholars have noted that the tradition of the Mandylion is conspicuously absent from both Eusebius' *History* (c. 326), and Egeria's account of her pilgrimage (c. 384). In place of it are letters reputedly sent between Abgar and Jesus, which were declared spurious by Rome c. 494. Cf. J. Wilkinson, trans. and ed., *Egeria's Travels to the Holy Land*, rev. ed. (Jerusalem: Ariel, 1981). Some sindologists argue that the Mandylion is, in fact, the Shroud of Turin, folded so that only the face is shown. This is an effort to explain the loss of the Mandylion. Interestingly, the Holy Face icons and the Shroud both show Jesus with a cleft beard.

[7] The name "Veronica" is commonly considered to be a corruption of *vera icona*, meaning "true image". I do not know if the name predates the Christian tradition.

[8] Ouspensky, *Theology of the Icon*, 53.

Today, of course, we have not only lost the idea of the sacred image, but even the word *icon* has taken on new and materialistic meanings in common parlance. In our computer jargon, *icon* has come to mean an image on a screen. Its current use, however, does have a meaning analogous to the original idea. An icon on the computer screen is a sort of window to another level of information. This usage is surprisingly faithful to the original meaning, for in mystical theology an icon is a sacred image that is a sort of window to another level of spiritual understanding, through which one contemplates a spiritual reality. The importance lies not in the object but in its subject, just as the value of the computer icon is only in providing access to something else. The holy icon represents a thing invisible, such as a saint now in heaven or a biblical event, and is used as a tool to contemplate the event.

Iconoclasm

The Church periodically has had to uphold the place of sacred images against "iconoclasm"— the heresy of "image-breaking"—which rejects as idolatry the proper veneration of sacred images. The apostolic letter *Duodecimum saeculum*, by Pope John Paul II, is only the most recent restatement of the Church's perennial teaching. Perhaps the most dire and direct attack came at the beginning of the eighth century with the Iconoclastic Controversy. Pope John Paul II succinctly explains the Iconoclasts' position:

In breaking with the authentic tradition of the Church, the iconoclast movement considered the veneration of images as a return to idolatry. Not without contradiction or ambiguity, they forbade representations of Christ and religious images in general but continued to allow profane images, in particular those of the Emperor with the signs of reverence that were attached to them. The basis of the iconoclast argument was of a Christological nature. How was it possible to depict Christ, who unites in his person, without separating or confusing them, the divine nature and the human nature? To represent his unfathomable divinity would be impossible; to represent him in his humanity would only be to divide

him, to separate the divinity and the humanity in him. To choose one or the other of these options would lead to the opposed Christological heresies of Monophysitism and Nestorianism. For, in trying to represent Christ in his divinity, one would necessarily have to absorb his humanity; in showing only a human picture, one would hide the fact that he is also God.[9]

In response to these arguments, the Second Council of Nicaea reaffirmed the hypostatic union and in light of that dogma defended and explained the legitimacy of making and venerating the images of Christ and his saints. The Council drew upon the Fathers—notably Saint Basil, who wrote, "The honour paid to the image passes on to the prototype, and he who reveres the image reveres in it the hypostasis represented",[10] and Saint John Damascene, who wrote, "The representation is something different from that which is represented"[11]—to defend the validity of iconic representation and distinguished it from idolatry. These teachings have been continually upheld: immediately after Nicaea II against the Western emperor Charlemagne as well as against the Eastern emperor Leo the Armenian, and later still at the Council of Trent against the Calvinist and Zwinglian iconoclasts of the Reformation.[12]

To this day, the Church continues to commend the making and venerating of sacred images. Vatican II states: "Those decrees, which were given in the early days regarding the cult images of Christ, the Blessed Virgin and the saints, [are to] be religiously observed."[13] Pope John Paul II has also affirmed the place of icons in Catholic worship: "Just as the reading of material books allows the hearing of the living word of the Lord, so also the showing of the painted icon allows those who contemplate it to accede to the mystery of salvation by the sense of sight."[14] The prominence given

---

[9] John Paul II, *Duodecimum saeculum* (Dec. 4, 1987), no. 8 [= DSa].

[10] John Saward, "Christ, Our Lady, and the Church", *Chrysostom* 8, 1 (spring 1988): 6. By *hypostasis*, St. Basil means "person".

[11] *Third Treatise*, chap. 17; quoted in Ouspensky, *Theology of the Icon*, 149.

[12] Trent, session 25 (Dec. 3–4, 1563).

[13] Vatican II, *Lumen Gentium* (Nov. 21, 1964), no. 67 [= LG].

[14] DSa, no. 10.

the discussion of icons in the *Catechism* suggests it is still a major concern for the Magisterium, especially in this age of neo-iconoclasm:

> Since the Word became flesh in assuming a true humanity, Christ's body was finite. Therefore the human face of Jesus can be portrayed; at the seventh ecumenical council (Nicaea II in 787) the Church recognized its representation in holy images to be legitimate.[15]

The divine injunction included the prohibition of every representation of God by the hand of man. *Deuteronomy* explains: "Since you saw no form on the day that the LORD spoke to you at Horeb out of the midst of the fire, beware lest you act corruptly by making a graven image for yourselves, in the form of any figure. . . ." It is the absolutely transcendent God who revealed himself to Israel. "He is the all," but at the same time "he is greater than all his works." He is "the author of beauty."

Nevertheless, already in the Old Testament, God ordained or permitted the making of images that pointed symbolically toward salvation by the incarnate Word: so it was with the bronze serpent, the ark of the covenant, and the cherubim.

Basing itself on the mystery of the incarnate Word, the seventh ecumenical council at Nicaea (787) justified against the iconoclasts the veneration of icons—of Christ, but also of the Mother of God, the angels, and all the saints. By becoming incarnate, the Son of God introduced a new "economy" of images.

The Christian veneration of images is not contrary to the first commandment which proscribes idols. Indeed, "the honor rendered to an image passes to its prototype," and "whoever venerates an image venerates the person portrayed in it." The honor paid to sacred images is a "respectful veneration," not the adoration due to God alone: "Religious worship is not directed to images in themselves, considered as mere things, but under their distinctive aspect as images leading us on to God incarnate. The movement toward the image does not terminate in it as image, but tends toward that whose image it is."[16]

Thus the Church continues to uphold the incarnational basis of Christian art. The dignity of man demands it. We human beings are

7.5 Medieval Crucifix, Notre-Dame de Paris, 1163–1250.

composed of body and soul. We have senses as well as will and intellect, memory and imagination. We were created to respond to religious art so that our hearts could be moved by the portrayal of beauty and truth. Through the visible image our hearts are lifted up to the invisible. The veneration of images is rooted in the truths of divine revelation, in the dogmas of creation, the Incarnation, and redemption. As the Holy Father summarizes, "Art can represent the form, the effigy of God's human face, and lead the one who contemplates it to the ineffable mystery of God made man for our salvation."[17]

The crucifix as an icon

We have already considered the historical and liturgical aspects of the crucifix in chapter 4. Here it is appropriate to make a few remarks about the theological significance of the crucifix *qua* icon, for it can help us to gain a better general understanding of the icon.

---

[15] *Catechism of the Catholic Church* (San Francisco: Ignatius Press, 1994), no. 476 [= CCC].

[16] CCC, nos. 2129–32. The final quotation is from St. Thomas Aquinas, *Summa Theologiae* II–II, 81, 3 ad 3.

[17] DSa, no. 9.

7.6 Altar Crucifix, St. Louis Cathedral, Missouri.

to the mystery of the Incarnation: that Jesus came to bring redemption through his sufferings by offering himself as the innocent Victim for the salvation of the world. That is the central message of the crucifix and the reason it is central to the divine liturgy [fig. 7.6]. That is why bare crosses beggar the Liturgy of the Altar, because they do not fully engage us in the act of our redemption.

Moreover, the crucifix speaks to the theology of transfiguration: in Christ there is a new (or, perhaps, restored) relationship between matter and spirit. Christ unites all things "in heaven, and on earth, and under the earth" (cf. Phil 2:10). The mystery of the Transfiguration, a mystery that reveals to us the magnificence of the Incarnation, shows us that matter can be sanctified and become an instrument of sanctification. Now we can participate in the mystery of God with our senses, our imagination, our emotions, our will, and our intellect. But what is even more important, the Transfiguration alludes to the completion of our divinization in the glory of the Resurrection. In Christ, man is called to a personal "transfiguration", to be "changed into his likeness from one degree of glory to another; for this comes from the Lord who is the Spirit" (2 Cor 3:18), when "we shall be like him, for we shall see him as he is" (1 Jn 3:2), and when he "will change our lowly body to be like his glorious body, by the power which enables him even to subject all things to himself" (Phil 3:21).[19]

This process of transformation through material objects, the heart of iconology, is the key to unlocking the medieval understanding of Gothic cathedral symbolism, a process known as "anagogic contemplation", which we shall consider in the next chapter. For now, let us conclude the discussion of the crucifix as an icon with a summary from Pope John Paul II, who writes: "The iconography of Christ involves the whole faith in the reality of the Incarnation and its inexhaustible meaning for the Church and the world. If the Church practices it, it is because she is convinced that the

In many ways, the crucifix is the central icon of the Faith. It has been said that the crucifix "embodies the theology of the icon, which is a theology of incarnation and transfiguration".[18] It speaks most eloquently of the Incarnation, for God the Son has become man, and as man he was crucified for our salvation. He has taken on flesh, and this is apprehensible to our senses: the Word became flesh and is thus capable of being depicted.

Without this new revelation in Christ, we would have to accept the Mosaic and Islamic injunctions against images of the unseen Deity. But in the light of the Incarnation, we can glory in the fact that God became man and that he is "the image of the invisible God" (Col 1:15). This image of the Crucified also speaks

---

[18] Joseph Cardinal Ratzinger, *The Feast of Faith* (San Francisco: Ignatius Press, 1986), 143.

[19] For other scriptural references about this, see Rom 8:17–18; 1 Cor 15:51-54; 2 Cor 5:4-17; Col 3:4; and 2 Pet 1:4.

God revealed in Jesus Christ has truly re-deemed and sanctified the flesh and the whole sensible world, that is, man with his five senses, to allow him to be ever renewed in the image of his Creator (cf. Col 3:10)." [20]

The role and placement of images

The practice of placing sacred images in churches so that they can be venerated by the faithful is to be maintained. Nevertheless their number should be moderate and their relative positions should reflect right order (*Sacrosanctum concilium*, no. 125).

With Vatican II calling for the continued use of sacred images, it is necessary to consider what this means for the modern parish. First and foremost, it is not optional. At Nicaea II, as J. Saward notes, "The establishment of icons in churches . . . is not simply permitted, it is de-creed. . . . For Catholics and Orthodox, Chris-tian images are not a decorative option but a dogmatic obligation." [21] As Pope Pius XII stated in *Mediator Dei*, "It would be wrong, for example, to want . . . pictures and statues ex-cluded from our churches", although he like-wise reproved "an unreasoned multiplicity of pictures and statues". [22] So, while sacred im-ages are a necessary part of the environment of Catholic worship, their number should be moderated, lest the idea of the image lose its potency by sheer repetition. These icons, whether painted, sculpted, or glazed, are meant to give architectural expression to the passage from Hebrews, "We are surrounded by so great a cloud of witnesses" (Heb 12:1). The devotion to the communion of saints should not be lost to a modern iconoclasm, and it is clear from the example set by the Holy See in fostering this devotion. In this regard, it is worth noting that John Paul II has canonized more saints than any previous pope, and it is probable that by the end of his pontificate he will have canonized more saints than all of his predecessors combined! [23] These examples, as well as the ongoing work of the Vatican's Com-mission on New Martyrs, give us more models of holiness and self-sacrifice in an increasingly egocentric age.

7.7 Jeremiah the Prophet, Mosaic, Santa Maria in Trastevere, Rome.

7.8 St. Clare Window, St. Mary's Basilica, Phoenix, Arizona.

7.9 King David, St. John Lateran, Rome.

In keeping with the papal emphasis on the *communio sanctorum*, the role of the *ecclesia triumphans* should be reconsidered. Through-out the history of the Church, the saints have always had their place in fresco, mosaic, glass, and sculpture [figs. 7.7 to 7.9]. From the earliest

[20] DSa, no. 9.
[21] Saward, "Christ, Our Lady, and the Church", 7.
[22] Pius XII, *Mediator Dei* (Nov. 20, 1947), nos. 66 and 201.
[23] M. Walsh, "What Makes a Saint?" *The Tablet*, April 22, 1989, 453.

7.10 St. Paul, Via
Anapo Catacombs,
4th cent.

"a great multitude which no man could number, from every nation, from all tribes and peoples and tongues, standing before the throne" (Rev 7:9). The "traditional" reasons for images in churches are still pertinent: images still serve as reminders of the Faith, they help us teach our children, and, perhaps just as importantly, they continue to give the wandering mind an object of devotion on which to rest and contemplate.

Vatican II gives the role of the saints and the promotion of their honor a strong and renewed emphasis in both *Sacrosanctum concilium* and *Lumen Gentium*. In the light of these documents, the postconciliar removal of statues and the recent fascination with abstract stained glass seem both radically incorrect and even iconophobic. Whereas the graphic image is playing an increasingly important role in modern society, as seen in movies, rock videos, television, glossy magazines, and the advertising media, there seems to have developed an equally deep-rooted reluctance toward sacred images within the Church, a sort of iconophobia. In his book *Moments of Vision*, Kenneth Clark gives an interesting history and analysis of iconophobia, citing philosophical, religious, societal, and stylistic causes for this phenomenon throughout the ages.[25] I do not think, however, that his thesis answers the problems of a specifically Catholic iconophobia (though, of course, it was not his intention to do so). I would offer that the modern Catholic problem is twofold. First, it is a reaction to all the bad "repository art". More than fifty years ago Maritain lamented "the disgraceful sentimentality of so many commercial products" that testified only to "the infinite number of Christians with bad taste."[26] A painted plaster Madonna—although through it "God alone can touch men's hearts with a feeling of piety... as much as before the most sublime masterpiece"[27]—may have been rightly dis-

days, the Church has honored martyrs not only by the preservation of their relics but also by vivid portrayals in the catacombs, *martyria*, and churches. Ancient paintings in the Roman catacombs show various saints entering heaven, accompanied by other saints or angels.[24] And though early Christian sculpture does not often depict the saints, the frescoes and Byzantine mosaics adorning the early churches and baptisteries clearly establish the validity of their representation [fig. 7.10].

Throughout the history of church building, the presence of images of the saints has been upheld as a reminder of the spiritual reality beyond the material world, professed in the Nicene Creed to have been created by God, the "maker of heaven and earth, of all that is seen and unseen". Traditionally these images serve several functions: to instruct the faithful who cannot read, to remind the faithful of their vocation, to serve as objects for contemplation, and to depict the house of God as a representation of the heavenly Jerusalem with

---

[24] R. Milburn, *Early Christian Art and Architecture* (London: Scolar, 1988), 45.
[25] Cf. Kenneth Lord Clark, "Iconophobia", *Moments of Vision* (London: John Murray, 1981), 30–49.
[26] Jacques Maritain, "Some Reflections upon Religious Art", *Art and Scholasticism*, trans. J. F. Scanlan (London: Sheed and Ward, 1930), 146.
[27] Ibid., 147–48, quoting Paul Cazin.

carded as bad art. The problem today, however, is that the plaster Madonnas and kitsch stations have often been replaced by abstractions that fail to communicate the spiritual realities of the subject. Second, much of the negative reaction to images is probably due to a desire to be "respected" and "accepted" by a society-at-large that equates religious images with sentimentality, superstition, and idolatry. But we should keep in mind that Christians are called to be "a sign of contradiction" in imitation of the Lord. There has been a certain comfortable acceptance gained by the Church since Vatican II, a sort of "mainstreaming", which few are willing to give up.[28] It seems to me that only if and when we overcome these inhibitions the images of the saints can once again find their rightful place in the house of God.

General guidelines

But what, then, is the "rightful place"? Though the problem of images crowding the side altars (which brought about the censures of *Mediator Dei*) nowadays seems remote, clearly there still needs to be a hierarchical understanding of their place. The only image that is *required* for Mass, of course, is the crucifix, but the other images suitably found in any church are those of the Virgin Mary, the titular saint, and the stations of the Cross. There are, fortunately, broad guidelines for the incorporation of a robust iconographic program in a church.

When planning for the provision of images, there are several things to consider. The *General Instruction* simply states that images should be placed "in such a way that they do not distract the people's attention from the celebration".[29] While what may be "a distraction" is somewhat subjective, it does suggest some objective responses. First and foremost, *an image must never be on the altar*, but one of the titular saint of the church or of the altar should be placed in some relational but subordinate position within the sanctuary. The size of any image must be carefully considered relative to the size of the sanctuary and the scale of the church: neither so big as to dominate nor so small as to lose significance. Some authors advise that it is better

not to place other images within the sanctuary, although it is not forbidden to do so.[30]

The *General Instruction* also states: "There is need . . . to limit their number. . . . There is to be only one image of any saint." "Limit their number" is also a rather subjective guideline, which the Church recognizes by qualifying, "In general, the devotion of *the entire community* [emphasis added] is to be the criterion regarding images in the adornment and arrangement of a church."[31] The injunction against more than one image of a particular saint is meant, I think, to address the use of statues in veneration shrines, rather than to be an outright forbidding of replication. That is to say, it does not seem that to have a titular representation of Saint John the Baptist in an apsidal mosaic, a painted icon depicting the Baptism of Christ in the baptistery, a place of veneration with a titular statue of the Baptist, and perhaps even another stained-glass portrait would violate the intention of the rule. The point of the injunction is to have only one place of veneration, typically with votive candles, for any particular saint. The injunction does not apply to crucifixes and multiple images of our Lord, or even of our Lady insofar as she appears under her various titles. Were this the case, both St. Peter's in Rome and the Shrine of the Immaculate Conception in Washington, D.C., would have to undergo thorough cleansings.

IMAGES OF OUR LORD

It is interesting that, while there are obvious differences in the composition and placement of images across the ages and around the globe, common to almost all Classical examples is the centrality of Christ. This is to remind us that the role of the saints in the Church is always to lead to Christ: they reflect and transmit the Lord's glory, in whose glory

---

[28] This is my observation mainly of the United States, but I think it is largely true of Europe as well. Conversely, in areas of great persecution or evangelical outreaches, the Church often thrives where she is seen as being counter to the prevailing culture.

[29] *General Instruction of the Roman Missal*, 4th ed. (Mar. 27, 1975), no. 278 [= GIRM].

[30] Fr. J. O'Connell, *Church Building and Furnishing, the Church's Way* (London: Burns and Oates, 1955), 105.

[31] GIRM, no. 278.

7.11 Apsidal Mosaics, Santa Maria in Trastevere, Rome.

the saints now share (cf. Phil 3:21; 2 Th 1:10). It was with this understanding that the medievals filled their houses of God with images of the saints and angels: not only in mosaic or stone, but also in stained glass, where the sun's light shining through the image gave analogy to the light of Christ shining through and illuminating the saints. As put forth in *Lumen Gentium*, "Every authentic witness of love, indeed, offered by us to those who are in heaven tends to and terminates in Christ, 'the crown of all the saints,' and through him in God who is wonderful in his saints and is glorified in them." [32]

The use of images should in some way lead back to Christ. In the history of the Church there have been many effective ways of displaying images of the saints so as to support the liturgy and not cause distraction. Among them the Byzantine apsidal mosaics [fig. 7.11], the iconostasis, stained glass, carved Romanesque capitals [fig. 7.12], Gothic chancel screens [fig.

7.13], and even the perimeter statuary niches at St. John Lateran [fig. 7.14], all serve to present to the faithful an aspect of the saints in relationship to the liturgy and the Church at large, yet in a clearly supportive and subordinated role to that of Christ in the liturgy. This idea of the saints leading to Christ is common in medieval iconography. In the Church of San Apollinare Nuovo, in Ravenna, above the colonnades are two famous processions of saints in mosaics. The frieze on the right shows twenty-six martyrs all advancing to Christ [figs. 7.15, 7.16], while on the left there are twenty-two virgin saints processing toward the Virgin Mary, who holds the Holy Child in her lap [figs. 7.17, 7.18]. This example shows a thoroughly orthodox understanding of the role of the saints: they serve as models and reminders to lead the faithful to Christ. The martyrs imitate Christ by sharing in his suffering, while the virgins share in the

---

[32] LG, no. 50.

7.12 Capital with Christ and Apostles, *c.* 1175, Victoria and Albert Museum, London.

7.13 *The Baptism of Christ*, Chancel Screen, Chartres, 1220.

7.15 *Procession of the Martyrs*, San Apollinare Nuovo, Ravenna, 6th cent.

7.14 St. Bartholomew, St. John Lateran, Rome.

7.16 *Christ Enthroned*, San Apollinare Nuovo, Ravenna, 6th cent.

Lord's life by imitating the example of his Virgin Mother, who likewise receives grace and glory from her Son. The center of the domes of the Neonian and Arian baptisteries in Ravenna show Jesus being baptized by John, while the images of the twelve apostles radiate around the sides, thus compositionally supporting the figure of Christ while being clearly subordinated to it [fig. 7.19]. Other examples, whether the dome of Saint Zenon's chapel [fig. 7.20], the tympanum at Saint-Denis [fig. 7.21], the rose window at Orvieto [fig. 7.22], the glorious west façade at Wells Cathedral [fig. 7.23], or the smaller but related façade at Bath Abbey [fig. 7.24], also express the centrality and dominance of Christ. These medieval examples serve to illustrate a key consideration when placing contemporary images: that the place of the Redeemer—whether as the Crucified or the Pantocrator—is given prime importance in the church, and all other images are to be subordinated to it.

IMAGES OF OUR LADY

The Virgin has a special role in church iconography and is commended "to the particular and filial veneration of the Christian faithful" as "Blessed Mary ever Virgin, the Mother of God, whom Christ established as the Mother of the

7.17 *Procession of the Virgins*, San Apollinare Nuovo, Ravenna, 6th cent.

7.18 *The Virgin and Child*, San Apollinare Nuovo, Ravenna, 6th cent.

7.19 *The Baptism of Christ*, Arian Baptistery, Ravenna, 6th cent.

7.20 *Christ the Pantocrator*, St. Zenon's Chapel, Santa Prassede, Rome, 818–824.

7.21 Tympanum, Saint-Denis, Paris, 1140.

7.22 Rose Window, Orvieto Cathedral, 1290.

human race".[33] Hers is among the most ancient and widespread of images, dating back even to the late first or early second century, as evidenced in the catacomb of Priscilla in Rome [fig. 7.25].[34] Today the place of the Blessed Virgin should not be underemphasized, as is made clear by the place given Saint Mary by the Council Fathers in *Lumen Gentium* (the entire eighth chapter) and by the encyclical *Redemptoris Mater*. Pope John Paul II writes:

> Images of the Virgin have a place of honor in churches and houses. In them Mary is represented in a number of ways: as the throne of God carrying the Lord and giving him to humanity (*Theotókos*); as the way that leads to Christ and manifests him (*Hodegetria*); as a praying figure in an attitude of intercession and as a sign of the divine presence on the journey of the faithful until the day of the Lord (*Deësis*); as the protectress who stretches out her mantle over the peoples (*Pokrov*); or as the merciful Virgin of tenderness (*Eleousa*). She is usually represented with her Son, the child Jesus, in her arms: it is the relationship with the Son which glorifies the Mother. Sometimes she embraces him with tenderness (*Glykophilousa*); at other times she is a hieratic figure, apparently rapt in contemplation of him who is the Lord of history.[35]

Furthermore, the Pope goes on to explain the relationship of the Blessed Virgin to the liturgy, which is vital to understanding the consequent placement of her images:

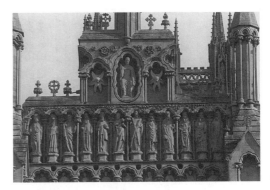

7.23 West façade, Wells Cathedral, *c.* 1185–1239.

7.24 West façade, Bath Abbey, *c.* 1499–1537.

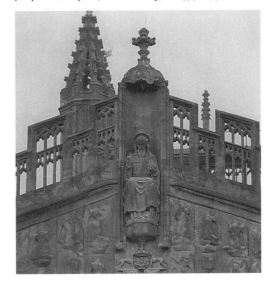

[33] *Code of Canon Law* (1983), can. 1186.
[34] Ouspensky, *Theology of the Icon*, 77.
[35] John Paul II, *Redemptoris Mater* (Mar. 25, 1987), no. 33 [= RM].

7.25 *Madonna and Child*, Catacomb of Priscilla, Rome.

7.26 *The Gathering of the Apostles*,
Greek, 17th cent.

Her motherhood is particularly noted and experienced by the Christian people at the *Sacred Banquet*—the liturgical celebration of the mystery of the Redemption—at which Christ, his *true body born of the Virgin Mary*, becomes present.

The piety of the Christian people has always very rightly sensed a *profound link* between devotion to the Blessed Virgin and worship of the Eucharist: this is a fact that can be seen in the liturgy of both the West and the East.[36]

Similarly in *Lumen Gentium*, the place given the Blessed Virgin in the Church is "the highest after Christ and also closest to us".[37] From these citations it is proper to deduce that images of the Mother of God should be given special prominence in or near the sanctuary. This location would also facilitate the presentation of the Marian bouquet, which is often a part of wedding ceremonies. The image of the titular saint can sometimes be effectively juxtaposed to the Marian statue on the opposite side of the chancel.

IMAGES OF THE SAINTS

Within the tradition of sacred depiction, there is a subtle and complex language of symbols, forms, and colors. The apostles and evangelists have their own language of depiction, and not without reason. By having a constant language of forms, whether in icons, statuary, or stained glass, the illiterate believers could easily recognize the images. Therefore, one often sees Saint Peter as a swarthy and stocky man with dark curly hair and beard; Saint Bartholomew with black and grizzled hair, fair complexion, large eyes, straight nose, and long beard; Saint Paul, older and balding with a long, wispy, white beard; Saint John as a young and unbearded man; Saint Mark, middle-aged, with a furrowed brow, a large nose, fair hair, a long beard, and a few gray hairs; Saint John the Baptist as a hermit in camel skins; and so on. Each apostle is usually shown with the instrument of his martyrdom or other insignia, as seen in Rusconi's nave statues at St. John Lateran: Saint Peter with the keys [fig. 7.27]; Saint Bartholomew,

[36] RM, no. 44.
[37] LG, no. 54.

7.27 St. Peter, St., John Lateran, Rome.

7.28 St. Bartholomew, St. John Lateran, Rome.

7.29 St. Philip, St. John Lateran, Rome.

who was flayed alive [fig. 7.28]; Saint Paul with his sword of beheading; Saint James with the seashells to recount his body miraculously washing ashore at Compostela; and Saint Philip, who, "like his Master, whom he had preached, was nailed to a cross" [fig. 7.29].[38]

Other martyrs also have their instruments of execution (e.g., Saint Lawrence with the gridiron [fig. 7.30], Saint Sebastian with arrows, and Saint Stephen with a pile of rocks at his feet) and often are depicted with palm branches, alluding to the passage "the righteous flourish like the palm tree . . . in the courts of our God" (Ps 92:12–13).

The four evangelists are represented by the four beasts of Revelation, the bull, the lion, the man, and the eagle (Rev 4:7) [fig. 7.30]. Saint Matthew is depicted as a man, for he begins with the genealogies and writes of Jesus' humanity, his birth, and his early years [fig. 7.31]. Saint Mark is symbolized by the Lion of the Tribe of Judah, for several reasons [fig. 7.32]. First, his is the depiction of Christ as the Royal King. Secondly, Saint Mark's Gospel opens with "a voice crying out in the desert", which the Fathers have likened to the lion, which roars in the desert. Thirdly, because of Saint Mark's description of the Resurrection, of which the lion is a symbol, owing to the legend that a lioness resuscitates her cubs by breath-

7.30 Tympanum, Duomo in Genoa, showing Christ, the Four Beasts, and St. Lawrence.

7.31 St. Matthew, Orvieto Cathedral.

7.32 St. Mark, Orvieto Cathedral.

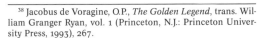

---

[38] Jacobus de Voragine, O.P., *The Golden Legend*, trans. William Granger Ryan, vol. 1 (Princeton, N.J.: Princeton University Press, 1993), 267.

7.33 St. Luke, San Clemente.

7.34 St. John, by Eric Gill.

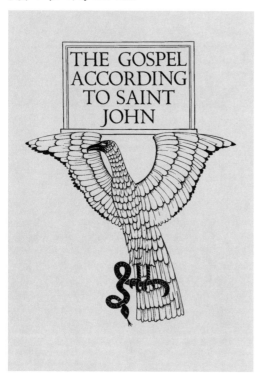

ing on them. Similarly, Saint Luke is the ox [fig. 7.33], the symbol of priestly sacrifice, for he begins his Gospel with the priest Zechariah, he develops the Lord's genealogy through the Levitical priesthood, and he dwells eloquently on Christ's Passion and sacrifice. Finally, the eagle symbolizes Saint John [fig. 7.34], because his Gospel soars to the divinity of Christ, opening with "In the beginning was the Word. . . ."

In this intricate language of symbol, the New Testament writers (the evangelists and Saints Paul, Jude, James, and Peter) are sometimes portrayed with books. Open books signify perfect knowledge, that the apostolic writers were perfectly instructed by the Lord himself.[39] This widely used language, though by no means universal or absolute, is still in use by responsible iconographers because it allows the artist to avoid the issue of personality and to work within the traditions of his art.

IMAGES OF THE ANGELS

One exception I would propose to the rule concerning images in the sanctuary is the placement of images of angels. Angels have a uniquely significant place in Scripture, in salvation history, and in the liturgy. It is certainly interesting that the first images God *commanded* to be made were those of incorporeal beings, the cherubim on the Ark of the Covenant. They flank and support the Mercy Seat, one on each side (Ex 25:18), as they also guard the entry to the garden of Eden (cf. Gen 3:24). This theme is continued in the decorative program of Solomon's Temple, where they are portrayed on the ten stands, carved into the wall paneling and the doors, and, most importantly, depicted as protecting the entry to the Holy of Holies (1 Kings 6:23). Here were set two large cherubim, with wings more than seven feet long (five cubits), guarding the entrance, in obvious reference to the cherubim with "a flaming sword", who guard the entry of Eden.

Throughout the Scriptures, the angels are not only signs of God's presence (e.g., 1 Sam 4:4, Ps 80:2 and 99:1, Lk 1:35) but are even par-

---

[39] Bishop Guillaume Durand, *The Symbolism of Churches and Church Ornaments: A Translation of the First Book of the* Rationale divinorum officiorum, trans. J. M. Neale and B. Webb (Leeds: T. W. Green, 1843; reprint New York: AMS Press, 1973), bk. 1, chap. 3, nos. 9ff.; also see bk. 7.

7.35 *above* St. Wendreda's, March, Cambs., Hammerbeam roof.

7.36 *right* Angels, Ely Cathedral, 1080–1322.

ticularly noted when the evangelist speaks of the Christian liturgy: "You have come to Mount Zion and to the city of the living God, the heavenly Jerusalem, and to innumerable angels in festal gathering, and to the assembly of the first-born who are enrolled in heaven, to a judge who is God of all, and to the spirits of just men made perfect, and to Jesus, the mediator of a new covenant, and to the sprinkled blood that speaks more graciously than the blood of Abel" (Heb 12:22–24). It is with this understanding that the new *Catechism* states: "The whole life of the Church benefits from the mysterious and powerful help of angels. In her liturgy, the Church joins with the angels to adore the thrice-holy God. She invokes their assistance", asking in the First Eucharistic Prayer, "Almighty God, we pray that your angel may take this sacrifice to your altar in heaven", and in the funeral rite, "May the angels lead you into Paradise." [40]

Fr. Jean Daniélou writes eloquently of the angels' assistance at the sacrifice of the Mass, citing numerous Fathers in corroboration:

But the angels are present especially at the Eucharistic sacrifice. The Mass is, actually, a sacramental participation in the liturgy of heaven, the cult officially rendered to the Trinity by the full host of the spiritual creation. The presence of the angels introduces the Eucharist into heaven itself. They help to surround it with a sacred mystery. "The angels surround the priest," writes St. John Chrysostom. "The whole sanctuary and the space before the altar is filled with the heavenly Pow-

ers come to honor Him who is present upon the altar." And elsewhere: "Think now of what kind of choir you are going to enter. Although vested with a body, you have been judged worthy to join the Powers of heaven in singing the praises of Him who is the Lord of all." "Behold the royal table. The angels serve at it. The Lord Himself is present." [41]

Fr. Daniélou concludes his discussion of the angels in the liturgy with another remarkable passage from Saint John Chrysostom: "The angels are present here. The angels and martyrs meet today. If you wish to see the angels and the martyrs, open the eyes of faith and look upon this sight. For if the very air is filled with angels, how much more so the Church! And if the Church is filled with angels, how much more is that true today when their Lord has risen into heaven! The whole air about us is filled with angels." [42] The exuberance of this statement has found its architectural expression throughout the history of church architecture. One of the most poetic applications is seen in the late Gothic hammerbeam roof of St. Wendreda's [fig. 7.35], March, Cambridgeshire, where over a hundred angels soar above the nave in a glorious choir of angelic hosts. This theme is also seen in the ceiling decoration of the nearby Ely cathedral [fig. 7.36]. In more Baroque statements, the angels that crowd Bernini's San Andrea al Quirinale and

---

[40] CCC, nos. 334–35.

[41] Jean Daniélou, S.J., *The Angels and Their Mission*, trans. David Heimann (reprint Westminster, Md.: Christian Classics, 1993), 62–63.

[42] Ibid., 66–67.

7.37 High Altar, San Andrea al Quirinale, by Bernini, 1658–1670.

7.38 Cupola, San Andrea al Quirinale,
by Bernini, 1658–1670.

7.39 Putti, San Andrea al Quirinale,
by Bernini, 1658–1670.

7.40 High Altar, San Ivo della Sapienza,
by F. Borromini, 1642–50.

7.41 Pediment, San Ivo della Sapienza,
by F. Borromini, 1642–50.

7.42 Cupola, San Ivo della Sapienza, by F. Borromini, 1642–50.

Borromini's San Ivo della Sapienza give expression to the Scripture that we are "surrounded by so great a cloud of witnesses" [figs. 7.37 to 7.42].

This sort of understanding leads me to conclude that, in the light of the angels' special place in the life of the Church, their representation is not only appropriate in the sanctuary but even to be recommended, because they signify our participation in the heavenly banquet of the Lamb. Throughout the church, the sanctuary and nave and baptistery should be filled with images of the angels in vivid depiction of the unseen spiritual reality! Beyond stating the spiritual truth, which should be sufficient justification, images of the angels, as well as those of the saints, help us to remember that our parish assembly is not solitary and disconnected but joined to the worship of the whole Mystical Body of Christ. Here and now, in this parish Mass, we are caught up into the heavenly liturgy of the Church Triumphant with all the angels and saints through Jesus our high priest, in the power of the Holy Spirit, to the glory of the Father Almighty. This is why images of angels have filled churches throughout the ages in fresco and mosaic and bronze and glass and stone: they bear witness to the reality of our place in the Kingdom of God and remind us of their intercession, protection, and ministry.

THE STATIONS OF THE CROSS

Another important series of images to consider is the stations of the Cross [fig. 7.43], representations of the traditional stages of our Lord's Passion. The stations are usually arranged around the perimeter of the nave, allowing for a procession that recalls the *via dolorosa*, the Way of the Cross through the streets of Jerusalem [fig. 7.44]. This devotion was not common in churches until the seventh century and is not required to be in the church proper. If the stations are in the church nave, as opposed to the narthex or an outdoor garden, they should be in harmony with the

7.43 *Christ Is Condemned*, Cathedral of the Madeleine, Salt Lake City.

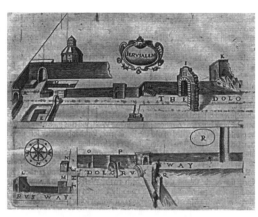

7.44 *Via Dolorosa*, Jerusalem, from *George Sandy's Travels*, London, 1652.

7.45 *Jesus Falls a Third Time*, Westminster Cathedral, London, by Eric Gill.

size and style of the church and always subordinated to the liturgical requirements. Hence, an outdoor set of stations may give the artist more latitude in design. Fr. O'Connell, undoubtedly familiar with the problems of kitsch stations, suggests it is "better to be content with the cross alone (accompanied by the title of each Station) unless it is possible to have worthy images."[43] This decision should not be too swiftly taken, and every effort should be made to find worthy, beautiful representations of the stations of the Cross.

---

[43] O'Connell, *Church Building*, 109.

7.46 *Jesus Greets His Mother*, St. Timothy's, Mesa, Arizona.

CHAPTER EIGHT

Domus Dei: *The Church as Icon*

Recovering an iconic architecture

The idea that the church building should in some way express the Kingdom of God is perhaps the most difficult and challenging area of ecclesial design. Many modern authors have attempted to offer directions for an iconic approach to church architecture. Rudolf Schwarz went to great lengths in devising architectural models representative of Christ's life. Some, like Hammond and the team of Maguire and Murray, have addressed the problem analytically or "functionally", but they have failed to propose fruitful direction. Others, for instance, Fr. R. Kevin Seasoltz, seem to acquiesce in modern iconoclasm: "The secular building which characterizes this modern man is the industrial building, the steel-frame structure. Likewise, to a great extent, modern churches are steel-frame buildings designed primarily for function. . . . Apart from the community which gathers in these churches, the buildings have little meaning."[1]

There is great difficulty in this aspect of church design for numerous reasons. One cannot simply create a new language and expect it to be apprehensible. Nor can one expect comprehensive answers from functional models when both the building and the human users are much more complicated entities. But much less does the Church need to resign herself to the economically driven cultural impoverishment that surrounds her. One of the difficulties here is that this is where we cross that boundary between mere building and architecture. The building is easy enough: func-

tion, technology, and everything else that goes into serving the body. But, as Eric Gill wrote, "The mind . . . and the body. . . are the two components of man, spirit and matter, both real and both good."[2] And, in one sense, this concept is useful when we seek to distinguish architecture from mere building. Architecture is intended to serve the whole man, body and soul. Its "function" is not only to accommodate the physical, material, and utilitarian requirements of the program but also to nourish the intellect and the aesthetic appetite with meaning and beauty. Whether or not it does so depends on whether it is good architecture or bad architecture; but, to be considered architecture, a building must at least make a claim to serve the whole person.

Irrespective of an architect's world view, be it Christian or Buddhist, Marxist or nihilist, what is common to all architecture is that it makes a claim beyond the mere building. The building may address the *Zeitgeist*, the Marxist dialectic, the power of the state, the authority of nature, a metaphysical appreciation of beauty, a relativistic view of historicity, or even the deconstructionist's belief in an "absolute" lack of order in the universe. The two things common to all of these approaches are that they are extraneous to the material functioning of the building and that they achieve their aims only if they are apprehended and understood.

---

[1] R. Kevin Seasoltz, *The House of God* (New York: Herder and Herder, 1963), 125–26.
[2] Eric Gill, *Beauty Looks after Herself* (London: Sheed and Ward, 1933), 53.

168

That they are successful only if apprehended and understood presupposes rational participants, an audience. The building addresses a rational audience, and it speaks of the values and ideology and world view of the architect and the prevalent social milieu. This is true whether the building be an Egyptian pyramid, a Georgian country estate, or a modern shopping mall. As a cultural expression, architecture is inseparably rooted in the values of the culture in which it is created. The building speaks to those values, it incarnates those values, and it furthers those values. The contemporary church architect, working in a complex and pluralistic society, must use a good deal of discernment and discrimination to filter the values that are appropriate to the Church.

The other obvious difficulty for the contemporary church designer is that Modernism in architecture is essentially asymbolical: it has no language with which to speak. It is iconoclastic in the root sense of this word—it "breaks images". The abstract has replaced the symbolic. Hence, one must question whether a modernist approach *can* be appropriate for liturgical architecture. Furthermore, because of the materialist and empiricist mind-set of this age, we have largely lost the ability to *read* buildings. These attitudes and circumstances present profound difficulties that must be overcome in order to regain an iconographic understanding of the church building.

The iconic program that the Church gives the architect is simply this: "The places and requisites for worship should be truly worthy and beautiful, signs and symbols of heavenly realities."[3] This simple statement, however, is packed with direction for the church architect. As "signs and symbols of heavenly realities", church buildings are to be a sign of the Kingdom of God, the body of Christ, the heavenly Jerusalem, and the architect must find some symbolic expression for these ideas. Furthermore, there is no place for the expedient, the utilitarian, or the mediocre; rather, the Church requires that the highest quality of workmanship and greatest design effort be expended in achieving this expression. In an age that values "return on investment", quantity over quality,

economic expediencies, and so forth, the Church must stand for the value of quality. However, the Church must do so without being either archaic or eccentric.[4] This means that the symbolism of the church must work within the prevailing cultural symbolism, and the church building must be understandable as a modern construction.

To some degree, Peter Hammond understood the modern problem of symbolism, writing: "The church must be a symbolic structure: it must be informed from the outset by a theological understanding of its purpose.... The church will take on the nature of a symbol only in so far as the architect understands its *raison d'être*."[5] Unfortunately, Hammond concluded that what was needed was "radical functional analysis", believing that "if the layout of the church is governed by an adequate theological programme, and if the building is an honest piece of construction, free from sham and irrelevant ornament, then its symbolic aspect can be left to take care of itself."[6] Apart from such problematic phrases as "an honest piece of construction", one must ask if this wasn't a dead end from the start. How can something be truly "symbolic" if it is not *intended* to communicate an idea? If its symbolic aspect is "left to take care of itself", is it a true symbol? Or is it only whatever the viewer infers it to be? As Maguire and Murray pointed out, "If the meanings are not made manifest in the architecture, then the symbolic means of architecture will be 'speaking' of something different."[7] So, in the end, Hammond only paid lip-service to the problem of symbolism by writing, "The task of the modern architect is not to design a building that *looks like a church*. It is to create a building that *works* as a place for liturgy."[8] Hence, the real question of the *symbolic function* of the building goes

---

[3] *General Instruction of the Roman Missal*, 4th ed. (Mar. 27, 1975), no. 253.

[4] Joseph Rykwert, *Church Building* (London: Sheed and Ward, 1966), 125–26.

[5] Peter Hammond, *Liturgy and Architecture* (London: Barrie and Rockliff, 1960), 155.

[6] Ibid., 30.

[7] R. Maguire and K. Murray, *Modern Churches of the World* (London: Studio Vista, 1965), 9.

[8] Hammond, *Liturgy and Architecture*, 9; emphasis in the original.

begging. What the building *looks like*, both inside and outside, is an intrinsic part of the quality of the worship environment and of its symbol-value to both the believer and the community at large.

Against this "radical functionalism", which has proven counterproductive, we must explore new directions in church design. It was a dead end, and a costly one at that, since thousands of banal churches have been erected on its principles. At least we ought to learn from its errors. But beyond this we must now "seek first the Kingdom of God" (βασιλεία τοῦ θεοῦ). The Latin word *basilica* comes from this same Greek word, βασιλεία, and refers to the Roman building that served as a hall of justice and commercial exchange; from this structure comes the basilican form of ecclesiastical building. So we will proceed to examine the iconic value of the church building—searching for an architecture that respects the agenda of the Second Vatican Council and an architecture that speaks of the Church to today's society—with some scriptural assurance that if we "seek first his kingdom . . . all these things shall be yours as well" (Mt 6:33).

The church as icon: Consecration

To understand the symbolic implications of the church building, we will look first at the church's consecration and orientation and then at the relationship between theology and the built form throughout the centuries. The consecration of a church has long been seen as a particularly solemn event. Hugh of Saint-Victor considers it analogous to the sacrament of baptism: "We must speak of the dedication of a church, just as of the first baptism by which the church itself in a manner is baptized, that in it after a fashion men may be baptized to be regenerated unto salvation. . . . Regeneration is first symbolized in the dedication of a church; then it is exhibited in the sanctification of a faithful soul." [9]

Much of our understanding of the church's symbolism is expressed, or at least alluded to, in the dedication ceremony. We can see the same pattern both in recent documents and in historical accounts. In the *Rite of Dedication*

of a Church and an Altar, we see that from the beginning of construction, when the cornerstone is laid, the gathered faithful are told that "the structure built of stone is . . . a visible sign of the living Church, God's building, which is formed of the people themselves." [10] Likewise, the prayer at the commencement of building recalls that the universal Church is a structure "founded upon the apostles with Jesus Christ its cornerstone" and that the building is a foreshadowing of the "heavenly city". [11] Hence, the church building "stands as a special sign of the pilgrim Church on earth and reflects the Church dwelling in heaven." [12] Throughout this document, rich scriptural metaphors of the building are to be found: "The very stone which the builders rejected has become the cornerstone" (Mk 12:10); "For no other foundation can any one lay than that which is laid, which is Jesus Christ" (1 Cor 3:11); "Jesus Christ of Nazareth, whom you crucified . . . is the stone which . . . has become the cornerstone" (Acts 4:10-11); and "On this rock I will build my church" (Mt 16:18). As an aside, the symbolic significance of this last Gospel reading was made manifest when Pope John Paul II, while still bishop of Krakow, consecrated the church in Nowa Huta, with its cornerstone cut from walls of St. Peter's in Rome [fig. 8.1]. This gesture is all the more profound in that the church was the first to be built in Poland since the Communist enslavement, built by men and women who risked life and livelihood to stand against their oppressors, and built in Nowa Huta, a new, industrialized city that was to be exemplary of the "socialist worker's paradise". Their heroic action unwaveringly stated the supremacy of the eternal Faith over the transiency of political machinations.

We have two excellent medieval manuscripts that both describe and explain the consecra-

---

[9] Hugh of Saint-Victor, *De Sacramentis*, bk. 2, pt. 5, 1, in *Hugh of St.-Victor on the Sacraments of the Christian Faith*, trans. R. J. Deferrari (Cambridge, Mass.: Mediaeval Academy, 1951).

[10] Sacred Congregation for the Sacraments and Divine Worship, *Dedication of a Church and an Altar* (May 29, 1977), chap. 1, no. 1 [= DOCA].

[11] DOCA, chap. 1, no. 1.

[12] DOCA, chap. 2, no. 2.

8.1 *Arka Pana*, Nowa Huta, Poland, 1965–1977 (after Rodzina).

tion ceremony, one by Hugh of Saint-Victor (*c.* 1134) and the other by Bishop Guillaume Durand of Mende (*c.* 1290). Hugh tells us that the bishop first blesses the water and mixes salt in with it to represent the baptismal waters and the power of the gospel. Then the bishop, followed by the clergy and laity, encircles and sprinkles the church three times, to represent the threefold immersion of baptism. Inside the church a solitary deacon has lighted twelve lamps, which are likened to the twelve apostles, who have illuminated the world with the light of Christ. The bishop then approaches the closed doors of the church and three times strikes the lintels while intoning Psalm 23: "Lift up your gates, O ye princes, and be ye lifted up, O eternal gates"; to which the deacon inside asks, "Who is this King of Glory?" The bishop responds, "The Lord of hosts, he is the King of Glory!" On the third knock—each strike representing Christ's domination of heaven, of earth, and of hell—the doors then open, indicating the removal of sin. The bishop enters, announcing, "Peace be to this house", to recall the command of the Lord in Luke 10:5 and to remind us that Christ entered into the world to make peace with fallen man.[13]

In the Middle Ages, there was an interesting ceremony in which the bishop wrote the alphabet on the floor of the church in an X-cross, from the northeast to the southwest and from the southeast to the northwest. Bishop Durand tells us that the cross shape is laid with ashes and sand to represent man, referring to

the words of Abraham, "Shall I speak to my Lord, [I] who am but dust and ashes?" (Gen 18:27), and that the alphabets are written in Greek and Latin.[14] This part of the rite is rich in allusion: Hugh tells us that the alphabet is the teaching of the Faith written on the pavement of the human heart. The chiastic form traverses the cardinal points of the compass to indicate that in Christ the first shall be last and the last shall be first; that what was first given to the Jews has now been given to the Gentiles; and that, after the fulfillment of the gospel among the Gentiles, all Israel shall be saved. For Bishop Durand, the ceremony also shows that "the pages of both Testaments . . . [are] fulfilled by the Cross of Christ. . . . In these few letters . . . all knowledge is contained; and the alphabet is written crosswise, because one Testament is contained in the other."[15] Another medieval author, Bishop Jacobus de Voragine, writes: "The alphabet is written on the floor, and this represents the joining of the two people, the Gentiles and the Jews, or it stands for a page of each Testament, or for the articles of our faith. That alphabet, inscribed within the cross in both Latin and Greek letters, represents the union in faith of the pagan and the Jewish people that was wrought by Christ by means of the cross." And, as the material building is always a representation of the human person, who is called to become the true temple of God, Jacobus tells us the spiritual application of this as well: "Fourthly, a spiritual alphabet, i.e., a spiritual scripture, is written in this temple of the heart. What is written there is threefold—the rules governing our actions, the testimony of the divine benefactions, and the accusations of our own sins."[16]

Such depth of symbolism has largely been lost to us. There are still, however, important vestiges in our contemporary rite that can be reincorporated into our consciousness. When

[13] Hugh of Saint-Victor, *De Sacramentis*, bk. 2, pt. 5, 2–3.

[14] Bishop William Durand, *The Symbolism of Chruches and Church Ornaments: A Translation of the First Book of the* Rationale divinorum officiorum, trans. J. M. Neale and B. Webb (Leeds: T. W. Green, 1843; reprint, New York: AMS Press, 1973), bk. 1, chap. 6, no. 20.

[15] Ibid., bk. 1, chap. 6, no. 22.

[16] Jacobus de Voragine, O.P., *The Golden Legend*, vol. 2, trans. William Granger Ryan, vol. 2 (Princeton, N.J.: Princeton University Press, 1993), 182, 392, and 395.

8.2 Consecration Cross, Chartres, 1220.

8.3 Consecration Cross, Sainte-Chapelle, Paris, Upper Church, 1242–1248.

a church is consecrated, the walls are anointed by the bishop to signify that the building is dedicated "entirely and perpetually to Christian worship". This ancient custom is traced back to at least the eighth century.[17] Bishop Durand writes in this regard: "Next, when the Altar has been anointed with chrism, the twelve crosses painted on the walls of the church are also anointed. . . . For crosses be the banners of Christ and signs of his triumph. Crosses, therefore, are with reason painted there that it may be made manifest that place has been subdued to the dominion of Christ."

As Émile Mâle noted: "The liturgical writers taught that when the bishop consecrated a church he should mark twelve columns in the nave or choir with twelve crosses in token that the twelve apostles are the true pillars of the temple" [fig. 8.2].[18] This association of the Twelve goes back at least to Eusebius (fourth century), who remarked that the twelve columns in the basilica next to the Anastasis in Jerusalem reminded him of the apostles.[19] In explicit expression of this idea, the medieval sculptors placed in the choir of Sainte-Chapelle twelve statues of apostles, each carrying a stone consecration cross [fig. 8.3]. This theme is echoed in the lower chapel at Sainte Chapelle, where the twelve apostles are depicted in enamelled medallions on the side walls [fig. 8.4]. They can also be seen elsewhere, as in the consecration medallions at the Spitalkirche, Innsbruck [fig. 8.5].

The twelve anointings are to be made on consecration crosses distributed around the interior walls, usually two at the sanctuary, two at the entrance, and the remaining crosses on the side walls. While it was once required that the crosses be cut into the stone walls (or be of stone, set into a wall of another material), the crosses may now be of stone, brass, or any suitable material permanently set into the wall. Beneath the cross there should be a bracket to

---

[17] Fr. J. O'Connell, *Church Building and Furnishing, the Church's Way* (London: Burns and Oates, 1955), 6, footnote.

[18] Émile Mâle, *The Gothic Image* (London: Fontana, 1961), 21.

[19] Richard Krautheimer, "Introduction to an 'Iconography of Mediaeval Architecture'", *Journal of the Warburg and Courtauld Institutes* 5 (1942): 11.

8.4 Consecration Medallion, Sainte-Chapelle, Paris, Lower Church, 1242–1248.

8.5 *right* Consecration Cross, Spitalskirche, Innsbruck, Austria.

receive a candleholder for the consecration ceremony and the anniversary observances.[20] While traditionally twelve anointings are made, nowadays four anointings may be used, to signify that the church represents the holy city of Jerusalem (if four anointings are used, they should be placed, if possible, one on each wall: north, south, east, and west).

The church as icon: Orientation

As we have previously seen, the ancient tradition of the Church has been to *orient* buildings so that the Mass is celebrated facing east, expressing the cosmological significance of the Church worshipping toward the *oriens*. Since the earliest days of Christianity, the sun has been seen as a symbol of Christ—as Saint John recounts, "His face was like the sun shining in full strength" (Rev 1:16)—thus the rising of the sun is seen as the light of Christ dispelling the darkness. The early Church expressed this theme by placing a cross on the east wall of meeting places to orient the worship. One early reference to the church building, obviously referring to the *domus ecclesiae*, describes it as "locus in parte domus ad orientem versa",[21] literally, "the place in the part of the house turned toward the east". Conversely, as

Saint Cyril of Jerusalem wrote, "Since the West is the region of sensible darkness, and he being darkness has his dominion also in darkness, therefore, looking with a symbolical meaning towards the West, you renounce that dark and gloomy potentate." This is not, however, originally a Christian interpretation but one received from the Greeks, who also placed Hades in the west.[22] This cosmological symbolism has other expressions as well. The main doors of the church face west, expressing the idea of the faithful leaving behind the darkness. And the baptistery is placed in the north, the region of darkness and paganism, so the candidates will leave the darkness of paganism to enter the light of the faith.

Some scholars, again Fr. Seasoltz, for instance, diminish the importance of liturgical orientation in the history of the Western Church and consider it more an Eastern Christian practice.[23] There seems to be enough evidence to suggest its importance in both the East and the West. One of the earliest sources for this direction is the *Apostolic Constitutions*, which state, "Let the building be long,

[21] *Didascalia*, ii, 57; quoted in Seasoltz, *House of God*, 84.
[22] Quoted in Fr. Jean Daniélou, S.J., *The Bible and the Liturgy* (London: Darton, Longman and Todd, 1960), 27.
[23] Seasoltz, *House of God*, 161–63.

with its head to the east, and with its vestries on both sides at the east end." Hugh of Saint-Victor seems to take this arrangement for granted.[24] Jacobus de Voragine, Bishop of Genoa, writes that "In our churches, however, we worship facing the East."[25] Bishop Durand, in a matter-of-fact manner, states that "The foundation must be so contrived that the head of the Church may point due east."[26] He elsewhere writes: "Albeit God is everywhere, yet ought the priest at the altar and in the Offices to pray toward the east: according to the constitutions of Vigilius, Pope."[27] There is also evidence that in medieval Great Britain the practice was of orienting the major axis of the church toward the sunrise *on the feast day of the church's patron saint*. This makes the particularly beautiful statement that the saint participates in his own way to help bring the light of Christ into the world.[28] Even as late as the Counter Reformation, Saint Charles Borromeo recommends the practice of orientation when possible.[29]

The historical documents show us the importance of liturgical orientation and building orientation throughout the centuries, in both the East and the West. We have all but lost these understandings. In chapter 4 we considered the value of liturgical orientation in the ordering of the church to help facilitate the true active participation that Vatican II seeks. In conjunction with this, we need also to rediscover the iconic value of the building's orientation.

In this traditional orientation, the church takes its place in the order of the universe as a fitting place for the Lord's sacrifice. For the eastward direction has historical precedent precisely because of the profound scriptural and traditional allusions to the east. As we see in the following two medieval explications for orientation, there is a divergence of opinion on the direction Christ faced on the Cross. Nevertheless, both authors use their opinion as a basis for determining liturgical direction. First, Bishop Durand:

The Temple . . . of Solomon and the Tabernacle of Moses had their entrance from the east. We pray, therefore, toward the east, being mindful first that he, who is the splendor of

eternal light, has illuminated *those who sit in darkness and in the shadow of death.* . . .

Second, that our souls are thereby taught to turn themselves to the things that are more desirable.

Third, because they who praise God ought not to turn their backs on him.

Fourth, according to John Damascene (who gives also the following three reasons) to show that we seek our Country.

Fifth, that we may look upon Christ crucified, who is the True East.

Sixth, that we may prove that we expect him to come to be our Judge. For Damascene says in that place, *God planted a garden eastward,* whence man's sin made him an exile, and instead of paradise made him to dwell in the west: therefore looking to our ancient home we pray toward the east.

Seventh, because our Lord, at his Crucifixion, looked toward the east: and also when he ascended into heaven, he ascended toward the east: and thus the apostles adored him: and thus "He shall come again *just as you saw him go up into the heavens.*"

Eighth, Daniel likewise in the Jewish Captivity prayed toward the Temple.[30]

Citing the same source, Bishop Jacobus de Voragine gives three reasons for orienting the building for worship:

First, it is our way of showing that we seek our true country; second, we look towards Christ crucified; third, we demonstrate our waiting for the coming of the Judge. So Damascenus says: "God planted the Garden of Eden in the East, and when he sent man into exile, God made him live to the west away from paradise. So, seeking and looking toward our ancient homeland and toward God, we worship facing the East. Moreover, the crucified Lord faced toward the west, so we worship looking back to him; and when he ascended, he was borne toward the East, thus the apostles adored him, and he will come again as they saw him going

---

[24] Hugh of Saint-Victor, *De Sacramentis*, bk. 2, pt. 5, 2–3.

[25] Jacobus de Voragine, *Golden Legend*, 387.

[26] Durand, *Rationale*, bk. 1, chap. 1, no. 8.

[27] Ibid., bk. 5, chap. 2, no. 57, appendix B.

[28] Ibid., bk. 1, chap. 1, no. 8, n. 17.

[29] Saint Charles Borromeo, *Instructiones Fabricae et Supellectilis Ecclesiasticae* (Instructions on ecclesiastical buildings), trans. Evelyn Carol Voelker, Ph.D. diss., Syracuse University, 1977 (Ann Arbor, Mich.: University Microfilms International, n.d.) 124 and 378.

[30] Durand, *Rationale*, bk. 5, chap. 2, no. 57, appendix B.

into heaven. Therefore we too pray to him facing the East, awaiting his coming."[31]

We see in this that the God who ordered the universe also uses that order in the mystery of our salvation. Catholics have traditionally designed their churches with this in mind, so that the local church is ordered to the universal order. That is why it is most appropriate for the ministerial priest, acting *in persona Christi*, also to face east for the Consecration. In this way, the building can contribute a universal dimension to the individual act of liturgical worship. With priest and people both facing east, the local gatherings of Christians express themselves in union with the whole body of Christ in a common act of divine worship. As Cardinal Joseph Ratzinger notes:

> We ... need to be reminded that liturgy involves the cosmos—that Christian liturgy is cosmic liturgy. In it we pray and sing in concert with everything "in heaven and earth and under the earth" (Phil 2:10), we join in with the praise rendered by the sun and the stars. Thus in church architecture, for instance, we should see to it that churches are not designed merely with human utility in mind, but that they stand in the cosmos, inviting the sun to be a sign of the praise of God and a sign of the mystery of Christ for the assembled community. A rediscovery of the value of the church building's eastward orientation would help ... in recovering a spirituality which embraces the dimension of creation.[32]

In this way the whole building can become part of the liturgy, for, as Hammond wrote, "The whole structure, no less than the altar, the font or the chalice, is an instrument of worship."[33] By orienting the building traditionally—and this presupposes educating the assembly congregation about the reason for it— the building becomes an iconic aid to help the people focus on the true and deeper meaning of the Lord's sacrifice. Yet, contrary to what Hammond wrote, for the building to work as an instrument of worship, it must *look* like an instrument of worship. It must address the idea of church to the faithful, and to society, within the context of the urban fabric. As J. Rykwert wrote, "The cold forms must also have the power to speak to the worshipper. The mes-

8.6 Christian Basilica, Ruins at Kursi, Israel.

sage which the church building carries must therefore be comprehensible to the worshipper if it is to be of any value; and not only to the worshipper but also, if possible, to the ordinary passer-by."[34]

The church as icon: History and theology

Throughout the building history of Christianity the Church has sought for ways to make the "cold forms" speak. At a rather simple level, this can be seen in the adoption of the pagan basilica as a building type. This was not accidental. The Church chose this building form and gave it a deeper meaning. Thus for the Christian, the basilica, which was the Roman law court, now expressed the justice of Christ, with the bishop, as Christ's representative, sitting in the place of Caesar's representative, the judge. Similarly, the altar of incense became the altar of the true sacrifice as the guarantor of justice [fig. 8.6].[35]

There are, as well, other contemporaneous architectural forms that the Church used and sometimes amalgamated in bits and pieces:

[31] Jacobus de Voragine, *Golden Legend*, 387.
[32] Joseph Cardinal Ratzinger, *The Feast of Faith* (San Francisco: Ignatius Press, 1986), 143.
[33] Hammond, *Liturgy and Architecture*, 29.
[34] Rykwert, *Church Building*, 11.
[35] Ibid., 13.

8.7 The House of Peter, Capernaum, Israel.
top: 1st-century domus ecclesia.
bottom: 4th-century domus ecclesia.

8.8 *below* Octagonal Church over the
House of Peter, Capernaum, Israel, 6th cent.

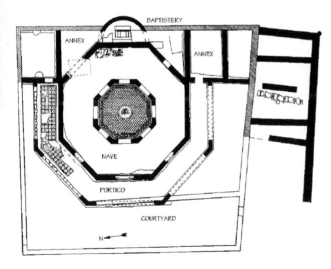

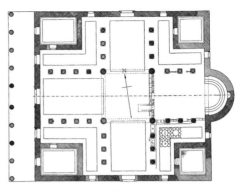

8.9 Church of the Prophets, Apostles, and
Martyrs, Gerasa.

8.10 Santa Costanza, Rome,
4th cent., Plan and Section.

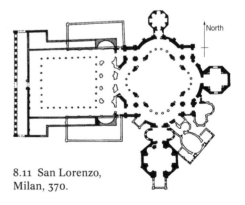

8.11 San Lorenzo,
Milan, 370.

the synagogue, the Mithraic temple, the mausoleum, and the private house. These were not strictly copied but were altered and adapted so that, while still carrying the symbolical content, they sought also to address the needs of Christian worship, the piety of the local community, and the technical abilities of the builders. Later, as we have seen in the case of baptisteries, the postapostolic and patristic builders used symbolic geometries to govern the arrangements of the buildings. Thus, apart from the basilicas, centralized churches (these are generally *martyria*) were built configured as octagons (the House of Peter, Capernaum [figs. 8.7, 8.8]), octagons-in-squares (such as at St. George's in Ezra), cruciform colonnades-in-squares (such as the Church of the Prophets, Apostles, and Martyrs at Gerasa [fig. 8.9]), circular churches (such as Santa Costanza in Rome [fig. 8.10]), the quatrefoil-in-square (San Lorenzo, Milan, *c.* 370 [fig. 8.11]), and many other combinations. All these shapes—the octagon, the hexagon, the square, the circle, and the cross—had obvious symbolic meanings for the Christians of their day.

Rather than catalogue the numerous and subtle variations of the early churches, let us consider in greater depth one building that iconically addressed the issues of the day in an architecturally complex and thoroughly orthodox manner: the Church of San Vitale at Ravenna.

SAN VITALE AS AN ANSWER TO ARIANISM

The Church of San Vitale [fig. 8.12] is often said to be an orthodox architectural response to the Arian controversy, and the building does speak eloquently of the orthodox faith.[36] Various points of orthodoxy are "defended" or "promoted" through a careful language of mosaic depiction, architectonic reference, and spatial organization. Justly famous for its mosaics, the themes at San Vitale depict the sacrificial nature of the Mass by referring to the prototypical sacrifices of Abel and Melchizedek [fig. 8.13]. These sacrifices are offered on a square and, therefore, Christic altar, and they are shown to be found pleasing to God by the hand of blessing from above. A regal *Agnus Dei* surrounded by four angels is also promi-

8.12 San Vitale, Ravenna, 525–548.

8.13 *Sacrifice of Abel and Melchizedek*, San Vitale, Ravenna.

nently shown in the center medallion in the vault over the altar and refers to the real sacrifice of Jesus and its continuation in the Eucharist [fig. 8.14]. The famous mosaic portraits of the Emperor Justinian and his court next to the portraits of Saint Vitalis and Bishop Ecclesius speak to the imperial power as patron and protector of the Church and to the intimate link between Church and state

---

[36] W. MacDonald, *Early Christian and Byzantine Architecture* (New York: George Braziller, 1962), 32; also J. Rykwert writes, "San Vitale is the great statement at Ravenna of Catholic doctrine against the Arians" (*Church Building*, 47).

8.14 *Agnus Dei*, San Vitale, Ravenna.

8.15 *Emperor Justinian and His Court*, San Vitale, Ravenna.

8.16 *Christ with St. Vitale and Bishop Ecclesius*, San Vitale, Ravenna.

necessary for the maintenance of a stable and just society [figs. 8.15, 8.16].

Like many other churches, San Vitale is overtly trinitarian: there are three windows puncturing each wall, triple arcades between each of the large interior piers, and the common Byzantine tripartite arrangement of chancel with the flanking *diakonikon* and prothesis. In plan we see that the building is also divided into three concentric zones of an outer ambulatory, a transitional zone of the seven semicircular arcades, and an octagonal nave in the center [fig. 8.17]. Furthermore, in section the building is divided into three distinct levels as well. The lower two levels comprise a double-stacked triple arcade. This arrangement perhaps refers to the hypostatic union (that in the Person, or the *hypostasis*, of the Word the two natures of humanity and divinity are united without confusion or separation).

The octagonal shape also speaks to certain ideas. Most obviously, as the church is dedicated to Saint Vitalis and other local martyrs, the traditional *martyrium* is the dominant ordering device. There may also be, as von Simson points out, other meanings as well. Remembering the harmonious world view of the ancients, which held that the universe was ordered numerically, as shown by musical tones, proportions, and so forth, the octagon is the architectural equivalent of the octave. Hence, this form can also speak of "perfect consonance". In this tradition, for instance, is the cathedral at Antioch—Constantine's "Golden Octagon"—which was built after Constantine's victory over Licinius and dedicated as "the church of concord". The octagon served to express the restoration of peace throughout the empire. For Justinian, who understood himself to be the successor of Constantine the Great, the octagon had perhaps a prophetically symbolic value. Since Ravenna was still in the hands of heretical enemies, the Ostro-Goths, the shape spoke to the goal of reuniting the East and West under an orderly *pax Iustiniana*, which did occur fifteen years later, when Belisarius captured the city for Justinian. Hence, the "perfect consonance" of this tiny jewel of Catholic orthodoxy spoke of the peaceful con-

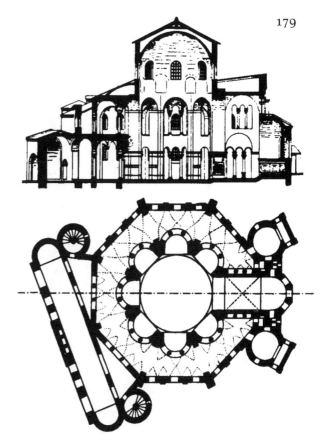

8.17 San Vitale, Ravenna, 525–548, Plan and Section.

cord that would be found across the empire, safeguarded by the Church in concert with the imperial state. As von Simson summarizes, "No other symbol could have better conveyed the abiding political aspirations of Justinian, i.e., the reunion of all parts of the imperium under his scepter through the elimination of heresy and the restoration of the one undivided Christian faith." [37]

Buildings with such subtlety, richness, and complexity as San Vitale are open to multivalent interpretations. What I find most significant about San Vitale, however, is that even the spatial arrangement—with its complex interpenetration of volumes—seems to address the theological problems of its day. While at first glance the building seems to be centralized, as

[37] Otto von Simson, *Sacred Fortress* (Chicago: University of Chicago Press, 1948), 8–9.

8.18 San Vitale, Ravenna, 525–548,
view from upper gallery.

would be typical of a baptistery, a *martyrium* (e.g., Santa Costanza, Rome), or a church commemorating a site (such as the Holy Sepulcher in Jerusalem), the interior is actually highly directional [fig. 8.18]. Rather than being truly centralized, San Vitale is a masterly and subtle manipulation of a centralized nave penetrated by a directional sanctuary that cuts through the ambulatory [see fig. 8.12]. Certainly, the shape is problematic: rather than being a site memorial or *martyrium* (although it may have been built over the site of an earlier *martyrium*), San Vitale is thought by some to have been used only as a parish church. Von Simson writes that it was, in fact, the site of the sepulcher of its three tituli, Saints Vitalis, Gervase, and Protase, which accounts for its mausoleum form.[38] Other authors disagree, conjecturing from the overtly imperial mosaics and

the hybrid form that it may have been a royal chapel.[39] This question still goes begging for an answer and also raises another question: why a spatial organization was chosen that so thoroughly and organically expresses both the liturgical movement of a directional church and the immanence of a centralized church. To answer this question it is helpful to look first at the problem of Arianism.

Arianism began about the year 315 with the heretical teachings of Arius, an Alexandrian priest. In 325, the first ecumenical council of the Catholic Church was convened at Nicaea specifically to condemn Arianism. Even though several subsequent councils also condemned Arianism, in later times this heresy so gripped the Church that at one point the majority of bishops ascribed to it. While Arianism eventually split into several schools of thought, endemic to all was the contention that the Logos was not eternal and consubstantial with the Father—"There was a time when the Son was not."[40] Thus Arianism denied the true divinity of Christ. And while both the councils of Nicaea I (325) and Constantinople I (381) anathematized Arius and his followers, the heresy continued to pervade the Church for centuries under various manifestations.

One of these recurrences was during the fifth and sixth centuries, when Ravenna was the capital of the Arian Ostro-Gothic Empire. Because Ravenna was the center of his empire, the Emperor Theodoric built several large and important Arian churches in Ravenna, including San Apollinare Nuovo and the Church of Spirito Santo (as the Arian cathedral with its adjacent Arian baptistery). In his later years Theodoric was either tolerant of the orthodox Catholics or too weak to prevent them from building. Either way, the Church of San Vitale was begun by Bishop Ecclesius in 525, the year before Theodoric's death. The church was built in the time of transition between Arian Ostro-Gothic rule and the Catholic Byzantine Empire. When Theodoric died in 526, the

---

[38] Ibid., 15.
[39] Cf. R. Milburn, *Early Christian Art and Architecture* (London: Scolar, 1988), 177. This is not, however, Milburn's opinion.
[40] Cf. Henry Bettenson, *Documents of the Christian Church*, 2d ed. (London: Oxford University Press, 1963), 40.

Arian Empire began to collapse. In 540 the Byzantine army under Belisarius laid siege to Ravenna and captured it. The Byzantine Empire then set up Ravenna as its western seat, governed by a local exarch. The Church of San Vitale was consecrated on April 19, 548, by Bishop Maximian. With this chronology in mind, it seems reasonable to view San Vitale not only as a product of its time but, more importantly, as a statement of orthodox Catholicism against the errors of Arianism. Though, of course, it is inevitably somewhat conjectural to "read" a building, there seems to be much at San Vitale that addressed the problems of its day.

Arianism contained both trinitarian and christological errors: trinitarian because it taught that the Word was a creature of the Father, albeit an exalted one; and christological in denying that the Word assumed a human soul. The consequence of this thinking had a radical impact on the state of mankind's relationship with God, for it concerned the question of whether or not man was redeemed by Jesus' death and Resurrection. The Fathers' argument is that only if Christ is true God can he save us, only then can he *divinize* us. We have seen how the mosaics and the architectonic devices give expression to a Catholic understanding of the Trinity and the sacrifice of the Mass. In San Vitale and other Justinian churches, I see an architectural response to controversies about the Trinity and the Incarnation. I believe that these churches are an architectural expression of the trinitarian and christological doctrine of "co-inherence", or *perichoresis*.

When explaining the relationships within the Trinity and the divine and human natures in the second Person, the Fathers of the Church spoke of the co-inherence, or *perichoresis*, of the triune God and of the incarnate Word. The Greek *perichoresis*, like its Latin equivalent *circumincessio*, is a theological term whose christological sense was first developed in the early sixth century by Leontius of Byzantium and which was later used as a trinitarian formulation to express the unity found in the Trinity.[41] It refers to the "mutual interpenetration of the Persons of the Godhead, so that although each Person is distinct in relation to the others, nevertheless, each participates fully in the being of the others. The being of the Godhead is thus one and indivisible."[42] The original Greek word has the more subtle and poetical sense of "dancing around", a joyous term used to describe this mystical communion of the Divine Persons. This is the indwelling of the Divine Persons to which our Lord refers in the Gospel of Saint John: "Do you not believe that I am in the Father and the Father is in me?" (Jn 14:10; cf. 17:21). Saint Paul likewise says that the Holy Spirit dwells in the Father and the Son, for he "searches everything, even the depths of God" (1 Cor 2:10). This idea of co-inherence, which was later expressed by the term *perichoresis*, was a powerful weapon against the Arians and was employed by the Fathers even before the word itself was established as a technical term. For example, Saint Basil the Great says that "the whole Son is in the Father and has all the Father in himself".[43] Later, as the theological sense of the word developed in the sixth and seventh centuries, the Fathers zealously taught the *perichoresis* of the Trinity and the Incarnation against Arianism. Since Ravenna in the first half of the sixth century was the center of the Arian Ostro-Gothic Empire, and since the Church has always had a tradition of using images to fight heresies, especially against the Arians, Nestorians, and Monophysites, it is not unreasonable to assume that some architectural expression for this teaching was found.[44]

There is, of course, a danger in thinking of co-inherence, or *perichoresis*, in spatial terms when pondering the Trinity. However, since sacred architecture is concerned with trying to find architectural expression for theological

---

[41] The term *perichoresis* has a very complex history, marked by a wide range of uses and various related words (e.g., ἀντιπεριχωρέω, περιχωρέω, χωρητικός, χωρέω, χωρεῖν, περικεχώρηκε, περιχωρήσασα) employed by many of the Fathers from the fourth to the seventh century (Macarius of Egypt, Gregory of Nazianzus, Gregory of Nyssa, Leontius of Byzantium, Maximus, Pseudo-Cyril) when grappling with the question of co-inherence. Cf. G. L. Prestige, *God in Patristic Thought* (London: S.P.C.K., 1952), chap. 14, passim.

[42] V. A. Harvey, *A Handbook of Theological Terms* (New York: Macmillan, 1964), 181.

[43] St. Basil, *Ep.* 38, 8; PG 32, 340C.

[44] L. Ouspensky, *The Theology of the Icon* (Crestwood, N.Y.: St. Vladimir's Seminary Press, 1978), 105–6.

ideas, it seems perfectly appropriate to ask what theological ideas are being expressed. In San Vitale, the penetration of the sanctuary into the nave and ambulatory is a kind of *perichoreses*: each one of the three, by analogy with the Trinity, is contained in the others. The interdependence of the nave and sanctuary, with the encompassing ambulatory, creates an organic unity and gives a sense of stability in contrast to the restless movement found in the longitudinal basilica.

One might say that this church building is an icon of the "unity without confusion" that lies at the heart of the mysteries of the Trinity and the Incarnation. The Church worships the Trinity in Unity and the Unity in Trinity, "without either confusing the persons or dividing the substance."[45] Likewise, as the Second Council of Constantinople (convoked by Justinian in 553) taught, reaffirming Chalcedon, in the incarnate Word there is a unity of Divine Person without any confusion of the two natures: "For the Church of God repudiates and condemns equally those who introduce a separation or division and those who introduce a confusion into the mystery of the divine Incarnation."[46]

By its unifying of distinct elements, San Vitale bears witness to *perichoreses* in the three Divine Persons in the one nature of the Godhead and to *perichoresis* in the two natures in the one Divine Person of the Word Incarnate. This was a powerful affirmation of orthodoxy in the heart of the Arian capital, a kind of architectonic refutation of the major heresies of the previous two centuries–not only Arianism but also Nestorianism and Monophysitism.

There is the danger that this is a back-formed explication. There are often certain consonances found in medieval architecture between the building form and the symbolic content of the building. Undoubtedly this is often quite intentional, as in the case of Saint Ambrose explaining that the cruciform plan of the Holy Apostles Church in Milan symbolizes Christ's victory via the Cross. In other cases, it is probable that symbolic meanings were subsequently attributed to existing forms. In this regard, Krautheimer writes:

Probably the relationship between pattern and symbolic meaning could be better described as being determined by a network of reciprocal half-distinct connotations. Rather than being either the starting point or else a *post festum* [sic] interpretation, the symbolic significance is something which merely accompanied the particular form which was chosen for the structure. It accompanied it as a more or less uncertain connotation which was only dimly visible and whose specific interpretation was not necessarily agreed upon. Yet as a connotation it was nearly always coupled with the pattern which had been chosen. Its very vagueness explains the variety of interpretations given to one and the same form either by one or several authors.[47]

Since we have no explicit evidence of the architect's intention, we must put the present interpretation of San Vitale as an expression of *perichoresis* in the latter, indeterminate category. And yet, this explanation does answer the formal questions posed by the building. This may be seen by looking at another Justinian church: Hagia Sophia [see fig. 2.2]. The Great Church of Hagia Sophia, which is contemporaneous with San Vitale, is another Byzantine church that even more subtly integrates the directional and centralized forms. The plan is of a great dome centered in a square, and the space seems to be centralized because of the tremendous dome above: yet in plan the length of the nave is seen to be almost three times its width [fig. 8.19]! Thus, depending on one's location in the building, one senses being in either a vast, centralized space or a long, axial hall [figs. 8.20, 8.21]. It seems likely that Justinian's architects (and theologians) could afford a more subtle statement in the Byzantine capital city, where the threat of Arianism had long passed, whereas at Ravenna, the center of the Arian Empire, a more dramatically obvious statement would have been made.

Given its unique historical setting, the contemporaneous theological controversy, and the agility of the patristic mind, it seems

---

[45] "The Pseudo-Athanasian Symbol *Quicumque*", in J. Neuner, S.J., and J. Dupuis, S.J., *The Christian Faith in the Doctrinal Documents of the Catholic Church* (London: HarperCollins, 1983), 11.

[46] Ibid., 161.

[47] Krautheimer, "Introduction", 8–9.

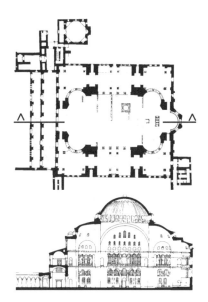

8.19 Hagia Sophia, Istanbul, 532–537, Plan and Section.

8.20 Hagia Sophia, Istanbul, 532–537, Interior.

8.21 Hagia Sophia, Istanbul, 532–537, Interior.

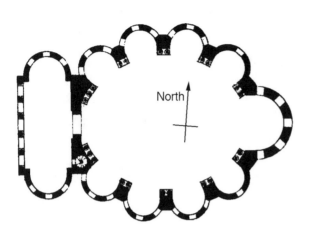

8.22 St. Gereon, Cologne, 380.

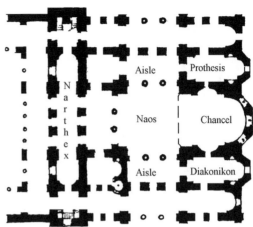

8.23 Nea Ecclesia, Istanbul, 880.

reasonable to view the Church of San Vitale, with its organic expression of the longitudinal sanctuary penetrating to the centralized nave, as a sort of "architectural *perichoresis*" that directly answered the challenge of Arianism. And in this way the Church would have been continuing the tradition of using architectural forms to express theological concepts, speaking to the needs of the day in a language that the people of the day would understand.

ICONOGRAPHY IN THE EASTERN
CHURCH MODELS

San Vitale can be seen, then, as a rather comprehensive architectural statement of the orthodox faith. Such a complex statement, while founded in and expressing the theology of the patristic age, is rather isolated. Most of the early churches can be understood as developmental stages toward the more conventional and now-familiar forms: typically the basilican form in the West, with various cruciform adaptations, and the more centralized cross-domed churches in the East, again with seemingly endless variations.[48] These two forms developed—both liturgically and symbolically—in conjunction with developments in their respective liturgies.

Across the ages, many types of Christian churches were built throughout the East and West. We find centralized buildings in the West from the fourth century (San Lorenzo in Milan,

c. 378, and Saint Gereon in Cologne, c. 380, [fig. 8.22]), and we even find longitudinal Eastern basilicas in the fourteenth century (e.g., Staro Nagoricane, 1313). However, in the Christian East the integration of architectural arrangement and liturgical requirement found perfection in the "nine-square" or cross-domed church. The archetypical arrangement is a building ordered by a three-by-three grid, with a dome over the central square, as exemplified in the ninth-century Nea Ecclesia in Constantinople [fig. 8.23]. The three eastern bays serve the clergy, with the typical Byzantine tripartite arrangement of the *diakonikon* and *prothesis* flanking the sanctuary. The *diakonikon* on the south is used to store the Scriptures and icons. The *prothesis* on the north serves as both a sacristy for the eucharistic elements and as a place of preparation of the gifts in the clerical ceremony also known as the Prothesis, which occurs prior to the arrival of the laity. (The Prothesis was evidently also found in the medieval Western Church, though its use was obviously waning: as Bishop Durand recounts, "For when they bear the bread of Prothesis to the Lord's table and the Mysteries, they understand not its signification more than brute beasts which carry bread for the use of others.")[49]

---

[48] Cf. Richard Krautheimer, *Early Christian and Byzantine Architecture*, 3d ed. (Hannondsworth, England: Penguin, 1979), 299–315, for development of the cross-domed church.
[49] Durand, *Rationale*, Proeme, no. 3.

The sanctuary, as we have seen, is the representation of the Mercy Seat in the Mosaic Tabernacle, the Holy of Holies in the Solomonic Temple, and even the very throne of God in heaven. It is connected to the nave (*naos*) by the iconostasis: the screen symbolizes the Veil, which is a barrier against profanation; and the central portal, called the royal doors, unites the two spaces and is used liturgically to represent the manifestation of Christ in the world [fig. 8.24]. The central square, the *naos*, is the center of the building physically, liturgically, and symbolically. It is expressed as such by a dome surmounting it [fig. 8.25]. This dome recalls the heavens, for the room symbolizes the redeemed world of the "new heaven and new earth" (2 Pet 3:13). On the dome is the image of the Redeemer as Pantocrator, he who holds all things together in heaven and on earth [see fig. 7.11]. But the dome also suggests that the *naos* is the womb of the Virgin, as well as the holy cave of Bethlehem and the holy cave of the Sepulcher. Thus it evokes many images of places where the Church is vivified by the Spirit, born into the world, and redeemed into the glory of the Lord. The lay faithful have their place in the side aisles and are ministered to by the clergy from the *naos*, whence the Scriptures are read and Communion distributed. Historically, the women were often segregated in the *gynaikon*, the gallery above the aisles. The entrance to the church is usually through the narthex in the three western bays. The narthex is symbolically the unredeemed world, hence it is the place for the catechumens and penitents. Traditionally the laity were relegated to it and to the aisles that are the north and south bays on each side of the central *naos*.

The whole building comes into its own with the great liturgical processions found in the Christian East. There are two processions, the "Little Entrance" of the Gospels and the "Great Entrance" of the Eucharist. They each signify Christ coming into the world in particular manifestations. At the Little Entrance, which usually begins in the *diakonikon*, the book of the Gospels is brought in procession around the church, through the *naos*, and up to the altar, where prayers are offered in front

8.24 Iconostasis, St. Ann's, Harrisburg, Penn.

8.25 Hagia Sophia, Salonika, 8th cent.

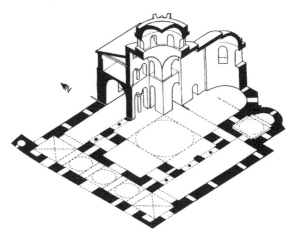

of the place where the Gospel is proclaimed. The book of the Gospels is then brought into the *naos* through the royal doors, thus symbolizing the beginning of Christ's ministry, and presented to the laity.[50] A fourteenth-century commentator on the Divine Liturgy of Saint John Chrysostom writes:

While this [the third antiphon] is being sung, the Gospels are brought in [from the *diakonikon*]; the holy book is carried in by the

---

[50] There is frequently widely divergent interpretation in the Eastern Fathers. For instance, whereas Maximus and Germanos see the Little Entrance as Christ coming into the world, Nicholas of Andida and Nicholas Cabasilas think it representative of his baptism in the Jordan and the beginning of his ministry, while Symeon of Thessalonike interprets it as the Resurrection, Ascension, and Pentecost. *See* Hugh Wybrew, *The Orthodox Liturgy* (Crestwood, N.Y.: St. Vladimir's Seminary Press, 1990), 182.

deacon, or, if he be not present, by the priest himself, surrounded by a procession of acolytes bearing candles and incense. The priest, just before he enters the sanctuary, standing immediately in front of the holy gates [royal doors], prays, while waiting for the chant to end, that God will send his holy angels to escort him to the altar and offer sacrifice with him and take part in the praise of the Lord. . . . When he has prayed thus, he goes into the sanctuary and places the Gospels on the altar. The [third] antiphon is like an encounter before the Lord who draws near and appears; that is why it is chanted while the Book of the Gospels is brought in and shown, since it represents Christ. . . . When these are over, the priest, standing in front of the altar [in front of the sanctuary; i.e., in the *naos*], raises the Gospel-book and shows it to the people, thus symbolizing the manifestation of the Lord, when he began to appear to the multitudes.[51]

Similarly, at the Great Entrance the clergy process from the prothesis through the church with the eucharistic elements. The priest and his deacons then enter into the altar behind the iconostasis, where the Sacrifice is offered, and then return to the *naos* to distribute Communion from its perimeter. As this event is recorded and explained:

The priest, having said the doxology aloud, comes to the altar of preparation [the Prothesis], takes the offerings, and reverently holding them head-high departs. Carrying them thus, he goes to the altar, after walking in slow and solemn procession through the nave of the church. The faithful chant during this procession, kneeling down reverently and devoutly, and praying that they may be remembered when the offering is made. The priest goes on, surrounded by candles and incense, until he comes to the altar. This is done, no doubt, for practical reasons; it was necessary to bring the offerings which are to be sacrificed to the altar and set down there, and to do this with all reverence and devotion. This is the way in which kings of old brought their gifts to God; they did not allow others to do it for them, but brought their offerings themselves, wearing their crowns. Also, the ceremony signifies the last manifestation of the Christ, which aroused the hatred of the Jews, when he embarked on the journey from his native country to Jerusalem, where he was to be sacrificed; then he rode into the Holy City on the back of an ass, escorted by a cheering crowd.[52]

So we can see a deep-rooted integration of liturgical and architectonic symbolism in the cross-domed church. It is a symbolism rooted in the same medieval thought that produced and venerated the icons, and it is thus to be considered with the same understanding. In fact, the patristic tradition indicates that both the church building and the liturgy are to be understood iconographically. "The entire church is an image of the Universe, of the visible world, and of man; within it, the chancel represents man's soul, the altar his spirit, the *naos* his body. The bishop's Entrance into the church symbolizes Christ's coming into the flesh, his Entrance into the bema Christ's Ascension to heaven. The Great Entrance stands for Revelation, the Kiss of peace for the union of the soul with God; indeed every part of the liturgy has a symbolic spiritual meaning."[53] Saint Maximus the Confessor sees the *cathedra* as Christ's heavenly throne, the canopy over the altar as commemorating the site of the Crucifixion, and the deacons in their golden dalmatics symbolizing the angels as "ministering spirits sent forth to serve, for the sake of those who are to obtain salvation" (Heb 1:14), moving between the altar and the *naos*. Although some of these ideas may seem to us obvious and others subtle or abstruse, it is important to remember that for the patristic mind the symbol was meant to communicate the spiritual reality, as the material world was already but a symbol of the true reality by way of theophany. As to the effect of such symbolism, Krautheimer writes: "No doubt, only a small group of laymen was fully conscious of all this sophisticated symbolism. The general ideas, however, permeated to a wider public. In entering the church, the average believer was aware, we may be sure, that he entered Heaven; and he saw, in the procession

[51] Nicholas Cabasilas, *A Commentary on the Divine Liturgy*, trans. J. M. Hussey and P. A. McNulty (London: S.P.C.K., 1978), chaps. 15, 19–20, pp. 51–52, 57, and 59.
[52] Ibid., chap. 24, p. 65.
[53] Krautheimer, *Early Christian Architecture* (Baltimore, Md.: Penguin, 1965), 212.

8.26 St. Paul's-outside-the-Walls, Rome, View of Nave.

of the clergy, the angelic host about to offer the sacrifice of the heavenly altar."[54]

ICONOGRAPHY IN THE WESTERN CHURCH MODELS

Similar ideas were developed at the same time in the West, although along different lines. The imagery of the church found rich, subtle, complex, and not infrequently abstruse expression by the medieval mind. From the patristic period (third century) through the Gothic Schoolmen (thirteenth century), metaphoric meaning was ascribed to seemingly each and every component of the church building. We will explore this thousand-year span from Eusebius to Guillaume Durand in two major phases: the themes of the medieval builders through the Romanesque period, and those of the Gothic cathedral builders. This is not to suggest any major shift in direction. Quite to the contrary, many of the symbolical themes continued even through the Renaissance and Baroque ages. There are, however, important and truly profound innovations in the Gothic that cannot be found in the Romanesque and that therefore require separate treatment. So, while the Gothic builders continued many of their predecessors' iconographic traditions, they brought the full glory of their lucid and articulated metaphysics to shine on the buildings they built. We will, therefore, consider the

earlier symbolical language first and separately from the Gothic innovations.

The basilican form was used from the beginning of the widespread Christian building effort after the Edict of Milan. The early Christians used the basilican form to take the law courts of the Roman Empire and impart to them the idea of true justice under Christ's domain. The basilican form was probably first used in 313 at the huge Roman cathedral of Christus Salvator, now known to us as St. John Lateran [see fig. I.2]. In the Mediterranean religions, whether Greek, Roman, or Jewish, there had always been a separation between the forecourt, where the laity were allowed, and the sanctuary, or "Holy of Holies", where members of the the priestly class were allowed. In the Christian basilica, however, we find the innovation of priest and people in one space and under one roof.[55] Although the space was still divided [fig. 8.26] in a hierarchical expression of relative degrees of sacredness, because Christianity was not a mystery religion (that is, for the initiates), the people could now participate directly in the sacrifice.

A further development to the basilica was the addition of a large lateral *bema* at the east

[54] Ibid., 213.

[55] Christian Norberg-Schulz, *Meaning in Western Architecture* (New York: Praeger, 1975), 123. Archaeological evidence suggests that this may, however, have been derived from the Mithraeum, as can be seen beneath San Clemente in Rome.

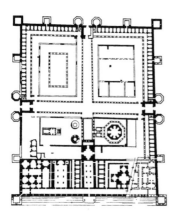

8.27 Palace of Diocletian, Split.

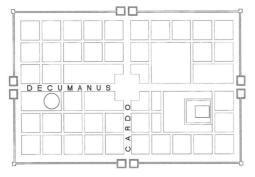

8.28 Roman city plan.

this *imago mundi* is found in widely varied cultures in city planning and in religious and ritualistic architecture [fig. 8.27].[56] Hence, this cosmological order, the way in which the gods ordered the visible world, became the basis for the way in which the Romans ordered their domain. In Roman town planning the cities were typically square or rectangular and subdivided into four quadrants by two great roads running at right angles. The *cardo*, which ran north to south, represented the world's axis, and the *decumanus* traced the path of the sun from east to west. At each end of the two main streets was one of the four city gates [fig. 8.28].

Norberg-Schulz argues that this was a deliberate expression of the *pax Romana*, bringing order throughout the world. The *civitas*, therefore, became a microcosm of the universal (Roman) order. Thus it was that traitors, who had tried to usurp the Roman order, and criminals, who had disobeyed the laws of that order, were crucified. The cross, which was a symbol of that order, became their instrument of execution.[57] If this explanation was both real and widely held, the early Christian must have seen a certain irony in that the One through whom the universe's order was created was put to death on a symbol of that order, thus bringing about the true redemption of that order.

After the Edict of Milan, the Christians took the form of the cross and again used it, this time perhaps to symbolize Christ's victory over the pagan Roman order and the establishment of the true universal order of all things united under the Lord's reign (cf. Phil 2:9–11) [fig. 8.29]. As early as A.D. 382, Saint Ambrose intentionally ordered a church in a cruciform plan to symbolize the victory of Christ. Other forms were also used, and these seem to be closely connected with the dedication of the church. For instance, Marian churches tend to be centralized, as do those dedicated to Saint Michael [fig. 8.30], which also tend to be on hills or promontories.[58] But because the sym-

end. This created the cruciform plan that began the association of the church's plan with the Body of the Lord on the Cross [see fig. 1.16]. At this point the building began to take on an iconographic imagery of the church as the body of Christ: the heart of the Lord represented at the crossing, where the altar of sacrifice stood; the head represented by the seat of power in the episcopal *cathedra* at the apse; and his torso, arms and legs, and hands and feet represented by the people gathered in the nave and transepts.

Christian Norberg-Schulz suggests that the cross had particular symbolic meaning not just for the Christians but for the Romans as well. For the Romans, as for many other traditional societies, the cross was a symbol of the *cosmos*: it represented the juncture of the north-to-south axis of the earth with the east-to-west path of the sun. Eliade shows us that

---

[56] Mircea Eliade, *The Sacred and the Profane: The Nature of Religion*, trans. Willard R. Trask (New York: Harcourt, Brace, 1959), 42ff.

[57] Norberg-Schulz, *Meaning in Western Architecture*, 84 and 146.

[58] Krautheimer, "Introduction", 21.

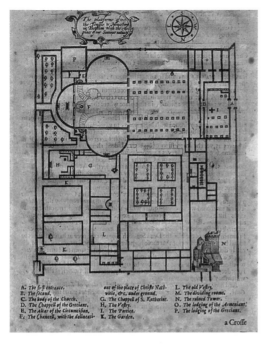

A. The first entrance.
B. The second.
C. The body of the Church.
D. The Chappell of the Grecians.
E. The Altar of the Circumcision.
F. The Chancell, with the delineati-

out of the place of Christs Nati-
vitie, &c. under ground.
G. The Chappell of S. Katherine.
H. The Vestry.
I. The Portico.
K. The Garden.

L. The old Vestry.
M. The dividing rooms.
N. The ruined Tower.
O. The lodging of the Armenians.
P. The lodging of the Grecians.

a Crosse

8.30 St. Michael's, Littlemore, Oxfordshire.

8.29 Church of the Nativity, Bethlehem, 6th cent.,
George Sandy's Travels, London, 1652.

bol of the cross is so obviously and inextricably linked to the Christian Faith, the representation of the Crucified in the floor plan was to remain the primary formal determinant for Latin-rite Catholic churches well into the twentieth century.

The ordering of the church to the cross is but one, and perhaps the most obvious, example of medieval symbolism. For the comprehensive medieval mind, though, there were seemingly no boundaries to the spiritual interpretation of material things. This way of thinking, of course, goes back to Scripture. Christ taught in parables, creating analogies by using the things around him to explain the things of the Kingdom to his disciples (cf. Mt 13:10–15; Mk 4:10–12; and Lk 8:9–10). The apostolic writers continued this tradition, using metaphors of the body, of armor, of ships, and of buildings.

We are going to examine briefly the use of building metaphors, as it is a theme that recurs across the ages and bears directly on the focus of this chapter. Bypassing Jesus' parable of the "man who built his house on sand", the idea of specifically developing architectural analogies certainly gains a place in the Church with the writings of Saint Paul. In 1 Corinthians 3:10–17, he draws out the analogy both to encourage the faithful and to teach eschatologically:

According to the commission of God given to me, like a skilled master builder I laid a foundation, and another man is building upon it. Let each man take care how he builds upon it. For no other foundation can any one lay than that which is laid, which is Jesus Christ. Now if any one builds on the foundation with gold, silver, precious stones, wood, hay, stubble— each man's work will become manifest; for the Day will disclose it, because it will be revealed with fire, and the fire will test what sort of work each one has done. If the work which any man has built on the foundation survives, he will recieve a reward. If any man's work is burned up, he will suffer loss, though he himself will be saved, but only as through fire.

Do you not know that you are God's temple and that God's Spirit dwells in you? If any one destroys God's temple, God will destroy him. For God's temple is holy, and that temple you are.

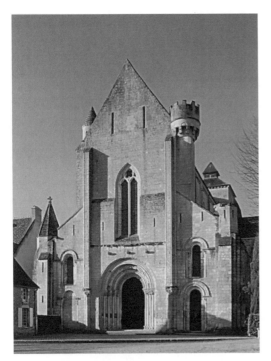

8.31 "The Church as the City of God", Abbeye de Fontgombault, 11th cent.

8.32 "It Was Lit by the Radiant Glory of God", Abbeye de Fontgombault, 11th cent.

Again, in Ephesians 2:20–22, he takes the theme of a building to explain the structure of the Church: "[You are] built upon the foundation of the apostles and prophets, Christ Jesus himself is the cornerstone, in whom the whole structure is joined together and grows into a holy temple in the Lord; in whom you also are built into it for a dwelling place of God in the Spirit."

This explanation of the Church in the language of building is then continued in Saint John's Revelation, when he takes it to the scale of the whole City of God [fig. 8.31]: "The wall of the city had twelve foundations, and on them the twelve names of the twelve apostles of the Lamb" (Rev. 21:14). It is a city that "has no need of sun or moon to shine upon it, for the glory of God is its light, and its lamp is the Lamb" (Rev 21:23) [fig. 8.32].

The theme of the Church, the people of God, comprising a great building or a city was continually developed. In the writings of Eusebius, Constantine the Great's court historian, there is an interesting passage that explains the places in the Church for different persons depending on their gifts, strengths, and vocations:

Building truly in righteousness, [a particular bishop] equitably divided the whole people in accordance with their powers. With some, he walled round the outer enclosure—that was enough for them—making unwavering faith the protective barrier. This accounted for far the greater part of the people, who were not strong enough to support a greater edifice. To some he entrusted the entrances to the church proper, giving them the task of waiting at the doors to guide those entering, since he justifiably regarded them as gateways to the house of God. Others he made under-props to the first outer pillars that form a quadrangle round the court, bringing them for the first time into touch with the letter of the four gospels. Others he joined to the basilica along both sides, still under instruction and in process of advancing, but not very far removed from the divine vision that the faithful enjoy of what is innermost. From these last he chooses the undefiled souls, purified like gold by divine washing; these he makes under-props to pillars much grander than the outer ones, drawing on the innermost teachings of

8.33 Hugh of St.-Victor.

Holy Writ, while others he illumines with openings towards the light. With one huge gateway, consisting of the praise of our Sovereign Lord, the one and only God, he adorns the whole cathedral; and on both sides of the Father's supreme power he supplies the secondary beams of the light of Christ, and the Holy Ghost. As to the rest, from end to end of the building he reveals in all its abundance and rich variety the clear light of the truth in every man, and everywhere and from every source he found room for the living, securely laid, and unshakable stones of human souls. In this way he is constructing out of them all a great and kingly house, glowing and full of light within and without, in that not only their heart and mind, but their body too, has been gloriously enriched with the many-blossomed adornment of chastity and temperance.[59]

We see this idea that different persons have different places in the building, recalling Saint Paul's analogy of the Body, both continued

and enriched almost a millennium later in the writings of Hugh of Saint-Victor. Hugh's treatise titled *The Mystical Mirror of the Church* is important, for it gives us an insight into the iconographic understanding right at the beginning of the Gothic period.[60] Where Bishop Durand, as we shall see, continues much of Hugh's thought one and a half centuries later in a Middle Gothic treatise, Hugh, who was Abbot Suger's friend and contemporary, gives us an accounting at the close of the Romanesque period and thus is a demonstrable link in the continuity of thought between the two epochs [fig. 8.33].

Hugh starts his treatise with a description of the composition of the Church in the language of church buildings: "The material church in which the people come together to praise God signifies the Holy Catholic Church, which is built in heaven of living stones." Continuing the scriptural teachings, Jesus is the Cornerstone, upon which is the foundation of the apostles and prophets, and the Church's lay faithful members, whether Jew or Gentile, are the stones that make up the walls and must be "polished and squared . . . and placed so as to last forever by the hands of the Chief Workman." These stones, however, are not all equal in either strength or position: "Of these, some are borne and do not bear, as the more simple folk in the Church; some are borne and also bear, as the middling sort; and others only bear and are not borne except by Christ alone." The cement that joins all the stones together is charity, and the bond is one of peace.

Hugh then takes a tour around the building, noting that "The towers are the preachers and prelates: who are her wards and defense" [fig. 8.34]. At the highest point of the building is traditionally found an emblem of a rooster sitting on an iron rod, placed above a cross sitting on a sphere. Each of these has meaning: the cock is the preacher who wakes the children from their sleep, sleep being a metaphor for sin; the iron rod represents the straightforward speech of the preacher, who speaks according to the Word of God; the rod is above the cross

---

[59] Eusebius, *The History of the Church*, trans. G. A. Williamson (New York: Dorset Press, 1984), bk. 10, chap. 4, 67ff.
[60] The text is taken from Durand, *Rationale*, pp. 197–209.

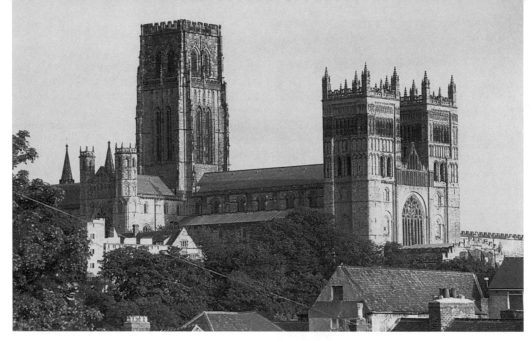

8.34 "The towers are preachers and prelates", Durham Cathedral, 1093–1133.

to show that the words of Scripture are "consummated and confirmed by the Cross: whence our Lord said in his Passion, 'It is finished.'" The sphere signifies both the world redeemed by the Cross[61] and, by its perfect roundness, the perfection with which the Catholic Faith is to be preached and practiced. The bells in the towers also receive this studied treatment: bells are also a type of preacher, for it is by their voice "that the people are called together to the church". If the bell is the preacher, then Hugh sees the clapper, "which causes sound from the two sides of the bell", as the tongue of the preacher, "which causes both Testaments to resound". In this schema, the wood frame supporting the bells is like the Cross; the cramps (which fasten the bell to the frame) are charity, "by which the preacher is bound fast to the Cross"; the rope is the humble life of the preacher; and the rings on the rope are "perseverance and the crown of reward".

In taking us inside the building, Hugh notes that the doors, of course, represent Christ. The windows are seen as the Holy Scriptures for two reasons. As windows repel wind and rain, so do the Scriptures protect us from evil; and, as windows let in the sun's light, so the True Sun illuminates our hearts with the Word. Even that masonry adjacent to the windows that is splayed on the interior is given interpretation: "These are wider on the inside than from the outside, because the mystical sense [of Scripture] is more ample and preeminent than the literal sense." The interior pillars are the Doctors of the Church, "who spiritually uphold the Temple of God by their doctrines" [fig. 8.35], and the columns are the evangelists—"silver columns: for according to the Song of Songs, 'He made the pillars there of silver'" (Song 3:10).

Hugh continues his consideration of other elements in the church: the choir seating, the chancel, the altar, the altar coverings, the steps, and so on. The richness with which he interprets the church building is a treasure for us. It is not, however, I think, a question of Hugh's innovation, but rather a summary of the themes common to the medieval understanding. We have seen a similar method of interpretation in the Eastern Church through the writings of Saint Maximus the Confessor and Nicholas Cabasilas. Therefore, it seems reason-

---

[61] This certainly argues against the fatuous but prevalent modern notion that pre-Renaissance men thought the world was flat!

able to take even later sources, such as the thirteenth-century *Rationale* by Bishop Durand and the sixteenth-century *Fardle of Facions*, to see how these ideas were continued and developed across the centuries.

Bishop Durand, to whom I have referred throughout this book, was a French cleric who was born around 1230 and who died in Rome on the Feast of All Saints, 1296 [fig. 8.37]. His accomplishments in the intervening sixty-six years speak to his character, his abilities, and his determination. Guillaume Durand was a canonical jurist who wrote several scholarly treatises on canon law. In the course of his career, he was at various times chaplain to Pope Clement IV, auditor of the Sacred Palace, Gregory X's papal legate at the Council of Lyons, a captain of the papal forces, and papal ambassador to the Sultan. In 1286, Durand was ordained bishop of Mende and later was offered the archbishopric of Ravenna, which he declined in the year he died. Among his accomplishments, Durand left us a vast and impressive account of the architectural, liturgical, scriptural, and sacramental symbolism of the Western Church. The eight-volume opus, entitled *Rationale Divinorum Officiorum*, is perhaps our most comprehensive account of Christian symbolism yet written, and certainly the most comprehensive of the symbolism of the medieval church. In it, Bishop Durand explicitly hoped to set forth "the reasons of the variations in Divine Offices and their truths . . . manifested: which the prelates and priests of churches ought faithfully to preserve in the shrine of their breasts."[62] His intent was to cover the whole of Christian symbolism as it pertained to encouraging and edifying the Church: symbolism found in church buildings, in the duties and places of the members of the body of Christ, in the vestments, in the liturgy, in the other offices, in the Sunday and holyday celebrations, in the liturgical calendar, and in the dedication ceremonies of churches.[63] Today we are seeing a renewed interest in the work of Bishop Durand. Although relatively little of the eight-volume work has been translated and published in

8.35 "who spiritually uphold the Temple of God", Durham Cathedral, 1093–1133.

8.36 *below* Durham Cathedral, 1093–1133, Plan.

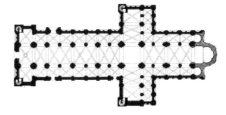

8.37 The Tomb of Guillaume Durand, Bishop of Mende, Santa Maria-sopra-Minerva.

---

[62] Durand, *Rationale*, Proeme, no. 18.
[63] Ibid., no. 19.

English, a definitive Latin text is now being prepared, which should yield considerable fruit for liturgists interested in rediscovering and understanding the symbolic languages of the medieval liturgy, its environment, and its accoutrements.[64]

Bishop Durand begins much like Hugh of Saint-Victor by clarifying the twofold meaning of the word *church*: "the one, a material building, wherein the Divine Offices are celebrated; the other, a spiritual fabric, which is the collection of the faithful.... For as the material church is constructed from the joining together of various stones, so is the spiritual Church by that of various men."[65] Like Eusebius and Hugh before him, Bishop Durand considers the places and roles of the faithful in terms of building construction, again amplifying and enriching the analogy:

> The faithful predestined to eternal life are the stones in the structure of this wall, which shall continually be built up unto the world's end. And one stone is added to another when masters in the Church teach and confirm and strengthen those put under them; and whosoever in Holy Church undertakes painful labors from brotherly love, he as it were bears up the weight of the stones that have been placed above him. These stones, which are of larger size and polished, or squared, and placed on the outside and at the angles of the building, are men of holier life than others, who by their merits and prayers retain weaker brethren in Holy Church.[66]

Again, Bishop Durand considers polished and squared stones to be like holy and pure lives, which must be placed "by the hands of the Great Workman into an abiding place in the Church".[67] Whereas for Hugh cement was simply charity, Bishop Durand breaks it down into its component parts, assigning each a spiritual meaning:

> The cement, without which there can be no stability of the walls, is made of lime, sand, and water. The lime is fervent charity, which joins itself to the sand, that is, undertakings for the temporal welfare of our brethren: because true charity takes care of the widow and the aged, and the infants and the infirm.... Now the lime and the sand are bound together in the wall by an admixture of water. But wa-

ter is an emblem of the Spirit. And as without cement the stones cannot cohere, so neither can men be built up in the heavenly Jerusalem without charity, which the Holy Ghost works in them.[68]

Bishop Durand then considers the components of the church building: the four walls are the doctrines of the four evangelists as well as the four cardinal virtues; and as each wall has length and breadth and height, so the height is both courage and hope aspiring to heaven, the length is the fortitude that "patiently endures till attaining its heavenly Home", and the breadth is the charity that "loves its friends in God, and its foes for God".[69] The foundations are faith, for they are things unseen; the roof is charity, for it "covers a multitude of sins" (1 Pet 4:8); the door is obedience, as the Lord said, "If thou wilt enter into life, keep the commandments" (Mt 19:17); and the pavement is humility, "for the Psalmist says, 'My soul cleaveth to the pavement'" (Ps 119:25).[70]

Bishop Durand continues much of Hugh's work, copying entire explanations about the glass windows, the piers and columns, the roof ornaments, the bells, the choir stalls, and so forth. Some of his analogies certainly seem rather overreaching, more in the method of allegory than true symbolism. The roof tiles, for instance, are compared to soldiers who protect the church from enemies as tiles do from rain, and the crypt is seen to represent hermits living in solitude. Other analogies seem abstruse and contrived, such as his explanation that the spiral staircases built in the walls "point out hidden knowledge which they only have who ascend to celestial things". Other passages have a beautiful poetry about them, such as the passage on the sacristy, which is likened to "the womb of the Blessed Mary, where Christ

---

[64] Currently the only texts available in English known to this author are the 1843 translation of the first book by Rev. J. M. Neale and Rev. B. Webb of Trinity College, Cambridge (which has been reprinted in a 1973 facsimile edition by AMS Press in New York), and another brief passage, "On the Sacred Vestments", published in 1899 by Thomas Baker in London.

[65] Durand, *Rationale*, chap. 1, no. 1.

[66] Ibid., chap. 1, no. 9.

[67] Ibid., chap. 1, no. 10.

[68] Ibid., chap. 1, no. 10.

[69] Ibid., chap. 1, no. 15.

[70] Ibid., chap. 1, no. 16.

put on his robes of humanity. The priest, having robed himself, comes forth into the public view, because Christ, having come from the womb of the Virgin, proceeded forth into the world." [71]

Space limitations allow only a small sampling of Bishop Durand's reflection of the medieval understanding of architectural and liturgical iconography. The reader is encouraged to seek out this source and glean what he may, as it comprises a fascinating and fecund account from which one can benefit greatly in learning to understand the medieval symbolic language of church building and liturgies. We also know that this type of symbolic language was continuously used far past the Gothic age, as is evidenced in the architectural imagery of the Renaissance humanists in Italy and in the *Fardle of Facions*, a sixteenth-century British work that briefly touches on the subject.

Parenthetically, one common question in interpreting the iconography of medieval cruciform churches concerns the frequently noticed axial deviation between the choir and the nave, which supposedly symbolized the fact that Christ inclined his head when he died. After careful and prolonged consideration, Émile Mâle, the noted French medievalist, concluded that this deviation was not intentional, so explications of its symbolic value are not valid. Mâle cites necessities of site and measuring errors as two plausible explanations, and, what is more important, the axial deviation "always corresponds to a break in the work".[72] It is interesting that Mâle also cautioned against trying to read too much into the cathedral as a symbol of the Lord's Body. He recounts the instance of one archeologist who tried to demonstrate that the small door on the side of the nave at Notre-Dame de Paris represented the lance wound in the right side of the Lord.

THE METAPHYSICAL ICONOGRAPHY
OF GOTHIC ARCHITECTURE

Not infrequently, architectural historians and theorists tend to juxtapose the Romanesque to Gothic, more to show differences than similarities. Norberg-Schulz, for instance, seeing the Gothic as the fulfillment of the Roman-

esque vision, suggests that where the Romanesque church spoke of pilgrimage, transcendental aspiration, and a desire for the *civitas Dei*, the later Gothic age took the same forms one step farther and expressed the realization of these goals. Thus, where the Romanesque church is often found in monasteries—built in the hinterlands around which towns later grew—the Gothic cathedral is found in the center of the city, expressing the integration of the Church and society in the City of God.[73] Von Simson, on the other hand, regards Gothic "not as the heir but the rival of Romanesque, created as its emphatic antithesis", and sees it springing from the anti-Cluniac (and thus anti-Romanesque) polemics of Saint Bernard.[74] In another reading, Norberg-Schulz sees that where the Romanesque mass and solidity expressed the church as a stronghold that protected man in an evolving society, the dematerialization of the Gothic suggested a transparent building that could interact with its stable urban environment, thus extending the presence of the Church to the city at large.[75] Quite to the contrary, Martienssen argues that "the interior of a Gothic church is more enclosed than the Romanesque, for the latter, by the very piercing of its dark wall surfaces, refers all the time to the light and space outside. The Gothic never invites the imagination to stray beyond its own self-sufficient organization of interior space."[76]

Having looked at the iconographic language of church buildings through the writings of Eusebius, Hugh of Saint-Victor, and Bishop Durand and seeing how this language was used and explored over the course of ten centuries, we can see that architectural languages from the patristic through the Gothic ages—let alone between the Romanesque and Gothic periods—seem to have far more in common than they have separating them. I do not think, therefore, that comparison and contrast have

---

[71] Ibid., chap. 1, nos. 19, 36–38.
[72] Mâle, *The Gothic Image*, 22.
[73] Norberg-Schulz, *Meaning in Western Architecture*, 185.
[74] Otto von Simson, *The Gothic Cathedral*, 2d ed. (New York: Pantheon Books, 1962), 61.
[75] Norberg-Schulz, *Meaning in Western Architecture*, 185.
[76] Heather Martienssen, *The Shape of Structures* (London: Oxford University Press, 1976), 87.

8.38 Flying Buttresses, Nantes Cathedral, 15th cent.

much to offer our present discussion. Yet, just as so much inchoate thought from earlier times came to flower in the later Middle Ages—whether in theology, science, or the arts—so there are marked advances in the architectural iconography of the Gothic builders.

To enter in depth into the richness of the Gothic cathedral is beyond the scope of this chapter. However, certain points of iconography deserve consideration. Certain themes are clearly continued: the building as the body of Christ, as the City of God, as the Temple of the New Covenant, as the Ark, as the *domus Dei*, and so on. I propose now to look at the Gothic building through the lens of medieval metaphysics, to examine the language of symbols and forms and building elements in the light of contemporaneous understanding of theology and, particularly, of divine beauty.

The Gothic cathedral as an expression of the heavenly Jerusalem was not an attempt at "stylistic" or aesthetic expression. Nor was it a theatrical presentation made possible by the evolving technology of the age. Instead, it was a very real religious image—at least in the mind of Abbot Suger of Saint-Denis, the builder the first "Gothic" building—of the celestial city on earth, "a spectacle in which heaven and earth, the angelic hosts in heaven and the human

community in the sanctuary, seemed to merge."[77] Nor were all the elements that went into the Gothic style—the pointed arch, the highly articulated verticality, the ribbed vault, the flying buttress [fig. 8.38], the stained glass—merely artistic ends in themselves; rather, they were means to the end of expressing the church as the heavenly Jerusalem [fig. 8.39].

Like the urban fabric of a city, the Gothic cathedral was a harmonious amalgamation of smaller structures: chapels, towers, piers, chantries, shrines, choir stalls, windows, and arches. The whole building, inside and out, was an assembly of shrines, "aedicular structures", and articulated elements that sought to express the mystery of the Church as the city of the Lord or, as Psalm 48:2 calls it, "*civitas Regis magni*", the "city of the great King".[78] And it was a city unlike anything anyone had ever seen! For the first time the structure shone forth, the ornament was "entirely subordinated to the pattern produced by the structural members, the vault ribs and the support shafts",[79] so that the whole of the structure

---

[77] Von Simson, *Gothic Cathedral*, xix, citing Suger's treatise on the dedication of the choir at Saint-Denis.

[78] Sir John Summerson, *Heavenly Mansions* (New York: W. W. Norton, 1963), cf. chap. 1.

[79] Von Simson, *Gothic Cathedral*, 5.

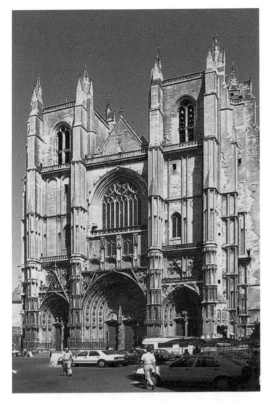

8.39 *The Heavenly Jerusalem*, Nantes Cathedral, 15th cent.

was articulated by the sun's light. Thus the building shone with "the glory of God, its radiance like a most rare jewel, like a jasper, clear as crystal", and its "wall was built of jasper, while the city was pure gold, clear as glass" (Rev 21:11, 18). This Scripture passage is most appropriate, for the model in Abbot Suger's mind was, as he readily recorded, the heavenly Jerusalem of Saint John's Revelation. This in itself was nothing new, for every church building, regardless of style, somehow or other tried to evoke the Kingdom of God. It is clear that Saint Augustine viewed the basilica as an image of heaven. So did Saint Maximus the Confessor, who wrote extensively about the mystical imagery of both the church building and the liturgy performed within.[80]

What sets Gothic apart was the *way* this was evoked: the conceptual principles of design that determined the architecture were first and foremost expressions of the contemporaneous theological, metaphysical understanding of beauty. The Gothic builders were inspired by a

definite and integrated metaphysical system, and they allowed that system to inform the design process and the language of the architecture. Here we are not discussing a "medieval concept of aesthetics"; rather, it is much more precise to speak of a whole "theology of beauty". For it was clearly in the mind of the Gothic builders to build in such a way that the building itself would in some measure share in the divine beauty of that heavenly Jerusalem that "has no need of sun or moon to shine upon it, for the glory of God is its light" (Rev 21:23) [fig. 8.40].[81] The Gothic expression, then, is not an "illusory" image of the heavenly Jerusalem. Rather, we must be mindful of the whole medieval view of symbol and reality, where the symbol, whether an icon or building, is a representation of the ultimate reality. Remembering the medieval concept of the symbol as "the only objectively valid definition of reality", we should consider that, for men like Abbot Suger, the building could participate in the divine beauty and could reflect the celestial city because it was designed with the same ordering principles in mind. Building with the same principles was a way of entering into the invisible reality to which the material world only alluded.

This way of understanding spiritual reality through material objects is a process known to the medieval authors as *anagogic contemplation*. Bishop Durand tells us, "*Anagoge* is so called from *ana*, which is 'upward,' and *goge*, 'a leading': as it were an upward leading. Whence the anagogic sense is that which leads from the visible to the invisible."[82] Durand is merely continuing the thought of Dionysius, who wrote, "For it is quite impossible that we humans should, in any immaterial way, rise up to imitate and to contemplate the heavenly hierarchies without the aid of those material means capable of guiding us as our nature requires."[83] This use, then, of material things to contemplate the spiritual realities—to use what

[80] Cf. St. Augustine, *Sermones*, 362; also St. Maximus, *Mystagogia*.

[81] Von Simson, *Gothic Cathedral*, 13, 51, 102, and 131.

[82] Durand, *Rationale*, Proeme, no. 12.

[83] Dionysius, *The Celestial Hierarchy*, in *Pseudo-Dionysius: The Complete Works*, trans. Colm Luibheid (New York: Paulist Press, 1987), 146.

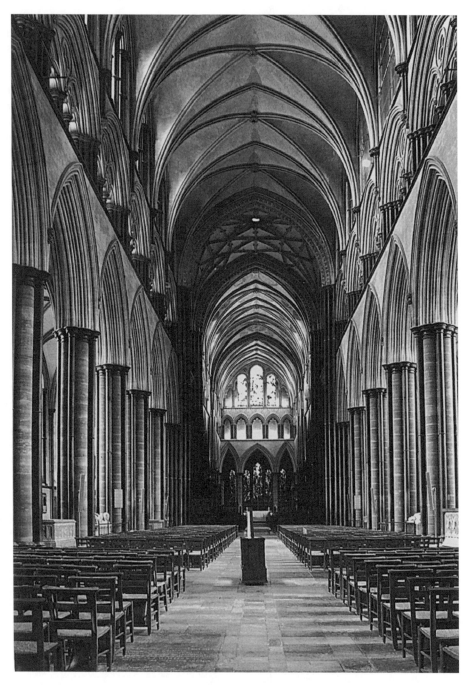

8.40 "Neither sun nor moon for light", Salisbury Cathedral, 1220–1266.

is below to study the things that are above—is the same as what we have seen in understanding the icon, recalling Dionysius' expression that the material world is but a "theophany". Through the *anagogicum mos* (literally translated, "the upward-leading method"), one participates in the divine life, in goodness and truth and beauty, and comes to a knowledge by way of contemplation and prayer that nourishes the mind in the pursuit of theological formulation.

The "theology of beauty", founded in the writings of Pythagoras and Plato, the thread of which can be traced through the writings of Saints Augustine and Maximus the Confessor, Dionysius, Boethius, and John Scotus Erigena, is an integral part of the medieval concept that ordered the cathedral. For the Schoolmen, all physical beauty—indeed, all of existence—comes from the beauty of God: "Ex divina pulchritudine esse omnium derivatur" (the existence of all things is derived from the divine beauty).[84] In God and in his creatures, beauty has three characteristics: integrity (*integritas*), radiance (*claritas*), and proportion or consonance (*proportio sive consonantia*).[85]

From textual sources, we can see how these three criteria were formative in the minds of the medieval builders in achieving the beauty and theological integrity of Gothic architecture. Here we are not concerned with the stylistic elements (flying buttress, pointed arch, ribbed vault, stained glass, and so on), but rather with the theological principles and philosophical method that determined the architecture. Each of these stylistic elements had existed before Abbot Suger built Saint-Denis. While it is true that Suger first brought these elements together at Saint-Denis in a cohesive building to create the Gothic style, more pertinent to the question of architectonic iconography is that the building is a direct architectural manifestation of the tripartite definition of beauty later articulated by the Angelic Doctor.[86] Here is a church with integrity in its structural elements, perfect proportion in its ruling geometries, and a radiance that activates its material composition.

When considering the metaphysics of the Gothic style, it is important to keep in mind that the central architectural theme, for Suger and the other medievals, was the expression of the heavenly Jerusalem. This distinction bears directly on understanding the relationship between the Scholastics' use of the term "integrity" and the way in which the Gothic structure was articulated. Saint Thomas equates integrity with perfection (*integritas sive perfectio*): "Perfection is present when the thing has all that makes up its substance. The whole object's form is its perfection and arises out of the integrity of its parts."[87] Thus Saint Thomas defines a thing as perfect when it has that which it needs to be what it was meant to be. The perfection would be lacking if there were either an excess or a privation.

This quality of "integrity" of the cathedral refers to its expression as the heavenly Jerusalem, the *domus Dei*, rather than as merely a building of stone. This distinction is important because we must separate what we would expect the form of a stone building to be from the form of a building designed "for purely spiritual expression . . . with structural intentions conceived artistically and independently of stone, and for which stone was only the external and submissive means for realization". As W. Worringer points out, a stone building implies weight, and it is built in a language that respects the nature of stone:

> The primitive builder used the weight of the stone only for practical purposes, the Classical builder employed it artistically as well. . . .

[84] Jacques Maritain, *Art and Scholasticism*, trans. J. F. Scanlan (London: Sheed and Ward, 1930), 25; quoting St. Thomas, *Comment. in lib. de Divin. Nomin.*, lect. 5 (with gratitude to Carol Downer for the Latin translations in this section).

[85] *Summa theologiae*, I, 39, 8.

[86] Obviously, other work has been done in this area; notably, W. Worringer's *Form in Gothic*, trans. *Herbert Read* (London: Alec Tiranti, 1957), E. Panofsky's *Gothic Architecture and Scholasticism* (New York: Meridian Books, 1960), and Umberto Eco's *The Aesthetics of Thomas Aquinas*, trans. Hugh Bredin (Cambridge, Mass.: Harvard University Press, 1988). Panofsky argues that the mental habit of the Scholastics had a causal effect on Gothic architecture and that the same mindset that sought theological clarification (*manifestatio*) brought about the Gothic "principle of transparency". My own focus is particular to the relationship between the medieval understanding of beauty and how it may have been *iconographically* expressed in the architecture of the Gothic cathedral.

[87] *Summa theologiae*, I, 73, 1c; quoted in Eco, *Aesthetics*, 99.

8.41 Bundled Columns, Chartres, 1220.

8.42 Ribbed Vaulting, Chartres, 1220.

All expression to which Greek architecture attained was attained *through* the stone, *by means of* the stone; all expression to which Gothic architecture attained, was attained . . . *in spite of* the stone. Its expression was not derived from the material but from the negation of it, by means only of its dematerialization.[88]

The dematerialization of a stone building was the first step necessary to take that Gothic leap from a building that symbolized the body of Christ to one that could express heaven itself. Thus every nuance and subtlety of the medieval mason's stone-working skill went toward diminishing the sense of being in a building of stone. Where the Romanesque is an architecture of mass, the Gothic structure is articulated into line. The mass of the pier is dissolved into a bundle of slender and soaring shafts [fig. 8.41]. The vertical line created by these soaring shafts becomes a rib to support the vault [fig. 8.42]; but even this is illusory, since the vault forces are not actually taken by the rib but by the unseen flying buttress [fig. 8.43].[89] Furthermore, the stone mass is seemingly reduced by splaying the walls at the windows, galleries, and tympana to give the impression of paper thinness [fig. 8.44]. These are all visual effects—and, as von Simson notes, often at the cost of "functional efficiency"—designed to create an illusion of negating gravity (in both its physical and metaphorical senses). These devices, which might have been seen as destroying the integrity of a stone building, are precisely what serve to express the integrity of a building that is the image of heaven. They are means to the end, rather than ends in themselves, so that the building becomes a true symbol of heaven by effecting the vision of Saint John's city "whose walls were like glass" [fig. 8.45]. So we can see that the Gothic concept of linearity, with its consequent dematerializing effect, was employed in the pursuit of *integritas*: it served to diminish one's awareness of being

8.43 Flying Buttress, Chartres, 1220.

8.44 "Paper thinness", Notre-Dame de Paris, 1163–1250.

8.45 "Whose walls were like glass", St. Vitus Cathedral, Prague, 1344–   .

---

[88] Worringer, *Form in Gothic*, 105–6. Emphasis in original.

[89] The ribbed vault, nevertheless, had certain technical advantages in allowing the vaults to be laid freehand, thus saving timber for framework, and in reducing the thickness of the vaults required. Cf. Panofsky, *Gothic Architecture and Scholasticism*, 53.

in a building of stone, since one had entered the heavenly sanctuary.

Furthermore, we can say that the Gothic cathedral architectonically expresses the *integritas* of the heavenly city. That is to say, the parts of the building analogously refer to the mystical understanding of heaven. Even briefly we should note that the comprehensive iconic package involved both statuary and depictive stained glass throughout. Thus at Chartres, for example, the patriarchs, saints, and virtues shown in the magnificent glasswork [fig. 8.46] give architectural expression to the scriptural idea that "we are surrounded by so great a cloud of witnesses" (Heb 12:1). Within this subtle iconographic tradition, Saint Peter, the appointed Rock on whom the Church is built, is correlated to the virtue of fortitude; while Saint Paul, author of 1 Corinthians 13, expresses the virtue of charity. As heaven could not be heaven if it lacked any perfection, so these saints and virtues also help to complete the sense of the *integritas* of the heavenly Jerusalem as evoked through the complex symbolism of Gothic iconography.

This search for integrity sometimes took the Gothic builders to extremes. Abbot Suger recounts how, during the consecration ceremony of the foundations at Saint-Denis, precious stones and gems were actually placed in the foundation walls while the choir chanted, "Lapides preciosi omnes muri tui" ("All thy walls are precious stones"). This was done to be faithful to Saint John's description that "the foundations of the wall of the city were adorned with every jewel . . . jasper . . . sapphire . . . emerald . . ." (Rev 21:19–20). For Suger, this even went to the extreme that—as Scripture dictates—only Christ can lay the cornerstone. Hence, he records: "The Most Serene King himself stepped down [into the excavations] and with his own hands laid his [stone]."[90] In this act he was figuratively recalling that "no other foundation can any one lay than that which is laid, which is Jesus Christ" (1 Cor 3:11).

More moderately, there are other analogical statements, such as a continuation of Eusebius' notion of the twelve apostles as the twelve pillars of the Church, which is ex- pressed at Saint-Denis by the twelve large columns supporting the chevet, while the twelve smaller ambulatory columns represent the minor prophets [fig. 8.47].[91] As we have seen, this idea is expressed at Sainte-Chapelle by the statues of the Twelve carrying consecration crosses, which surround the nave.[92] Even the scriptural metaphor that Jesus is the Keystone of the Church is given special expression by the numerous depictions of the Lord on the keystones of Gothic vaults [fig. 8.48].[93]

One often sees astrological symbols incorporated into the iconographic program of a church, such as at the north porch of Chartres [fig. 8.49]. Some like to ascribe this fact to the practice of magic, to medieval superstition, or to a pagan substrain coexisting in the Church, often through the Masonic guilds. Such explanations are obviously fatuous, as a closer study of the topic will indicate. The Church has always recognized that part of God's creation was the cyclical year. As Saint Cyril of Jerusalem writes:

Men ought to have been astonished and amazed, not only at the structure of the sun and moon, but also at the well-ordered movement of the stars and their unfettered courses, and the timely risings of each of them; how some are signs of summer, others of winter; how some indicate the time for sowing, others the beginning of navigation; and man, sitting in his ship and sailing amid the boundless waves, guides his ship by observing the stars. For concerning these things, Scripture says: "Let them serve as signs and for the fixing of seasons, days and years," not for astrological fables of birth.[94]

And it is clear from examining the sculptures that this is just the message intended. At Chartres, for instance, the astrological symbols are plainly juxtaposed to representations of everyday life throughout the course of the year—planting in the springtime, harvesting in

[90] Suger, *De Consecratione*, iv, trans. Erwin Panofsky in *Abbot Suger on the Abbey Church of St.-Denis and Its Art Treasures*, 2d ed. (Princeton, N.J.: Princeton University Press, 1979), 103.

[91] Von Simson, *Gothic Cathedral*, 134; citing Suger's *De Consecratione*, iv, 226.

[92] Mâle, *Gothic Image*, 21.

[93] Von Simson, *Gothic Cathedral*, 134.

[94] *Catecheses*, ix, 8; quoting Gen 1:15.

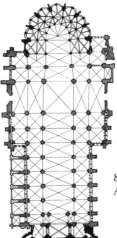

8.47 Saint-Denis, Paris, by Abbot Suger, 1140–   , Plan.

8.46 Stained Glass, Chartres, 1220.

8.48 Christ as the Keystone, Wells Cathedral, *c.* 1185–1239.

8.49 *Signs of the Zodiac*, North Porch, Chartres, 1220.

8.50 Main Portal, Saint-Denis,
by Abbot Suger, 1140–   .

That the building as whole was to be understood as the heavenly Jerusalem is made clear at first from the entrance of Saint-Denis, an entrance Suger had understood in both the literal and symbolic senses. The entrance to the sanctuary is, as we have seen, to be understood as an entrance through the gate of heaven. It is also a gateway through which men's minds are brought to the truth of the gospel. So it was that Abbot Suger modeled the whole façade of Saint-Denis on the gates of a Roman city. Suger continued this theme through the statuary at the entrance, which addressed the theme of the Last Judgment—Christ as the Divine Judge with six apostles at each side and two figures, representing the wise and foolish virgins from the Gospel of Saint Matthew, in the corners [fig. 8.50]. Finally, the symbolism of entering heaven was driven home by an inscription on the great gilded bronze door that encouraged the visitor to "marvel not at the gold and expense" of the doors, but to realize that the doors, "being nobly bright, . . . should brighten the mind, so that they may travel through the true light to the True Light (*per lumina vera . . . ad verum lumen*), where Christ is the True Door." This intriguing inscription not only challenged the pilgrim to enter into the city of the great King with the proper disposition but even went on to express explicitly the anagogical method by which this was to be done: "The dull mind rises to truth through that which is material, and, in seeing this light, is resurrected from its former submersion" [fig. 8.51].[96]

The citation above, which speaks of Christ as "the true light", hints at the second metaphysical iconographic feature of the Gothic church: physical light symbolizes "the divine immanence", the light of Christ. This is an idea common to the two main branches of Platonism, both Augustinian and Dionysian, that so shaped the Middle Ages. Dionysius had identified the Godhead as "the superessential light", calling God the Father "*Pater luminum*", and the Son "*claritas*", for "he has revealed the Father to the world [*Patrem clarificavit mundo*]."[97] Other early medievals,

the autumn. These symbols speak, not of magic and superstition, but of the nobility and divine ordination of human endeavors, the integration of daily human activity into the life of the Church, and the magnificent systems with which God has ordered his creation. They represent what Eliade might call "the consecration of human life itself, the sacrality . . . [of] man's vital functions (food, sex, work and so on)."[95] The cycles God has ordained—the yearly cycle, the life cycle, the daily cycle, the planting cycle—are all sacramental cycles, for they connect the individual and society with the divine manifestation; they are all parts of our "communion with the sacred". Thus the presence of the astrological symbols in church ornamentation is yet another expression of the *integritas* of the heavenly Jerusalem, for they represent an integral part of the material world given to man by God.

[95] Eliade, *Sacred and Profane*, 14.
[96] Panofsky, *Abbot Suger*, 46–49.
[97] Ibid., 19.

notably Maximus of Turin, developed very vivid and graphic analogies of Christ as the "new Sun" (*novus sol*) and compared the physical properties of the material sun with the spiritual effects of the Lord.[98] But light was more than just a symbol of Christ—"the true light that enlightens every man" (Jn 1:9)—it was also an indispensable element in the medieval concept of beauty. The language of the Scholastics is rich with allusions to light in beauty: "lux pulchrificat, quia sine luce omnia sunt turpia" (light makes beauty, because without light all things become base),[99] or "claritas est de ratione pulchritudinis" (clarity is the order of beauty),[100] or "pulchritudo ... consistit in resplendentia formae" (beauty consists in the resplendence of form).[101] The *"claritas"* of Thomistic metaphysics pertains not only to the shape of the object but to its sharing in the divine luminescence, "the presence of an incorporeal light which is reason and form".[102] Ultimately, God is the source of all beauty: "He is beauty itself, because He imparts beauty to all created beings", and every created form is "a certain irradiation proceeding from the first brightness, a participation in the divine brightness".[103]

Abbot Suger, when recording his intentions for the work at Saint-Denis, wrote, "The entire sanctuary is thus pervaded by a wonderful and continuous light entering through the most sacred windows."[104] That the Gothic builders would find the play of light especially important to a building that sought participation in the divine beauty is not surprising. For Erigena all material things, whether artificial or natural, "are images of the intelligible lights and above all of the True Light Itself" (imagines sunt intelligibilium luminum, super omnia ipsius verae lucis).[105] Furthermore, in Augustinian, Dionysian, and Thomistic metaphysics, the second Person of the Trinity, the Light of the World, is specifically considered as the archetype of Beauty. As Maritain summarizes: "As for integrity and perfection, He has truly and perfectly in Himself, without the least diminution, the nature of the Father. As for due proportion or consonance, He is the express image of the Father, a perfect likeness. ... As for brilliance, He is the Word, the

8.51 Tympanum, Saint-Denis, by Abbot Suger, 1140– .

light and splendour of the mind, 'perfect Word, lacking nothing and, so to speak, art of the Almighty God.'"[106] The importance of light as an anagogical expression of Christ's presence and beauty is made clear in an interestingly ambivalent quote of Suger, who writes, "And bright is the noble edifice (*opus nobile*) which is pervaded by the new light (*lux nova*)." While Suger is ostensibly talking about the light that radiated in the Gothic sanctuary, von Simson thinks that he is working on two other levels as well. First, metaphysically, the Divine Beauty that is Christ is made manifest by the presence of physical light and therefore causes the whole building to participate in this Divine Beauty; and second, metaphorically, because the *opus nobile* is also the human soul,

[98] M. C. Conroy, *Imagery in the* Sermones *of Maximus, Bishop of Turin* (Washington, D.C.: Catholic University of America, 1965), 16, 35, 61, 158, and 173.

[99] From Maritain, *Art and Scholasticism*, 24; quoting St. Thomas, *Comment. in Psalm, Ps* 25:5.

[100] From Maritain, *Art and Scholasticism*, 24; quoting St. Thomas, *Comment. in lib. de Divin. Nomin.*, lect. 6.

[101] Albertus Magnus, *De Pulchro et Bono*; quoted in Eco, *Aesthetics*, 112–13.

[102] Maritain, *Art and Scholasticism*, 160; quoting Plotinus, *Enneades*, i, 6, 2.

[103] Maritain, *Art and Scholasticism*, 31; citing *Summa theologiae*, I, 39, 8c; and St. Augustine, *De Doctr. Christ.*, I, 5.

[104] *De Consecratione*, iv, 225; quoted in von Simson, *Gothic Cathedral*, 100.

[105] Panofsky, *Abbot Suger*, 24.

[106] Maritain, *Art and Scholasticism*, 32.

which is likewise made beautiful by the light of Christ.[107]

Not surprisingly, the last of the three requisites for beauty, proportion, is also the third determining principle. Its place as an architectural determining principle is evidenced most clearly by an account of the building of the Milan Cathedral (begun 1386), where an argument ensued as to whether the square or the equilateral triangle should be used to project the elevations, since the square had already been used to determine the ground plan. Though these proportioning systems were kept secret by the guilds, two centuries later Matthew Roriczer—the master mason of the Regensburg Cathedral—showed how the elevations of the building could be derived from a single square taken from the ground plan . The whole building and all its component parts could be derived by inscribing within a square a second square turned at 45 degrees and, within the second, a third at 45 degrees, parallel to the first. Before Arabic numbers became commonplace, and before standard units were universal, this simple device allowed the system of 1:√2 to be employed in the ordering of buildings [figs. 8.52, 8.53].[108]

The two main proportioning systems, one based on the square and the other on the equilateral triangle, had not only practical aspects but symbolic ones as well. The triangle was, of course, a symbol of the Trinity, and the square, as we have seen, was a symbol of the Son. Moreover, the forms were seen as part of the universal fabric that ordered the world: they were all part of the divine truth of creation, for "thou hast arranged all things by measure and number and weight" (Wis 11:20).

This revealed truth, which expressed the order of the whole universe, gave coherence through geometry to both music and architecture. In fact, the Christian Platonic tradition viewed the musical law as one of the sources of beauty. For the early medievals, Augustine, Dionysius, and Boethius, among others, the beauty that permeated music was intrinsically connected to the truth that ordered geometry, and the two were united in architecture. This tradition, as ancient as Pythagoras and Plato, came to Abbot Suger through John Scotus

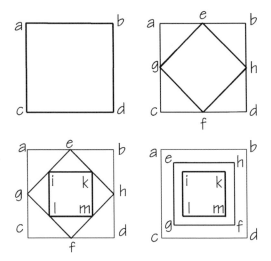

8.52 Gothic Proportions (after M. Roriczer).

Erigena's translation of Dionysius' *Corpus areopagiticum*. Erigena's own writings and translations, it should be noted, were the keen study of Suger's great friend Hugh of Saint-Victor.[109]

Within this tradition, the ratio 1:1 was considered closest to perfection. Then there were ratios of "perfect consonance": 2:1 in the octave, 3:2 in the fifth, and 4:3 in the fourth. The ratio of the side of a square to the diagonal yields 1:√2, which was considered, "according to true measure". These laws were directly applied—and not without great authority—to the architectural ordering of the buildings. For God, "the great architect of the universe", had revealed certain sacred proportions to Noah for the ark of the deluge (Gen 6:15) and to Moses for the Ark of the Covenant (Ex 25:10). Also considered "revealed" and therefore "perfect" were the proportions with which Solomon built the Temple (2 Chron 3:3ff.) and those with which Ezekiel described the heavenly Temple (Ezek 40:5–43:17).

Given such great authority, it is hardly surprising that the medieval builders brought these ideas into the ordering of their churches. So it was that in Saint Bernard's abbey church

[107] Von Simson, *Gothic Cathedral*, 119.
[108] Ibid., 14–19; also Rykwert, *Church Building*, 90.
[109] Von Simson, *Gothic Cathedral*, 115 and 125.

8.53 Façade of the Duomo, Milan.

at Fontenay, the octave of 1:2 determines both the plan and the elevation, while the distance between the upper and lower string courses on the elevation was "determined according to true measure". Elsewhere in the building, the crossing is at the ratio of 1:1; the ratio of the width of the crossing to its length, including the choir, is 2:3; and the ratio 3:4 relates the width of the side aisles and nave to the length of the transept. Likewise, as von Simson notes, *The Pilgrim's Guide to Santiago de Compostela* "devotes an entire chapter to the 'measure' of the church, [and] calls attention to the harmony that prevails among the well-proportioned dimensions of width, length and height (*latitudine, longitudine et altitudine congruenti*)."[110] And, of course, that most notable of Gothic devices, the pointed arch, is formed by projecting arcs from the bottom two points of an equilateral triangle that converge at the top point.

So it was, as we have seen in the cases of *integritas* and *claritas*, that by the careful use of *proportio* the medieval builder sought to cause the building to share in that beauty and order which not only permeated the universe and (however mystically) expressed the heavenly Jerusalem but which ultimately was founded in and reflected the divine beauty of the Almighty God. This theological aesthetic,

so consonant with the prevalent Scholastic mind-set and world view, is intrinsic to the formation and understanding of Gothic architecture.

The Gothic church was uniquely a product of its age. It perhaps could only have happened with the medieval world view that differentiated—not to contrast but to clarify, and not to prove exclusion but to demonstrate integration—between nature and metaphysics, arts and science, geometry and music, and so on. Gothic architecture probably would never have happened without the intellectual foundation laid by Plato, Augustine, Boethius, and Dionysius, for the Platonic understanding of the metaphysics of light and of beauty contributed greatly to the implementation of Abbot Suger's vision. Nor, as Panofsky points out, could the structural lucidity have been achieved apart from the Scholastic sense of orderly organization, which also affected such diverse areas of human endeavors as manuscript illumination, poetry, tympanum design, musical notation, architectural graphic representation, double-entry accounting systems, and theological treatises.[111] It was the comprehensive genius of the age that transformed these metaphysical

---

[110] Ibid., 48–50 and 132.
[111] Panofsky, *Gothic Architecture and Scholasticism*, 38–43.

qualities of divine beauty—radiance, integrity, and proportion—into a hard architecture of light activating form ordered by geometry.

Also, the technology and the resources came together at precisely the right time. There was a ready supply of quarry-cut stone; as Suger recounts, "Through the gift of God, a new quarry, yielding very strong stone, was discovered as in such quality and quantity had never been found in these regions." [112] This new supply allowed a thinner vault than the rubble vault of the Romanesque. And along with this, the combination of the pointed arch, the flying buttress, stained glass, and the cross-ribbed vault (none of them purely Gothic innovations) brought to Suger all the necessary means to implement the vision in his mind's eye. Furthermore, the integration of the Church in society conjoined with popular piety to create a social environment that allowed everything to come together. It is not surprising, then, that the end of the Gothic age was contemporaneous with a diminishing of the Church's place in an increasingly pluralistic society as well as with the discarding of Scholastic metaphysics, the advance of humanistic studies, and an increasingly anthropocentric world view.

The Renaissance

This increasingly anthropocentric world view of the Renaissance was soon manifested in architecture. In 1439 the whole metaphysical foundation laid by Augustine and Dionysius on Plato, and later integrated by Saint Thomas Aquinas with Aristotle, was discarded. George Gemistus, a now obscure Byzantine philosopher, took the name Plethon and proclaimed Plato as *the* philosopher. He evidently lectured widely in Italy and convinced Cosimo de' Medici to advance the cause of Platonism. With this financial backing, Platonic academies were established in many major cities to advance the neoplatonic ideals, and Plethon's arguments swept through southern Europe.[113] But it was a rather skewed and gnostic neoplatonism.

Many of the humanists of the age, such as Pico della Mirandola and Ficino, were involved in alchemy and astral magic as well and were influenced by the cabala and Hermeticism. It is interesting that Dionysius, that fecund source of so much advancement in medieval theology and architecture, was a continuing influence in the Renaissance. But whereas the humanists treated Dionysius with equal, and perhaps even greater, respect than had their Scholastic predecessors, they had their own strong and deliberate agenda in doing so. Pico considered Dionysius not only an exemplary Platonist but a Christian cabalist— one to whom was entrusted the spiritual secrets of the apostles: "You must never speak of nor divulge divine things to the uninitiated."[114] For Pico, Saint Paul and Plato were two equal and necessary transmitters of the divine truths. Since Dionysius drew on both and married them in a religio-philosophical synthesis, he was awarded by Pico a place in this trinity. Similarly Ficino, who worked on his own translations of *The Divine Names* and *The Mystical Theology*, vigorously argued that Dionysius was the same inheritor of this Platonic-Pauline mysticism as the Dionysius whom Saint Paul had instructed in Athens. Despite historical, stylistic, and textual evidence to the contrary— for instance, none of the earlier Latin or Greek Fathers quote Dionysius—this leap was polemically necessary to connect Dionysius with Saint Paul, thus building the case for a gnostic-Christian transmission of a rarefied divine wisdom. The Dionysian strain of Platonism in the Renaissance, unlike the Augustinian Platonism that informed the Scholastics and equally unlike the Scholastics' use of Dionysius, was infected with the gnostic, cabalistic, and Hermetic agenda. Luther, for instance, at one point calls the negative theology method of *The Mystical Theology* "*vera cabala*".[115] As Umberto Eco remarks in his novel *Foucault's Pendulum*, "The men of secular modernity, once they had emerged from the darkness of the Middle Ages, had found nothing better to

---

[112] Panofsky, *Abbot Suger*, 90–91.

[113] W. Lesnikowski, *Rationalism and Romanticism in Architecture* (New York: McGraw-Hill, 1982), 19.

[114] Cf. *Divine Names*, chap. 1.

[115] K. Froelich, "Pseudo-Dionysius and the Reformation of the Sixteenth Century", in *Pseudo-Dionysius: The Complete Works*, trans. Colm Luibheid (New York: Paulist Press, 1987), 33–46.

do than devote themselves to cabala and magic."[116]

This neoplatonism had its own problems. With the shift in consciousness toward materialism and away from a metaphysical understanding of creation, the idea of anagogy was lost. The symbol lost its potency to convey the reality that it signified. Rather, the symbol took on an almost concrete reality (as when Plato is misinterpreted so that the "Platonic solids" are thought to have existed *materially* as archetypes for him). And so, the expression of a symbol became that symbol (in the sense that a cube was an abstraction of the reality of Cube). So it was that, with the rejection of metaphysics, the anagogical power of the icon lost its force. No longer could earthly items speak of and lead us to the things of heaven. And the gap between the heavens and the earth, the spiritual and the material, God and man, widened.

But more than this was responsible for the cultural changes that brought about the new forms in music, arts, and architecture that we now call the Renaissance. At this time humanistic studies, notably philology and archeology, were developing. Philology brought about a change in methodology. Whereas the Scholastics argued from authority, the humanists tended to argue from precedent. The advancement of archeology afforded artists and architects the opportunity to study ancient buildings. Both of these new fields contributed, no doubt, to the architects' new interests in architectural precedent. It was also during this time that, due to the advent of the printing press, the texts of the ancient Roman architectural theoretician Vitruvius (which had been kept safe in the monasteries during the so-called Dark Ages) were widely published. Soon a wealth of Classical detail was available. Although the architects shamelessly discarded the Gothic style as a corrupt accretion worthy only of the "Germans", they were instantly attracted to Roman precedents because there was little early Christian architecture on which to base their ideas. These newly found details and building forms, however, were not seen as merely a storehouse from which to copy and amalgamate as de-

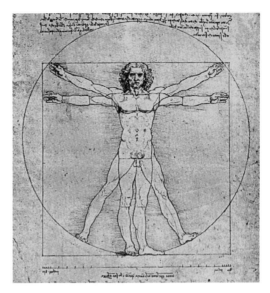

8.54 *Homo ad Circulum*, by da Vinci.

sired. They were understood as the architectural embodiment of the truths of Pythagoras and Plato and were seen to represent the high ideals of the whole of Greek civilization. The fact that they were Roman "corruptions" was not yet understood. (Jacob Burckhardt mentions that the Greek antiquities were of interest only to collectors and archeologists. Even the Greek ruins in Italy, such as at Paestum, seem to have been ignored.)[117]

At the same time the place of man in the world was elevated: the Vitruvian ideal of *homo ad circulum*, showing a man within a circle, spoke of Man as an "image of the World". Because man's body could be circumscribed by a circle or a square, it was seen as the earthly perfection of proportion [fig. 8.54]. Man was also the only part of visible creation that shared in a dialogue with the Creator, and Holy Writ did say that man was "made in God's image". While the idea of man as a microcosm is already found in the Fathers, this anthropocentric view permeated the age and had impact

---

[116] Umberto Eco, *Foucault's Pendulum*, trans. William Weaver (New York: Harcourt Brace Jovanovich, 1981), 172.

[117] Jacob Burckhardt, *The Architecture of the Italian Renaissance*, ed. Peter Murray (Harmondsworth, England: Penguin, 1987), 26.

8.55 Collegio di Propaganda Fide, Rome,
by Borromini, 1662.

on the arts and sciences and architecture. This can be seen in the widespread prominence given to centralized churches, where elementary geometries became architectural determinants, which seemed especially appropriate for the buildings in which God and man met.

The Renaissance is often portrayed as the rise of "neopaganism". Various authors, recently W. Lesnikowski, argue that the study of man usurped the study of God, that Plato was given equal status with Christ, that the Church served only for dogmatic promulgations, and so on. While there are obviously gnostic themes in many of the humanists' ideas, the humanism of the Renaissance cannot be considered in any sense monolithically. After all, it was also the age of the great Christian humanists, such as Erasmus and Saint Thomas More. Giorgio Vasari, in his *Lives of the Artists*, shows many of his contemporaries to be devoutly Christian, students of the Scriptures, and true sons of the Church.[118] Thomism was still a vibrant intellectual force throughout Europe. Even the Gothic style, with its roots in Scholas-

ticism, continued in Italy, albeit in modified and decidedly noncanonical expressions, such as at Milan's cathedral. Throughout the Renaissance and into the Baroque age we see continuing influences of the Gothic style. Borromini had great respect for its ordering principles and structural integrity, as his Collegio di Propaganda Fide demonstrates [fig. 8.55]; and Philibert Delorme saw the Gothic proportioning systems as "revealed" and lamented late in life the fact that his Renaissance buildings did not participate in these systems.[119]

While the rejection of late medieval Scholasticism, the reintroduction of Classical elements, the dominance of elementary geometries, and the centralization of churches all have reductionist and humanistic implications, we need not conclude that they were done for "worldly" or "pagan" reasons. That there was a significant change in thinking at the Renaissance is beyond dispute. No doubt, the methodology brought about by the philologists was bound to produce different fruit for a different age. It is important to consider, however, that while the *subject* of thinking changed, the *object* was still much the same. It was not a wholly *radical* change, since both the roots and objectives were the same. To demonstrate this, let us consider the architect who was one of the seminal figures in Renaissance iconography, a devout Catholic priest named Leon Battista Alberti.

Alberti's predilection for centralized churches had little to do with the apotheosis of man. His concerns were rather for precedent, liturgical propriety, and iconography. Alberti saw that much of nature was centrally organized. The earth and stars, many animals and their nests, all share a centralized organization or radial structure. Alberti specifically mentions the honeycomb as a form in which nature "delights".[120] It should also be remembered that the longitudinal Gothic basilican form was seen as an aberration from Classical temple architecture. The Renais-

[118] Cf. G. Vasari, *The Lives of the Artists*, trans. George Bull (Harmondsworth, England: Penguin, 1965), passim.
[119] *Le Premier tome de l'architecture*; cited in von Simson, *Gothic Cathedral*, 28 and 235.
[120] Leon Battista Alberti, *On the Art of Building in Ten Books*, trans. J. Rykwert, N. Leach, and R. Tavernor (Cambridge, Mass.: MIT Press, 1988), bk. 7:4.

8.56 Stonehenge, Salisbury Plain, Wiltshire.

sance men wanted to reestablish the universal traditions of sacred architecture. Some believed from the evidence of antiquity that Classical temples were usually circular, hence there was a bias that sometimes clouded their research. Inigo Jones, for instance, held Stonehenge to be a Roman temple dedicated to Uranus [fig. 8.56].[121] Some thought that early Christian buildings that were centralized, such as San Stefano Rotondo, Santa Costanza, and the Lateran baptistery, were pagan buildings converted for Christian worship (as was the Pantheon). Thus, as Wittkower infers, Alberti mistakenly took the circular form as a continuation of the ancient tradition of sacred architecture and applied it to Christian churches.[122]

The use of the centralized form was also a reaction to the medieval proliferation of altars found in the Gothic cathedrals and monasteries. Alberti wanted to express the unity of the liturgy by giving the high altar its due prominence and by returning to the ancient practice of celebrating Mass only once a day at the central altar. "There would be a single altar, where they would meet to celebrate no more than one sacrifice each day"[123]—a theme recently revived in some postconciliar liturgical planning guidelines.

To appreciate Alberti's iconography, we should first consider his understanding of beauty. For Alberti, as Wittkower summarizes,

beauty consisted in "a rational integration of the proportions of all the parts of a building in such a way that every part has its absolutely fixed size and shape and nothing could be added or taken away without destroying the harmony of the whole."[124] This definition clearly owes much to Aquinas. But while the notions of "integrity" and "proportion" are certainly rooted in Scholasticism, obviously lacking is the metaphysical appreciation of "radiance" as necessary to beauty. This is hardly surprising, since Scholastic metaphysics had been sidelined. It does, however, give an important clue as to why the Renaissance church differed so radically from its immediate predecessor.

As Wittkower attests, in spite of their humanist agenda, the Renaissance artists were firmly rooted in the tradition of thought that went from Pythagoras and Plato to Saint Augustine and Dionysius. They taught that geometry ordered the universe and that beauty was found in harmonic proportions. So again we see that it was not the object of thought that changed, but the method. While humanist thinking was more in tune with finding conso-

[121] Robert Tavernor, *Palladio and Palladianism* (London: Thames and Hudson, 1991), 138–39.

[122] R. Wittkower, *Architectural Principles in the Age of Humanism*, 3d ed. (London: Alec Tiranti, 1962), 5.

[123] Alberti, *Art of Building*, 7:13.

[124] Wittkower, *Architectural Principles*, 7.

8.57 Tempietto di San Pietro in Montorio, by Bramante, 1502.

nances in nature than with metaphysical abstraction, the humanists nonetheless sought these consonances with the same belief as the medievals—that God "arranged all things by measure and number and weight" (Wis 11:20). Although their approach to architecture was similar, in likewise proportioning buildings with spatial units, since they had lost the concept of *claritas*, they understandably placed more emphasis on the science of geometry than had their predecessors. The Renaissance architects sought perfection in geometry, believing that "without that organic geometrical equilibrium where all the parts are harmonically related like the members of a body, Divinity cannot reveal itself!"[125]

With this understanding, it is now easy to see why the Renaissance architects turned to the circle. We have seen the argument from nature that Alberti used, but the circle is also an ancient symbol of God, because at once it suggests form, unity, integrity, and wholeness. This continues the thought of the Fathers and medievals, who saw the circle as symbolic of virtue (Saint Augustine) and of the Church (Eigil), because of the qualities of perfection, eternity, and plentitude associated with the circle.[126] Ficino regarded God as "the true center of the universe, the inner core of everything, but at the same time as the circumference of the universe, surpassing everything immeasurably". The circular or centralized form was thought to be the proper shape for churches because the geometrical pattern would be seen to be "absolute, immutable, static, and entirely lucid". In this the form of the church could be, according to the formula of Vitruvius, "analogous to the character of the divinity". So it was also for Palladio that the circular building expressed most perfectly "the unity, the infinite essence, the uniformity and the justice of God".[127]

This being the case, it is surprising that, apart from the obvious case of Bramante's Tempietto [fig. 8.57], few truly circular churches were erected in the Renaissance or by the Mannerist and Baroque artists. And, in fact, the Tempietto is circular because it follows the traditional language of the *martyrium*, as it was built to honor the site of Saint Peter's crucifixion. The emphasis of the age was rather on centralized structures that supported domes [fig. 8.58]. These centralized structures were commonly cruciform—thus continuing that ancient Christian form—using both the Greek cross, such as at Santa Maria della Consolazione in Todi and Santa Maria delle Carceri in Prato, and the Latin cross, of which notable examples are Il Gesù in Rome and Palladio's Il Redentore in Venice. There were also endless variations with elliptical domes over rectangles (Vignola's San Andrea in Rome), circular forms with pronounced apses suggesting a cross (Palladio's Tempietto Barbaro at Maser), and the highly complex arrangement of two squares centered at 45 degrees to one another with a dome over a Greek cross, such as both Bramante and Michelangelo proposed for St. Peter's [fig. 8.59]. One can only speculate at the future of subsequent

[125] Ibid.
[126] Krautheimer, "Introduction", 9.
[127] Wittkower, *Architectural Principles*, 7, 22–23, and 28.

8.58 Dome, San Andrea al Quirinale, by Bernini, 1658–1670.

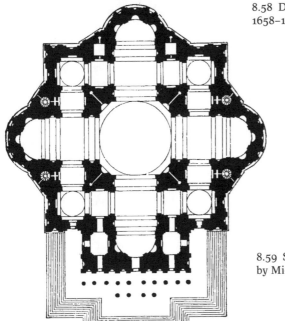

8.59 St. Peter's, Original Plan, by Michelangelo, 1546–1564.

8.60 St. Peter's, Vatican, Façade, by C. Maderno, 1606–1612.

8.61 St. Peter's, Vatican, Nave.

8.62 Piazza San Pietro, Vatican, by Bernini, 1656–   .

Western churches had St. Peter's remained a Greek cross, without the later accretion of the longer nave that transformed it to a Latin cross (this was done by Maderna, evidently to return to the traditional basilican form in response to the Council of Trent's interest in a *retour aux sources*!) [figs. 8.60, 8.61].

With this Renaissance concern for geometrical perfection, it is also easy to understand why the artists of the age adopted the Classical elements for the decorative treatment of façades and interiors. The medieval precedents were rejected as corrupt: the word "Gothic" was used at first as a pejorative term that denigrated the style as worthy only of the barbarians from the north. As there were few early Christian models on which to base their architecture, the architects took the Classical detail and forms being discovered, surveyed, and published and applied them to their designs. The architects had no qualms about embellishing their Christian buildings with architectural devices from the pagan temple. While this may seem to us to be indiscriminate or even syncretistic, the men of the Renaissance considered all sacred architecture—whether pagan or Christian—to be part of the same continuum. In this light we can understand why Alberti and others used the term "temple" when writing about Christian churches. Moreover, as the Classical orders were seen as products of the same civilization that produced Plato, and since there was a certain harmony in the Classical orders, great authority was vested in them as being expressive of universal and transcendental truth. Indeed, they were seen as reflections of God's order. So it is not surprising that the humanists of the day employed Classical ornament in the construction of churches.

Even so, these Renaissance classicists took the orders and imparted to them deeper meanings as part of the iconographic programs. Sebastiano Serlio (1475–1554) recommended that Doric be used for churches dedicated to male, extroverted saints: the evangelists, missionaries, and martyrs. Hence, at St. Peter's in Rome, we see the gigantic Doric colonnade speaking to the manliness, the militancy, and the martyrdom of the first pope [fig. 8.62].

8.63 Santa Maria della Pace, Rome,
by P. da Cortona, 1656–1657.

8.64 Santa Maria Novella, Florence,
by L. Alberti, 1456–1470.

8.65 San Andrea, Mantua, by L. Albert, 1470– .

Similarly, at Bramante's Tempietto de San Pietro, Doric is used to the same austere effect [see fig. 8.57]. Ionic was to be used for churches dedicated to matronly female saints or contemplative, educated males; and the Corinthian order, with its feminine and delicate detailing and slight proportions, was considered to be most appropriate for churches dedicated to the virgin-martyrs, such as at Santa Susanna in Rome, and most especially for churches dedicated to the Blessed Virgin. That said, it would not require much effort to compose a long list of Renaissance and Baroque buildings where this language was entirely ignored, such as the Church of Santa Maria della Pace, with its aggressive and manly Doric portico [fig. 8.63], or the (albeit ponderously gigantic) Corinthian pilasters that dominate the façade of St. Peter's [see fig. 8.60].

One problem that continued to plague the architects was that of trying to order the basilican form with Classical details, since the central nave was typically higher than the two side aisles. Early on, before the sophisticated use of Classical elements, Alberti used two large scrolls on the façade of Santa Maria Novella (c. 1458) to make the transition between aisle and nave [fig. 8.64]. Later, when Alberti had become more proficient at the manipulation of Classical elements and forms, he covered both the nave and the aisles at San Andrea in Mantua (c. 1470) with one large temple front, but with the barrel vaulted nave rather curiously poking above [fig. 8.65].

8.66 San Francesco della Vigna, Venice, by A. Palladio, *c.* 1562.

8.67 San Giorgio Maggiore, Venice, by A. Palladio, *c.* 1566.

8.68 Il Redentore, Venice, by A. Palladio, *c.* 1576.

Various attempts were made by practically every noteworthy architect to reconcile these two traditions. Some used monumental orders, others stacked temple façades one on another in different permutations. It was almost one hundred years after Alberti's first attempt before Palladio made the decisive breakthrough. Rather than stacking the façades, Palladio layered two façades one on the other; a low and broad one that covered the nave and aisles and a taller and more monumental one across the nave alone. First at the Church of San Francesco della Vigna [fig. 8.66], then at San Giorgio Maggiore [fig. 8.67], and lastly at Il Redentore [fig. 8.68], he masterfully interlocked two temple fronts of different scales to express the interior structural arrangement. The higher nave is expressed as a complete, proportioned façade. This is superimposed over a lower "temple" that is also a complete but rather irregular façade, comprising the combined width of the nave and the side aisles. By this device it was possible to accommodate differing widths and heights, still maintain the integrity of the individual façades, and express the unity of the two together. The difference in height between the two façades also allowed for the typical basilican clerestory windows. And most interesting is the interpretation J. Rykwert suggests: the lower form is not a temple as such but, after Palladio's Villa Theine, a stylized "house of human nature", whereas the taller and properly proportioned façade is the true temple, the house of God, the Church. With this interpretation, and set against the background of the Council of Trent, the model takes on the significance of expressing the role of the Church in protecting and sheltering human society. So, under the care of the Church, "the house of nature is raised to a higher state, is mirrored and harmonized by the exalted columns of the temple." [128] These three buildings, then, can be seen iconographically—in the same tradition as San Vitale—as expressing important points of contemporaneous orthodoxy that were attacked by the Protestants: one, that the Church is necessary for an ordered society; and two, that "grace perfects nature."

THE BAROQUE AGE AND THE GOTHIC REVIVAL

It is interesting that the main source of information about the ordering of Catholic Counter Reformation churches, Saint Charles Borromeo's *Instructiones*, has little to say about architectural symbolism per se. In it he makes a few comments about the strong preference for cruciform buildings as opposed to centralized churches, the former being in use "back almost to Apostolic times", whereas the latter, "was used for pagan temples and is less customary among Christian people". He did not, however, forbid centralized buildings, insofar as "on the advice of the architect, the site requires another form of building in preference to an oblong building", and the decision "conforms to the judgment of the bishop".[129] Saint Charles recommends, where possible,

---

[128] Joseph Rykwert, "Palladio: Venetian Churches", *Domus*, Sept. 1980, 28–31.
[129] St. Charles Borromeo, *Instructiones*, 51–52.

continuing the tradition of orienting the building to the east, particularly in line with the sunrise at equinox and not the summer solstice.[130]
And while cautioning against decoration having too much resemblance "to the work of the
heathens", he explicitly allows for "the Doric,
or the Ionic, or the Corinthian style, or of any
similar work", without commenting on the
symbolism of the orders.[131] In describing the
baptistery, Saint Charles took for granted that
the form "should be round, octagonal, or hexagonal or any other style within the confines
of a perfect circle"—without addressing the
patristic symbolism behind these forms—but
he did require that the font be sunken by at
least three steps so that "it should bear some
resemblance to a sepulchre."[132] Finally, in apparent opposition to Suger's explicit intention,
Saint Charles rejected the idea that the church
doors should represent a city gate but positively encouraged the associations with the
Temple of Solomon.[133] His lack of commentary about the symbolic aspects of the church
is conspicuous, especially as he is clearly writing in the tradition of Bishop Durand and
Hugh of Saint-Victor. In fact, Saint Charles
owned a 1572 Venetian reprint of Durand's
Rationale, and he referenced it frequently. This
suggests that the architectonic language of his
time must have been stable and that he had no
concern for either rejection of the traditions
or bizarre innovation. Throughout the *Instructiones*, Saint Charles seemed content to remind the reader that, for instance, "the
symbolic meaning set forth by the Fathers suggests [a particular] form", without reminding
him about the meaning of the form.[134]

Perhaps Saint Charles had little reason for
concern, because throughout the Baroque age
the iconographic themes of the Renaissance
and medievals were built upon, extended, and
complicated. Churches continued to be ordered
iconographically, and sometimes quite inge-
niously, as in the case of Bernini's San Andrea
al Quirinale, which is planned on the diagonal
cross of Saint Andrew [fig. 8.69]. Some have
seen Bernini's colonnade at St. Peter's as a gigantic keyhole, alluding to the Keys of the Kingdom entrusted to Peter by the Lord [fig. 8.70].
And certainly the spiraling columns in his

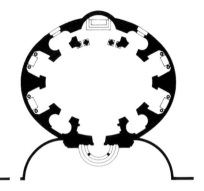

8.69 San Andrea al Quirinale, Rome,
by Bernini, 1658–1670.

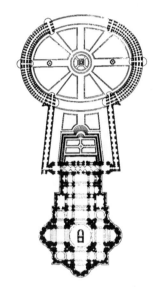

8.70 Piazza San Pietro, Vatican,
by Bernini, 1656– .

civory at St. Peter's refer to the Temple of
Solomon in Jerusalem, which speaks of the fulfillment of the Old Covenant in the sacrifice of
the New Covenant [see figs. 4.12 and 8.61].

Similarly, Borromini, Bernini's contemporary and rival, continued, adapted, and
invented iconographic expressions. He was

---

[130] Ibid., 124 and 358.
[131] Ibid., 450.
[132] Ibid., 248 and 250.
[133] Ibid., 37–38.
[134] Ibid., 41.

8.71 St. Thomas, St. John Lateran, Rome.

8.73 Palm Tree, Synagogue, Capernaum, 4th cent.

8.72 Corinthian Capital, St. John Lateran, Rome, by F. Borromini, 1646–1669.

evidently familiar with Bishop Durand's *Rationale*, as many of his allusions are direct. The use of the twelve pilasters in his Collegio di Propaganda Fide certainly recalls the tradition of Eusebius regarding the apostles. What is implied at this chapel is made explicit in the nave of St. John Lateran, which Borromini remodeled. Here, the twelve apostles are portrayed in monumental statuary, ringing the nave, with the consecration crosses at their sides [fig. 8.71]. The names are written on the bases in what Blunt suggests is a reference to Revelation 21:14, where "the wall of the city had twelve foundations, and on them the twelve names of the twelve apostles of the Lamb." Blunt notes that the Vulgate word *fundamenta* can mean both bases or foundations, hence the plausibility of his interpretation.[135] What I believe makes this even more convincing is that St. John Lateran is actually consecrated as Christus Salvator, that is, to Christ the Savior; and, as the Pope's cathedral, it is the Mother Church of Rome, hence most appropriate as an expression of the heavenly Jerusalem.

Borromini often went to subtle and ingenious lengths in his iconography. Themes of

[135] Anthony Blunt, *Borromini* (Cambridge, Mass: Harvard University Press, 1979), 146.

8.74 San Ivo della Sapienza, by F. Borromini, 1642–1650, Façade.

8.75 Cornice Molding, San Ivo della Sapienza, by F. Borromini, 1642–1650.

8.76 San Ivo della Sapienza, by F. Borromini, 1642–1650, Plan.

the heavenly city, such as symbols of date palms, stars, and cherubs' heads, enliven his façades and interiors, as Bishop Durand recommended.[136] In the nave capitals at St. John Lateran, the Corinthian capitals are transformed into palm branches, with pomegranates below [fig. 8.72]. These same themes are found in the carvings of the fourth-century synagogue at Capernaum, both of them recalling the Temple of Solomon [fig. 8.73]. At San Ivo della Sapienza, Borromini transformed the Classical egg-and-dart molding into cherub's heads, with their wings taking the place of the darts [figs. 8.74, 8.75]. It has been suggested that the whole church is an iconographic statement of divine wisdom: the church is ordered on a six-pointed star, the Star of David, which recalls the wisdom of Solomon, the Temple in Jerusalem, and the fulfillment of the Temple in the heavenly Jerusalem [fig. 8.76]. The original

[136] Durand, *Rationale*, bk. 1, chap. 3, no. 14.

8.77 *above* San Ivo della Sapienza,
by F. Borromini, 1642–1650, Section.

8.78 *right* San Ivo della Sapienza,
by F. Borromini, 1642–1650, Cupola.

8.79 *below* Vierzehnheiligen,
by B. Neumann, 1743–1772, Plan.

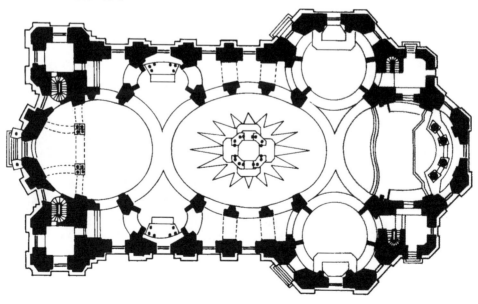

plans called for seven pillars behind the high altar, in reference to the passage from Proverbs 9:1: "Wisdom has built her house, she has set up her seven pillars." Around the perimeter are twelve niches, originally meant to take statues of the apostles [fig. 8.77]. When these are understood in the context of the whole schema, with the symbol of the Holy Spirit in the lantern above, it becomes evident that Borromini is recreating the setting of Acts 2, when God's Holy Spirit anointed the early Church with wisdom at Pentecost.[137] Even the bizarre, spiraling tower atop the building is understood as a testament to wisdom [fig. 8.78]. Though the form is originally a sort of Tower of Babel, it is transformed (in keeping with the art of the day) into a *turris sapientiae*, a tower of wisdom, with the flamelike structure recalling the "tongues of fire" of Pentecost surmounted by the familiar model of the cross on top of the globe.[138]

There were also, of course, other important developments in ecclesial design. The Baroque and Rococo churches often had exuberant plays of light in highly complex and plastic interiors. Intersecting ellipses and warped domes were used in conjunction with naturalistic ornament and ceilings covered in fantastical paintings representing heaven to create dematerialized interiors. This was done, no doubt, largely as a polemic against the gnostic austerity and iconoclasm of the Calvinist reformers.[139] Many churches of the time continued and reinterpreted the ideas of the past. Thus at Neumann's Vierzehnheiligen (1743–1772) [figs. 8.79 to 8.81] the basilican section and the cruciform plan were reworked with complex circular and elliptical geometries to reinterpret the past forms to a rather histrionic effect.[140] Fischer von Erlach's Karlskirche in Vienna (1716) layers the cruciform with a large centralized elliptical dome depicting a vision of heaven in *trompe-l'oeil*. The twin towers in the front are direct allusions to the

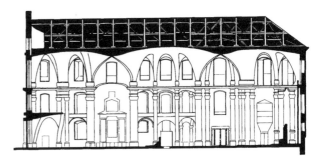

8.80 Vierzehnheiligen, by B. Neumann, 1743–1772, Section.

8.81 Vierzehnheiligen, by B. Neumann, 1743–1772, Interior.

---

[137] Blunt, *Borromini*, 116–21. See also L. Steinberg, *Borromini's San Carlo alle Quattro Fontane* (New York: Garland, 1977), 374ff.

[138] Blunt, *Borromini*, 126.

[139] Paul Johnson, *Pope John Paul II and the Catholic Restoration* (London: Weidenfeld and Nicolson, 1982), 7.

[140] Norberg-Schulz, *Meaning in Western Architecture*, 311.

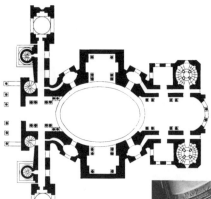

8.82 Karlskirche, Vienna,
by F. von Erlach, 1716,
Plan.

8.83 Karlskirche, Vienna,
by F. von Erlach, 1716,
Dome.

8.84 Karlskirche, Vienna,
by F. von Erlach, 1716,
Exterior.

Boaz and Jachin pillars in front of Solomon's Temple mentioned in 1 Kings 7:21 [figs. 8.82 to 8.84].

The Baroque age was an age of great theater and of grand opera, and the church building, it is often said, was but another theater. (Fr. Louis Bouyer, for instance, makes the point that churches came to resemble theaters both in form and decoration.)[141] Many modern liturgists now see this age to have been an unfortunate time, when the Mass was often divorced from pastoral concerns, where the people are seen to have been passive spectators to the priests acting out the Eucharist, and when liturgical music had more to do with the talent of professional choirs than with lay participation. Even if the Baroque Mass was in a sense "reactionary", shoring up the people against the attacks of Protestant polemic, the fact remains that it provided a stable environment in which the divine liturgy could have its transforming effect. Furthermore, one simply cannot deny the efficacy of the Eucharistic Sacrifice in the nurturing, healing, reconciliation, and sanctification of the faithful during this age! Thus it seems quite unfortunate, and even revisionist, for Fr. Bouyer to write that the Baroque liturgy was "embalmed".[142] In their own way, with the interior ornament, the play of light and the representational paintings, the Baroque and Rococo architects sought to communicate to their age a sense of heaven, and because of this their buildings can take their rightful place in the continuum of sacred architecture. However, the method of communicating this sense of heaven, which was truly "otherworldly", often seems more a question of fantastical representation than one of continuing the iconographic traditions.

The Gothic Revival of the nineteenth century, which we discussed in the first chapter, was clearly a case of reactionary architecture. The so-called age of Enlightenment and the Industrial Revolution had brought about, in the eyes of many, a fragmented and increasingly materialistic society that destroyed both land and family with its "dark, satanic mills". Against this, the Romantic movement saw in the Middle Ages the ideal of a society where Church and state were integrated, where the

8.85 St. Nicholas in Mala Strana, by Dientzenhofer, 1702, Interior.

8.86 St. Nicholas in Mala Strana, by Dientzenhofer, 1702, Plan.

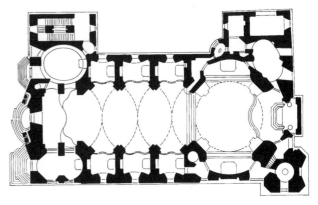

family was the basic unit of polity, when the agrarian society worked in harmony with the land, when man earned his living through the craft of his hand whether as a shoemaker or stonecutter, and when the faith that burned brightly in the monasteries brought about the "Christian" or "pointed" architecture of the Gothic cathedral. During this time the Church was also condemning the errors of Modernism in the *Syllabus of Errors* of Pope Pius IX and in the agenda of the First Vatican Council.

---

[141] Fr. Louis Bouyer, *Life and Liturgy* (London: Sheed and Ward, 1956), 7.
[142] Ibid., 8.

8.87 Cathedral of Santhome, Chennai, India, 19th cent.

Pope Leo XIII's celebrated encyclical *Rerum novarum* was also promoting the dignity of the working man against dehumanization, whether by industrialization or by Marxist socialism. Moreover, the Church was not just criticizing the errors of Modernism but was actively promoting the revival of Scholastic metaphysics, such as through Leo XIII's *Aeterni Patris*, which restored Saint Thomas Aquinas to the place of "the Catholic philosopher".

Seen in this milieu, the writings and work of men such as Pugin can be seen as both reactionary and "corrective". The Gothic Revival represented "high Christian values that, if properly understood and adapted, could result in the birth of a new, proper and modern society".[143] Despite the writings of Ruskin and Morris and the art of the Pre-Raphaelites, the ideology never really got off the ground, and the neo-Gothic style simply settled into the eclecticism of the Victorian age [fig. 8.87]. As a style for churches it was quite popular. The Gothic Revival movement was taken up by the monastic orders, particularly the Benedictines, who at the end of nineteenth century also began a Romanesque revival. This then brings us full circle, as it was largely through the Benedictines that the Liturgical Movement spread, the history of which we traced in the first chapter.

---

[143] Lesnikowski, *Rationalism and Romanticism*, 122; also Rykwert, *Church Building*, 115–20.

CHAPTER NINE

Catholic Architecture in the Third Millennium

The question of form

We at last turn to the final consideration: What form should our churches take? Étienne Gilson, the eminent modern Thomist, wrote: "Religious architecture is remarkably free. . . . Perhaps it is the freest of all forms of architecture. A temple, or a church, or a chapel can assume any conceivable form, provided only that it includes an altar and a pulpit, covered with a roof and isolated by walls."[1] To this one may well say, "yes and no". It is certainly free, given Gilson's criteria. In the same breath, it is also obvious that there are unique symbolic opportunities available to the church designer that are intrinsic to a successful design. Clearly, Gilson was not arguing for any sort of iconoclasm. Yet against the iconoclastic impoverishment that "radical functionalism" has brought, I propose that a vital part of the church building's "work" is "to look like a church".

In addition to the purely utilitarian requirements that serve the needs of the congregation, the church building also has an iconic function. The church, as a building type, has a unique relationship to other building types in the urban fabric, for it is "a sign and symbol of heavenly things"; it stands "as a special sign of the pilgrim Church on earth and reflects the Church dwelling in heaven".[2] The church existentially represents and creates a break in the urban fabric of profane and nonreligious life. It is a sacred zone, a *temenos*, a precinct where the Divine Presence is manifested. It is an interruption not only in space but also in time: the church building and the Eucharistic Presence unite the temporal with the eternal, the material to the spiritual, and the immanent with the transcendent. Therefore, the building itself serves as a sign of the eternal: it is an icon of the Divine Presence in the banal cityscape.[3] So with Wren's steeples, which punctuate the skyline of London; or the quiet dominance of St. Peter's, sitting like a mother hen over Rome; or the jewel-like Sacré-Coeur, shining on Montmartre above Paris [fig. 9.1]; or the mountainous presence of Chartres, rising above a small village on the Plaine de Beauce—the church building accentuates the cityscape as a reminder of the City of God. Though one may contend that the church can (or should) no longer tower over the city, for it cannot compete with the economic efficiencies of high-rise office buildings, the church still has a rightful and necessary place in the urban fabric.

To allow contemporary churches to take their rightful place in the architectural dialogue, the building must be at once both "modern" and "traditional". Though these terms are commonly understood as being contradictory, we must consider that "tradition" in the Church is not a static deposit of concretized laws, definitions, and rituals (much less, of architectural styles) but a living and growing

---

[1] Étienne Gilson, *The Arts of the Beautiful* (New York: Scribner, 1965), 160.

[2] Sacred Congregation for the Sacraments and Divine Worship, *Dedication of a Church and an Altar* (May 29, 1977), chap. 2, nos. 1–3 [= DOCA].

[3] Mircea Eliade, *The Sacred and the Profane: The Nature of Religion*, trans. Willard R. Trask (New York: Harcourt, Brace, 1959), passim.

9.1 Sacré-Coeur, Paris, by P. Abadie, 1875–1919.

appreciation of the things of God.[4] As the *Catechism* beautifully expounds, quoting the Fathers of the Second Vatican Council: "This living transmission, accomplished in the Holy Spirit, is called Tradition. . . . Through Tradition, 'the Church, in her doctrine, life and worship perpetuates and transmits to every generation all that she herself is, all that she believes.'"[5] The living and working principle of the Church is one of "continuity in tradition": that is, of maintaining and protecting the deposit of faith entrusted to her, while making prudent pastoral adaptations to the new circumstances of the ever-changing world. As we noted at the beginning of this book, the Church is always, to use Saint Augustine's phrase, "the Church of today". Hence, the Church is necessarily and simultaneously "modern" and "traditional".

The architectural implication is simply that the buildings, like all other parts of the Church, must be rooted in the common language of the Church, which in the case of buildings is the language of historical precedent. And yet there is clearly room, and it is indeed necessary, to adapt the forms to be pertinent to the present conditions. For just as the Fathers of the Second Vatican Council spoke "at a far different time in the world's history" than did the Fathers of Trent (and yet they spoke of the same truths), so might today's church buildings speak differently of the same truths.[6]

To say that churches must be both "modern" and "traditional" may require some further ex-

planation and clarification. We should understand the term "modern" in the sense of being "contemporary", rather than in the stylistic or ideological sense. One can fall into a real muddle when going beyond this. For instance, one noted architect wrote, "Architects of today must reflect this century in the churches they design, using the materials and techniques with which we are familiar. If we do not build churches in keeping with the spirit of the age, we shall be admitting that religion no longer possesses the same vitality as our secular building."[7] Despite his impassioned rhetoric, this polemic really says very little. This begs the question of just how much "vitality" most modern secular buildings have, but his passage does raise some other significant concerns. How can a modern building *not* reflect this century? Even if we discarded all modern tools, materials, and techniques and *copied* an existing structure, we cannot fail to build a church "of our time".[8] On the other hand, simply because a material or technique is modern does not render it *appropriate* for a church building. Why *must* we use panelized or component systems and "high-tech" materials for the churches we build? Either the Faith is alive and relevant to the worshipper, or it isn't. No use of "modern materials" will give "vitality" to a building, much less to a religion.

One can argue that economic realities, the availability of materials, and other market forces, such as the availability of skilled craftsmen, might dictate certain building techniques over others. However, one need not appeal to the "spirit of the age" to justify this. If the term signifies more than a careful ex post facto

[4] Cf. Vatican II, *Dei Verbum* (Nov. 18, 1965), no. 8.

[5] Catechism of the Catholic Church (San Francisco: Ignatius Press, 1994), no. 78, quoting *Dei Verbum*, no. 8.

[6] *General Instruction of the Roman Missal*, 4th ed. (Mar. 27, 1975), intro., no. 10 [= GIRM].

[7] Edward Mills, *The Modern Church* (London: Architectural Press, 1956), 16; quoted in Peter Hammond, *Liturgy and Architecture* (London: Barrie and Rockliff, 1960), 6.

[8] Even in the way one designs—one's aesthetic appreciation of form, proportion, and articulation—it is difficult to divorce oneself from present-day sensibilities. Hence, in one celebrated case, a supposedly ancient artifact found in the 1930s was exposed as a forgery years later because it exhibited certain Art Deco characteristics. At the time of the forgery the curators and critics (as well as the forgers) were blind to the stylistic similarities that were seen as obvious only after the prevailing aesthetic had changed.

selection of buildings pointing to a perceived preconception (for if there truly is a *Zeitgeist*, it should be manifested in all products—both good and bad, traditional and "progressive"—and not only in those which "demonstrate" its existence),[9] it should probably be dismissed out of hand for Catholic Church buildings! Any such transient "spirit of the age" will be at odds with the "spirit of Christ", who is the "same yesterday and today and forever" (Heb 13:8). Hence one should discard anything imbued with the "spirit of the age" as inappropriate. As Chesterton succinctly put it: "The Catholic Church is the only thing which saves a man from the degrading slavery of being a child of his age." [10]

It is quite a different assertion, however, to insist with J. Rykwert that a church design "must operate in forms that are essential to the architecture of its own day." [11] This is what is meant by "contemporary". For it is a question of architectural language. And although any living language changes, it changes by evolution and not radically. So the church architect must simultaneously translate between two languages—one, "the modern language of architecture",[12] and the other, a "traditional" language of historical forms that are often imbued with ancient symbolic meanings—to let them both profit from the architectural dialogue. For there are serious problems incurred by ignoring either language.

It is difficult, as well as suspect, to try to divorce contemporary church forms from historical precedents. Certain forms have come to be associated with certain meanings, and if these are ignored, then the symbolic aspect of the building may be "speaking" of something unintended, and there will be conflicting messages.[13] For centuries the Church has continued certain ideas by continuing the use of representative symbols. The liturgical vestments worn by the clergy still plainly show this. The priest's stole, which was taken from the Roman law courts as a symbol of authority, became the "yoke that is easy".[14] The alb signifies that the priest "puts on Jesus Christ" and is shown to be *alter Christus* at the Eucharist. The chasuble (from *casula*, "a little house"), an ancient priestly symbol, is worn over the other

vestments to signify that charity is the supreme law.[15] Likewise, the bishop's pallium is an ancient imperial symbol of authority, as well as "a symbol of unity and a sign of [his] communion with the Apostolic See", which even today the bishop receives as "taken from the tomb of Peter".[16] The bishop's crook signifies that he is the shepherd of the diocese, and his double-pointed miter symbolizes the knowledge he should have of both the Old and New Testaments, with the two ribbons a reminder that Scripture must be interpreted according to both its letter and spirit.[17] And beyond the vestments, both the eucharistic liturgy and the sacrament of baptism are rich in representative symbolism. What we saw in the oriental liturgical iconography of Saint Maximus the Confessor holds equally true in the Christian West, as is evidenced by the works of Hugh of Saint-Victor and Bishop Durand.

Therefore we must question the modern tendency to ignore historical architectural forms associated with church buildings. Since we have come to associate certain ideas with certain words and symbols and forms, we must work within these vocabularies. One cannot simply construct an entirely new language or iconography (as Rudolf Schwarz attempted) and hope for it to be understood (and therefore meaningful). Even though, as the case may be, most people are "functionally illiterate" in the language of architecture—which holds equally true for churches and for secular buildings—it should be a question of how best to educate the people rather than of discarding the language.

[9] Roger Scruton, *The Aesthetics of Architecture*, 2d ed. (Princeton, N.J.: Princeton University Press, 1980), 54.

[10] From *The Catholic Church and Conversion*, new ed. (London, 1960); quoted in John Saward, *Christ the Light of the Nations* (Hoddesdon, England: Crux, 1986), 7.

[11] Joseph Rykwert, *Church Building* (London: Sheed and Ward, 1966), 121.

[12] To use Bruno Zevi's phrase.

[13] R. Maguire and K. Murray, *Modern Churches of the World* (London: Studio Vista, 1965), 9.

[14] Hugh of St.-Victor, *De Sacramentis*, bk. 2, pt. 4, x, in *Hugh of St.-Victor on the Sacraments of the Christian Faith*, trans. R. J. Deferrari (Cambridge, Mass.: Mediaeval Academy, 1951).

[15] Émile Mâle, *The Gothic Image* (London: Fontana, 1961), 19–20.

[16] "Rite of Reception of the Bishop in the Cathedral Church", in *The Rites of the Catholic Church*, vol. 2 (New York: Pueblo, 1970), 298–99.

[17] Mâle, *Gothic Image*, 20.

There are, likewise, dangers in ignoring the modern idiom and imitating only historical styles. Modern man, for better or for worse, no longer thinks like his medieval or Renaissance counterpart. The architecture of the Middle Ages, for instance, is imbued with an integrity of thought reflecting the cosmological world view symbolized in a complex iconography—much of which is lost to the modern mind. One can, of course, build a "bare bones" Gothic abstraction: the pointed arch still retains its potency. However, as we can see from de Baudot's Saint-Jean-de-Montmartre, much is lost when modern materials are used to build in the architectural style of another period [fig. 9.2]. The building winds up looking decidedly impoverished and barren because we no longer have the skill, sensitivity, or social structure to build with the attention to detail, proportion, iconography, integration of art and ornament, and so forth, demanded by the style.

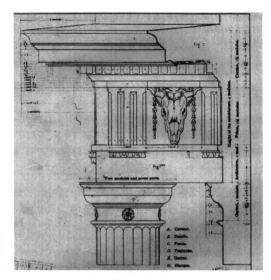

9.3 Buchrane, from Vignola.

9.4 Egg and Dart Molding, British Museum.

Similarly, one can fabricate Classical ornament out of plastic resins or reconstituted stone, but—independently of the question of whether or not this is "honest"—the symbolism contained in the Classical orders should cause us to question their use in modern Catholic churches. As we have seen, the Classical orders were applied to church design during the Renaissance because the architects were unaware of any historical Christian precedents to use. Indeed, the orders came to be seen as a reflection of God's order. However, as G. Hersey suggests in his book *The Lost Meaning of Classical Architecture*, the various elements of Classical detail all perhaps originally alluded to various

9.2 Saint-Jean-de-Montmartre, Paris, by J. de Baudot, 1894–1904.

aspects of the pagan sacrificial rituals. Some of the representations are obvious, such as the *bucrane* (*bucranium*), or carved ox skull, often found on the Doric metopes [fig. 9.3], the egg-and-dart molding that refers to the sacrificed birds and eggs (the "darts" being, perhaps, "claws") [fig. 9.4], and the dentil course that suggests the teeth of oxen. Other symbols are less apparent, such as the triglyph and guttae, which may abstract the ox femur cut into three pieces (τρί-γλύφος means "thrice-cloven") and the dripping "sacred fluids" that were collected on the altar [fig. 9.5]. Hersey thinks that, by decorating the temple with images of various pieces of the sacrificed animals, the Greeks sought to perpetuate the sacrifice and accord the victim a place of immortality. Even the columns refer to the tree trunks of the sacred groves in the *temenos* of primitive Greek religious cultures.[18]

If Hersey's thesis is correct, then one should question the place of such ornament in a modern place of Christian worship. This is not to criticize the use of Classical columns from pagan temples in the early Christian basilicas, nor is it a criticism of the ideological use of Classical elements in Renaissance churches. The pertinent issue is that symbolism of the Classical orders, if reflective of *pagan* sacrifice, blurs the distinctiveness of the Sacrifice of the Eucharist. We do not seek to diminish the value of Classical ornament but to respect it for what it symbolizes. Though one may say that the pagan and Jewish sacrifices prefigure the Eucharist, the Christian symbol of sacrifice is the crucifix.

To make the Classical orders pertinent to the Church, one would practically have to construct anew an order symbolic of Eucharistic Sacrifice. Over the ages this has been attempted. As the emancipated fourth-century Church undertook her extensive building program, pagan temples were quarried for architectural elements: columns and entablatures were reused to form the colonnades in the new basilicas [fig. 9.6]. On other occasions suitable pagan temples were used as Christian churches; the Pantheon is one

9.5 Elements of Pagan Sacrifice, from Vignola.

9.6 Column Capitals from Pagan Temples, Santa Maria in Trastevere, Rome.

[18] George Hersey, *The Lost Meaning of Classical Architecture* (Cambridge, Mass.: MIT Press, 1988), 14–20, 31–36.

9.7 The Pantheon, Rome, 118–128.

notable example, rededicated in 610 to Santa Maria ad Martyres [fig. 9.7]. Given the great wealth of Classical forms from which to choose, the basilica builders, as J. Onians demonstrates in *Bearers of Meaning*, frequently developed a language of hierarchic relationships with the various orders.

The chief Greek orders used were Ionic and Corinthian [fig. 9.8]. Doric was rare in Rome (it was considered crude by the Romans), and perhaps it was used at San Pietro in Vincoli only to express robustly the manly nature of the church's dedication in accordance with Vitruvius' schema. The Composite order was a Roman invention developed as the "perfection" of the orders (superimposing with little subtlety the Corinthian over the Ionic over the

Doric). This order, therefore, represented the dominance and superiority of the Roman Empire—militarily, politically, culturally, aesthetically—over all other civilizations. Thus the Romans used this order across the Empire as an expression of the *pax Romana*, albeit an imposed peace, which spoke as well to victory and subjugation. The Church adopted this order to symbolize Christ's victory over the world.

While not reinventing the orders, the early Christians evidently took some consideration in the placement of the existing orders and so adapted the architectonic language for their own use. Constantine's original basilica of St. Peter's on the Vatican hill, for instance, shows this progression. There were Ionic capitals in the forecourt, Corinthian columns down the nave, and the Composite order was found around the sanctuary. The Solomonic order was reserved here for the *confessio* at the Tomb of Saint Peter, representing, of course, the Temple and the heavenly Jerusalem. This hierarchy gave subtle but clear expression to the transition from the mundane world to the glory of heaven. By placing the Composite columns around the sanctuary and especially around tombs (for instance, at Santa Costanza), the early Christians were able to transfer the symbolic message of the moral, religious, and cultural perfection of the Catholic Faith over the pagan world. These columns also spoke of the victory of Christ, a victory over the world, and, in using this order around the tombs of the martyrs, victory over death.[19]

From the fifth-century basilica at Callatis in Mangalia, there is an interesting transformation of a Composite-order capital, where the corner volutes become rams' heads, perhaps alluding to the sacrifice of the Lord as perfection of the Old Testament "scapegoat" [fig. 9.9].[20] Romanesque capitals, such as at Vézelay, sometimes depict parables. Similarly, at Chartres, the column capitals on the west front depict scenes from the life of Christ [fig. 9.10]. At St. Paul's Outside the Walls, one of the Gothic capitals shows a bearded man, perhaps Christ or one of the evangelists [fig. 9.11]. After the Middle Ages, as we have seen, Serlio ascribed typological attributes to the various Classical orders, and Borromini (among others) transformed Classical details with symbols of Solomon's Temple and the heavenly Jerusalem. In the Baroque and Baroque Revival churches, cherubim were sometimes substituted for *bucrane*, foliage such as pomegranates and palm leaves alluded to Christian themes, and so forth; yet many examples still vestigially show dentil courses and the garlands worn by cattle during the sacrificial procession to the *temenos*. Subtly, in a side chapel at St. John Lateran, the Ionic scroll is

9.8 The Five Orders, from Vignola.

9.9 Rams' Head Ionic Capital, Callatis, 5th cent. (after Condurachi).

9.10 Gospel Story Capital, Chartres, 1220.

---

[19] John Onians, *Bearers of Meaning* (Princeton, N.J.: Princeton University Press, 1988), 59ff.

[20] Cf. Emil Condurachi and Constantin Daicoviciu, *Romania*, Archaeologia Mundi, trans. James Hogarth (Geneva: Nagel, 1971), plate 179.

9.11 Composite Capital,
St. Paul's-outside-the-Walls, Rome.

9.12 Pelican Ionic Capital,
St. John Lateran, Rome.

9.13 Eve as Caryatid Column,
Our Lady of Tal Mellieha,
Malta.

9.14 Adam as Atlas Column,
Our Lady of Tal Mellieha,
Malta.

9.15 Caryatid,
British Museum.

9.16 Solomonic
Column, Basilica
Museum, St. Peter's,
Vatican, 4th cent.

transformed into the image of a pelican feeding her young [fig. 9.12]. The pelican was understood from the medieval bestiaries as a symbol of Christ, because, as Christ shed his blood for his flock, so it was thought that the pelican in times of famine would let her own blood to feed her young.

In a more figurative and poetic approach the architect of the Shrine of Our Lady Tal Mellieħa in Malta took the Classical forms of the caryatid and atlas, female and male columnar figures, to portray Eve and Adam, on each side of the chancel arch [figs. 9.13 to 9.15]. They are on the nave side of the arch, thus banished from the glory of the sanctuary and turning their heads away in shame, not daring to look upon the wonder of the paradise restored in the redemptive sacrifice. On a more academic level, the Spanish Jesuit architect Villalpando theorized on the orders of the Temple of Solomon to construct an order founded on Judeo-Christian revelation. The Solomonic order was a back-formation from a long-standing, but murky, tradition of spiraling columns that were purportedly in the Temple of Solomon. The original Constantinian columns from the *confessio* of Saint Peter allude to this tradition. They may be seen today high on the piers [figs. 9.16, 9.17] that support the dome over the crossing in the present church, and they were obviously Bernini's model for the gigantic baldacchino. The motif of the spiraling columns referring to Solomon's Temple is also found in the contemporaneous fourth-century synagogue at Capernaum [fig. 9.18]. It is interesting that Villalpando based his work on the belief that the Hellenic orders were derived from a Jewish precedent! Thus he could argue that the whole of the Hellenistic architectural tradition was derived directly from revelation.[21]

Amid the growing dissatisfaction with the "whitewashed barns" of the past seventy years, we are seeing a return to academic studies in the Classical orders and even new churches being built incorporating Classical devices. This is an area that may hold great potential. Simply applying Corinthian columns, Baroque

9.17 Solomonic Columns, St. Peter's, Vatican, 4th cent.

9.18 Solomonic Columns, Synagogue, Capernaum, Israel, 4th cent.

[21] Cf. Joseph Rykwert, *On Adam's House in Paradise*, 2d ed. (Cambridge, Mass.: MIT Press, 1981), 121–36.

scrolls, dentil courses, and egg-and-dart molding, as beautiful as they are, is insufficient. The challenge for the designers today—as it was then for Borromini—will be to find ways to transform the language of the orders by means of the message of the gospel, thus to revivify the Classical forms with meaning and beauty comprehensible to the modern mind. Only then will these Neoclassical efforts, whether academic or practical, succeed in producing lasting fruit.

The iconography of Rudolf Schwarz

Perhaps the only architect since the Baroque to propose a "New Iconography" for churches was Rudolf Schwarz. Because of his prominence both as a theoretician and as a practicing architect, and because of his large *oeuvre* of significant Catholic churches, Schwarz deserves special mention, and his ideas deserve particular consideration in any discussion of modern ecclesial architecture. In the book *Vom Bau der Kirche*, published in English as *The Church Incarnate*, Schwarz argues that when the medievals built a church modeled on the body of Christ, they had a particular idea of what *body* meant—an idea steeped in an iconographic thinking that we no longer have:

Nowadays we no longer see the body as people formerly saw it, with luminous head, tall, radiant and buoyant. Our body is inert and heavy, bound to the spot.[22] And so it is that when we speak of the sacred body our only possibility is to think either completely honestly of this our body as we see it . . . or to think of something generally solemn. He who calls the church a "work of God" either means precisely what is meant today by the word "work," or he means something completely vague, which means that he doesn't think at all but only has feelings.[23]

So, for the modern thinker, "the sacred is invisible and the old words refer to miracles." Schwarz therefore leads his readers through a series of meditations—on the hand, the eye, painting, sculpture, and various building systems—to reacquaint them with the lost understandings of "sacredness", "body", and "work". Schwarz then develops his iconography by imparting meanings to simple, geometric forms. These meanings are related to various stages in Christ's life, which he also extends to the Pilgrim Church as the body of Christ.

The first plan, the circle of "sacred inwardness", speaks of the life of Christ before his ministry began [fig. 9.19]. For Schwarz it connotes the Church gathered around the Christ-altar in an intimate bonding, immanent but closed. The second plan is the open ring, a three-quarter circle focused on the open side [fig. 9.20], which signifies the beginning of Christ's ministry:

The meaning of this plan is parting, setting forth.

This plan raises to lasting condition the moment in which the closed form "parts," bursts open. The people are on the point of going out into the openness, they wish to take the first step but they tarry a moment "on the threshhold" between security and the way. The sheltering forms are still at hand but now they have broken open and are beginning to disappear—they are no longer valid.[24]

This plan transforms into the third plan, the "chalice of light", by domes cut open and surmounted by other domes or cupolas, such as at Hagia Sophia or in the Baroque churches [fig. 9.21]. This for Schwarz suggests Christ's baptism, the illumination from above that strengthened him and equipped him with the Holy Spirit for his journey to Golgotha. The fourth plan is the sacred journey, thus it is axial [fig. 9.22]. It is concerned with the movement and procession of the pilgrimage community: "A people whose destiny is 'common way' lives without rest, almost without body, on this earth. But they live in a great and daring way. They have risked their whole existence on the

---

[22] One thinks of St. Isidore of Seville: "For his head points to the sky, and he has two eyes, just like the two luminaries the Sun and Moon. . . . Man has been made straight and erect so that he may contemplate heaven, not like the cattle which are bent and inclined to earth"—*Differentiarum*, 2:48 and 50. Quoted in Umberto Eco, *The Aesthetics of Thomas Aquinas*, trans. Hugh Bredin (Cambridge, Mass.: Harvard University Press, 1988), 254, n. 12.

[23] Rudolf Schwarz, *The Church Incarnate* (Chicago: Henry Regnery, 1958), 10–11.

[24] Ibid., 70-71. One could ask why the previous form is given the status of a plan if it is "no longer valid".

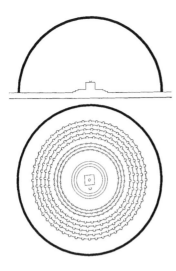

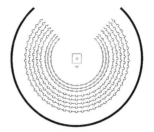

9.20 "The Open Ring", from Schwarz's *Vom Bau der Kirche*.

9.19 "Sacred Inwardness", from Schwarz's *Vom Bau der Kirche*.

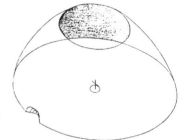

9.21 "The Chalice of Light", from Schwarz's *Vom Bau der Kirche*.

goal." Its form is the basilican church, row upon row of people united in a great "trellis" or "net" processing toward the apse.[25] But it is a lonely path, isolated from God, and similar to the way the Israelites followed the cloud of God's presence in the desert: "As long as they continue on their way, God is remote from them, he is outside, going on ahead of them and they direct their procession toward him."[26]

9.22 "The Sacred Journey", from Schwarz's *Vom Bau der Kirche*.

In the fifth stage, the pilgrim people, thinking they are home at last, come to the open arms of Christ, represented by the open ends of a parabola [fig. 9.23]. But for Schwarz it is Gethsemane: the glory of salvation cannot be realized yet, for the Passion has yet to occur. "The powerful ascent at the beginning gradually tires as it reaches the dead end point in the apex, then opposing forces come into play and finally the movement comes to a standstill." Thus the parabola becomes "the dark chalice", the cup Christ prayed might pass. The people

9.23 "The Dark Chalice", from Schwarz's *Vom Bau der Kirche*.

---

[25] One wonders whether Schwarz's use of the "net" imagery is not an allusion to St. Cyril of Jerusalem, who admonished the baptismal candidates who had come for instruction with less than satisfactory motives: "Maybe you did not know where you were going, or what sort of net it was in which you were to be caught. You are a fish caught in the net of the Church. Let yourself be taken alive: don't try to escape. It is Jesus who is playing you on His line, not to kill you, but, by killing you, to make you alive"–*Protochatechesis*, 5.

[26] Schwarz, *The Church Incarnate*, 125–26 and 132.

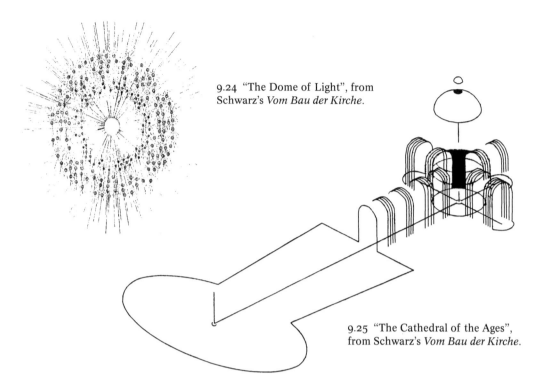

9.24 "The Dome of Light", from Schwarz's *Vom Bau der Kirche*.

9.25 "The Cathedral of the Ages", from Schwarz's *Vom Bau der Kirche*.

are sent or, rather, *thrown* back into the world in the "sacred cast". It is

a cast into death. A form of anguish, and also a form of existence thought out to the very end and of sacred way carried out to the very end. Certainly not everyone is charged to live in this form. But he who has reached this ultimate insight is not free to choose whether he will acknowledge it or not. He must decide whether to hold out with the Lord in the everlasting agony of the dark chalice which the Lord must forever drink, or whether, despairing, he will fall back into the dumb fear of the animals in which the gloom of undivided darkness abides.[27]

The sixth plan is again a circle [fig. 9.24], "but this time it is a dome of sheer light. The building consists of light, light breaking in from all sides, light shining forth from all things, light infused with light, light turning to face light, light the answer to light." Thus Schwarz tries in the sixth plan to express architecturally the joys of the Resurrection, the Parousia, and the beatific vision of the soul's union with God, when "heaven is everywhere, earth everywhere, the one melting into the other."[28]

Having established the six plans, Schwarz then examines the cathedral. In the cathedral these six plans come together because, for Schwarz, the cathedral uniquely expresses the wholeness of the Church [fig. 9.25]. Since Schwarz also means this historically, the six stages or "plans" are strung together, one after the other. It is "the composite form of sacred history—within it the first six plans are only limbs, period and phase. Three great elements go to make it up. The first and the last are centric and between them the way takes its course."[29] So, as the Church continues the journey through the ages of mankind, each age expresses its own cathedral within the art of its culture, until the consummation of the world. Thus the process of building the cathedral goes on, and it grows because the Church grows, until the end of time.

---

[27] Ibid., 178–93.
[28] Ibid., 180–81.
[29] Ibid., 193.

Schwarz's work is brilliant, poetic, and original. But precisely because it is so utterly original (and not even ostensibly rooted in tradition), it is also problematic. Schwarz was so very much intent on developing a "New Iconography" that one can hardly understand his language without reading his work. One senses that the theory is so abstruse that the worshipper is probably isolated from the building's iconographic message. So, while his buildings stand as good examples of the architecture of the Liturgical Movement, they also stand in a certain isolation from other works of ecclesial architecture.

Another difficulty is Schwarz's methodology. In basing his plans on the life of the Lord, which he calls "the great model of sacred architecture",[30] Schwarz commits himself to a rather peculiar interpretation of Christ's life. He is clearly convinced, and is quite emphatic, that in these six stages there is an objectivity to his work, that these are the "precisely determined number of such . . . plans, no more and no less."[31] And yet, in a seemingly facile manner, these six stages come together in a "Cathedral of the Ages" that is obviously modeled on St. Peter's in Rome. One must wonder how Schwarz arrived at this: Was it an honest "revelation" that his six plans strung together expressed the *parti* of the Mother Church in Rome? This would certainly help confirm the authority of his schema. Was there a certain amount of "massaging" the forms and stages to arrive at such a coherent system? Or were the six stages a back-formation based on the elements of St. Peter's? Did Schwarz's analysis begin with the complex string of architectural forms found at the Vatican basilica and then develop consonances between the individual parts and his chronological model of Christ's ministry?

Putting aside the obvious difficulty of maintaining the position that these are the "precisely determined" plans, in seeing the plans in relation to the life of Christ one does not get a particularly orthodox understanding of the mission of the Lord. In fact, one is surprised to detect similarities with early heterodox Christologies. The first ring of "sacred inwardness" seems to suggest that Jesus is unaware of his

divinity until the "open ring" brings about the "chalice of light", which is his baptism, when he either receives or realizes his divinity. The "sacred journey" is a rather joyless way, utterly bereft of the Father's consolation. The "sacred cast" is Gethsemane; it is, for Schwarz, emblematic of despair and confusion: "The Son of God is dead and . . . nothing but his corpse remains."[32] Yet it is interesting that Schwarz so decidedly avoids the traditional cruciform, for it is the Cross and the redemption it symbolizes that is at the heart of orthodox Christianity. And it is precisely because the Eucharistic Sacrifice is a re-presentation of the sacrifice at Golgotha that the Church so easily adopted the cruciform as the predominant architectural model throughout the ages. Finally, the "dome of light" is a sort of resurrection—yet Schwarz's words do not conjure images of the truly bodily, corporeal Resurrection. It is more the Jesus who walked through walls, but not quite the Jesus who bade Thomas to probe his wounds.

If my reading of Schwarz's work is accurate, one must decide whether to "correct" his thesis with a more orthodox Christology to determine the true Christian "plans" or to use his system of thought with a more historically rooted architectural language or else to dismiss it as a brilliant but fundamentally flawed exercise. For there is a great chasm between the Vitruvian ideal that the form of the church should be analogous to the character of the Divinity and Schwarz's contention that "Church architecture is . . . the imitation of the Lord in the language of building and with the material of architecture."[33] One must first consider whether Schwarz asked the right questions: *Is* the historical model valid for determining plans? *Can* we find objective plans based on the life of Christ? *Can* a "cathedral of all time" be created simply by connecting the historical models together? And *does* this method produce a usable iconography?

While there is great poetry in Schwarz's models, one would be hard put to argue for an

---

[30] Ibid., 191.
[31] Ibid., 227.
[32] Ibid., 164.
[33] Ibid., 228.

iconographic form based on a historical model. The question does not have to do first with "form" but with "nature", since nature determines form.[34] But Schwarz denied that church architecture was about theology or liturgical practice[35] and therefore could not concern himself with the ecclesiological nature of the parish community or with the liturgical ramifications of the Mass, or with what sacramental theology might suggest about the ordering of the church. Schwarz's denial notwithstanding, we have already seen the place of theology in developing coherent iconographies from the patristic age to the Renaissance. If we are to give meaningful expression to the architectural form of the churches we build, we must first concern ourselves with the nature of the Church, the liturgy, the sacraments, the parish community, and even with human nature.

Rediscovering the iconic

> ... Like a householder who brings out of his treasure what is new and what is old (Mt 13:52).

Having seen some of the difficulties in finding an appropriate modern language for church architecture, what can we positively propose as a direction for modern Catholic churches? Let us begin by recalling the guidelines given by the Vatican Fathers for the correct reformation of the liturgy: "In order that sound tradition be retained, and yet the way remain open to legitimate progress, a careful investigation—theological, historical, and pastoral—should always be made . . . and care must be taken that any new forms adopted should in some way grow organically from forms already existing."[36] Applied to ecclesial design, this passage certainly suggests that new churches be rooted to some degree in historical architectural precedent. Given the immense number of Catholic churches built over the centuries, one could hardly argue that this guideline would limit creativity. The Church also requests that "the general plan of the sacred building should be such that it reflects in some way the whole assembly."[37] That is, the spatial arrangements

"must express a hierarchical arrangement and the diversity of offices" and simultaneously "form a complete and organic unity, clearly expressive of the unity of the entire holy people".[38] Only an arrangement derived from such an understanding can begin to address the iconographic concern of the building representing the Church as the body of Christ and the people of God.

We can also examine afresh the structural metaphors for the Church, both biblical and traditional, to explore new and relevant ways of expressing the ancient images of the Faith. Images such as "the holy mountain" of the Psalms,[39] the heavenly Jerusalem of Revelation, the womb of the Virgin, the Upper Room, and the cruciform body of the Lord are but a few of the scriptural metaphors rich with meaning and architectural potential. Other recurring images show the Church as the ark of Noah or as a ship. This idea, which has continued since Saint Justin Martyr in the second century, has been expressed through the timber ceilings of medieval churches (which were likened to upside-down hulls) and, in the recent past, with the great "prow" at Le Corbusier's Ronchamp [see fig. I.6]. It is certainly interesting, though hardly surprising, that in recent surveys of new church buildings few if any cruciform plans—either Latin or Greek crosses—are to be found. What was once the primary church model has now virtually fallen into oblivion.

We can also reconsider the relationship between massing and function as a method of

---

[34] Put briefly, *nature*, as "the first principle of the operations for the performance of [that for] which the thing has come into being" (Maritain), is shown to be concerned with a being's *purpose*. Form, as that which "determines the real character of any being and gives it being" (Rahner and Vorgrimler), and arranges individual elements into distinct objects (Gilson), both determines and realizes the material thing. Since the form gives material existence, it must be in-formed as to *what the thing is*; and what it is, its *essence*, is understood in its nature. The thing's nature, which orders its activities toward its proper end, therefore also determines its form. Cf. K. Rahner and H. Vorgrimler, *Concise Theological Dictionary* (London: Burns and Oates, 1965), s.v. "form"; Jacques Maritain, *An Introduction to Philosophy*, trans. E. I. Watkin (New York: Sheed and Ward, 1937), 202; and Gilson, *Arts of the Beautiful*, 4.

[35] Schwarz, *Church Incarnate*, 212.

[36] Vatican II, *Sacrosanctum concilium* (Dec. 4, 1963), no. 23.

[37] DOCA, chap. 2, no. 3.

[38] GIRM, no. 257.

[39] See Ps 43:3 and 87:1–2.

9.26 San Apollinare in Classe, Ravenna, 534–549.

9.27 San Vitale, Ravenna, 525–548.

9.28 Hagia Sophia, Istanbul, 532–537.

articulating the building. Though historically an important determinant in church design, the relationship between a functional space and its formal expression has been all but lost in modern church architecture. For example, the apse is a special space within the building that defines a particular function and that can be "read" from the exterior elevation as an interdependent form. Throughout the history of Christian building, one sees (despite significant stylistic differences) this common approach to the massing of the building. This idea is first seen in the simple basilica, with its major spaces all clearly expressed as harmoniously intersecting forms. San Apollinare in Classe, for instance, is a simple and elegant form of a prominent central nave and articulated side aisles with an adjoining apse, narthex, and campanile [fig. 9.26]. All these elements are clearly defined, and the success of the building lies in this simplicity. Even in later, more complex structures, such as Hagia Sophia or San Vitale, the intersecting massing forms lucidly express the modulation of spaces within. At San Vitale, for instance, one can clearly associate the higher octagonal lantern as defining the central nave, around which is the wider and lower octagonal ambulatory, with the gallery above [figs. 8.12 and 9.27]. The intersecting roof forms express the sanctuary cutting through the ambulatory, while the organic interplay of gable-ends, cylinders, and octagons masterfully masses together the apse and the side chapels. Likewise at Hagia Sophia, the complex interior volume can be understood from the exterior massing as a great dome centered on a square with a series of smaller domes, half-domes, and apses around the perimeter [fig. 9.28]. Thus, the

9.29 Paray-le-Monial, 12th cent.

massing of the building expresses all the major internal subdivisions.

This approach was continued throughout the Romanesque age. At Paray-le-Monial the ambulatory chapels radiating around the chancel are each given organic architectural expression, which gives external form to the function within [fig. 9.29]. Likewise, at the immense pilgrimage church of Santiago de Compostela the building mass articulates all the major spaces: it is a great cruciform basilica, with a central lantern defining the crossing; the clerestory about the apse hints at the ambulatory around which radiate the apsidal chapels; side chapels mass against the transepts; and towers announce the entrance and punctuate the corners of the building. Similarly, one can see the same idea in the Gothic cathedral. The Gothic cathedral can be described as "the heavenly Jerusalem" or "the Body of Christ" because it is like a city or body in that it has a harmony of separate parts, all of which find organic integration in its formal expression. The front façade typically has two towers, which both order the tripartite internal division of nave and side aisles and also recall the city gates [figs. 9.30, 9.31]. As in the Romanesque cathedrals, each chapel around the ambulatory is structurally expressed as a distinct "building" within the cathedral. The most prominent of these is frequently the Lady chapel, which from the exte-

9.30 Notre-Dame de Paris, 1163–1250.

9.31 Notre-Dame de Paris, 1163–1250.

9.32 Ely Cathedral, 1080–1322.

9.33 Regina Coeli, Malta.

rior reads as a significant volume [fig. 9.32]. As Sir John Summerson points out, the whole cathedral, both internally and externally, is a combination of "aedicular structures" that are ordered within the urban framework of the City of God.[40] Each function is given a special place and a special form: altars, confessionals, chantry chapels, tombs, and so on, are given due prominence within the organic composition. And likewise, throughout the Renaissance, Baroque, and Revivalist epochs we find this relationship of massing to distinct volume with a concomitant separation and expression of the individual function of the place [fig. 9.33]. In fact, we have lost this approach to church design only in this century; it has been lost to the "universal space" of the Modern movement [fig. 9.34].

To have the building forms define the separate functional volumes within is precisely in keeping with the Church's guidelines. As we have seen, the baptistery is to be a clearly defined place reserved for the sacrament; the sanctuary is to be clearly distinguished from the rest of the church by, among other possibilities, a "special shape"; the shape of the church is to recall the form of the assembly; the tabernacle is to be in a place that is "truly prominent"; and so on. In the language of architecture, things are given prominence and

---

[40] Sir John Summerson, *Heavenly Mansions* (New York: W. W. Norton, 1963), chap. 1.

9.34 St. Timothy's, Mesa, Arizona.

distinction by assigning them special forms. With this in mind, the plan can generate the building massing so that these special functions and relationships are perceptible from both the interior and the exterior [fig. 9.35].

Furthermore, this approach presents an opportunity for the architectural forms to nuance a liturgical or theological idea. For instance, the baptistery can express the transition from the world to the Kingdom by being placed at the entrance to the church, between the narthex and nave, or even as a separate and special entry into the building. The confessionals can become architectural reminders of the need for personal preparation by being placed at the entrance to the nave. Hence, the building itself can not only express the form of the assembly, but its major elements (viz., baptistery, nave, sanctuary, confessional) can express the relationships between the sacraments and the people of God. This appreciation of function, volume, and massing is, I think, vital to building churches in the tradition of Christian church architecture and to building churches that communicate the idea of "Church".

For decades, thanks to the Liturgical Movement, we have tried to solve the problem of how to design a church "that *works* as a place for liturgy". Much of this book is my contribution toward that answer. But there is another, equally important concern that has gone begging for a half-century: namely, how to design a building *that looks like a church*. And so the question today is: "What does a church look like?" From our heritage of Western civilization we have a huge and ready supply of symbol-laden building forms from which to draw. It is quite appropriate that these forms be organi-

cally modified to accommodate the needs of the modern parish and the recent developments in the communal appreciation of the Eucharist. There are also profound understandings of the Church to be rediscovered in Scripture and in patristic and medieval writings, many of which can nourish an architecture expressive of structural metaphors germane to church building.

And, finally, we can return to the practice of building churches that express the structure of the internal relationships through the external massing of the building. With these means I think we can return to the great tradition of Catholic architecture that has produced churches and cathedrals that go far beyond the mere functional requirements of accommodating the various aspects of parish life. This tradition is one of building churches that speak both to society and the individual of the Faith, communicating in a language of built forms about the Kingdom of God, the heavenly Jerusalem, the Body of Christ, and the importance and meaning of the sacraments. In the end, for a church to serve only functional utility is, to a certain degree, to be useless. Mankind has a higher calling, and the mission of the Church is therefore higher as well. The church building is a message to the world of that calling. It is, therefore, to use a favorite phrase of Pope John Paul II, to be a "sign of contradiction" to the world in the architectural dialogue with the urban fabric. But it is not just to the world that the gospel is announced but within the Church as well, and therefore the building must speak to the faithful of their place in the people of God:

As the Old Testament speaks of the Temple, the Church is to be the place of "glory", and as such, too, the place where mankind's cry of distress is brought to the ear of God. The Church must not settle down with what is merely comfortable and serviceable at the parish level; she must arouse the voice of the cosmos and, by glorifying the Creator, elicit the glory of the cosmos itself, making it also glorious, beautiful, habitable and beloved.[41]

---

[41] Joseph Cardinal Ratzinger, *The Feast of Faith* (San Francisco: Ignatius Press, 1986), 124.

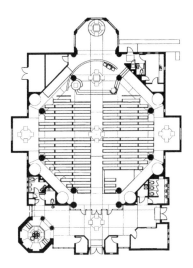

9.35 St. Therese, Collinsville, Oklahoma,
by S. Schloeder, Model.

9.36 *right* St. Therese, CoIlinsville, Oklahoma,
by S. Schloeder, Plan.

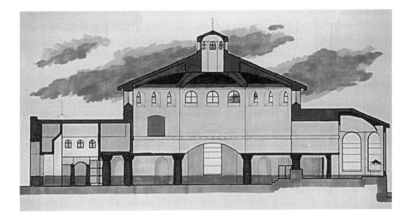

9.37 St. Therese, Collinsville,
Oklahoma, by S. Schloeder,
Section.

9.38 St. Therese,
Collinsville, Oklahoma,
by S. Schloeder,
Aerial of Model.

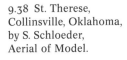

Bibliography

Adam, Karl. *The Spirit of Catholicism*. London: Sheed and Ward, 1929.

Alberti, Leon. *On the Art of Building in Ten Books*. Translated by J. Rykwert, N. Leach, and R. Tavernor. Cambridge, Mass.: MIT Press, 1988.

Bettenson, Henry. *Documents of the Christian Church*. 2d ed. London: Oxford University Press, 1963.

——. *The Early Christian Fathers*. London: Oxford University Press, 1956.

——. *The Later Christian Fathers*. London: Oxford University Press, 1970.

Biéler, André. *Architecture in Worship*. Translated by Donald and Odette Elliot. Philadelphia: Westminster Press, 1965.

Blunt, Anthony. *Borromini*. Cambridge, Mass.: Harvard University Press, 1979.

Borromeo, Saint Charles. *Instructiones Fabricae et Supellectilis Ecclesiasticae (Instructions on Ecclesiastical Buildings)*, trans. Evelyn Carol Voelker. Ph.D. diss., Syracuse University, 1977. Ann Arbor, Mich: University Microfilms International, n.d.

Bouyer, Fr. Louis. *Life and Liturgy*. London: Sheed and Ward, 1956.

——. *Liturgy and Architecture*. South Bend, Ind.: University of Notre Dame Press, 1967.

Burckhardt, Jacob. *The Architecture of the Italian Renaissance*. Edited by Peter Murray. Harmondsworth, England: Penguin, 1987.

Cabasilas, Nicholas. *A Commentary on the Divine Liturgy*. Translated by J. M. Hussey and P. A. McNulty. London: S.P.C.K., 1978.

Camara, Dom Helder. *Race against Time*. Translated by Della Couling. London: Sheed and Ward, 1971.

The Canons and Decrees of the Council of Trent. Translated by H. J. Schroeder, O.P. St. Louis: Herder, 1941.

Chinigo, M., ed. *The Teachings of Pope John XXIII*. Translated by A. A. Coppotelli. London: George G. Harrap and Co., 1967.

Clark, Kenneth. *Moments of Vision*. London: John Murray, 1981.

Condurachi, Emil, and Constantin Daicoviciu. *Romania*. Translated by James Hogarth. Archaeologia Mundi. Geneva: Nagel, 1971.

Conroy, M. C. *Imagery in the Sermones of Maximus, Bishop of Turin*. Washington, D.C.: Catholic University of America Press, 1965.

Constant, Caroline. *The Palladio Guide*. London: Butterworths, 1987.

Cyril of Jerusalem, St. *Works*. Translated by L. P. McCauley, S.J., and A. A. Stephenson. Washington, D.C.: Catholic University of America Press, 1969–1970.

Daniélou, Jean, S.J. *The Angels and Their Mission*. Translated by David Heimann. Westminster, Md.: Christian Classics, 1993.

——. *The Bible and the Liturgy*. London: Darton, Longman and Todd, 1960.

Davies, J. G. *The Architectural Setting of Baptism*. London: Barrie and Rockliff, 1962.

——. *A New Dictionary of Liturgy and Worship*. London: SCM, 1988.

——. *The Secular Use of Church Buildings*. New York: Seabury, 1968.

Dionysius the Pseudo-Areopagite. *Pseudo-Dionysius: The Complete Works*. Translated by Colm Luibheid. New York: Paulist Press, 1987.

Durand, Bishop Guillaume. *The Symbolism of Churches and Church Ornaments: A Translation of the First Book of the* Rationale Divinorum Officiorum. Translated by J. M. Neale and B. Webb. London: T. W. Green, 1843. Reprint. New York: AMS Press, 1973.

Eco, Umberto. *The Aesthetics of Thomas Aquinas*. Translated by Hugh Bredin. Cambridge, Mass.: Harvard University Press, 1988.

——. *Foucault's Pendulum*. Translated by William Weaver. New York: Harcourt Brace Jovanovich, 1989.

Eliade, Mircea. *The Sacred and the Profane*. New York: Harcourt, Brace, 1959.

Elliott, Peter. *Ceremonies of the Modern Roman Rite*. San Francisco: Ignatius Press, 1995.

Eusebius. *The History of the Church*. Translated by G. A. Williamson. New York: Dorset Press, 1965.

Flannery, Austin, O.P. Introduction to *Contemporary Irish Church Architecture*, by R. Hurley and W. Cantwell. Dublin: Gill and Macmillan, 1985.

——, ed. *Vatican Council II*. Dublin, 1975.

——. *Vatican Council II: The Conciliar and Post Conciliar Documents*. Vol. 2. New York: Costello Publishing, 1982.

Fletcher, Sir Banister. *A History of Architecture*. 19th ed. Edited by J. Musgrove. London: Butterworths, 1987.

Frere-Cook, G. *Decorative Arts of the Christian Church*. London: Cassell, 1972.

Froelich, K. "Pseudo-Dionysius and the Reformation of the Sixteenth Century". In *Pseudo-Dionysius: The Complete Works*. Translated by Colm Luibheid. New York: Paulist Press, 1987.

Gamber, Msgr. Klaus. *The Reform of the Roman Liturgy*. San Juan Capistrano: Una Voce, 1993.

Gill, Eric. *Beauty Looks after Herself*. London: Sheed and Ward, 1933.

Gilson, Étienne, O.S.B. *The Arts of the Beautiful*, New York: Scribner's, 1965.

Gough, T. "Corpus Christi, Aachen". *Church Building*, autumn 1988.

Green, Michael. *Evangelism in the Early Church*. London: Hodder and Stoughton, 1970.

Hammond, Peter. *Liturgy and Architecture*. London: Barrie and Rockliff, 1960.

Hargreen, J. "Confessionals for the New Rite", *The Clergy Review* 67, no. 9 (September 1982).

Harvey, V. A. *A Handbook of Theological Terms*. New York: Macmillan, 1964.

Hersey, George. *The Lost Meaning of Classical Architecture*, Cambridge, Mass.: MIT Press, 1988.

Hugh of Saint-Victor. *On the Sacraments of the Christian Faith (De Sacramentis)*. Translated by R. J. Deferrari. Cambridge, Mass.: Mediaeval Academy, 1951.

Jacobus de Voragine, O.P. *The Golden Legend*. Vols. 1 and 2. Translated by W. G. Ryan. Princeton, N.J.: Princeton University Press, 1993.

John Chrysostom, St. *Baptismal Instructions*. Translated by P. W. Harkins. Westminster, Md.: Newman Press, 1963.

Johnson, Paul. *Pope John Paul II and the Catholic Restoration*. London: Weidenfeld and Nicolson, 1982.

Johnson, Fr. Stephen, and Fr. Cuthbert Johnson. *Planning for Liturgy*. Farnborough, England: St. Michael's Abbey Press, 1983.

Jungmann, Josef [Joseph], S.J. *The Early Liturgy* Translated by Francis A. Brunner. South Bend, Ind.: University of Notre Dame Press, 1959.

——. *The Mass*. Translated by Julian Fernandes. Collegeville, Minn.: Liturgical Press, 1976.

——. *The Mass of the Roman Rite*. 2 vols. Translated by F. A. Brunner, C.SS.R. New York: Benziger Brothers, 1951.

Kelly, J., S.J. "The Sense of the Holy", *The Way* 13, no. 4 (October 1973): 249–58.

Krautheimer, Richard. *Early Christian and Byzantine Architecture*. Baltimore, Md.: Penguin, 1965; and 3d ed. Harmondsworth, England: Penguin, 1979.

——. "Introduction to an 'Iconography of Mediaeval Architecture' ", *The Journal of the*

Warburg and Courtauld Institutes 5 (1942).

Lampe, G. W. *A Patristic Greek Lexicon*. Oxford: Clarendon Press, 1965.

Lane, Dermot. *The Reality of Jesus*. New York: Paulist Press, 1975.

Lesnikowski, W. *Rationalism and Romanticism in Architecture*. New York: McGraw-Hill, 1982.

Lethaby, W. R., and H. Swainson. *The Church of Sancta Sophia, Constantinople: A Study of Byzantine Building*. New York: Macmillan, 1894.

Lossky, V. *The Mystical Theology of the Eastern Church*. Crestwood, N.Y.: St. Vladimir's Seminary Press, 1976.

MacDonald, William. *Early Christian and Byzantine Architecture*. New York: George Braziller, 1962.

Maguire, R., and K. Murray. *Modern Churches of the World*. London: Studio Vista, 1965.

Maldonado, Luis. "Liturgy as Communal Enterprise". In *The Reception of Vatican II*, edited by G. Alberigo et al. Translated by Matthew J. O'Connell. Washington, D.C.: Catholic University of America Press, 1987.

Mâle, Émile. *The Early Churches of Rome*. Translated by David Buxton. London: Benn, 1960.

——. *The Gothic Image*. London: Fontana, 1961.

Mango, Cyril. *Byzantine Architecture*. New York: Harry N. Abrams, 1976.

Maritain, Jacques. *Art and Scholasticism*. Translated by J. F. Scanlan. London: Sheed and Ward, 1930.

——. *An Introduction to Philosophy*. Translated by E. I. Watkin. New York: Sheed and Ward, 1937.

Martienssen, Heather. *The Shapes of Structure*. London: Oxford University Press, 1976.

Mersch, Emile. "The Whole Christ: On the Unity of the Church". *Communio* 14, no. 1 (spring 1987): 76.

Migliorino, M. "The Real Presence of Christ and Placement of the Tabernacle". *Christian Order* 29, no. 2 (February 1988): 118–26.

Milburn, R. *Early Christian Art and Architecture*. London: Scolar, 1988.

Mills, Edward. *The Modern Church*. London: Architectural Press, 1956.

Neuner, J., S.J., and J. Dupuis, S.J. *The Christian Faith in the Doctrinal Documents of the Catholic Church*. London: HarperCollins, 1983.

Norberg-Schulz, Christian. *Meaning in Western Architecture*. New York: Praeger, 1975.

O'Connell, J., Fr. *Church Building and Furnishing, the Church's Way*. London: Burns and Oates, 1955.

Onians, John. *Bearers of Meaning*. Princeton University Press, 1988.

Ouspensky, L. *The Theology of the Icon*. Crestwood, N.Y.: St. Vladimir's Seminary Press, 1978.

Panofsky, Erwin. *Gothic Architecture and Scholasticism*. New York: Meridian Books, 1960.

——, trans. *Abbot Suger on the Abbey Church of St.-Denis and Its Art Treasures*. 2d ed. Princeton, N.J.: Princeton University Press, 1979.

Pevsner, N., J. Fleming, and H. Honour. *A Dictionary of Architecture*. Woodstock, N.Y.: Overlook Press, 1976.

Pickstone, C. "Creating Significant Space". *Church Building*, autumn 1988.

Pieper, Josef. *Leisure: The Basis of Culture*. Translated by Alexander Dru. Mentor-Omega books. New York: New American Library, 1963.

Prestige, G. L. *God in Patristic Thought*. London: S.P.C.K., 1952.

"Pseudo-Athanasian Symbol *Quicumque*", in J. Neuner, S.J., and J. Dupuis, S.J. *The Christian Faith in the Doctrinal Documents of the Catholic Church*. London: HarperCollins, 1983.

Rahner, K., and H. Vorgrimler. *Concise Theological Dictionary*. London: Burns and Oates, 1965.

Ratzinger, Joseph Cardinal. *The Feast of Faith*. San Francisco: Ignatius Press, 1986.

——. *The Ratzinger Report*. San Francisco: Ignatius Press, 1985.

Ritz, Sandor, S.J. *L'insuperabile creazione del passaio, presente e futuro*. Rome: Edizione speciale riservata all'autore, n.d.

——. *La nuova Gerusalemne dell'Apocalisse.* Rome: Edizione speciale riservata all'autore, n.d.

——. *Il tempio perenne di Santo Stefano Rotondo in Roma.* Rome: Edizione speciale riservata all'autore, n.d.

Rykwert, Joseph. *Church Building.* London: Sheed and Ward, 1966.

——. *On Adam's House in Paradise,* 2d ed. Cambridge, Mass.: MIT Press, 1981.

——. "Palladio: Venetian Churches". *Domus,* September 1980.

Saward, John. "Christ, Our Lady, and the Church". *Chrysostom* 8, no. 1 (spring 1988).

——. *Christ the Light of the Nations,* Hoddesdon. England: Crux, 1986.

Schwarz, Rudolf. *The Church Incarnate.* Chicago: Henry Regnery, 1958.

Scruton, Roger. *The Aesthetics of Architecture.* 2d ed. Princeton, N.J.: Princeton University Press, 1980.

Seasoltz, R. Kevin. *The House of God.* New York: Herder and Herder, 1963.

Smith, Thomas Gordon. *Classical Architecture: Rule and Invention.* Layton, Utah: G. M. Smith, 1988.

Staniforth, Maxwell, ed. *Early Christian Writings,* Harmondsworth, England: Penguin, 1968.

Steinberg, L. *Borromini's San Carlo alle Quattro Fontane.* New York: Garland, 1977.

Suger, Abbot. *De Administratione.* In *Abbot Suger on the Abbey Church of St.-Denis and Its Art Treasures.* Translated by E. Panofsky. 2d ed. Princeton, N.J.: Princeton University Press, 1979.

Summerson, John. *Heavenly Mansions.* New York: W. W. Norton, 1963.

Tavernor, Robert. *Palladio and Palladianism.* London: Thames and Hudson, 1991.

Tsafrir, Yoram, ed. *Ancient Churches Revealed.* Jerusalem: Israel Exploration Society, 1993.

Tuzik, R., ed. *Leaders of the Liturgical Movement.* Chicago: Liturgy Training Publications, 1990.

Vasari, G. *The Lives of the Artists.* Translated by George Bull. Harmondsworth, England: Penguin, 1965.

Von Simson, Otto. *The Gothic Cathedral.* 2d ed. New York: Pantheon Books, 1962.

——. *Sacred Fortress.* Chicago: University of Chicago Press, 1948.

Walsh, M. "What Makes a Saint?" *The Tablet,* April 22, 1989.

Watkins, David. *Morality and Architecture.* Oxford: Clarendon Press, 1977.

Wheeler, M. *Roman Art and Architecture.* London: Thames and Hudson, 1964.

Wilkinson, J., trans and ed. *Egeria's Travels to the Holy Land.* Rev. ed. Jerusalem: Ariel, 1981.

Wittkower, R. *Architectural Principles in the Age of Humanism.* 3d ed. London: Alec Tiranti, 1962.

Wojtyla, Karol. *Sources of Renewal.* London: Collins, 1980.

Wormell, S. "Rudolf Schwarz and the Theology of Architecture". *Church Building,* autumn 1988.

Worringer, W. *Form in Gothic.* Translated by Herbert Read. London: Alec Tiranti, 1957.

Wybrew, Hugh. *The Orthodox Liturgy.* Crestwood, N.Y.: St. Vladimir's Seminary Press, 1990.

CHURCH DOCUMENTS

The Bishops' Conference of England and Wales. *The Parish Church.* London: Catholic Truth Society, 1984.

Code of Canon Law. January 25, 1983.

The German Liturgical Commission. *Guiding principles for the design of churches according to the spirit of the Roman Liturgy.* 1947.

"Rite of Reception of the Bishop in the Cathedral Church". In *The Rites of the Catholic Church.* Vol. 2. New York: Pueblo, 1979.

John Paul II. *Christifideles laici.* December 30, 1988.

——. *Dominicae cenae.* February 24, 1980.

——. *Duodecimum saeculum.* December 4, 1987.

——. *First Message to the World.* October 17, 1978.

——. *Love Your Mass.* Apostolic Letter on the 25th Anniversary of *Sancrosanctum con-*

cilium, December 4, 1988. London: Catholic Truth Society, 1989.

———. *Redemptor Hominis*. March 4, 1979.

———. *Redemptoris Mater*. March 25, 1987.

Paul VI. *Discourse to the Roman Clergy*. June 24, 1963.

———. *Mysterium fidei*. September 3, 1965.

———. The Credo *of the People of God*. June 30, 1968.

———. *Evangelica testificatio*. June 29, 1971.

———. *Ministeria quaedam*. August 15, 1972.

———. *Evangelii nuntiandi*. December 8, 1975.

Pius XII. *Mediator Dei*. November 20, 1947.

Sacred Congregation for Divine Worship. *General Instruction of the Roman Missal*. 4th ed. March 27, 1975.

———. *Liturgiae instaurationes*. September 5, 1970.

Sacred Congregation for the Doctrine of the Faith. *Pastoralis actio*. October 20, 1980.

Sacred Congregation for Doctrine and Worship. *Per initiationis Christianae*. 2d ed. June 24, 1973.

———. *Nomine parvulorum*. 2d ed. June 24, 1973.

Sacred Congregation of Rites. *Inter oecumenici*. September 26, 1964.

———. *Eucharisticum mysterium*. May 25, 1967.

———. *Musicam sacram*. March 5, 1967.

Sacred Congregation for the Sacraments and Divine Worship. *Dedication of a Church and an Altar*. May 29, 1977.

———. *Inaestimabile donum*. April 3, 1980.

———. *De verbi Dei*, or *General Introduction to the Lectionary for Mass*. January 21, 1981.

United States Catholic Conference. *Environment and Art in Catholic Worship*. Washington, D.C.: USCC, 1978.

Vatican II (1963–1965). *Sacrosanctum concilium*. December 4, 1963.

———. *Lumen Gentium*. November 21, 1964.

———. *Apostolicam actuositatem*. November 18, 1965.

———. *Dei Verbum*. November 18, 1965.

———. *Gaudium et spes*. December 7, 1965.

———. *Presbyterorum ordinis*. December 7, 1965.

Abbreviations

AA	*Apostolicam actuositatem*	GS	*Gaudium et spes*
CCC	*Catechism of the Catholic Church*	ID	*Inaestimabile donum*
CL	*Christifideles laici*	IO	*Inter oecumenici*
CIC	*Code of Canon Law*	LG	*Lumen Gentium*
DA	*A Dictionary of Architecture*	MD	*Mediator Dei*
DC	*Dominicae cenae*	MF	*Mysterium fidei*
DOCA	*Dedication of a Church and an Altar*	MS	*Musicam sacram*
DSa	*Duodecimum saeculum*	NDLW	*A New Dictionary of Liturgy and Worship*
DV	*Dei Verbum*		
EACW	*Environment and Art in Catholic Worship*	NP	*Nomine parvulorum*
		PA	*Pastoralis actio*
EM	*Eucharisticum mysterium*	PC	*The Parish Church*
GIRM	*General Instruction of the Roman Missal*	PIC	*Per initiationis Christianae*
		PO	*Presbyterorum ordinis*
GILM	*General Introduction to the Lectionary for Mass*	RH	*Redemptor Hominis*
		RM	*Redemptoris Mater*
		SC	*Sacrosanctum concilium*

Glossary

ambo A raised platform from which the Epistles and Gospel are read.

ambulatory In medieval churches, a semicircular or polygonal passage to access the apsidal chapels around the CHANCEL.

apse A semicircular or polygonal termination of the eastern end of a church.

arcosolium An arched cell in a Roman catacomb, where the lower half was the tomb covered by a stone slab.

atrium An open forecourt in front of an early Christian or Byzantine church, usually a colonnaded quadrangle.

aumbry A cupboard or recess for storing holy oils or sacred vessels. In the Middle Ages, it was also used to reserve the Blessed Sacrament. Also spelled *ambry*.

baldacchino A canopy over an altar, throne, or tomb, generally supported by columns. It is a traditional mark of respect for a high altar. Also called a *baldaquin*. See CIVORY.

balustrade A row of small posts joined by a rail that serves as an enclosure for a balcony, staircase, landing, or terrace.

baptistery 1. A usually round or polygonal building used in early times for baptismal services; 2. Now, a part of a church containing a font and used for baptismal services.

basilica 1. A church of rectangular shape with a broad and tall nave lighted by CLERESTORY windows, flanked by lower colonnaded aisles, and usually with an APSE at the east end; 2. *Major basilica*: One of the four major churches in Rome (St. John Lateran, St. Peter's, St. Mary Major, and St. Paul's Outside the Walls) with papal privileges. The church of St. Francis in Assisi is also a major basilica; 3. *Minor basilica*: One of many churches throughout the world accorded special privileges by the Pope, usually a historically or architecturally significant building.

bema 1. A raised platform for the clergy in early Christian churches; 2. In Byzantine churches, the raised area behind the ICONOSTASIS that contains the altar.

buttress A pier of brick or stone giving additional strength to the wall to which it is attached.

cancelli A low screen wall enclosing the CHOIR in early Christian churches. Also called a *septum* or *transenna*.

canopy See CIVORY.

cartibulum In pagan Rome, a private altar for sacrifice to the household gods.

casket See PYX.

catechumenon In early Christian architecture, a special room, associated with a BAPTISTERY, for instructing the catechumens.

cathedra The bishop's chair or throne in his cathedral church.

chancel The part of a church, traditionally the east end, containing the main altar and, in early and medieval times, the CHOIR. The term is often used to describe the continuation of the NAVE east of the CROSSING. Also called a SANCTUARY.

251

chancel arch The arch between the NAVE and the CHANCEL.

chancel screen In medieval churches, a large wall separating the CHANCEL and CHOIR from the NAVE and AMBULATORY, effectively creating a "church-within-a-church".

chantry In medieval churches, a small chapel, usually within the NAVE of a larger church or cathedral, that was endowed for the maintenance of priests and perpetual prayer for the donor.

choir That part of a church reserved for the singers.

ciborium 1. A covered dish for containing the consecrated Hosts, used for reservation and for distribution; 2. An altar canopy. See BALDACCHINO and CIVORY.

civory A canopy of wood, stone, etc., that rests on four columns, especially a canopy over an altar.

clerestory The upper part of the side walls of a building, especially a church, rising above the aisle roofs and pierced by windows.

confessio An area of the church, usually below an elevated altar, that shelters a saint's tomb or other relic and is accessible or visible from the NAVE.

conopaeum A veil that adorns the tabernacle where the Blessed Sacrament is reserved.

corbel A projecting block of stone or brick supporting a beam, or an upper wall projecting out beyond the wall beneath it.

credence table A small, movable table next to the altar to hold the unconsecrated bread and wine, the sacred vessels, and the liturgical books.

crossing The place in a cruciform (cross-shaped) church where the TRANSEPT crosses the NAVE, often surmounted by a dome, cupola, or crossing tower.

de Stijl movement An early-twentieth-century Dutch arts movement of painters, sculptors, architects, and designers who developed abstract cubism. The style sought to reduce elements to rectilinear forms and primary colors. It was the forerunner of the Bauhaus and the International Modern styles in architecture.

demotic model An ecclesiological model that emphasizes the role and position of the laity in the liturgy and architectural arrangements (from Greek *demos*, "common people").

dentil A Classical ornament of small, square, tooth-like blocks used in horizontal rows in cornices.

diakonikon In Byzantine architecture, a room adjacent to the SANCTUARY for the storage of icons, vessels, vestments, and liturgical books.

dove In the Middle Ages, a receptacle, shaped like a dove, used to contain the Blessed Sacrament, usually suspended above the altar. See PYX.

egg and dart A Classical decorative molding ornamented with egg shapes alternating with arrowhead shapes. Also called *egg and tongue*.

faldstool A portable, backless chair used by a bishop while officiating in a church other than his own or when not on his CATHEDRA. Also called a *faldistorium*.

flying buttress An arched support carrying the thrust of a vault to an outer buttress.

footpace A wide step at the base of an altar; the platform on which the altar sits.

gradine A shelf for candlesticks, located behind the altar.

groin vault A vault caused by the intersection at right angles of two barrel vaults.

guttae Small drop-like projections carved beneath the TRIGLYPH of a Doric entablature.

gynaikon The upper gallery in Byzantine churches into which the women were segregated during the Divine Liturgy. Also called a *matroneum* or *gynaeceum*.

hierarchic model An ecclesiological model that respects the order of the ministerial priesthood in relationship to the laity in the liturgy and architectural arrangements (from Greek *hiereus*, "priest").

iconostasis In Byzantine architecture, the high screen, decorated with icons and pierced by three doors, that separates the BEMA and SANCTUARY from the NAVE.

jubes The French name for ROOD SCREEN.

martyrium A church or chapel erected over an important Christian site (typically a biblical site or the site of a saint's martyrdom), usually centralized and compact like a mausoleum. Also called a *martyrion* or *martyr-shrine*.

metope The rectangular panel between two TRIGLYPHS in a Doric frieze, often carved with sculptural groups or ornament.

narthex A long colonnaded entrance porch or vestibule, traditionally at the west end of a church, as an antechamber to the NAVE and side aisles. In early Christian times, it was the area for catechumens, penitents, and pagans.

nave The main body of a church, generally flanked by aisles, traditionally located west of the CROSSING.

orans In early Christian art, a figure standing with outstretched arms as if in prayer. Sometimes portrayed as a woman to symbolize the Church as the Bride of Christ, though biblical figures and saints are also often shown in this posture.

pilaster A shallow pier or rectangular column, usually of the Classical orders, engaged in a wall and projecting slightly from the wall surface.

piscina See SACRARIUM.

pistikon In early Christian architecture, a special room for profession of faith; associated with a BAPTISTERY.

portfolio See PYX.

predella A FOOTPACE.

predelle A low seating or kneeling bench.

prothesis In Byzantine architecture, a room adjacent to the SANCTUARY that serves for the preparation of the eucharistic bread before the liturgy and where the Blessed Sacrament is reserved afterward.

pyx Generally, any container in which the Blessed Sacrament is kept; commonly, a small watch-sized receptacle used to carry the Blessed Sacrament to communicate the sick or house-bound.

reredos A carved or sculptural screen or decorated portion of wall located behind the altar.

rood screen In medieval churches, a screen or ornamental partition separating the CHOIR of a church from the NAVE and usually supporting the crucifix (from Middle English *rood*, "cross" or "crucifix").

sacrament tower In the late Middle Ages, a free-standing tower or pedestal with a built-in tabernacle for holding the reserved Blessed Sacrament. Also called a *sacrament house*.

sacrarium A basin with the drain leading directly to the earth, used for washing altar vessels. Also called a *piscina*.

sacristy A room in a church where sacred vessels and vestments are kept and in which the priest prepares for the liturgy. Sometimes called a VESTRY.

sanctuary The part of the church around the altar. Also called the CHANCEL.

sedile (*plural:* **sedilia**) In medieval churches, a niche generally containing three seats for clergy (for priest, deacon, and subdeacon), carved in stone in the south wall of the CHANCEL. Today, the term can be used for a seating bench in the chancel.

sedilla A movable bench.

septum See CANCELLI.

tester A flat canopy over a pulpit or altar, usually suspended from the ceiling.

transenna A carved grating or latticework of marble, usually around a CHOIR or tomb. See CANCELLI.

transept The transverse arms of a cross-shaped church, usually between the NAVE and the CHANCEL at the CROSSING.

triglyph A Classical ornamental panel separating the METOPES in the Doric frieze, carved with vertical channels to form three vertical bars, probably representing the divided femur of the sacrificed oxen (from Greek *tri-glyphos*, "thrice-cloven").

vault, cross-ribbed A vault in which solid ribs carry the vaulted surface.

vestry A room in which vestments are kept and where acolytes and choristers robe for the liturgy. Sometimes called a SACRISTY.

Index

Page numbers with an asterisk (*) indicate illustrations.
Page numbers with "n." indicate footnotes and are followed by the note numbers.

Illustration Credits

Australian National University (I.5, 2.1–2.2, 4.35, 5.5–5.6, 7.15–7.19, 8.12, 8.15–8.16, 8.18, 8.43, 8.65); Mr. William C. Burks, AIA (6.5); Cathedral of the Madeleine, Salt Lake City, Utah (1.22, 4.40–4.41, 5.13, 5.16, 7.43); Concrete Institute (1.9) Courtesy of the Conrad Schmitt Studios, Inc., New Berlin, Wisconsin (6.3–6.4, 6.6); Graphische Sammlung Albertina, Vienna (8.77); Sandor Ritz, S.J. (3.2, 3.10); Courtesy of Darrin Anthony Merlino, C.M.F. (4.14, 7.6); Courtesy of Martin de Porres Walsh, O.P. (4.48); Steven J. Schloeder (I.1–I.4, 1.2–1.6, 1.10, 1.18–1.21, 2.3, 2.5–2.9, 3.4, 4.1, 4.4–4.6, 4.8–4.9, 4.13, 4.15, 4.19, 4.21–4.24, 4.26–4.30, 4.32, 4.34, 4.36–4.39, 4.42, 4.45–4.47, 4.51–4.58, 5.1, 5.3–5.4, 5.9–5.12, 5.14–5.15, 5.17–5.18, 6.2, 6.8–6.11, 6.13–6.18, 7.2–7.3, 7.5, 7.7–7.9, 7.11–7.14, 7.20–7.24, 7.27–7.33, 7.35–7.42, 7.46, 8.2–8.6, 8.12–8.14, 8.30, 8.34–8.35, 8.37–8.42, 8.44–8.45, 8.48–8.53, 8.56–8.58, 8.65–8.68, 8.85, 8.87, 9.2, 9.4, 9.6, 9.10–9.18, 9.26–9.27,9.30–9.31, 9.33–9.38); Courtesy of Dr. Virginia Randall (4.18); Courtesy of Mr. Charley Tapley, AIA (4.43–4.44); Courtesy of Mr. William Tatum (4.12, 8.60–8.61); Courtesy of Prof. Stanley Tigerman, FAIA (from *The Architecture of Exile*, book I: 46) (3.1); Saint Ann's, Harrisburg, Pennsylvania (8.24); School of Architecture, University of Notre Dame (1.11, 1.13–1.14, 1.17, 3.5, 3.7, 3.9, 4.2, 5.8, 8.20–8.21, 8.62–8.63, 8.81); Courtesy of the Studium Biblicum Franciscanum (8.7–8.8); University of Pennsylvania (8.33).